BESTSELLING
BOOK SERIES

The Internet For Dum
6th Edition Starter Kit

Cheat Sheet

W9-BRU-055

Useful Web Pages

http://www.yahoo.com	Yahoo! Web directory
http://www.altavista.com	AltaVista Web search page
http://www.infoseek.com	Infoseek Web directory
http://www.tucows.com	The Ultimate Collection of Windows Software (also for Macs)
http://cws.internet.com	Stroud's Consummate Winsock Applications
http://www.infobeat.com	Sign up to get news via e-mail
http://home.netscape.com	Netscape Communications home page
http://www.microsoft.com/ie	Microsoft Internet Explorer home page
http://www.operasoftware.com	Opera home page
http://www.liszt.com	Liszt Directory of E-mail Mailing Lists
http://www.unitedmedia.com/comics/dilbert	Dilbert
http://www2.uclick.com/client/ucd/db	Doonesbury
http://people.yahoo.com	Yahoo (Four11) phone and e-mail directory
http://www.mapquest.com	Maps of U.S. street addresses
http://weather.yahoo.com	World weather info
http://www.usps.gov	U.S. Postal Service zip codes and postage rates
http://mail.yahoo.com and http://www.hotmail.com	Free e-mail via the Web
http://wwwscout.cs.wisc.edu/scout	InterNIC Scout Report
http://www.us.imdb.com	Internet Movie Database
http://net.gurus.com	Updates to this book

Types of URLS

file://pathname	File stored on local computer
ftp://hostname/pathname	File on FTP server
http://hostname/pathname	World Wide Web page
mailto:address	E-mail address
telnet:hostname	Computer to log in to using telnet program

E-Mail Mailing Lists

To find a list, go to http://www.liszt.com.

To subscribe, send a message to the administrative address (usually with username LISTSERV, ListProc, or Majordomo) containing the line "subscribe listname yourname" (for Majordomo, omit yourname) in the text of the message.

Read and save the welcome message you receive.

To sign off, send a message to the administrative address containing the line "signoff listname" (for LISTSERV and ListProc) or "unsubscribe listname" (for Majordomo) in the text of the message.

Acronyms to Know

BTW	By the way
RTFM	Read the manual
IMHO	In my humble opinion
ROFL	Rolling on floor, laughing
TIA	Thanks in advance
YMMV	Your mileage may vary
TLA	Three-letter acronym

IDG
BOOKS
WORLDWIDE

...For Dummies®: Bestselling Book Series for Beginners

The Internet For Dummies, 6th Edition Starter Kit

Cheat Sheet

Fill In Information about Your Internet Account

Your e-mail address: _____

@ _____

Your Internet provider's data phone number (the number your software dials):

_____

Your Internet provider's technical-support phone number (if you want to talk to a human being):

_____

Your Internet provider's technical-support department's e-mail address: _____

@ _____

For PPP accounts

Your IP address (you may not have one assigned):

_____

Your Internet provider's DNS (domain name server): _____

Your Internet provider's SMTP mail gateway (for outgoing mail): _____

Your Internet provider's POP mail server (for incoming mail): _____

Your provider's news server (for Usenet newsgroups): _____

Hostname Zones

This list shows you the three-letter last word of Internet hostnames; for two-letter country codes, see the Web page `http://net.gurus.com/countries`.

com	Company or individual
edu	Educational institution
gov	U.S. federal government
mil	U.S. military
net	Network organization
int	International organization
org	Nonprofit or other noncommercial organization

Netiquette Tips

- Remember that everyone else on the Net is human, too.
- Don't respond in anger or insist on getting the last word.
- DON'T TYPE IN ALL CAPS! It's shouting.
- Don't post messages to mailing lists if you don't have something new to add.
- Don't pass along chain letters (even virtuous-looking ones), online petitions, make-money-fast messages, avoid-this-virus warnings, or other bogus mail.

E-Mail Addresses

To Send To	With This Address	Type This
AOL	SteveCase	stevecase@aol.com
AT&T WorldNet	TedVail	tedvail@worldnet.att.net
CompuServe	77777,7777	77777.7777@compuserve.com
FIDONET	MarySmith 1:2/3.4	mary.smith@p4.f3.n2.zl.fidonet.org
MCI Mail	555-2468	5552468@mcimail.com
MSN	BillGates	billgates@msn.com
Prodigy Classic	ABCD123A	abcdl23a@prodigy.com
Prodigy Internet	dummies	dummies@prodigy.net

...For Dummies®: Bestselling Book Series for Beginners

TM

References for the Rest of Us!®

THE INTERNET FOR DUMMIES®

FOR

6TH EDITION STARTER KIT

by John R. Levine, Carol Baroudi, and Margaret Levine Young

IDG BOOKS WORLDWIDE

IDG Books Worldwide, Inc.
An International Data Group Company

Foster City, CA ♦ Chicago, IL ♦ Indianapolis, IN ♦ New York, NY

The Internet For Dummies®, 6th Edition Starter Kit

Published by
IDG Books Worldwide, Inc.
An International Data Group Company
919 E. Hillsdale Blvd.
Suite 400
Foster City, CA 94404
www.idgbooks.com (IDG Books Worldwide Web site)
www.dummies.com (Dummies Press Web site)

Library of Congress Catalog Card No.: 99-60184

ISBN: 0-7645-0507-6

Printed in the United States of America

10 9 8 7 6 5 4 3

6B/SQ/QY/ZZ/IN

Distributed in the United States by IDG Books Worldwide, Inc.

Distributed by CDG Books Canada Inc. for Canada; by Transworld Publishers Limited in the United Kingdom; by IDG Norge Books for Norway; by IDG Sweden Books for Sweden; by IDG Books Australia Publishing Corporation Pty. Ltd. for Australia and New Zealand; by TransQuest Publishers Pte Ltd. for Singapore, Malaysia, Thailand, Indonesia, and Hong Kong; by Gotop Information Inc. for Taiwan; by ICG Muse, Inc. for Japan; by Norma Comunicaciones S.A. for Colombia; by Intersoft for South Africa; by Eyrolles for France; by International Thomson Publishing for Germany, Austria and Switzerland; by Distribuidora Cuspide for Argentina; by LR International for Brazil; by Galileo Libros for Chile; by Ediciones ZETA S.C.R. Ltda. for Peru; by WS Computer Publishing Corporation, Inc., for the Philippines; by Contemporanea de Ediciones for Venezuela; by Express Computer Distributors for the Caribbean and West Indies; by Micronesia Media Distributor, Inc. for Micronesia; by Grupo Editorial Norma S.A. for Guatemala; by Chips Computadoras S.A. de C.V. for Mexico; by Editorial Norma de Panama S.A. for Panama; by American Bookshops for Finland. Authorized Sales Agent: Anthony Rudkin Associates for the Middle East and North Africa.

For general information on IDG Books Worldwide's books in the U.S., please call our Consumer Customer Service department at 800-762-2974. For reseller information, including discounts and premium sales, please call our Reseller Customer Service department at 800-434-3422.

For information on where to purchase IDG Books Worldwide's books outside the U.S., please contact our International Sales department at 317-596-5530 or fax 317-596-5692.

For consumer information on foreign language translations, please contact our Customer Service department at 1-800-434-3422, fax 317-596-5692, or e-mail rights@idgbooks.com.

For information on licensing foreign or domestic rights, please phone +1-650-655-3109.

For sales inquiries and special prices for bulk quantities, please contact our Sales department at 650-655-3200 or write to the address above.

For information on using IDG Books Worldwide's books in the classroom or for ordering examination copies, please contact our Educational Sales department at 800-434-2086 or fax 317-596-5499.

For press review copies, author interviews, or other publicity information, please contact our Public Relations department at 650-655-3000 or fax 650-655-3299.

For authorization to photocopy items for corporate, personal, or educational use, please contact Copyright Clearance Center, 222 Rosewood Drive, Danvers, MA 01923, or fax 978-750-4470.

is a registered trademark or trademark under exclusive license to IDG Books Worldwide, Inc. from International Data Group, Inc. in the United States and/or other countries.

About the Authors

John R. Levine was a member of a computer club in high school — before high school students, or even high schools, had computers, where he met Theodor H. Nelson, the author of *Computer Lib/Dream Machines* and the inventor of hypertext, who reminded us that computers should not be taken seriously and that everyone can and should understand and use computers.

John wrote his first program in 1967 on an IBM 1130 (a computer somewhat less powerful than your typical modern digital wristwatch, only more difficult to use). He became an official system administrator of a networked computer at Yale in 1975. He began working part-time, for a computer company, of course, in 1977 and has been in and out of the computer and network biz ever since. He got his company on Usenet (the Net's worldwide bulletin-board system) early enough that it appears in a 1982 *Byte* magazine article on a map of Usenet, which then was so small that the map fit on half a page.

Although John used to spend most of his time writing software, now he mostly writes books (including *UNIX For Dummies* and *Internet Secrets,* both published by IDG Books Worldwide, Inc.) because it's more fun and he can do so at home in the tiny village of Trumansburg, New York, where he is the sewer commissioner (Guided tours! Free samples!) and play with his small daughter when he's supposed to be writing. John also does a fair amount of public speaking. (See `http://iecc.com/johnl`, to see where he'll be.) He holds a B.A. and a Ph.D. in computer science from Yale University, but please don't hold that against him.

Carol Baroudi first began playing with computers in 1971 at Colgate University, where two things were new: the PDP-10 and women. She was lucky to have unlimited access to the state-of-the-art PDP-10, on which she learned to program, operate the machine, and talk to Eliza. She taught Algol and helped to design the curricula for computer science and women's studies. She majored in Spanish and studied French, which, thanks to the Internet, she can now use every day.

In 1975 Carol took a job doing compiler support and development, a perfect use for her background in languages. For six years she developed software and managed software development. For a while she had a small business doing high-tech recruiting (she was a headhunter). Though she wrote her first software manuals in 1975, her *job* since 1984 has been writing. Carol has described all kinds of software, from the memory-management system of the Wang VS operating system to e-mail products for the PC and Mac. For the past several years, she has been writing books for ordinary people who want to use computers. She enjoys speaking to academic, business, and general audiences about the impact of technology on society and other related topics. (Check out her home page at `http://iecc.com/carol` to see what she's up to.)

The mother of a fantastic 8-year-old, Carol loves acting and singing and will fly to Europe on any excuse. She believes that we are living in a very interesting time when technology is changing faster than people can imagine. Carol hopes that as we learn to use the new technologies, we don't lose sight of our humanity, and feels that that computers can be useful and fun but are no substitute for real life.

Unlike her peers in that 40-something bracket, **Margaret Levine Young** was exposed to computers at an early age. In high school, she got into a computer club known as the R.E.S.I.S.T.O.R.S. — a group of kids who spent Saturdays in a barn fooling around with three antiquated computers. She stayed in the field throughout college against her better judgment and despite her brother John's presence as a graduate student in the computer science department. Margy graduated from Yale and went on to become one of the first microcomputer managers in the early 1980s at Columbia Pictures, where she rode the elevator with big stars whose names she wouldn't dream of dropping here.

Since then, Margy has co-authored more than 16 computer books about the topics of the Internet, UNIX, WordPerfect, Microsoft Access, and (stab from the past) PC-File and Javelin, including *Dummies 101: The Internet For Windows 98*, *Dummies 101: Netscape Communicator*, *Internet FAQs: Answers to Frequently Asked Questions*, *UNIX For Dummies*, and *WordPerfect 8 For Windows 95 For Dummies* (all published by IDG Books Worldwide, Inc.). She met her future husband, Jordan, in the R.E.S.I.S.T.O.R.S. Her other passion is her children, Meg and Zac. She loves gardening, chickens, reading, and anything to do with eating and lives near Middlebury, Vermont (see http://www.gurus.com/margy for some scenery).

ABOUT IDG BOOKS WORLDWIDE

Welcome to the world of IDG Books Worldwide.

IDG Books Worldwide, Inc., is a subsidiary of International Data Group, the world's largest publisher of computer-related information and the leading global provider of information services on information technology. IDG was founded more than 30 years ago by Patrick J. McGovern and now employs more than 9,000 people worldwide. IDG publishes more than 290 computer publications in over 75 countries. More than 90 million people read one or more IDG publications each month.

Launched in 1990, IDG Books Worldwide is today the #1 publisher of best-selling computer books in the United States. We are proud to have received eight awards from the Computer Press Association in recognition of editorial excellence and three from Computer Currents' First Annual Readers' Choice Awards. Our best-selling ...For Dummies® series has more than 50 million copies in print with translations in 31 languages. IDG Books Worldwide, through a joint venture with IDG's Hi-Tech Beijing, became the first U.S. publisher to publish a computer book in the People's Republic of China. In record time, IDG Books Worldwide has become the first choice for millions of readers around the world who want to learn how to better manage their businesses.

Our mission is simple: Every one of our books is designed to bring extra value and skill-building instructions to the reader. Our books are written by experts who understand and care about our readers. The knowledge base of our editorial staff comes from years of experience in publishing, education, and journalism — experience we use to produce books to carry us into the new millennium. In short, we care about books, so we attract the best people. We devote special attention to details such as audience, interior design, use of icons, and illustrations. And because we use an efficient process of authoring, editing, and desktop publishing our books electronically, we can spend more time ensuring superior content and less time on the technicalities of making books.

You can count on our commitment to deliver high-quality books at competitive prices on topics you want to read about. At IDG Books Worldwide, we continue in the IDG tradition of delivering quality for more than 30 years. You'll find no better book on a subject than one from IDG Books Worldwide.

IDG
BOOKS
WORLDWIDE

John Kilcullen
Chairman and CEO
IDG Books Worldwide, Inc.

Steven Berkowitz
President and Publisher
IDG Books Worldwide, Inc.

WINNER

Eighth Annual
Computer Press
Awards ≥ 1992

WINNER

Ninth Annual
Computer Press
Awards ≥ 1993

Tenth Annual
Computer Press
Awards ≥ 1994

WINNER

WINNER

Eleventh Annual
Computer Press
Awards ≥ 1995

Dedications

John dedicates his part of the book (the particularly dumb jokes) to Sarah Willow, who still doesn't sleep after two and a half years and is impressively articulate when explaining why not, and to Tonia, who when not staying up with her, reminded him ever so politely that he really did have to finish revising this book.

Carol dedicates her part of the book to Joshua, with all her love, and to her friends, who remind her that there's more to life than writing books.

Margy dedicates this book to Jordan, Meg, and Zac, who make life worth living.

Authors' Acknowledgments

Colleen Totz moved our natterings through the editorial process while (no doubt at great personal cost) making us look like better writers than we are. Thanks also to the rest of the gang at IDG, especially those listed on the Publisher's Acknowledgements page.

Margy thanks Jordan and the Cornwall Elementary School. John likewise thanks Nancy Fuhr, who provided vital and high-quality attention and care to the aforementioned non-sleeping person.

The entire contents of this book were edited and submitted to the publisher using the World Wide Web; practicing what we preach. We thank our Internet providers: Finger Lakes Technologies Group (Trumansburg, NY. Hi, Paul!), Lightlink (Ithaca, NY. Hi, Homer!), Sovernet (Bellows Falls, VT), and shoreham.net (Shoreham, VT. Hi, Don and Jim!).

Finally, thanks to all the smarties (we wouldn't say wise-acres) who sent us comments on the previous editions and helped make this one better. If you have ideas, comments, or complaints, about the book, whisk them to us at internet6@gurus.com.

Also visit our web site at http://net.gurus.com for updates and more information about the topics in this book.

Publisher's Acknowledgments

We're proud of this book; please register your comments through our IDG Books Worldwide Online Registration Form located at http://my2cents.dummies.com.

Some of the people who helped bring this book to market include the following:

Acquisitions, Editorial, and Media Development

Project Editor: Colleen Totz

Acquisitions Editor: Mike Kelly

Technical Editor: Bill Karow

Media Development Editor: Joell Smith

Media Development Coordinator: Megan Roney

Editorial Manager: Mary C. Corder

Media Development Manager: Heather Heath Dismore

Editorial Assistants: Alison Walthall, Paul Kuzmic

Production

Project Coordinator: Karen York

Layout and Graphics: Angela F. Hunckler, Jane E. Martin, Brent Savage, Renee L. Schmith, Jacqueline J. Schneider, Brian Torwelle

Proofreaders: Christine Berman, Kelli Botta, Rebecca Senninger, Toni Settle, Janet M. Withers

Indexer: Richard Shrout

Special Help

Suzanne Thomas

General and Administrative

IDG Books Worldwide, Inc.: John Kilcullen, CEO; Steven Berkowitz, President and Publisher

IDG Books Technology Publishing Group: Richard Swadley, Senior Vice President and Publisher; Walter Bruce III, Vice President and Associate Publisher; Steven Sayre, Associate Publisher; Joseph Wikert, Associate Publisher; Mary Bednarek, Branded Product Development Director; Mary Corder, Editorial Director

IDG Books Consumer Publishing Group: Roland Elgey, Senior Vice President and Publisher; Kathleen A. Welton, Vice President and Publisher; Kevin Thornton, Acquisitions Manager; Kristin A. Cocks, Editorial Director

IDG Books Internet Publishing Group: Brenda McLaughlin, Senior Vice President and Publisher; Diane Graves Steele, Vice President and Associate Publisher; Sofia Marchant, Online Marketing Manager

IDG Books Production for Dummies Press: Michael R. Britton, Vice President of Production; Debbie Stailey, Associate Director of Production; Cindy L. Phipps, Manager of Project Coordination, Production Proofreading, and Indexing; Shelley Lea, Supervisor of Graphics and Design; Debbie J. Gates, Production Systems Specialist; Robert Springer, Supervisor of Proofreading; Laura Carpenter, Production Control Manager; Tony Augsburger, Supervisor of Reprints and Bluelines

Dummies Packaging and Book Design: Patty Page, Manager, Promotions Marketing

♦

The publisher would like to give special thanks to Patrick J. McGovern, without whom this book would not have been possible.

♦

Contents at a Glance

Cartoons at a Glance

By Rich Tennant

page 165

page 41

page 7

page 293

page 79

Fax: 978-546-7747 • E-mail: the5wave@tiac.net

Table of Contents

● ●

Introduction

*W*elcome to *The Internet For Dummies,* 6th Edition Starter Kit. Although lots of books are available about the Internet, most of them assume that you have a degree in computer science, would love to know about every strange and useless wart of the Internet, and enjoy memorizing unpronounceable commands and options. We hope that this book is different.

This book describes what you actually do to become an *Internaut* (someone who navigates the Internet with skill) — how to get started, what you really need to know, and where to go for help. And we describe it in plain old English.

We've made many changes for this new, sixth edition. When we first wrote *The Internet For Dummies, Starter Kit* a typical Net user was a student who connected from school or a technical worker who had access through work. Now, six years later, the Net has grown like crazy to include millions of (dare we say it?) normal people, connecting on their own nickel from computers at home, along with students ranging from elementary school to adult education. Now we focus on the parts of the Net that are of the most interest to typical users — the World Wide Web and how to find things there, including how to use Netscape, Internet Explorer, and Opera (the most popular and/or useful Web programs), send and receive electronic mail (e-mail) for person-to-person communications, shop online, chat online, and download interesting things from the Net.

About This Book

We don't flatter ourselves that you are interested enough in the Internet to sit down and read the entire book (although it should be a fine book for the bathroom). When you run into a problem using the Internet ("Hmm, I *thought* that I knew how to find somebody on the Net, but I don't seem to remember. . . ."), just dip in to the book long enough to solve your problem.

Pertinent sections include

- Understanding what the Internet is
- Knowing how to get connected to the Net
- Climbing around the World Wide Web

> ✔ Finding people, places, and things
> ✔ Communicating with e-mail (electronic mail)
> ✔ Getting stuff off the Net
> ✔ Finding services and software

How to Use This Book

To begin, please read the first three chapters. They give you an overview of the Net and some important tips and terminology. Besides, we think that they're interesting.

When you're ready to get yourself on the Internet, turn to Part II and pick the option that best suits you and your circumstances.

Parts III, IV, and V egg you on and provide extra support.

Although we try hard not to introduce a technical term without defining it, sometimes we slip. Sometimes, too, you may read a section out of order and find a term we defined a few chapters before that. To fill in the gaps, we include a glossary.

Because the Internet is ever-changing, we have expanded our book to include an online area to help keep it up-to-date. Whenever you see our special Whoosh icon, it means that we have more up-to-the-minute information available on our Web site, at

```
http://net.gurus.com
```

When you have to type something, it appears in the book like this: `Hello, Internet!` Or else we put in on a line of its own, like this:

```
cryptic command to type
```

Type it just as it appears. Use the same capitalization we do — many systems care deeply about CAPITAL and small letters. Then press the Enter or Return key. The book tells you what should happen when you give each command and what your options are.

If you have to follow a complicated procedure, we spell it out step by step wherever possible, with the stuff you have to do also highlighted in **bold-face**. We then tell you what happens in response and what your options are.

When you have to choose commands from menus, we write File⇨Exit when we want you to choose the File command from the menu bar and then choose the Exit command from the menu that appears.

Who Are You?

In writing the book, we assumed that

- ✔ You have or would like to have access to the Internet.
- ✔ You want to get some work done with it. (We consider the term "work" to include the concept "play.")
- ✔ You are not interested in becoming the world's next great Internet expert, at least not this week.

How This Book Is Organized

This book has five parts. The parts stand on their own — although you can begin reading wherever you like, you should at least skim Parts I and II first to get acquainted with some unavoidable Internet jargon and find out how to get your computer on the Net.

Here are the parts of the book and what they contain:

In Part I, "Welcome to the Internet," you find out what the Internet is and why it's interesting (at least why we think it's interesting). Also, this part has stuff about vital Internet terminology and concepts that help you as you read through the later parts of the book. Part I discusses how you get on the Internet, gives some thoughts about children's use of the Net, and talks about the latest rage in corporate intranet technology.

For the nuts and bolts of getting on the Net, read Part II, "Internet, Here I Come." For most users, by far the most difficult part of using the Net is getting to that first connection, with software loaded, configuration configured, and modem modeming. After that, it's (relatively) smooth sailing.

Part III, "Web Mania," dives into the World Wide Web, the part of the Internet that has powered the Net's leap from obscurity to fame. We discuss how to get around on the Web, how to find stuff (which is not as easy as it should be), how to shop online on the Web, and how to add your own home page to the Web.

Part IV, "Essential Internet," looks at the other important and useful Net services: sending and receiving electronic mail, instant messages, chatting, and getting stuff off the Net. You find out how to exchange electronic mail with people down the hall or on other continents, how to use electronic mailing lists to keep in touch with people of similar interests, and how to download things from the Net. We also cover the use of the Net from AOL and WebTV, two popular online services that offer Net access.

A compendium of ready references and useful facts is in Part V, "The Part of Tens" (which, we suppose, suggests that the rest of the book is full of useless facts).

The appendix provides all the information you need to install the programs on the CD-ROM.

What's on the CD-ROM

Here are some of the programs on the CD-ROM, with the chapters that describe them. For how to install the programs, see the What's on the CD Appendix.

✔ **Netscape Navigator 4.5** (for Windows 95/98, Windows 3.1, and the Mac) and **Microsoft Internet Explorer 4** (for Windows 95), the two most popular Web browsing programs. Chapters 6 and 7 explain in some detail how to use them.

✔ **Mindspring Service software** (for Windows 95/98, Windows 3.1, and the Mac) signs you up for an Internet PPP account with Mindspring, which has local phone numbers throughout the urban and suburban U.S.

✔ **AOL 4.0** (for Windows 95/98 and the Mac) signs you up for America Online. Chapter 17 discusses America Online in detail.

✔ **Trumpet WinSock** (for Windows 3.1) and **FreePPP** (for the Mac) are programs that you can use to connect to almost any Internet SLIP or PPP account, and are described in Chapter 5. Folks with Windows 95 or 98 can use Windows' built-in Dial-Up Networking.

✔ **Eudora Light** (for Windows 95/98, Windows 3.1, and the Mac) is our favorite freeware e-mail program; see Chapters 11 and 12 for how to use it.

✔ **Free Agent** (for Windows 95/98 and Windows 3.1) and **InterNews** (for the Mac) are newsreaders, which let you participate in Usenet newsgroups (discussion groups). See this Web page for more info:

        http://net.gurus.com/news

✔ **WS_FTP** (for Windows 95/98 and Windows 3.1) and **Anarchie** (for the Mac) are for downloading programs, graphics, and other files from the Net; see Chapter 16.

✔ **mIRC** (for Windows 95/98 and Windows 3.1) and **Ircle** (for the Mac) let you participate in Internet Relay Chat (IRC), a bunch of real-time world-wide conversations. See Chapter 15 for how to use these programs to get chatting.

        http://net.gurus.com/irc

- **NetTerm** (for Windows 95/98 and Windows 3.1) and **NCSA Telnet** (for the Mac) let you log in to other computers on the Net. See this Web page for more info:

```
http://net.gurus.com/telnet
```

- **HotDog Professional 5 Webmaster Suite** (for Windows 95/98 and Windows 3.1) and **BBEdit Lite** (for the Mac) help you create your own Web pages, as described in Chapter 10.

- **WinZip** (for Windows 95/98 and Windows 3.1) and **StuffIt Expander** and **DropStuff with Expander Enhancer** (for the Mac) can expand the zillions of compressed files you'll find on the Net. See Chapters 16 and 21.

- **Paint Shop Pro** (for Windows 95/98 and Windows 3.1) and **Graphic Converter** (for the Mac) let you create pictures for your Web site or look at pictures you download from the Net.

- **Adobe Acrobat Reader** (for Windows 95/98, Windows 3.1, and the Mac) lets you read and print documents formatted as Portable Document Format files, such as the Eudora Light manual on the CD-ROM.

- **ICQ** (for Windows 95/98 and the Mac) is an instant message and paging system that lets you exchange messages with friends who are online.

Icons Used in This Book

Lets you know that some particularly nerdy, technoid information is coming up so that you can skip it if you want. (On the other hand, you may want to read it.)

Indicates that a nifty little shortcut or time-saver is explained.

Gaack! We found out about this information the hard way! Don't let it happen to you!

Points out a resource on the World Wide Web that you can use with Netscape Navigator, Internet Explorer, or other Web software.

Points you to more up-to-the-minute information on our very own Web site. Hey, this book is *alive.*

The CD-ROM in the back of the book includes this program.

What Now?

That's all you need to know to get started. Whenever you hit a snag using the Internet, just look up the problem in the table of contents or index in this book. You'll either have the problem solved in a flash or know where you need to go to find some expert help.

Because the Internet has been evolving for almost 30 years, largely under the influence of some extremely nerdy people, it was not designed to be particularly easy for normal people to use. Don't feel bad if you have to look up a number of topics before you feel comfortable using the Internet. After all, most computer users never have to face anything as complex as the Internet.

Feedback, Please

We love to hear from our readers. If you want to contact us, please feel free to do so, in care of

IDG Books Worldwide
7260 Shadeland Station
Suite 100
Indianapolis, IN 46256

Better yet, send us Internet electronic mail at internet6@gurus.com (our friendly robot will answer immediately; the human authors read all the mail and answer as much as we can), or visit this book's Web home page, at http://net.gurus.com. These electronic addresses put you in contact only with the authors of this book; to contact the publisher or authors of other ...*For Dummies* books, visit the publisher's Web site, at http://www.dummies.com, or send e-mail to info@idgbooks.com, or send paper mail to the address just listed.

Part I
Welcome to the Internet

The 5th Wave   By Rich Tennant

"SINCE WE GOT IT, HE HASN'T MOVED FROM THAT SPOT FOR ELEVEN STRAIGHT DAYS. ODDLY ENOUGH THEY CALL THIS 'GETTING UP AND RUNNING' ON THE INTERNET."

In this part . . .

The Internet is an amazing place. But because it's full of computers, nothing is quite as simple as it should be. First, we look at what the Internet is and how it got that way. We tell you what's happening, what people are doing, and why you should care. We give special attention to family concerns and resources and take a quick look at intranets and extranets, which are Internet technologies gone corporate.

Chapter 1

What Is the Net?

*W*hat is the Internet? It depends (an answer you'll be seeing in this book more often than you might expect). The Internet and the technologies that make it work are changing faster than anyone can keep track of. In this chapter, we begin with the basics and tell you what the Internet is and, just as important, what has changed during the past couple of years so that you can begin to have an understanding of what it's all about.

If you're new to the Internet, and especially if you don't have much computer experience, *be patient with yourself.* Many of the ideas here are completely new. Allow yourself some time to read and reread. It's a brand-new world with its own language, and it takes some getting used to. Many people find it helpful to read through the entire book quickly one time to get a broader perspective of what we're talking about. Others plow through a page at a time. Whatever your style, remember that it's *new* stuff — you're not *supposed* to understand it already. Even for many experienced Internet users, it's a new world.

Even if you're an experienced computer user, you may find the Internet unlike anything you've ever tackled. The Internet is not a software package and doesn't easily lend itself to the kind of step-by-step instruction we could provide for a single, fixed program. We are as step-by-step as we can be, but the Internet resembles a living organism that's mutating at an astonishing rate more than it resembles Microsoft Word or Excel, which sit quietly on your computer and mind their own business. After you get set up and get a little practice, using the Internet seems like second nature; in the beginning, however, it can be daunting.

The Internet — also known as the *Net* — is the world's largest computer network. "What is a network?" you may ask. Even if you already know, you may want to read the next couple of paragraphs to make sure that we're speaking the same language.

A computer *network* is basically a bunch of computers hooked together somehow. In concept, it's sort of like a radio or TV network that connects a bunch of radio or TV stations so that they can share the latest episode of *The X-Files.*

Don't take the analogy too far. TV networks send the same information to all the stations at the same time (it's called *broadcast* networking); in computer networks, each particular message is usually routed to a particular computer. Unlike TV networks, computer networks are invariably two-way: When computer A sends a message to computer B, B can send a reply back to A.

Some computer networks consist of a central computer and a bunch of remote stations that report to it (a central airline-reservation computer, for example, with thousands of screens and keyboards in airports and travel agencies). Others, including the Internet, are more egalitarian and permit any computer on the network to communicate with any other.

The Internet isn't really one network — it's a network of networks, all freely exchanging information. The networks range from the big and formal (such as the corporate networks at AT&T, General Electric, and Hewlett-Packard) to the small and informal (such as the one in John's back bedroom, with a couple of old PCs bought through the *Want Advertiser*) and everything in between. College and university networks have long been part of the Internet, and now high schools and elementary schools are joining up. In the past year or two, Internet usage has been increasing at a pace equivalent to that of television in the early '50s; the Net now has an estimated 40 million computers and something like 150 million users, growing at 40 to 50 percent per year.

So What's All the Hoopla?

Everywhere you turn, you hear people talking about the Net — as though they're on a first-name basis. Radio shows give you their e-mail addresses, businesses give you their Web sites (starting with "www" and ending with the ubiquitous "dot com") and strangers ask whether you have a home page. People are "going online and getting connected." Are they really talking about this same "network of networks?" Yes, *and* there's more.

With networks, size counts for a great deal because the larger a network is, the more stuff it has to offer. Because the Internet is the world's largest computer network, it has an amazing array of information to offer.

The Internet is new communications technology that is affecting our lives on a scale as significant as the telephone and television. Some people believe that when it comes to disseminating information, the Internet is the most significant invention since the printing press. If you use a telephone, write letters, read a newspaper or magazine, or do business or any kind of research, the Internet can radically alter your entire world view.

When people talk about the Internet today, they're usually talking about what they can do, what they have found, and whom they have met. The Internet's capabilities are so expansive that we don't have room to give a complete list in this chapter (indeed, it would fill several books larger than this one), but here's a quick summary:

- **Electronic mail (e-mail):** This service is certainly the most widely used — you can exchange e-mail with millions of people all over the world. People use e-mail for anything for which they might use paper mail, faxes, special delivery of documents, or the telephone: gossip, recipes, rumors, love letters — you name it. (We hear that some people even use it for stuff related to work.) Electronic *mailing lists* enable you to join in group discussions with people who have similar interests and to meet people over the Net. *Mail servers* (programs that respond to e-mail messages automatically) let you retrieve all sorts of information. Chapters 11, 12, and 13 have all the details.

- **The World Wide Web:** When people talk these days about surfing the Net, they often mean checking out sites on this (buzzword alert) multimedia hyperlinked database that spans the globe. The Web, unlike earlier Net services, combines text, pictures, sound, and even animation and lets you move around with a click of your computer mouse. New *Web sites* (sets of Web pages) are growing faster than you can say "Big Mac with cheese," with new sites appearing every minute. In 1993, when we wrote the first edition of this book, the Internet had 130 Web sites. Today, it has many millions, and statistics indicate that the number is doubling every few months.

  The software used to navigate the Web is known as a *browser*. The most popular browsers today are Netscape Navigator and Microsoft Internet Explorer. We tell you all about them in Chapters 6 and 7, along with some other less popular but worthy competitors.

- **Chatting:** People are talking to people all over the globe about everything under the sun. They enter *chat rooms* with several other people or one special someone. They're using the America Online chat facility, CompuServe's version of the same thing, or *Internet Relay Chat (IRC)*, a chat facility available to almost anyone on the Internet. We tell you how in Chapter 15. We also discuss *paging* programs like ICQ and AOL Instant Messenger that let you send messages that "pop up" on the recipient's screen in Chapter 15.

✔ **Information retrieval:** Many computers have files of information that are free for the taking. The files range from U.S. Supreme Court decisions and library card catalogs to the text of old books, digitized pictures (nearly all of them suitable for family audiences), and an enormous variety of software, from games to operating systems.

Special tools known as *search engines, directories,* and *indices* help you find information on the Net. Lots of people are trying to create the fastest, smartest search engine and the most complete Net index. We tell you about two of the most useful, AltaVista and Yahoo, so that you get the picture. As mentioned in the Introduction to this book, you see a Web icon here and there; it points to resources you can retrieve from the Net, as described in Chapter 16.

✔ **Electronic commerce:** This term is just a fancy word for buying and selling stuff over the Net. It seems that everybody's doing it, and now the software is available to make the process of sending your credit card number over the Net safe and secure. You can buy anything from books to stock in microbreweries. We talk about the relevant issues later in this chapter and in Chapter 9.

✔ **Intranets:** Wouldn't ya know? Businesses have figured out that this Internet stuff is really useful. They're using e-mail and Web technologies on their own internal networks and calling them *intranets.* After companies figured out that Internet technology can be used inside their companies, some quickly cottoned to the idea that they could use this same stuff to work with their customers and suppliers and other companies with which they have business relationships. Because this technology goes outside their companies, they called this new permutation *extranets.* We talk about intranets and extranets in Chapter 2.

✔ **Games and gossip:** A type of multi-user game called a *MUD (Multi-User Dimension* or *Multi-User Dungeon)* can easily absorb all your waking hours and an alarming number of what otherwise would be your sleeping hours. In a MUD, you can challenge other players who can be anywhere in the world. Lots of other multi-user games are available on the Web, too, like AlphaWorld.

A Few Real-Life Stories

Seventh-grade students in San Diego use the Internet to exchange letters and stories with kids in Israel. Although it's partly just for fun and to make friends in a foreign country, a sober academic study reported that when kids have a real audience for their stuff, they write better. (Big surprise.)

For many purposes, the Internet is the fastest and most reliable way to move information. In September 1998, when special prosecutor Kenneth Starr suddenly delivered his report to the U.S. House of Representatives, the House quickly put the report online, allowing millions of people to read it the day it came out. (We can still debate whether it was a good idea to do that, but the Internet is what made it possible.) And Matt Drudge's *Drudge Report* online gossip sheet broke much of the scandal first.

During the 1991 Soviet coup, members of a tiny Internet provider called RELCOM sent out stories that would have been in newspapers, statements from Boris Yeltsin (hand-delivered by friends), and their personal observations from downtown Moscow.

Medical researchers around the world use the Internet to maintain databases of rapidly changing data. People with medical conditions use the Internet to communicate with each other in support groups and to compare experiences.

The Internet has more prosaic uses, too. Here are some from our personal experience:

When we began writing our megabook, *Internet Secrets* (published by IDG Books Worldwide, Inc.), we posted notices on the Net asking for contributions. We got responses from all over the world. Many of these contributors became our friends. Now we have people to visit all over the world. It could happen to *you.*

We get mail every day from all over the world from readers of our *...For Dummies* books and are often the happy recipients of readers' first-ever e-mail messages.

The Internet is its own best source of software. Whenever we hear about a new service, it usually takes only a few minutes to find software for our computers (various computers running various versions of Windows and a Power Macintosh), download it, and start it up. Most of the software available on the Internet is free or inexpensive shareware.

The Internet has local and regional parts, too. When John wanted to sell a trusty but tired minivan, a note on the Internet in a local for-sale area found a buyer within two days. Margy's husband sold his used computer within a half-hour of posting a message in the relevant Usenet newsgroup.

Why Is This Medium Different from Any Other Medium?

The Internet is unlike all the other communications media we've ever encountered. People of all ages, colors, creeds, and countries freely share ideas, stories, data, opinions, and products.

Anybody can access it

One great thing about the Internet is that it's probably the most open network in the world. Thousands of computers provide facilities that are available to anyone who has Net access. This situation is unusual — most networks are extremely restrictive in what they allow users to do and require specific arrangements and passwords for each service. Although pay services exist (and more are added every day), most Internet services are free for the taking. If you don't already have access to the Internet through your company, your school, your library, or a friend's attic, you probably have to pay for access by using one of the Internet access providers. We talk about them in Chapter 4.

It's politically, socially, and religiously correct

Another great thing about the Internet is that it is what one may call "socially unstratified." That is, one computer is no better than any other, and no person is any better than any other. Who you are on the Internet depends solely on how you present yourself through your keyboard. If what you say makes you sound like an intelligent, interesting person, that's who you are. It doesn't matter how old you are or what you look like or whether you're a student, a business executive, or a construction worker. Physical disabilities don't matter — we correspond with people who are blind or deaf. If they hadn't felt like telling us, we never would have known. People become famous in the Net community, some favorably and some unfavorably, but they get that way through their own efforts.

The Net advantage

Maybe it's obvious to you that Internet technology is changing so quickly that you have barely had time to crack the spine of *The Internet For Dummies,* 5th Edition, and here you are holding the 6th Edition. (We said the same thing last time.) "Could it possibly be all that different?" you ask yourself. Trust us — we've asked ourselves the same thing. The answer, by

Every continent?

Some skeptical readers, after reading the claim that the Internet spans every continent, may point out that Antarctica is a continent, even though its population consists largely of penguins, who (as far as we know) are not interested in computer networks. Does the Internet go there? It does. A few machines at the Scott Base on McMurdo Sound in Antarctica are on the Net, connected by radio link to New Zealand. The base at the South Pole is supposed to have a link to the United States, but it doesn't publish its electronic address.

At the time this book was written, the largest Internet-free land mass in the world is probably Queen Elizabeth Island in the Canadian arctic. We used to say New Guinea, but we got e-mail from a reader there in 1997 telling us about his new Internet provider.

the way, is a resounding "Yes." It's *that* different again this year. This year, we have to say that the Internet is totally mainstream, and you're falling further behind the curve faster if you haven't yet gotten started. Increasingly, news gets out on the Internet before it's available on other media, and the cyber-deprived are losing ground.

Here are some of the ways the Internet is being used:

- **Finding people:** If you've lost track of your childhood sweetheart, now's your chance to find him or her anywhere in the country. You can use one of the directory services to search the phone books of the entire United States. We tell you more about this subject in Chapter 8.

- **Finding businesses, products, and services:** New yellow page directory services enable you to search by the type of company you're looking for. You can indicate the area code or zip code to help specify the location. People are shopping for that hard-to-find, special gift item. A friend told us of her search for a bear pendant that led her to a company in Alaska that had just what she was looking for.

- **Research:** Law firms are realizing that a great deal of information they formerly paid $600 an hour to find from commercial services can be found for almost nothing when they go directly to the Net. Real estate appraisers use demographic data available on the Net, including unemployment statistics, to help assess property values. Genetics researchers and other scientists download up-to-date research results from around the world. Businesses and potential businesses research their competition over the Net.

- **Education:** Schoolteachers coordinate projects with classrooms all over the globe. College students and their families exchange e-mail to facilitate letter writing and keep down the cost of phone calls. Students do research from their home computers. The latest encyclopedias are online.

- **Travel:** Cities, towns, states, and countries are using the Web to put up (post) tourist and event information. Travelers find weather information, maps, transportation schedules and tickets, and museum hours online.

- **Marketing and sales:** Software companies are selling software and providing updates via the Net. (The folks making money from the manufacture of floppy disks are looking for new products. Aside from the large pile of AOL disks we now use as coasters, most software distribution is migrating to the Net.) Companies are selling products over the Net. Online bookstores and music stores enable people to browse online, choose titles, and pay for stuff over the Net.

- **Love:** People are finding romance on the Net. Singles ads and matchmaking sites vie for users. Contrary to Internet lore, the Net community is no longer just a bunch of socially challenged male nerds under 25.

- **Healing:** Patients and doctors keep up-to-date with the latest medical findings, share treatment experience, and give one another support around medical problems. We even know of some practitioners who exchange e-mail directly with their patients.

- **Investing:** People do financial research, buy stock, and invest money. Some companies are online and trade their own shares. Investors are finding new ventures, and new ventures are finding capital.

- **Organizing events:** Conference and trade-show organizers are finding that the best way to disseminate information, call for papers, and do registration is to do it on the Web. Information can be updated regularly, and paper and shipping costs are dramatically reduced. Registering online saves the cost of on-site registration staff and the hassle of on-site registration lines.

- **Nonprofits:** Churches, synagogues, and other community organizations put up pages telling about themselves and inviting new people. The on-line church newsletter *always* comes before Sunday.

Electronic Commerce

We hear many new buzzwords and phrases aimed at confounding the innocent and filling the pockets of would-be consultants. We hear about "digital commerce," "electronic commerce," "digicash," "virtual checks," and "smart cards." If you care, entire books are being written about these subjects. The one topic in this area that you need to know about is buying stuff over the Net. (If you plan to set up your own business and sell stuff over the Net, you need more info than we have pages in this book to cover it.) Chapter 9 tells you all about it.

The earth-shattering, startling new idea of how to buy things over the Net lies buried in the inner meaning of the following phrase: "Enter your credit card number." We're not saying that you shouldn't exercise caution, but our experience of buying stuff over the Net in the past year tells us that you have no great cause for alarm. What have we bought? Books, CDs, clothing, software, videotapes, encyclopedia subscriptions, and matchmaking subscriptions. Here's what you need to know.

Security in general

Some folks seem particularly wary of sending their credit card numbers over the Net. Despite all the foofaraw (technical term) about the risks of online credit card use, we haven't found one single case of a card number being stolen in transit over the Internet. On the other hand, every day, people hand their actual physical cards with their handwritten signatures to gas station attendants wearing distinctive outfits in bright colors not found in nature, to servers at restaurants and to clerks at all sorts of stores. Do you know what they do with the card before they give it back to you? Do you worry about it? We don't. We do know someone who used to run a restaurant and later ran an on-line store, who assures us that he had far more credit card trouble at the restaurant.

If you use a credit card, remember that the credit card companies are even more concerned than you are about the idea of any kind of credit card fraud, on or off the Net. All cards have a limit on the amount of fraudulent use for which you're liable; if you're a U.S. resident, the limit is $50 or less.

The point is, if you're comfortable using a credit card for other uses, you don't have to get really scared about using it over the Net just because it's new. Chapter 9 talks about shopping on the Net, with or without a credit card.

Security in specific

To avoid the possibility of bad guys or gals electronically listening to the bits of your private information whirring across the Net, stripping them off, and redirecting them to purchase their dream vacations, schemes have been invented to encode info sent over the Net so that even if the villains intercept the info, it doesn't do them any good. The information gets all mixed up and hidden in such a way that only the legitimate recipient can decode it. The software that processes this information safely, hiding everything from possible perverse perusal, is known as *SSL* (Secure Sockets Layer) or a *secure server.* Most Web browsers (you can read more about them in Chapter 6) have SSL built right in. If you're the least bit antsy about sending your card number over the Net, stick to secure servers.

Software that takes your credit card number (or any other information) over the Net without encoding it is known as an *insecure server*. Insecure servers are perfectly adequate for many transactions. We use them all the time so long as we know that the business behind the server is reliable.

Some Thoughts about Safety and Privacy

The Internet is a funny place. Although it seems completely anonymous, it's not. People all used to have Internet usernames that bore some resemblance to their true identity — their name or initials or some combination in conjunction with their university or corporation gave a fairly traceable route to an actual person. Today, with the phenomenon of screen names (courtesy of America Online) and multiple e-mail addresses (courtesy of many Internet providers), revealing your identity is definitely optional.

Depending on who you are and what you want to do on the Net, you may, in fact, want different names and different accounts. Here are some legitimate reasons for wanting them:

- You're a professional — a physician, for example — and you want to participate in a mailing list or newsgroup without being asked for your professional opinion.
- You want help with an area of concern that you feel is private and would not want your problem known to people close to you who might find out if your name were associated with it.
- You do business on the Net, and you socialize on the Net. You may want to keep those activities separate.

Safety first

The anonymous, faceless nature of the Internet has its downside, too.

We advise that you do not use your full name or ever provide your name, address, and phone number to someone you don't know over the Net. Never believe anyone who says that he is from "AOL tech support" or some such authority and asks you for your password. No legitimate entity will ever ask you for your password. Be especially careful about disclosing information about kids. Don't fill out profiles in chat rooms that ask for a kid's name, hometown, school, age, address, or phone number, since they are invariably used for "targeted marketing" (a.k.a. junk mail).

Though relatively rare, horrible things have happened to a few people who have taken their Internet encounters into real life. Many wonderful things have happened, too. We've met some of our best friends over the Net, and some people have met and gotten married — no kidding! We just want to encourage you to use common sense when you set up a meeting with a Net friend. Here are a few tips:

- ✔ Talk to the person on the phone before you agree to meet. If you don't like the sound of the person's voice or something makes you feel nervous, don't do it.

- ✔ Depending on the context, try to check the person out a little. If you've met in a newsgroup or chat room, ask someone else you know whether they know this person. (Women, ask another woman before meeting a man.)

- ✔ Meet in a well-lit public place. Take a friend or two with you.

- ✔ If you're a kid, take a parent with you. Never, ever meet someone from the Net without your parents' explicit consent.

The Net is a wonderful place, and meeting new people and making new friends is one of the big attractions. We just want to make sure that you're being careful.

Protect your privacy

Here in the United States, we've grown up with certain attitudes about freedom and privacy, many of which we take for granted. We tend to feel that who we are, where we go, and what we do is our own business as long as we don't bother anyone else. Well, it seems that a whole bunch of people are extremely interested in who we are, where we go (on the Net, at least), and, most especially, what we buy. Here are a few hints to control how much or how little info you give them.

Please pass the cookies

To enhance your online experience, the makers of Web browsers, such as Netscape and Internet Explorer, have invented a type of special message that lets a Web site recognize you when you revisit that site. They thoughtfully store this info, called a *cookie*, on your very own machine to make your next visit to the same site smoother.

Usually this info can in fact make your next transaction smoother. When you're using an airline-reservation site, for example, the site uses cookies to keep the flights you're reserving separate from the ones other users may be reserving at the same time. On the other hand, suppose that you use your credit card to purchase something on a Web site and the site uses a cookie to remember your credit card number. Suppose that you provide this information from a computer at work and the next person to visit that site uses the same computer. That person could, possibly, make purchases on your credit card. Oops.

It may be true that cookies can make your life more convenient. You have to be the judge. Every Web server can offer you cookies. You need to know that this kind of software exists so that if you're concerned about your privacy, you can take steps to protect it.

Cookie files usually have the name *cookie* associated with them — cookies.txt on Windows and MagicCookie on a Mac, for example. You can delete your cookie files — your browser will create a new, empty one. Modern browsers can tell you about cookies and ask you whether to accept them as servers offer them to you. When Carol checked her Macintosh, she found two cookie files — one from Netscape and one from Internet Explorer. If she hadn't been looking for them, she never would have known that they were there.

Contrary to rumor, cookie files cannot get other information from your hard disk, give you a bad haircut, or otherwise mess up your life. They collect only information that the browser tells them about.

In addition to the cookie file, Internet Explorer keeps a history file of where you've been on the Web. (Look in your Windows folder for a subfolder called History.) If anyone other than you uses the computer you use, you may want to delete its contents after your use, unless you don't care who sees it. Courts have ruled, by the way, that companies own their computers and their contents. You have no "right to privacy" at work, even though most of us find the idea creepy. Companies can eavesdrop on phone calls, read your e-mail (going and coming,) and read anything on your computer, including a history file detailing where you've searched. This can be problematical if you've done a little unofficial surfing at lunchtime.

Encryption and pretty good privacy

When you send information through the Internet, it gets relayed from machine to machine, and along the way, if someone really cares, she may be able to take a look at what comes across the wire. Whether you're sending your credit card number or sending e-mail love letters, you may feel more comfortable if the absolute secure nature of the transmission were guaranteed.

You can guarantee security by using encryption. *Encryption* is high-tech-ese for encoding — just like with a secret decoder ring. You know — codes, spies, secret messages. Software exists that helps you package up your message and send it in a way that nobody except the intended recipient can read it. Encryption is the virtual envelope that defies prying eyes. In practice, we rarely encrypt e-mail, though we're happy to know that the option exists. One reason we don't encrypt it is that, at this point, it's too darned cumbersome. Some e-mail software comes with encryption built-in, notably Microsoft Outlook Express, so many more people will choose to use it. Also check out PGP, which stands for *pretty good privacy*, the most widely used encryption scheme on the Net. Because it's complicated enough to require pages of explanation, we don't have room in this book to go into the details; check out our *E-Mail For Dummies* where we give you blow-by-blow details. New, easier-to-use versions of PGP come out every month or two, so a PGP add-in is probably available for your favorite mail program.

WHOOSH

Where did the Internet come from?

The ancestor of the Internet was the *ARPANET,* a project funded by the Department of Defense (DOD) in 1969, both as an experiment in reliable networking and to link DOD and military research contractors, including the large number of universities doing military-funded research. (*ARPA* stands for Advanced Research Projects Administration, the branch of the DOD in charge of handing out grant money. For enhanced confusion, the agency is now known as *DARPA* — the added *D* is for Defense, in case anyone had doubts about where the money was coming from.) Although the ARPANET started small, connecting three computers in California with one in Utah, it quickly grew to span the continent.

In the early 1980s, the ARPANET grew into the early Internet, a group of interlinked networks connecting many educational and research sites funded by the National Science Foundation (NSF), along with the original military ones. By 1990 it was clear that the Internet was here to stay, and DARPA and the NSF bowed out in favor of the commercially run networks that comprise today's Internet. Some of the networks are run by familiar companies like AT&T, Worldcom/MCI, IBM, GTE, and Britain's Cable and Wireless; others belong to specialist companies like PSI and Exodus networks. No matter which one you're attached to, they all interconnect, so it's all one giant Internet.

For yet more Internet history and gossip, visit our Web site at `http://net.gurus.com/history`.

Chapter 2

Intranets, Extranets, and Volleyball Nets

• •

In This Chapter

▶ What is an intranet?

▶ What is an extranet?

▶ What is a volleyball net? (Not in this chapter. Sorry.)

• •

*N*ow that lots of people have cottoned on to the idea that this Internet stuff is pretty cool, clever people have adapted all the cool features and put them to work inside companies and on private networks among companies. You may get the sense that even though the names keep changing, everybody's really talking about the same thing. You would be right. We give you some formal definitions so that you can't be bamboozled by jargon-slinging cybersnobs and so that you can sling jargon whenever you want.

Intranets and What They're Good For

Intranet? Are you sure that that's spelled right? Sure is. Now that everyone knows about the *Internet,* the marketroids have invented *intranet,* which is just the same except different. The idea is simple: Take all that swell technology that has been developed for the Internet during the past 20 years and use it directly inside your company on its own network.

An *intranet* is, specifically, a bunch of services, such as Web pages, that are accessible only within an organization. The World Wide Web works over the Internet with tens of thousands of *Web servers* (computers that store Web pages) serving up Web pages to the general public. An *intranet* works over an organization's internal network with Web servers serving up Web pages to folks within the organization. An intranet is sort of a private World Wide Web — an Organization Wide Web. (OWW! — another acronym!)

What's the big deal?

In one sense, intranets aren't very interesting because anything you can do on an intranet, people have probably been doing on the Internet for years. Departments in your organization create Web pages that other people in the organization can see. So what?

Intranets can be an extremely big deal. In many (if not most) companies, a mountain of important information about the business is locked up in big old databases on big old mainframes or minicomputers. The information would be of great use to people all over the company if only they could get at it. Another mountain of stuff is stuck in spreadsheets and word-processing files on people's computers all over the company. Intranets offer a new way to make that locked-up information available to the rest of the company.

After people within a company have a basic set of Web browsers (which we discuss in Chapters 6 and 7) and other Internet-style software on an intranet, it's surprisingly easy to write software glue (often known as *middleware,* as described in the upcoming sidebar, "You too can be an intranet consultant!") that lets people get at the formerly locked-up information. Lots of people have told us that they can make information available in weeks or months on an intranet that they would have had to spend months or years providing by using older software tools. We have also heard of many "skunkworks" projects in which small but useful intranets have been created quickly and with little or no budget by using a few spare PCs.

After an organization has an intranet — its own Web server and some Web pages — anyone in the organization can see the Web pages by using a browser. Product information, human-resources information, and other stuff is suddenly easy to find, read, and print by using the intranet.

Using intranets

What your organization can do on an intranet is limited only by the imaginations of the people in the organization. (We realize that this limitation is more severe in some organizations than in others, but we're optimists.) Here are some examples; the *italicized* words are all defined in the upcoming sidebar, "You too can be an intranet consultant!":

✔ Nearly all the paper memoranda circulated around a company can be sent more effectively as e-mail messages or as Web pages. This method saves paper and makes the information easier to file and find, and it keeps everyone up-to-date.

✔ Those big, dusty company manuals moldering on the shelf or perhaps holding up one corner of your desk if the floor is uneven work much better as Web pages. They're easier to search through to find the page you want. Also, the authors can update them as often as necessary so that everyone instantly has access to the most current version.

✔ Catalogs, parts lists, and the like are relatively easy to put on the Web by using *database publishing,* a technique that automatically creates Web pages, which contain the information from the *legacy system* in which the information is stored.

✔ If several people are working on a project, putting the project information on the Web lets each person look at and update the status of parts of the project, with everyone seeing up-to-date information. That's how the three authors and the editors of this book, who live in four different states, tracked our progress in updating the book and keeping ourselves moving in roughly the same direction, by using a little Web application John whipped up in an afternoon.

✔ If your company has a flair for multimedia, now you can have animation, video, and sound right on your desktop. Slightly less dramatic but perhaps more useful are new integrated intranet products that let you put "live" links to Web pages in your e-mail messages. Now you can send around a memo that refers to all types of different material with a link directly to that material. Your readers have to just click the link to see the information you're referencing.

All in all, we see the technology flowing both ways. As Internet technology, particularly e-mail and Web technology, combines with traditional databases, the ways in which companies manage information are bound to change. Paper memoranda will become about as common as the IBM Selectric, and large, metal file cabinets will fill much more slowly.

Extra, Extra Net, Net Net

Anything worth doing is worth doing in any number of ways. We start with the Internet; we bring it into the company — we get an intranet; we take the intranet out of the company, and — voilà — we get an *extranet.* Not that this net is *extra,* mind you: We mean *extra* as in "outside," as in *extra*terrestrial.

Here's the idea: Now that people are successfully using Internet technology (browsing, creating Web pages, and using e-mail, for example) *inside* companies, the logical extension is to expand these internal networks to include a company's customers, suppliers, and business partners. After intranets expanded outside the boundaries of one organization to include other entities, someone ingenious created a brand-new buzzword: *extranet.* As is the case with intranets, it's all the same technology — it's just used in a different way.

You too can be an intranet consultant!

A general rule in the computing industry says that a consultant is anyone more than 75 miles from home. Although we can't offer transportation, here are some handy buzzwords you will want to use if you want to sound like an intranet expert. (See if you can use all of them in one sentence.)

- **Client/server:** A type of computer system in which one program, the client, runs on your computer so that you can work with it directly; a separate program, the server, runs on another computer and manages all the important data; and a computer network connects the two. Although the Internet has always worked this way, it took the special insight of the large-scale business data-processing industry to realize that you could make a great deal of money in the process.

- **Database publishing (DP):** The process of taking a company's information that used to be locked away in databases where only the DP types and a few managers could see it and making it available to large numbers of people inside and even outside the company. DP makes it much easier to get your job done but makes managers nervous. ("If they know everything I know, how can I keep my job?")

- **Drill down:** To throw away all the confusing but important details and reduce something to one or two simple ideas a customer can understand, or conversely, to look at the underlying data from which a simple idea or number came. Yes, these are practically opposite definitions, which give you a lot of room to improvise.

- **Legacy:** Referring to something that's obsolete but still essential. "I'm looking for a pair of recapped whitewalls for my legacy vehicle here." Usually it's *legacy system,* a computer system that has been nursed along for the past 25 years, and everyone who remembers how it was originally put together has retired.

- **Middleware:** Software that connects one piece of software to another piece of software. In the movie *Apollo 13,* the air scrubbers in the command module are exhausted and the astronauts have to use spares from the lunar module. The spare air scrubbers are a completely different shape, so the astronauts concoct something from duct tape and wire and who-knows-what to make it fit — the concoction was middleware.

- **Platform:** The underlying computer hardware or software on which a system runs. "We're targeting a Netscape platform on a Windows 98 Pentium platform."

- **Solution:** A software package or a hardware and software combination that does something, preferably an expensive software package or combination.

Really, you care

Once again, you may be asking yourself, what does this stuff have to do with me? Well, Internet technology is changing the way our world operates. For example, you may notice that you're talking to your favorite companies over the Net instead of picking up the phone. Smart companies are realizing that they can cut costs in the areas of customer service, marketing, and sales by using Internet technology. Some of what you see will seem just like the Internet to you. The glue that's connecting the Internet site you see to the company or companies that are handling your transactions, however, is really an extranet — the linking of internal systems with the outside.

Another important aspect of extranets is that they can be designed with security in mind and allow only people with legitimate access to use the extranet facilities.

Let us count the ways

Here are some of the ways folks are using extranets. Your imagination can no doubt continue where we've left off:

- ✔ Newsletters, press releases, product announcements, and any other information a company would send out by snail mail (the kind that uses paper and a postage stamp) or fax can be e-mailed and put on a Web site.
- ✔ Catalogs and brochures can be placed on the Web to radically reduce printing costs and enable materials to be easily updated.
- ✔ Customers can place and track orders.
- ✔ Answers to frequently asked questions can be posted on a Web site to eliminate lots of phone calls.

Why This Is the Last You Will Hear from Us about Intranets and Extranets

Because no fundamental difference exists between intranets, extranets, and *the* Internet, we'll stop talking about them. The more you use these technologies, the more you're going to expect everyone around you to get smart and get with it. Buy those people a book. Internet and Web technology are much like the telephone — much more useful when everyone has them and uses them.

Chapter 3
The Net, Your Kids, and You

*W*ith more than a million kids already online and an estimated 7 million online by the turn of the millennium, we think that a discussion of families online is critical. Obviously, if this isn't your concern, just skip this chapter and go to the next.

Stop Making Sense

Most parents are trying to make sense of the Internet and what it means for them and their families. Although no one has the ultimate answer, we can talk about some of the major issues being raised, the benefits we see, and the problems. The Net has dramatic implications in the education, entertainment, and socialization of our children. The more we know and are actively involved, the better choices we can make.

What's in it for us?

We're just beginning to discover the myriad ways in which the Internet can be exciting in the context of our families' lives. Here are some of the ways in which we think that it enhances our lives:

- It provides information about every topic imaginable.
- It provides personal contact with new people and cultures.
- It helps develop and improve reading, writing, research, and language skills.
- It provides support for families with special needs.
- It is an exciting new outlet for artistic expression.

Not everything new is wonderful, and not everything wonderful is new. In talking about children, we have to make distinctions: Are they preschoolers or college kids? Because what makes sense for one group in this case usually doesn't map to another, the remainder of this section considers how the Internet works for different age groups.

The Internet for young children

We have to say up front that we are strong advocates of allowing children to be children, and we believe that children are better teachers than computers are. None of our kids watch commercial TV. Now that you know our predisposition, maybe you can guess what we're going to say next: We are not in favor of sticking a young child in front of a screen. How young is young? We believe that younger than age 7 is young. Many educators believe that unstructured computer time for kids younger than age 11 is inappropriate. We recommend that children get as much human attention as possible, and we believe that computers make lousy baby-sitters. At young ages, children benefit more from playing with trees, balls, clay, crayons, paint, mud, monkey bars, bicycles, and other kids.

Even if you do want to let your small kids use the Internet, frankly, not much is out there for the pre-reading set anyway.

The Internet for K–12

K–12 is the label given to all the education that happens in the United States between preschool (nursery school or day care) and college. It's a broad category. We use it here because many mailing lists and newsgroups use the K–12 designation, and it seems to be common ground for many people. We think that Internet access is more appropriate for somewhat older children (fourth or fifth grade and older), but your mileage may vary.

The Internet is an incredible way to expand the walls of a school. The Net can connect you to other schools and to libraries, research resources, museums, and other people. You can visit the Louvre (at `http://mistral.culture.fr/louvre`) and the Sistine Chapel; practice your French or Spanish or Portuguese or Russian or Japanese (using online chat); and hear new music and make new friends.

School projects such as the Global Schoolhouse connect kids around the world by working collaboratively on all types of projects. The first annual global learning project drew more than 10,000 students from 360 schools in 30 different countries. Since then, annual cyberfairs have brought together over 500,000 students from hundreds of schools in at least 37 countries!

You can send an e-mail message to the Global Schoolhouse at helper@gsn.org or check out the foundation's Web site at http://www.gsn.org. (We explain these funny-looking locations in Chapter 6, so you can come back here later and follow up on them.) From the Global Schoolhouse Web site, you can subscribe to lots of mailing lists. If you don't have Web access, you can subscribe to the Global Watch mailing list (Chapter 13 has all the details) by sending an e-mail message to lists@gsn.org that contains this single line in the body of the text: *subscribe global-watch.*

College and the Net

Although the Internet has had a home in universities for a long time, what's happening with the World Wide Web is new for everyone. Much of the inspiration and perspiration of the volunteers who are making information available to everyone is coming from universities, both students and faculty, who see the incredible potential for learning.

Many campuses provide free or low-cost access to the Internet for their students and staff. Campuses that enable you to register early sometimes give you that access when you register, even months in advance. If you're going to go anyway, you can get a jump on your Internet education before you even get to campus.

Checking out colleges on the Net

Most colleges and universities have or are rapidly creating sites on the Web. You can find a directory of online campus tours at http://www.campustours.com, with links to lots more info about the colleges and universities.

After you're a little more adept at using the Net, you can research classes and professors to get a better idea of what appeals to you.

The Internet (more specifically, e-mail) is a great way for parents and college kids to stay in touch. It's much cheaper than phoning home and easier than coordinating schedules. Forwarding mail to other family members allows for broader communication. We noticed another surprising benefit: In our experience, families tend to fight less when they're communicating by e-mail. Somehow, when folks have time to think about what they're going to say before they say it, it comes out better.

Finding a job through the Net

Not just for students, the Net is an incredible tool for finding a job. It's especially good for students because it provides a powerful, economical way to conduct a real job search. You can publish your résumé online for prospective employers. You can check out the Monsterboard, an impressive compilation of job-related information that enables you to search by discipline (the area of study — all searches need the other kind) or geography or a host of other criteria. You can find the Monsterboard at `http://www.monster.com`. You can also research companies to find ones you may want to work for.

Companies have found that posting their jobs on the Net is an effective, economical way to recruit talented people. Check out the home pages of companies that interest you, and look for their open positions. Many colleges and universities have career office home pages, many of which are grouped together for you on the Web. Ask a Web search engine such as AltaVista (which we visit in Chapter 8) to look for "career office home pages" to get college and university listings grouped by geography.

When the Net is college

It's no exaggeration to say that many people are learning more on the Net than they ever did in school. Although many factors have to be considered, the Net requires motivation, and motivated learning is much more fun. The Net provides equal opportunity beyond the imagination of those locked in physical settings. It is open to everyone of any color, height, belief, and description. People previously locked out of educational opportunities by physical handicap, economic need, conflicting work schedules, or geography find the Net an empowering, life-altering experience.

Beyond the informal education that's already available, organizations are actively working to establish formal online colleges. The Globewide Network Academy (at `http://www.gnacademy.org:8001/uu-gna`) may have been the first completely virtual incorporated educational institution. It serves as a clearinghouse for online courses available throughout the world.

Of Paramount Concern

High on the list of parents' concerns about the Internet is the question of children's access to inappropriate material, including businesses trying to market and sell directly to children. This concern is a legitimate one: As time has gone by, both the good stuff and the grody stuff on the Net have increased dramatically. We have no simple answers. One thing is crystal clear to us: Parents *have* to be involved. Considering the direction of education and edicts from on high, *kids will be involved* with the Internet, as schools hook up at a rapid clip.

Hey, Mom, what's on?

Parents who take the time to learn about access issues usually understand that, on one hand, the threat is not as great as some would have you believe, while some of the proposed solutions have severe problems of their own. Parents who have thought about the issues on a larger scale are extremely concerned that reactionary sentiment and hyperbole pose a real threat to our freedom of expression and that those reactions are ultimately a great danger to our children. On the other hand, a great deal of garbage lurks online. Parental involvement is essential; we talk about family strategy a little later in this chapter. If you're interested in thrashing out these issues, you can subscribe to the CACI (Children Accessing Controversial Information) mailing list by sending an e-mail message to `majordomo@cygnus.com` with the words *subscribe caci* in the body of the message. (We talk about sending e-mail in Chapter 11.)

Sell, sell, sell!

Another problem that has surfaced that *should* be of concern to parents but doesn't get much press is the targeting of children by marketing organizations. Children of middle- and upper-income families are considered the most lucrative target market, and the Net is being viewed as another way to capture this audience.

Targeting children isn't new. You're probably familiar with Joe Camel, the Camel cigarette campaign that many people claimed was aimed at kids. You may know about Channel One, which brings advertising directly to the classroom. If you have ever walked into Toys R Us, you've seen the unmistakable link between television shows and toys.

You should know that astute marketing types have already designed kid-friendly, fascinating, captivating software to help them better market to your kids. Delightful, familiar cartoon characters deftly elicit strategic marketing information directly from the keyboard in your home. You should be aware of this situation and teach your children about what to do when someone on the Web is asking for information. You can obtain a copy of the Center for Media Education report *The Web of Deception* by sending $25 to the organization, at 1511 K Street NW, Suite #518, Washington, DC 20005. The Federal Trade Commission has also weighed in on this topic. It is on the Web as well at `http://www.ftc.gov`; when you go there click Consumer Protection and then Children's Issues.

Who's there?

We strongly encourage families using the Net for personal reasons (distinct from businesspeople using the Net for business purposes) not to use their full or real names and never to disclose names, addresses, phone numbers, Social Security numbers, or account information — such as a password — to anyone who asks for it online or off. This advice applies especially when you receive information requests from people claiming to be in positions of authority, such as the instant messages AOL users have received from people claiming that they're from AOL tech support and need your password information. They're not and they don't.

People with real authority never ask those types of questions.

More than ever, children need to develop critical thinking skills. They have to learn how to evaluate what they read and see — especially on the Web.

Regrettably, we have to report that we have seen a great deal of trashy e-mail (*spam*) lately. This situation is likely to get worse until someone figures out an effective way to deal with unsolicited e-mail. Again, you have to be involved and teach your children what to do.

Parental Guidance Required

Parents, educators, and free-speech advocates alike agree that parental guidance has no substitute when it comes to the subject of Internet access. Just as you as parents want your children to read good books and see quality films, you also want them to find the good stuff on the Net. If you take the time to find out these things with your children, you have the opportunity to share the experience and to impart critical values and a sense of discrimination that your children need in all areas of their lives.

The good stuff on the Net vastly outweighs the bad. Software aids are being developed almost daily to help parents and educators tap the invaluable resources of the Net without opening Pandora's box. Remember that every child is different and that what may be appropriate for your children may not be appropriate for someone else's. You have to find what's right for you.

Establish rules for your family's use of the Net. Outline areas that are off-limits and inside the limits, limit the time that can be spent online, and be explicit about the types of information kids can give out over the Net.

Using the Internet, like watching television, is a solitary experience, so it takes extra effort from you to establish limits and at the same time give your child the freedom he needs to explore the cyberworld. Some families prefer to keep their computers in a family space as opposed to in kids' bedrooms. Wherever they are, check often; don't let the screen be your baby-sitter.

Kids need explicit rules about talking with and meeting people they meet on the Net. Never let your kids meet a cyberfriend by themselves. Keep an eye on your phone bill for unusual calls.

Setting limits

Now that most Internet service providers charge a flat rate for service, you can't rely on economic incentive alone to curb your Internet use. If you don't let your children watch unlimited television, don't let them have unlimited computer access either. Don't buy in to the hype that just because it's on a computer, it's educational. We're reminded of the cartoon featuring wishful parents reading the newspaper's Help Wanted section and finding that Nintendo players are making $70,000. Everyone knows kids whose lives seem to be lost in front of a screen. Don't let that be your kid.

Rating the ratings

Several schemes have been proposed that involve the rating of Internet content. Who will rate the material, and whose ratings will you trust? Is the author of a Web page or other online material the best person to assign the ratings? Probably not. Internet software designers have added provisions for third-party ratings so that you can choose or exclude material by the ratings, although the guidelines the raters use may not be the ones you would choose.

In an attempt to address the concern of controlling access while not caving in to censorship, the World Wide Web Consortium (W3C) has designed a standard for marking Web content so that third parties can rate the material. You can read all about the standard, called PICS (Platform for Internet Content Selection), at this Web address:

```
http://www.wellesley.edu/CS/JimMillerTalk/9601PICS/
        slide1.htm
```

Or see the W3C Web page about PICS, at

```
http://www.w3.org/PICS
```

Other software under development will let parents limit access by their own criteria. A parent who feels strongly about warthogs and asparagus, for example, will be able to block all material about those subjects. More realistically, they'll be able to block heavy fictionalized violence and still permit access to medical information about sexually transmitted diseases.

Consumer's choice

Because parents are paying for online services, services that want to remain competitive are vying for parental dollars by providing features to help families control Internet access. America Online, for example, enables you to block access to chat rooms that may not be appropriate for children and to restrict access to discussion groups and newsgroups based on keywords you choose. Parental blocking is available at no extra cost. WebTV enables the master account holder to restrict the material that subaccount holders can view.

Software sentries

More and more products are appearing on the market to help parents restrict access or monitor usage by some sort of activity report. If you choose to use one of these systems, remember that they're not a substitute for your direct involvement with your child's Internet experience; they all filter based on keywords and fixed lists of systems that the programs' authors believe to have objectionable material. None of them tells you exactly what they block, and your idea of what's appropriate and inappropriate may well not be the same as theirs. Many software sentries seem to have political agendas, blocking sites whose political opinions don't conform with those of the program's authors.

You can try before you buy by downloading evaluation copies of software-blocking packages. (You see how to do that when you find out how to navigate the Web in Chapters 6 and 7.) Here are a few blocking programs we're aware of:

✔ SurfWatch, from Spyglass

> **Phone:** 888-6SPYGLASS (888-677-9452)
> **E-mail:** info@surfwatch.com
> **URL:** www.surfwatch.com

Available for both Windows and Macintosh, SurfWatch screens for newsgroups likely to contain sexually explicit material and keeps a computer from accessing specified Web, FTP, Gopher, and chat sites.

✔ Net Nanny, from Net Nanny Software International, Inc.

Phone: 800-349-7177
E-mail: netnanny@netnanny.com
URL: www.netnanny.com

This PC-based product monitors all PC activity, both online and off the Net, in real-time. The parent- (or employer- or teacher-) defined dictionary enables you to determine what's not appropriate in your home. Net Nanny creates a log of children's activities.

✔ Cybersitter, from Solid Oak Software, Inc.

Phone: 800-388-2761
E-mail: info@solidoak.com
URL: www.solidoak.com/cysitter.htm

This Windows-based Internet filtering program blocks Web sites and newsgroups and filters e-mail. Cybersitter also generates a report of site visits.

For a list of all the filtering products known to human-kind, and a lot more helpful advice about ways to protect your kids, check out http://www.smartparent.com.

Internet Resources for Kids

As you may have guessed, the Internet is replete with resources for kids — and parents, by the way. As we have learned from writing this book five times in five years, nothing is as ephemeral as a Net address. To help keep this information as accurate as possible, we're putting our lists of resources on our Web site, both to keep them up-to-date and because they're too long to list here completely. From there, you can get right to the source, and we do our best to keep the sources current.

Visit http://net.gurus.com/kids, which puts you one mouse-click away from the pages described in this section.

Mailing lists for parents and kids

Chapter 13 tells you how to subscribe to mailing lists. Lots of mailing lists for and about kids are listed on our Web page.

Web sites for kids

Okay, we admit it. Web sites can be the coolest thing since sliced bread. Our Web site has links to sites from around the world especially for kids. To get to these sites, you have to know how to use a browser, such as Netscape, Internet Explorer, or Lynx. We tell you how in Part III.

When we're looking for fun, we tend to think that color and graphics make all the difference. If you spend a great deal of time on the Web, you probably won't be satisfied for long with plain text. To get the best from the Web, you need a color screen and a Net connection that gives you graphics. If those items aren't available to you now, by all means check stuff out anyway; just remember that you may have more fun in the text-based world of mailing lists and newsgroups, where content is more important than form.

Help for parents of kids with problems

One of the most heartening experiences available on the Net has to do with the help that total strangers freely offer one another. The bonds that form from people sharing their experiences, struggles, strengths, and hopes redefine what it means to reach out and touch someone. We encourage everyone who has a concern to look for people who share that concern. Our experience of participating in mailing lists and newsgroups related to our own problems compels us to enthusiastically encourage you to check things out online. You can do so with complete anonymity, if you want. You can watch and learn for a long time, or you can jump into the fray and ask for help.

Remember that everyone who gives advice is not an expert. You have to involve your own practitioners in your process. Many people have found enormous help, however, from people who have gone down similar paths before them. For many of us, it has made all the difference in the world.

Our Web site lists a few of the available online mailing lists and discussion groups. A mailing list or group specific to your needs almost certainly exists regardless of whether we list it, and new groups are added every day. If you're using a commercial provider, such as America Online or CompuServe, it has special forums that may interest you as well.

Notice that some lists are talk lists, which feature free-flowing discussion; some lists have focused discussions, and some lists are almost purely academic. The type of discussion is not always obvious from the name. If it looks interesting, subscribe and see what sort of discussion is going on there. It's easy enough to unsubscribe if you don't like it.

The Internet in Schools

As schools hook up to the Net, they are actively debating Internet access for their students. Find out as much as you can and get involved. The more you know, the more you can advocate for appropriate access.

Contractually speaking

Many kids are smart. Smart kids can find ways around rules, and smart kids can find ways around software systems designed to "protect" kids. Many institutions rely successfully on students' signed contracts that detail explicitly what is appropriate and what is inappropriate system use. Students who violate one of these contracts lose their Internet or computer privileges.

We believe that this approach is a good one. In our experience, kids are quicker and more highly motivated and have more time to spend breaking in to and out of systems than most adults we know, and this method encourages them to do something more productive than electronic lock-picking.

Real education

Used effectively, the Internet is a terrific educational resource. Used ineffectively, it's a terrific waste of time and money. The difference is research and planning. We were chatting with our local elementary school principal who'd just spent four hours one weekend afternoon searching the Net to help her son, who teaches third grade in a nearby district, develop a unit on Canada. Once you get a little familiarity with the Web and the ways to find things online (which we cover in Chapter 8), offer to help your teachers look for material to bolster their teaching.

Part II
Internet, Here I Come

The 5th Wave   By Rich Tennant

In this part . . .

After you're ready to get started, where do you start? Probably the hardest part of using the Internet is getting connected. We help you figure out which kind of Internet service is right for you and help you get connected.

Chapter 4

Picking Your Internet Service

● ●

In This Chapter

▶ Connecting to the Net

▶ Determining whether you're on the Net already

▶ Looking at types of accounts

▶ Deciding where to get an account

▶ Figuring out what kind of software you need

● ●

"*G*reat," you say, "How do I get to the Internet?" The answer is "It depends." The Internet isn't one network — it's 100,000 separate networks hooked together, each with its own rules and procedures, and you can get to the Net from any one of them. Readers of previous editions of this book pleaded (they did other things, too, but this is a family-oriented book) for step-by-step directions on how to get on, so we make them as step-by-step as we can.

Here are the basic steps:

1. **Figure out what type of computer you have or can use.**

2. **Figure out which types of Internet connections are available where you are.**

3. **Figure out how much you're willing to pay.**

4. **Set up your connection and decide whether you like it.**

Do You Have a Computer?

We used to say, "There's really no way around this one." In fact, it's still true. Because the Internet is a computer network, the only way to hook to it is by using a computer. Computers are starting to appear in all sorts of disguises, and they may well already be in your home, whether you know it or not.

Nope!

If you don't have a computer, you still have some options. If you have a computer at work, particularly if it's already set up to handle electronic mail, you may already have an Internet connection (see the following sidebar, "Are you already on the Internet?").

If you don't have the work option, the next most likely place to find Net access is in your public library, particularly if your local cable-TV company thinks that it wants to get into the Internet business: Because hooking up to the Internet over a TV cable turns out to be a technical nightmare, cable companies often set up one free connection at the library first to get the bugs out. (Because it's free, it's hard to complain when it doesn't work.)

Another possibility is a local community college, continuing-education center, or even high school, which often have short, inexpensive "Introduction to the Internet" courses. You may ask, "What kind of loser book tells people to go out and take a course?" A course can offer two things you can't possibly get from any book: A live demonstration of what the Internet is like and, more important, someone to talk to who knows the local Internet situation. You can certainly get on the Net without a class (we did, after all); if an inexpensive class is available, though, take it.

Popping up with surprising speed are cybercafés. You can now surf the Net while sipping your favorite beverage and sharing your cyberexperience. If you want to check out the Internet, cybercafés are a great place to try before you buy. If you decide to go the cybercafé route, check out the section about cybercafé etiquette in Chapter 22.

If you're trying to avoid buying a computer and you already own a television you're fond of, you may think about buying WebTV (a small computer in disguise). This option is somewhat cheaper than buying a computer, because it isn't a general-purpose computer and it uses your existing TV as a monitor. Although this option has drawbacks, of course, it may be just what you need, at least for your first date. We describe how to get connected using WebTV in the next chapter.

Yup!

Ah, you do have a computer. (Or maybe you're thinking about buying one.)

One approach (let's call it the geek, or deranged, approach) is to run network cables — held in place by duct tape, of course — all over your house, climb up on the roof, put up radio antennas, and fill up the attic with humming boxes full of routers and spread spectrum network adapters and channel service units and heaven knows what else. Although this approach can be made to work (John has done it, in fact, more than once), if you were the kind of geek who liked to do that sort of thing, you probably wouldn't be reading this book.

Another approach, the normal approach, is to use a computer and a phone line to dial in to an Internet service in which the geeks have already set things up for you. Margy favors this approach.

The snazzy approach, not yet available universally, is the cable modem approach. Your local cable company brings nifty equipment and connects your computer to a high-speed connection while you sit back and watch. Carol likes this approach best.

The couch potato approach involves buying a special box to connect to your TV. None of us likes this particular approach, though we know people whom we respect who do. Out of respect for them, and you, we tell you all about WebTV.

Let's Be Normal

To make the normal approach work, you need four things:

- ✔ A computer
- ✔ A modem to hook your computer to the phone line
- ✔ An account with an Internet provider to give your modem somewhere to call
- ✔ Software to run on your computer

We look at each of these items in turn.

Are you already on the Internet?

If you have access to a computer or a computer terminal, you may already be on the Internet. Here are some ways to check.

If you have an account on an online service, such as CompuServe, America Online (AOL), or Microsoft Network (MSN), you already have a connection to the Internet. At the least, you can send mail, and some online services provide relatively complete Internet connections.

If your company or school has an internal e-mail system, it may also be connected to the Internet. Ask a local mail expert.

If your company or school has a local computer network, it may be connected directly or indirectly to the Internet, either just for mail or for a wider variety of services. Networks of workstations usually use the same type of networking that the Internet does, so connection is technically easy. Because networks of PCs or Macs often use different types of network setups (most commonly Novell Netware or AppleTalk), it's more difficult, but still possible, for the people who run the network to hook it to the Internet.

Any Computer Will Do

People argue at great length about the advantages and disadvantages of various types of computers. We don't do that here (although, if you'll buy the beer, we'll be happy to argue about it after work). Almost any personal computer made since 1980 is adequate for at least some type of connection to the Internet, although some computers make it easier than others. If you're really going to buy a computer, we strongly encourage you to buy a new one, or at least not one that's more than a year old. New computers come with Internet software already installed and are configured for the latest in Web technology. If you buy an older computer, you will spend much more time and energy, and ultimately just as much money, just trying to get the thing to work the way you want. Unless you already own such a thing, therefore, we think that you're best off buying a brand-new computer. New computers are getting cheaper and cheaper, and you can get a downright good one for $1,000 or less.

The most popular computers are IBM-compatible computers running Windows 95 or 98 and Macintoshes. On either of those types of computers, you can get the spiffiest type of Internet connection (known as a PPP connection), which makes it possible to use the nicest point-and-click programs to get pictures, sounds, and even movies from the Net.

On any other type of computer, you can still have a text-only Internet connection that isn't as cool as the fancy ones but is still adequate for a great deal of both Net surfing and useful work.

Modems, Ho!

A *modem* is the thing that hooks your computer to the phone line. Because the usual way to hook up to the Internet is over the phone, you need a modem. Modems come in all sorts of shapes and sizes. Some are separate boxes, known as *external* modems, with cables that plug in to the computer and the phone line with power cords. Others are inside the computer, with just a cable for the phone, and some of the newest ones are tiny credit-card-size things you stuff into the side of your computer. (They still have a cable for the phone — some things never change.)

Matching the variety of physical sizes is an equally wide variety of internal features. The speed at which a modem operates (or the rate at which it can stuff computer data into a phone line) ranges from a low of 2,400 bits per second (bps, commonly but erroneously called baud) to 56,000 bps (usually abbreviated 56K, and the bps part is dropped.) Some modems can act as fax machines, and some can't. Some have even more exotic features, such as built-in answering machines.

Pretty much any modem made in the past ten years is adequate for an initial foray on the Net, and most computers sold in the past couple of years come with built-in modems. If you already have a modem, use it. If you have to buy a modem, get a 56K, since anything less won't be much cheaper. Be sure to get a cable to connect the modem to your computer, and be sure that it has connectors that match the computer — three different types of plugs may be on the back of a computer.

Note to laptop computer owners: If your computer has credit-card-size PC Card slots but no built-in modem, get a PC Card modem that fits in a slot so that you don't have to carry around a separate modem when you take your computer on the road. Although it costs more, it's worth it.

Providing That. . .

You have to pay to subscribe to a provider to give you your Internet connection. You use your computer and modem to call in to the provider's system, and the provider handles the rest of the details of connecting to the Internet.

You can choose from (wait — no, how did you guess?) many different types of Internet providers, with a trade-off among ease of use, range of features, and price.

Big ol' commercial providers

You can choose a big, commercial online service, such as America Online (AOL), CompuServe, or Microsoft Network (MSN). Each has its own software package that you run on your computer and that connects you to the service. AOL and CompuServe (which is now owned by AOL) have versions of the packages for Windows, Mac, and even DOS. AOL requires that you use its software, and MSN requires that you have Windows 95 or Windows 98.

Here are some good things about the big commercial services:

✔ They're relatively easy to get connected to and use.

✔ They claim to have lots of helpful people you can call when you get stuck. (Our firsthand experience doesn't necessarily substantiate these claims.)

✔ They offer flashy screen- and mouse-oriented programs to help you use them.

✔ They offer proprietary services and information not available elsewhere on the Net (although much of the material that used to be available solely via these services has now moved to public areas on the Net).

✔ Many give you a way to limit the material your kids can access.

Here are some bad things about the big commercial services:

✔ They limit you to whatever specific set of Internet services they choose to offer; if you want something else, you're out of luck.

✔ They make it more difficult or, in some cases, impossible to get to parts of the Net considered controversial. (Some people consider this restriction to be an advantage, of course.)

Figure 4-1 shows a typical screen from AOL.

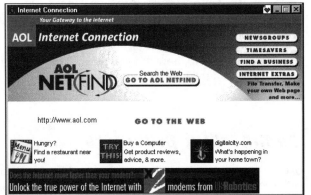

Figure 4-1:
America
Online is
on-screen.

The Internet, the whole Internet, and nothing but the Internet, so help us. . .

The next type of provider to look at is an *Internet service provider,* often abbreviated *ISP.* (We computer types just love TLAs — three-letter acronyms.) An ISP is similar to a commercial service, but with the important difference that its primary business is hooking people to the Internet. Because almost all ISPs buy their equipment and software from a handful of manufacturers, the features and services that one ISP offers are much like those of another, with important differences such as price, service, and reliability. Think of it as the difference between a Ford and a Buick, with the differences between your local dealers being at least as important in the purchase decision as the differences between the cars.

How much does this all cost?

You can spend a great deal of money on your Internet connection. Or you can spend practically none. Here are a few things to look out for.

Provider charges

Pricing schemes vary all over the lot. Most providers charge about $20/month and give you either unlimited hours or a large monthly allotment of 80 to 100 hours. Often there is a cheaper $5 rate that only includes 3 or 4 hours, with time beyond the included amount charged at $2/hour or so. Most people prefer a flat rate or at least a large enough allotment that they're unlikely to use it up. If you do pick one with limited free hours, studies have shown that the average Internet use is about 18 hours per month.

A few providers charge more for daytime use than for nights and weekends, although that's much less common than it used to be.

If you or your kids become regular online users, you will find that time stands still while you're online and that you use much more online time than you think you do. Even if you think that you will be online for only a few minutes a day, if you don't have a flat-rate plan, you may be surprised when your bill arrives at the end of the month.

Phone charges

If you're not careful, you can end up paying more for the phone call than you do for your Internet service. One of the things you do when you sign up for an online service is to determine the phone number to call. *If at all possible, use a provider whose number is a free or untimed local call.* If you use a local or regional Internet service provider, that provider will have a short list of phone numbers you can use. Of the national providers, IBM and AT&T have their own national networks of dial-in numbers; the rest piggyback on other networks, such as Sprintnet, from Sprint; Tymnet, from MCI; and Alternet and the CompuServe network from WorldCom. If one national provider has a local number, therefore, they probably all do because it's a Sprintnet, Tymnet, Alternet, or CompuServe number that works for any of them.

If you cannot find a provider that's a local call for you, your options are limited. If you have a long-distance plan, such as Sprint Sense (Sprint) or Friends and Family (MCI), you can put your provider's phone number on your list of frequently called numbers and get a low rate that should be less than ten cents per minute. (That's still more than $5 per hour.) Be sure to compare rates for in-state and out-of-state calls because an out-of-state call is cheaper in many cases even though it's farther away. Beware of 800 numbers, which almost always levy a stiff hourly surcharge.

Some providers give you software that automatically selects a local phone number to dial. Usually it chooses correctly, but we've heard enough horror stories that you should always verify that the number your computer is calling is in fact a local call. Check the front of your phone book or call the local business office.

If you're a long, expensive toll call from anywhere, take a look at MCI Mail, which offers only one service (electronic mail) but, uniquely, has 800-number access from anywhere in the country at no hourly charge.

ISPs provide two different types of access: PPP/SLIP and shell (see the "It's terminal" sidebar). Some ISPs offer both types, though shell access is a dying breed.

The standard type of connection to the Internet is known as *PPP* access. (An older, obsolete scheme called SLIP works similarly to PPP, but PPP is better.) When you connect to your provider with PPP, your computer becomes part of the Internet. You type stuff directly to programs running on your computer, and those programs communicate over the Net to do whatever it is they do for you.

This type of access lets programs running on your computer take full advantage of your computer's facilities so that the programs can draw graphics, display windows, play sounds, receive mouse clicks, and otherwise do all the fancy stuff that modern computer programs do. If your computer system can handle more than one running program at a time, as the Mac and Windows can do, you can have several Internet applications running at a time, which can be quite handy. You may be reading your e-mail, for example, and receive a message describing a cool new home page on the World Wide Web. You can switch immediately to your Web program (Netscape Navigator Internet Explorer, most likely), look at the page, and then return to the mail program and pick up where you left off. Most new e-mail programs highlight URLs (Web addresses) and enable you to go straight to your browser by clicking the URL in your e-mail message.

Another advantage of PPP is that you're not limited to running programs your Internet provider gives you. You can download a new Internet application from the Net and begin using it immediately — your provider is just acting as a data conduit between your computer and the rest of the Net.

The Beauty of Bandwidth

If you're the type of person who likes to live on the edge, technologically speaking, you're the type of person who wants the fastest Internet connection available so that you can play with all the fancy graphics and download sound and video. Graphics, video, and sound are all bits of information — lots and lots of bits of information — too many for most dial-up connections to handle. High-speed connections can provide greater *bandwidth,* the amount of data transferred in a specific amount of time. The good news is that high-speed connections are becoming available and affordable by mere mortals.

It's terminal

The older type of ISP account is *UNIX shell access.* Although it's less flexible than PPP, it's easier to set up. For shell access, the only software you need on your computer is a *terminal emulator,* a type of simple program found on nearly any computer shipped since 1970. Windows 95/98 users can use Hyperterminal, Windows 3.1 users can use Windows Terminal, and DOS users can use many shareware and freeware programs, such as ProComm.

With shell access, your provider's computer is considered part of the Internet, but your computer is not. When you connect to your provider, you type commands to its system that tell it what Internet or other functions you want to perform. The program on your provider's computer that receives and acts on the commands is known as a *shell* (hence the name). The shell and the programs it runs for you send back to your computer some text that is displayed on-screen.

You don't get graphics, but for text-only e-mail and Web browsing, shell access can be quite adequate. If you are so inclined, you can generally customize your account to do automatic mail sorting and other tasks even when you're not logged in. If you want the power of shell access but your ISP doesn't offer it, many shell ISPs have a less expensive *telnet* option in which you connect to your own ISP and then use the Internet terminal emulator called *telnet* to connect to the shell ISP.

Almost without exception, shell access providers are running some version of UNIX system software, perhaps Linux, so it eventually helps to understand a little about UNIX systems. We shamelessly recommend our *UNIX For Dummies* and *MORE UNIX For Dummies* (both published by IDG Books Worldwide, Inc.), of course.

At this point we don't know of any national providers offering shell access. (Netcom has some grandfathered shell users, but not to new users.) One of the largest regional shell providers, which may also be the nation's oldest ISP, is The World in Brookline, Massachusetts, run by Internet pioneer and peanut butter connoisseur Barry Shein.

Cable connections

Cable-television companies have been working to provide Internet access and are successfully providing service in some areas. If cable Internet access is available in your community, it's worth checking out. It's really fast, nominally 10 million bits per second, with downloads in practice often exceeding a million bps.

In most areas where cable connections are available, you call the cable company. The technician comes and installs a network connection doozus (technical term) where your cable comes into your house, installs a standard network card in your computer if it doesn't already have one, brings a cable modem (which can look like a laptop computer with a spike hairdo), and hooks them together. Magic.

If you have cable television, the cable is split, and one segment goes to your computer. If you don't have cable television, the cable company may have to install the actual cable, too. When the technician goes away, however, you have a permanent, high-speed connection to the Internet (as long as you pay your bill, about $40 a month). In addition to the speed and constant access at a fixed price, you aren't tying up a phone line.

Couch potatoes, ho!

By far, the cheapest entry to the Internet for people with a TV and no computer is WebTV. Now, if you're already a computer aficionado, this solution will probably leave you wanting the real thing. If you're a whiz with the remote control, however, and aren't ready to plop down a grand and buy a computer, this method just may be the ticket for you. You essentially buy the box in an electronics or department store, follow the directions, and pay a monthly fee to WebTV. We tell you all about it in Chapter 18.

ISDN, ADSL, and other four-letter words

The pair of phone wires that runs between your house and the phone company has remained unchanged in design since about 1900. This option works just fine for voice applications, such as ordering pizza, but leaves something to be desired for transmitting Internet data. In the early 1980s, AT&T developed what was supposed to be the next generation of telephones, called *ISDN,* alleged to be short for I Still Don't Know or Improvements Subscribers Don't Need. ISDN uses the same phone wires (which is important because phone companies have about 100 million of them installed) and puts boxes at each end that transmit *digital* data rather than the older *analog* data. In this arrangement, an ISDN line can transmit 128K bits per second, a considerable improvement over the 33K or 56K that a regular line permits.

Although the idea was good, phone companies utterly botched the way they made ISDN available. For one thing, the way in which ISDN is installed is fantastically complicated, so much so that we know full-time telecom managers who have been unable to find anyone at their local phone company who knows how to install it. For another, ISDN is overpriced in most places: In New York, for example, an ISDN line costs about twice as much as a regular line, and every call you make, even local calls, costs extra. For this reason, unless you have a local Internet provider that arranges the details of an ISDN connection for you and knows the incantations to mutter at the phone company to make the per-call charges go away (phrases such as multilocation Centrex), we don't think that ISDN is worth the bother.

If you're a student

Most colleges and universities provide some type of Internet access for their students. Which type of access varies a great deal. In some cases, it's just a few text-only terminals in a lab somewhere on campus. Others have a complete dial-up Internet service comparable to what you get from a commercial provider, often with direct Internet access into every dorm room.

In all cases, Internet access is inexpensive or free: If you're a student or otherwise affiliated

with a college or university, check out what's available on campus before you look elsewhere. In some areas, becoming a student is cheaper than paying for long-distance Internet access.

Some institutions even let alumni use their systems; if you live close to your alma mater, it's worth seeing whether it has some sort of alumni access.

But wait! ISDN uses 1970s computer technology, and things have moved ahead a wee bit since then. Now they have ADSL, SDSL, and HDSL (the DSL stands for Digital Subscriber Loop, and the first letter is a variation on the theme), which take the same pair of phone wires and run not at a piddling 128,000 bits per second but at two, three, and even five *million* bits per second using 1990s technology. ADSL was supposed to provide "video on demand"; but when customers demanded video, they were happy to meet that demand by turning on HBO or running down to the video rental store. ADSL has now been reborn as yet another high-speed Internet gateway.

Phone companies are still in the early stages of their ADSL roll-out strategies. (Or, in English, they're doing experiments.) They know that they have to do something pretty soon or else the cable-TV crowd will steal all their Internet customers. Stay tuned. If ADSL is available in your area, you order it through a local ISP who arranges for the ADSL installation, usually sharing the phone wire you already have.

Picking an ISP

After you have decided that you want to go with an ISP, the next question is *which* ISP. This question is relatively complicated because you have several thousand ISPs from which to choose. If you have access to the Internet through a friend or your library, you can find many on our Web site, at:

```
http://net.gurus.com/isp
```

A few lines about Linux

Linux is a new, completely free, UNIX-style operating system that runs on PCs. Because most servers on the Net run UNIX, most server software also runs on Linux or can be easily adapted for it by someone with a little programming experience. Although the process of getting Linux installed can be a pain, if you find yourself wanting to put your computer on the Net many hours a day or to test out a set of interrelated Web pages you have written, Linux is the system to use. By using advanced system-software techniques known since about 1961 (but not yet fully implemented in Windows — even in Windows 98), Linux protects running programs from each other so that if one program crashes, it almost never takes the system with it. Nobody thinks it at all unusual when Linux systems run continuously for a month or more without having to be restarted.

Although Linux is not as easy to set up as Windows, it's considerably cheaper and much more reliable for use as a server.

A few national ISPs are available, such as Concentric, Mindspring, GTE, Earthlink, and AT&T WorldNet. National ISPs have lots of dial-in numbers across the country, which can be handy if you travel, and usually (but, sadly, not always) have an extensive support staff to help you. Their price is usually in the range of $20 per month.

You can usually get a better deal from a regional or local ISP. They tend to compete in pricing more than the national ones do and, in many cases, because they stick to one geographic area, also offer community-oriented online materials. When you're doing your comparison shopping, consider these factors:

- ✔ **Price:** Ask about unlimited or at least 100-hours pricing if you plan to use the Net frequently, or lower pricing for a limited number of hours.

- ✔ **Support:** Call and talk to members of the support staff before you sign up. We think that good support means support available outside of just 9 to 5, not being put on hold for long periods, and, most important, support people who don't think that your questions are stupid and can actually answer them. (You can't take this one for granted.)

- ✔ **Load:** What is response time like at peak times, and do you get busy signals when you call?

- ✔ **Modem speed:** Some providers haven't upgraded their equipment in a long time. It does you no good to have a fast modem if your provider's modem speed can't match it.

How to find a local service provider

An important topic to consider in choosing your provider is the cost of the phone call, because calls to online systems tend to be long ones. You want to find a provider that has a phone number that's a local call for you.

Although a few providers have 800 numbers, their hourly rates have to be high enough to cover the cost of the 800 call. To dial direct and pay for the call, yourself is almost invariably cheaper than to use an 800 access number; someone has to pay for the 800 call, and that someone is you. Some local providers have local numbers for day-to-day use and a more expensive 800 number to use while traveling, or they belong to a network called iPass, which lets you use other ISPs' dial-in numbers when you're out of town.

Here are the best ways we know to find a provider close to home:

- ✔ Check the business pages of your local newspaper for advertisements from local-access providers.
- ✔ Ask your public library's research librarian or online services staff.
- ✔ Look in your local yellow pages under Internet Services.
- ✔ Use a friend's Internet account or a trial account from a commercial provider to access the World Wide Web. Search for "Internet service providers." You will find numerous lists of them that you can then search for something close to home. Check our Web page about ISPs (at `http://net.gurus.com/isp`) for Web sites that list ISPs by state, area code, or country.
- ✔ Ask anyone you know in your area who already has access what she's using and whether she likes it.

Many cities also have *freenets,* a type of local community computer system that usually has a link to the Internet. Except in Los Angeles, freenets are indeed free (although they don't turn down contributions if you want to support them). If you know anyone who already has access to the Web, or if you can use an Internet computer at the local library, check out the following location, which provides a list of freenets around the world:

`http://www.lights.com/freenet/`

Signing up

Many dial-in services list two numbers: a voice number and a modem number. We think that it's useful, if you're new at this stuff (some of us are new at it for *years* — don't take it personally) to call and talk to the human beings on the other end of the voice line to get their helpful guidance. Talking to a person enables you to ask the questions you have and in many cases goes a long way toward calming the trepidation that often accompanies this step. For a PPP account, talk to your provider about which software it provides or expects you to have. If you don't get understandable answers or the person you're talking to sounds like he has better things to do than answer customer questions, look for a different provider.

If you're an old pro or would rather talk to a machine, set up your communications software to dial the modem number and follow the instructions displayed on-screen. If your modem is dialing the correct number but you're not getting anything usable on-screen, try calling the voice line to verify the modem settings and to get any other useful advice from this service you're about to begin paying for.

Sign-up generally involves providing your name, address, and telephone number along with billing information, almost invariably including a credit card number. Access is often granted immediately, or the service may call you on the phone to verify that you are who you said you were.

Back to Software

The type of access you have is intimately related to the type of software you need.

Commercial providers

All commercial providers (such as America Online, CompuServe, and Microsoft Network) give you program disks with software that works with their particular systems. Chapter 17 describes America Online (AOL). We tell you how to use AOL and how to get and install the software required to access them.

PPP access

If you use an ISP with PPP access, you need PPP software. If your provider doesn't give you software to install, you still have plenty of alternatives:

- Windows 95 and 98 have an adequate set of PPP software built right in. It's called Dial-Up Networking, and you can see Chapter 5 for advice about setting it up.

- The most popular access software for Windows 3.1 is Trumpet Winsock. It's shareware, and many ISPs give their customers disks with copies of it. (Most of them, unfortunately, forget to mention that if you use the software on the disk, you owe a registration fee to the program's author in Tasmania.)

> ✔ For Mac users, most of the necessary Internet software, called MacTCP, is a standard part of System 7 and later. The missing parts are the dial-up access software and the applications, both of which are available from most ISPs and also bound in the back of some books, including the Starter Kit edition of this very book.

> ✔ If you use Linux or a workstation running some version of UNIX, all the necessary software is part of the standard system.

Sign in, Please

If the computer you use is already connected to a network, you're probably familiar with such terms as user ID and login name. If you're not, keep reading.

A hundred million people are on the Internet. Because only one of them is you, it would be nice if the other 99,999,999 couldn't go snooping through your files and e-mail messages. No matter which type of provider you use, you have to use a security procedure to prove that you are who you say you are.

Winsock? Like at an airport?

No, Winsock is short for *Windows sockets*. It's like this: Back in the dark ages of PC networking, about 1990, several different software vendors wrote PC Internet packages. Each package provided functions so that other people could write Internet applications of their own that worked with the vendor's package.

Because each vendor's functions were, unfortunately, slightly different in the details, even though functionally they all did the same things, applications that worked with one didn't work with another. Some vendors boasted that they had compatibility libraries for four or five other vendors so that programs that expected to use the other vendors' libraries would work. (It's similar to the situation with electrical appliances in Europe: Although all the power is the same, all the plugs are different. If you take an English sewing machine to France, for example, you can't use it unless you can find an adapter plug.)

In 1991, all the network vendors were gearing up to produce Windows Internet packages. One day, a bunch of them got together at a trade show and thrashed out a common, standard set of functions for Windows Internet applications. Every Internet software vendor, even Microsoft, quickly agreed to support this Windows sockets standard, or Winsock. (It's called *sockets* because its design is based on a well-established UNIX package by that name.)

In practice, therefore, any Windows Internet application you find that uses Winsock (whether it's commercial, shareware, or free) should work with any Windows Internet package. In the annals of software development, this degree of compatibility is virtually unprecedented, so let's hope that it's a harbinger of things to come.

Your provider gives each user an account, kinda like a bank account. The account has your account name and a secret password associated with it.

Your account name may also be called your user ID, or your login or logon name. Your account name is unique among all the names assigned to your provider's users. It's also your e-mail address, so don't pick a name like *snickerdoodle* unless that's what you want to tell your friends and put on your business cards.

Your password is secret, and it's the main thing that keeps bad guys from borrowing an account. Don't use a real word or a name. A good way to make up a password is to invent a somewhat memorable phrase and turn each word in the phrase into a single letter or digit. "Computers cost too much money for me" turns into Cc2m$4m, for example. *Never tell anyone else your password.* Particularly don't tell anyone who claims to be from your ISP; they're not.

How to Get Off the Internet

After you have gotten yourself on the Internet, you're inevitably placed in the position of having to get off. You can do this in more and less graceful ways — and, depending on how far you have gone, you may have layers of systems to exit from.

The most common exit sequences include the ones in this list:

- ✔ Click the Disconnect button in the program you used to connect.
- ✔ Choose File⇨Disconnect from the menu bar.
- ✔ Type **exit**, **logout**, or **bye** in a terminal emulator.
- ✔ Press Ctrl+D (popular on always excessively terse UNIX systems).

If you use a PPP account, you may have a bunch of programs running, including your Web browser and your e-mail program. Only one of these programs, however, is the program that connects you to the Internet. That's the one you have to talk to when you're disconnecting from the Internet.

Fire at the wall

Lots of PCs in big companies are loaded up with Internet software and have network connections with a hookup to the Internet, so if you're so blessed, you can run programs on your computer and hook right up to the Net. Right? Not quite.

If you're in a large organization that has (not altogether unreasonable) concerns about confidential company secrets leaking out by way of the Internet, a *firewall* system placed between the company network and the outside world may limit outside access to the internal network.

Because the firewall is connected to both the internal network and the Internet, any traffic between the two must go through the firewall. Special programming on the firewall limits which type of connections can be made between the inside and outside and who can make them.

In practice, you can use any Internet service that is available within the company; for outside services, however, you're limited by what can pass through the firewall system. Most standard outside services — such as logging in to remote computers, copying files from one computer to another, and sending and receiving e-mail — should be available, although the procedures, involving something called a *proxy server,* may be somewhat more complicated than what's described in this book.

Often, you have to log in to the firewall system first and from there get to the outside. It's usually impossible for anyone outside the company to get access to systems or services on the inside network (that's what the firewall is for). Except for the most paranoid of organizations, e-mail flows unimpeded in both directions.

Keep in mind that you probably have to get authorization to use the firewall system before you can use *any* outside service other than mail.

Some phone numbers

Here are the voice phone numbers for some of the national providers we have listed in this chapter.

America Online: 800-827-6364

AT&T WorldNet: 800-967-5363

CompuServe: 800-739-6699

IBM Global Network: 800-455-5056

Juno Online: 800-654-5866 (free e-mail)

MCI Mail: 800-444-6245 (e-mail with 800 access)

Microsoft Network: 800-FREE-MSN (the CD with software is free, not the account)

Chapter 5

Connecting to the Internet

● ●

In This Chapter

▶ What is PPP, and why do you care?

▶ What you need to connect to the Internet

▶ Connecting from Windows 98 and Windows 95

▶ Connecting from Windows 3.1

▶ Connecting from a Mac

▶ Connecting to AOL

▶ Connecting with WebTV

● ●

*T*o connect your computer to the Internet, you have two major choices — or three, if you're lucky:

✔ **Choice 1: Sign up with an online service, such as America Online.** Online services tend to be easier to use, and they provide information in a more organized way. They usually don't give you the full range of Internet services, however. Unless services have a flat rate for unlimited use, they can be expensive if you use them for more than a few hours a month. Because demand is growing faster than some providers are able to support, access is sometimes very slow.

✔ **Choice 2: Sign up with an Internet provider for an Internet account.** These days, most providers provide you with a PPP account (we promise to explain PPP again in a few paragraphs). You need PPP to use all the cool, new programs, such as Netscape Navigator, Internet Explorer, and Eudora. Luckily, many Internet providers now have zoomy, automated sign-up programs that are just as easy to use as the one America Online uses.

✔ **Choice 3 (if you're lucky): Sign up for cable or ADSL access.** We say "if you're lucky" because cable and ADSL access are not widely available yet. If either is available in your area, however, all you have to do is call your cable company or Internet provider and arrange for someone to come and install a network card in your computer and, if you don't already have cable TV wiring in your house, the cable connection to your home, or some extra equipment on your phone line, for ADSL. If you choose this option, you can skip the rest of this chapter and just gloat. You don't need a phone, you don't need a modem, and you don't need a TV.

If you're interested in using America Online to access the Internet, skip ahead to the middle of this chapter. First, we describe The Real Thing: an honest-to-goodness Internet account. It's not just any account, either — it's a PPP account, the kind that lets you use cool programs, such as Netscape Navigator and Internet Explorer and their multimedia add-ons.

If you don't have or want to buy a computer, you still have a chance. The last section of this chapter describes WebTV, a gadget that connects you to the Internet by using your television set.

PPP (And SLIP)

We had better explain what PPP and its obsolete predecessor SLIP are. Here are the three incomprehensible acronyms you need to know about:

- ✔ *PPP (Point-to-Point Protocol)* enables your PC to connect to the Internet not as a terminal but as a full-fledged member of the Net, at least while your computer is on the phone to its Internet provider.
- ✔ *SLIP (Serial Line Internet Protocol)* is an obsolete version of the same thing.
- ✔ *CSLIP (Compressed SLIP)* is a faster version of SLIP.

Because these three protocols are very similar and provide you with the same function, henceforth we refer to them all as PPP. All three are versions of IP (Internet Protocol), the underlying part of TCP/IP (Transmission Control Protocol/Internet Protocol), which is the way all computers on the Internet communicate with each other. All three make your own computer part of the Net instead of acting as a terminal to someone else's big computer — programs running on your own computer can do much better sound, graphics, and animation than a terminal can.

You provide the programs

To use a PPP account, you need two types of programs:

- ✔ **A program to get you connected to the account:** The technical term for this type of program is a *TCP/IP stack,* although normal mortal human beings usually call it something like an Internet dialer program. Windows 95 and 98 come with one, called Dial-Up Networking. Windows 3.1 users have to get an Internet dialer from somewhere; we tell you how, in the section "Connecting, for Windows 3.1 Users" later in this chapter. Macintoshes have the basic TCP/IP stuff, called MacTCP, built in as of System 7 and later. You also need MacPPP, to handle the telephone dialing stuff. (New Macintoshes come with an Internet connection program already installed.)

✔ **Programs to use various Internet services:** These programs give you access to e-mail, the Web, and information over the Internet. They're known as *client programs* because they're part of a two-part strategy: Part of the programs run on your computer; the other part, the *server programs,* run on your provider's computer and other Internet host computers. You want an e-mail program to read and send e-mail, a Web browser to surf the Web, and a newsreader program to read Usenet newsgroups. Or you can get a program, such as Netscape Navigator, that does all three. If you use Windows, you can use any *Winsock-compatible* program (that is, any program that works with the WINSOCK.DLL file that's part of your Internet dialer program). If you use a Mac, you can use any MacTCP-compatible program.

Cool programs you can use

All the cool Internet programs you have heard about are either Winsock- or MacTCP-compatible, and many work on both Windows and Macs. Here are some famous programs available for Windows 98, Windows 95, Windows 3.1, and the Mac:

✔ **Netscape Navigator and Internet Explorer:** The former is the world's most popular Web browser; the latter, the Microsoft answer to Netscape (Chapters 6 and 7 tell you how to use them).

✔ **RealAudio and Shockwave:** You have to be running Netscape Navigator or Internet Explorer to use these and lots of other cool plug-in programs for Netscape Navigator and Internet Explorer (see Chapter 7).

✔ **Eudora Light:** This remains our favorite e-mail program. Pegasus and Outlook Express are other e-mail programs that share the advantage of being free (Chapters 11 and 12 describes how to use them).

✔ **Free Agent (for Windows) and Newswatcher (for the Mac):** These programs are great for reading Usenet newsgroups; see our Web site for an introduction to newsgroups:

```
http://net.gurus.com/usenet
```

✔ **mIRC (for Windows) and Ircle (for the Mac):** These programs let you participate in Internet Relay Chat (IRC) for online, real-time, flying purple conversations with lots of people at the same time. These programs are discussed in Chapter 15, or you can look at our Web site:

```
http://net.gurus.com/irc
```

PPP connections are easy enough to use, but unless your Internet provider gives you a good, automated sign-up program, they can be tricky to set up. In fact, connecting can be the most difficult part of your Internet experience. Installing and setting up TCP/IP software can require that you enter lots of scary-looking numeric Internet addresses, host names, communications ports — you name it. Make sure that your provider is helpful and available, or choose another provider. If you can bribe or coerce a friend or relative into helping you, do so. (*Hint:* Look for someone roughly between the ages of 12 and 16 — they can be very knowledgeable and very patient, after you get past your humiliation. Chocolate chip cookies always help.)

Because each provider is just a tad different from the next, we can't go into exact step-by-step directions for everyone. We give the usual steps, help you understand the terms, and coax you through the whole process. If you find this process totally impossible and have no one you can press into service or just don't like the thought of doing it, don't despair. Consider using MindSpring, America Online, AT&T WorldNet, Concentric, CompuServe, or another account that comes with an automated sign-up program.

Getting Connected

Okay, you're raring to go. What are the steps you have to follow? What hardware and software will you need?

Do you have what it takes?

Hardware-wise, here's what you need to cruise the Net:

- ✔ **A modem that connects your computer to a phone line:** The faster the modem, the better. Try to get a modem that talks at least 28.8 Kbps (kilobits per second), or preferably 56 Kbps; otherwise, things will be sluggish. Slower modems are no longer much cheaper, so go with the fastest.

- ✔ **A phone line (you probably guessed that):** Make sure that your phone line doesn't have call waiting. If it does, you have to type ***70** or **1170** at the beginning of your provider's phone number to tell your phone company to turn off call waiting for this phone call; otherwise, an incoming phone call will disturb your Internet connection.

   If you're lucky enough to be in an area that has cable access to the Internet, you don't need a phone line — just the cable the cable company provides.

✔ **A computer capable of running Winsock- or MacTCP-compatible programs:** Any computer that can run Windows 3.1 or Windows 95 or 98 or any Macintosh does fine. The World Wide Web is full of pictures that can take up a lot of space in your computer. To get the full effect, you probably want more than the minimal amount of memory that came with older machines, and you may need more disk space. Before you upgrade an older machine, look at the brand-spanking-new ones — for what an upgrade would cost you can probably buy a whole new computer. If you have no computer at all and hardly any money to speak of and you have a TV, consider WebTV to get yourself started.

The big picture, sign-up-wise

To get your Windows PC set up for PPP, follow these steps:

1. **Arrange for a PPP account from a provider with local access.**

   In Chapter 4, we give you ideas about how to choose an Internet provider. Unless you're running Windows 98 or a version of Windows 95 that includes Internet Explorer, you'll need some extra software to get started. Most providers have a software disk; ask for one if they don't send it automatically.

2. **Get the basic TCP/IP software loaded into your computer somehow, either from a disk or over the phone.**

   Use the software already in your computer, the disk your provider gave you, or get a friend to download it from the Internet for you and give it to you on a floppy disk. Most providers mail you a disk or tell you to buy a book that comes with a disk full of programs (*The Internet For Dummies,* 6th Edition Starter Kit, for example).

   Later in this chapter are sections about TCP/IP and dialer software for Windows 98, Windows 95, Windows 3.1, and the Mac.

3. **Type about a thousand setup parameters, if you're not lucky.**

   Your Internet provider (if it provided the software) or the software vendor should have given you instructions for when to type what. If you're lucky, your software has an automatic configuration program to set most or all of the setup parameters. In the following section, "Many mysterious numbers," we tell you as much as we know about the parameters you may encounter.

4. Crank up your TCP/IP program and fiddle with it until it works.

Miracles have been known to happen and sometimes it works the first time. If it doesn't, call and ask your provider to help you. Having only one phone line and having to hang up to call your provider may be difficult and frustrating. We can only sympathize and tell you that, yes, it's a real pain, it shouldn't be this difficult, and, one day, in the bright future, it won't be. For now, it is.

Many mysterious numbers

Your TCP/IP program uses a bunch of scary-looking technical information to connect to your PPP account. Although in theory you should never need any of this information after your account is first set up, we find that it's useful to have on hand, particularly if you have to call your provider for help. Feel free to write it all down in Table 5-1 (except for your password — just store that one in your head).

Table 5-1	Information about Your PPP Connection	
Domain name _____	The name of your Internet provider's domain. It's the last part of your Internet address and usually ends with .net or .com (in the United States, anyway).	gurus.com
Communications port _____	The communications port on your own PC to which your modem is attached, usually COM1 or COM2. (Mac owners don't have to worry about this stuff.) Even if your modem lives inside your computer and doesn't look as though it's connected to a port, it is.	COM1
Modem speed _____	The fastest speed that both your modem and your Internet provider's modem can go. If your modem can go at 56 Kbps or 33.6 Kbps, for example, but your Internet provider can handle only 28.8 Kbps, choose 28.8 Kbps.	28.8.Kbps
Modem _____	The type of modem you have. Windows 95/98 has info on about 15 million modems, but most dialer packages are only dimly aware of the details of different types of modems. A regular PC-type modem is probably similar enough to a Hayes model to fool the programs you use if your modem isn't on the list.	Hayes

Your Information	Description	Example
Phone number	The number you call to connect to your Internet provider, exactly as you would dial it by hand, including **1** and the area code, if needed. If you have to dial 9 and pause a few seconds to get an outside line, include **9,** at the beginning. (Each comma tells your modem to pause for two seconds, so stick in extra commas as necessary to get the timing right.) Many modems have speakers so that you can hear them dialing. The noise is useful when you're trying to figure out whether you have succeeded in getting an outside line when you dial out.	1-340-555-1234
Username	The name on your account with your Internet provider, also called a *login name.*	`myoung`
User password	The password for your account. (But don't write it down here!)	3friedRice
Start-up command	The command your Internet provider should run when you call in. Your Internet provider can tell you this command. Many packages start automatically, so you can probably leave this entry blank.	PPP
Domain name server (DNS) address	The numeric Internet address of the computer that can translate between regular Internet addresses and their numeric equivalents (between `net.gurus.net` and `205.238.207.74`, for example). Your Internet provider should give you this address, although the software may set it automatically when your computer connects.	`123.45.67.99`
Interface type	The exact type of interface your provider uses. The three choices are PPP, CSLIP, and SLIP. Some TCP/IP packages can't handle them all. If your software and provider handle PPP, use it; the next-best choice is CSLIP; the worst (but still okay) choice is SLIP.	PPP
Your own host name	The name of your computer. Although most Internet providers don't give each user's computer a name, if yours does, make it short and spellable and perhaps cute.	meg

Where Does All This Software Come From?

You can find in several places a TCP/IP program that connects your computer to the Internet by using a PPP account:

- ✔ **Your operating system may supply it.** Windows 95 and 98 already have all the software you need to connect with a PPP account. Newer versions of MacOS have it, too.

- ✔ **Your Internet provider may offer it on a disk.** If your Internet provider gives you software, use it. That way, when you call for help, your provider knows what to do (you hope!). Note that the software your provider gives you is probably shareware — which means that if you use it, you're honor-bound to send a donation to the author, who is probably on the other side of the world in Tasmania (yes, really).

- ✔ **You can buy it.** If you buy Netscape Navigator in a box from a store, for example, the program (a Web browser) comes with a TCP/IP program and dialer program. The Starter Kit edition of this book comes with it on a CD in the back of the book.

- ✔ **You can get someone to download it from the Internet for you.** If you have a friend with an Internet account, induce him to download the programs you need, copy them on one or more diskettes, and give them to you. Then buy your friend lunch.

Read the rest of this chapter to find out exactly which programs you may need, depending on which type of computer system you use (Windows 98, Windows 95, Windows 3.1, or the Mac).

A Home for Your Programs

Before you begin filling your computer's hard drive with network software, make a folder in which to put it. (Windows 3.1 users, make a directory.) You can use this folder for the programs you download in this chapter in addition to useful little programs you find on the Net.

In Windows 95 or 98, run My Computer or Windows Explorer, move to the Program Files folder, and choose File⇨New⇨Folder from the menu.

In Windows 3.1, run File Manager, move to the directory in which you want to create the new directory (probably the root, a.k.a. C:\), and choose File⇨Create Directory.

On a Macintosh, choose New Folder from the File menu.

If you don't already have a folder or directory for storing things temporarily, you should make one. You need it when you install the software you download from the Internet. On a PC, we recommend calling the directory C:\temp.

Connecting, for Windows 98 Users

Amazingly, Windows 98 comes with all the software you need to connect to a PPP account, using its Dial-Up Networking program. Windows 98 also comes with automated sign-up programs for several Internet service providers, including AT&T WorldNet and Prodigy Internet, as well as for America Online, CompuServe, and Microsoft Network (in the United States, anyway). To sign up for an account or to use an existing account with one of these services, click the Start button and choose Programs⇔Online Services, and then choose the service.

If you want to use an account other than the ones with automated sign-up programs (and the service didn't send you an automated sign-up CD), you can run the Internet Connection Wizard to configure Dial-Up Networking to work with your account. Run the wizard by clicking the Connect to the Internet button on your Windows desktop, if there is one, or by clicking the Start button and choosing Programs⇔Internet Explorer⇔Connection Wizard, which should display a window similar to Figure 5-1. (This is the Internet Explorer 5 version of the wizard, your version may look somewhat different.) If you have no account set up and want Windows to look for an Internet provider in your area, click the top button. If you've already arranged for an account, click the middle button whether or not you've set it up on another computer before. If you tried the middle button and your provider is not in the list that Microsoft suggests, quite likely if you're using a local provider, click the bottom button. Setting up your account manually isn't as scary as it sounds; it mostly means that you have to type in the provider's phone number and your login and password yourself. (Wow, makes our fingers hurt just to think about it. Not.)

When you're done, you should have a Dial-Up Networking icon and a choice on the Programs menu for your Internet provider. To call your account, run the Dial-Up Networking program and click the Connect button.

Windows 98 comes with Microsoft Internet Explorer, a reasonably good Web browser. (Chapter 6 explains how to use it.) Windows 98 also comes with a good e-mail program called Outlook Express. See Chapter 11 for instructions.

Figure 5-1:
Windows
tries to help
you get
connected.

Even though Windows 98 comes with Internet Explorer and Outlook Express, you can still use Netscape Navigator, Eudora, and other Winsock programs.

Connecting, for Windows 95 Users

The good news is that Windows 95 comes with Dial-Up Networking. The bad news is that at least three major sub-versions of Windows 95 exist, and what they call Dial-Up Networking varies a lot.

Except in the earliest version of Windows 95, you get the Internet Setup Wizard, which helps you configure Dial-Up Networking to work with your account. You may be able to run the wizard by clicking the Start button and choosing Programs➪Accessories➪Internet Tools➪Internet Setup Wizard (if you don't see the wizard there, look around your Programs menus for it). If you can start the wizard at all, it'll work like the Windows 98 wizard, described previously, although perhaps without some of the options.

Recent versions of Windows 95 come with Microsoft Internet Explorer (see Chapter 7). It also comes with Microsoft Exchange, an e-mail program we've always considered rather confusing. If you have Internet Explorer 3.0, you should download a later version. We also recommend that you download a better e-mail program, such as Eudora Light or Outlook Express (the latter comes with Internet Explorer 4.0); see Chapter 16 to find out how to download and install programs, and Chapter 11 for instructions for using Eudora Light.

To sign up for and connect to an account, of course, you can always use the automated sign-up CDs that you can get from MindSpring, AOL, Concentric, and other services.

Connecting, for Windows 3.1 Users

Windows 3.1 lacks the software you need to connect to a PPP account. Most Internet providers give you a copy of the Trumpet Winsock shareware TCP/IP package or else the Shiva TCP/IP package that comes with Netscape. Trumpet Winsock is freely available shareware (we thought that you would like that, although you should register and pay for it if your provider hasn't done so for you). They may also give you a copy of Eudora Light, the freeware version of the popular Eudora e-mail program, and possibly Netscape Navigator or Internet Explorer.

Some Internet providers give you an automated sign-up program; AT&T WorldNet, Concentric, and other nationwide providers do, which makes setting up your account easy. (The Starter Kit edition of this book comes with sign-up software from MindSpring, a nationwide Internet provider.) Otherwise, your Internet provider should give you detailed installation and configuration instructions. If they do the latter, plan to spend some time on the phone getting your software set up correctly.

After you're done setting up Trumpet Winsock, you have a Trumpet icon in one of your Windows program groups. Double-click the Trumpet icon and follow the instructions your Internet provider gave you to get connected.

Your provider should also have given you, at the very least, an e-mail program and Web browser. If your provider gave you Netscape Navigator (Version 2.0 or later), you have an excellent Web browser and an acceptable e-mail and newsreader program. Because Microsoft Internet Explorer also runs on Windows 3.1 and is free, your provider may give it to you along with Outlook Express, an e-mail program. Parts III and IV of this book tell you how to use these programs.

Connecting, for Mac Users

Mac users already have most of the software they need to connect to the Internet because System 8 comes with MacTCP. Upgrade to System 8 to get it. You also need a Mac TCP/IP modem program, such as FreePPP, MacPPP, or InterSLIP, which your Internet provider should be able to give you. (If not, consider finding a provider who has more of a clue about Macs or else you will always be on your own when you have problems.) Most newer Macs come with modem software installed.

Using a UNIX shell account

In the early days of the Internet, before Netscape, before America Online, before the World Wide Web itself (can you remember back that far? — we're talking about 1989), intrepid Internet explorers dealt with the Internet by using UNIX accounts. UNIX is an operating system that, in its purest form, requires you to type short, cryptic, and totally unmemorable commands to get anything done. Although UNIX is a powerful system and programmers love it, most mere mortals find it a pain in the neck to use. Because most of the computers on the Internet run UNIX, however, early Internet users didn't have any choice. UNIX accounts are also called *shell accounts*, for the name of the part of UNIX that listens to the commands you type.

UNIX accounts used to be widely available, before PPP accounts took the world by storm. Some Internet providers can still give you one, if you ask specifically. Some providers give you one when you sign up for a PPP account.

One big advantage of UNIX accounts is that you don't need any fancy programs on your computer to get connected. All you need is a *terminal emulator* program, one that dials the phone and pretends to be a terminal attached to the UNIX computer at the other end of the phone line. Almost every computer comes with a terminal emulator program; Windows 3.1 comes with Windows Terminal, Windows 95 and Windows 98 come with HyperTerminal, and Macs come with MacTerminal.

When you use a UNIX account, all the programs you run (except for the terminal emulator) run on the Internet provider's computer, not on your computer. To read your e-mail, you run a UNIX e-mail program on your Internet provider's computer; the most popular UNIX e-mail program is called Pine, which we describe in Chapter 11. To browse the Web, you run a UNIX browser, usually one called Lynx, which we describe in Chapter 6. To read Usenet newsgroups, you run a UNIX newsreader program, such as trn or tin. Because these programs don't do graphics and you don't use your mouse, you end up learning lots of one-letter commands.

Using Microsoft Network

When Microsoft introduced Windows 95, it also introduced Microsoft Network (MSN), the new online service that was going to eat America Online and CompuServe for lunch. Several years later, MSN is still undergoing growing pains, has given up its original proprietary design, and is moving to become an Internet provider with special Web pages that you can see only if you're an MSN subscriber.

Signing up with MSN is easy if you use Windows 95 or Windows 98 because an MSN icon sits right on your desktop. MSN is not available if you use any other operating system — Windows 3.1 and Mac users are out of luck (or in luck, depending on your point of view). For more information, take a look at the MSN Web page, at `http://www.msn.com`.

Connecting to America Online

America Online (AOL, to its friends), the world's largest online service, provides access to both the Internet and its own proprietary services. AOL has more than 12 million subscribers and is still growing. To use AOL, you use software it provides. (Windows 98, Windows 95, Windows 3.1, Mac, and even DOS versions are available.) You can also use other software with your AOL account, such as Netscape Navigator and Microsoft Internet Explorer. This chapter describes the AOL Internet-related capabilities, including e-mail and the World Wide Web.

This section describes Version 4.0 of the AOL software. Because AOL updates its software and the graphics that appear in its dialog boxes all the time, your screen may not match exactly the figures in this chapter.

Signing up for America Online

Ready to sign up? No problem! If you have Windows 98, click Start and choose Programs⇨Online Services⇨AOL; otherwise, in the unlikely event that you don't already have a stack of AOL disks or CD-ROMs lying around, call 800-540-9449 and ask for a trial membership. Specify whether you want the CD-ROM or a floppy disk with the Windows version (Windows 3.1, Windows 95, or Windows 98), the Mac version, or the DOS version. The introductory package has instructions and a disk containing the AOL access program. After you have the introductory package, follow the instructions on its cover to install the program and sign up for an account. You need a credit card to sign up.

The pros and cons of AOL

AOL is easier to use than most commercial online services and Internet accounts because one big AOL access program does it all for you. AOL also does a nice job of providing users with online software updates — it can update your AOL access software for you right over the phone, and connect-time is usually free when it does so.

Signing up for an AOL account is easy, too — many magazines come with free AOL sign-up disks. AOL also has lots of discussion groups and information available only to AOL subscribers.

With the AOL flat rate of about $20 per month, it's competitive with regular Internet PPP accounts and provides both AOL-specific content and adequate Internet access.

On the other hand, getting connected can be a pain because many AOL phone lines are perennially busy. Getting technical support can be a trick — you can wait a long time for phone support, and getting help from the online tech-support chat rooms can be painfully slow and not always informative. If you do sign up for AOL, canceling your account later can be difficult — you have to be forceful.

Note: America Online, despite its name, is available outside America. AOL has access numbers in major Canadian cities, at no extra charge. Although you can also use AOL from other parts of Canada or from other countries, you pay a steep surcharge.

The installation program creates a cute triangular icon named America Online. If you have trouble installing the AOL software, call AOL at 800-827-3338.

Running AOL from Windows and the Mac are similar processes. Although we took pictures of the Windows version, we don't think that it matters much. You can always tell that you're on the correct Mac screen.

Setting up your AOL account

After you have installed the AOL software, you can use it to sign up for an account. When you sign up, you have to tell it which *screen name* (account name) you want to use and how you want AOL to bill you after you have used up your free hours.

Follow these steps to set up your account:

1. **Double-click the America Online icon.**

2. **Follow the instructions on-screen.**

    First, AOL calls up an 800 number to find out the local-access number closest to you. Then it asks for your *registration certificate,* which comes with AOL disks and CD-ROMs — it's a long number with a couple of dashes. (Ours was *SPECS-RICHES,* and our editor's was *ANGER-PASTRY.* Who or what thinks up these things?)

3. **Choose an account name (which AOL calls a *screen name* — sounds glamorous) for yourself, along with a password.**

   Your screen name can be as long as ten characters and can contain spaces. You can use a combination of capital and small letters, as in MargyL or LoveAOL. When AOL asks you to enter your screen name, it checks its list of existing names. If someone is already using that name (John Smith, for example), you have to invent another one. By now, the 12 million most obvious names have been taken, so get creative. If the screen name you want is already taken, try adding a number to the end to make it unique. For example, if NetHead is taken (and we're sure that it is), you can be NetHead3236.

4. **Enter a credit card number and expiration date.**

   When you finish, you see the Sign On window in the America Online window, as shown in Figure 5-2. You're ready to boogie!

The America Online window always displays the menu bar and, underneath it, the *Flashbar* (a row of cute little icons).

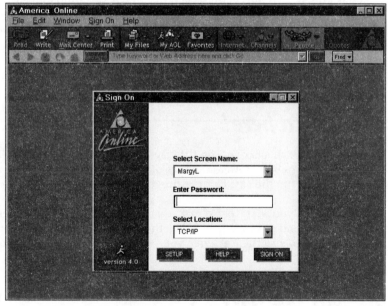

Figure 5-2:
The America Online Welcome window suggests that you log right in!

GO America!

To connect your computer to AOL:

1. **Type your password in the Enter Password box.**

2. **Click the SIGN ON button.**

   A window appears, showing the progress of the connection. The graphic changes as the AOL program dials the phone, establishes a connection with the big AOL computer in the sky, and logs you in.

   You see the online Welcome window. Behind the Welcome window is the Main Menu window. (Its edges peek out from behind the Welcome window.)

   Now you're connected to AOL. You can click the buttons to read the day's news stories. If e-mail is waiting for you, you can click the You Have Mail button.

3. **Minimize the Welcome window by clicking its Minimize button (in the upper-right corner of the window).**

   You see the Channels window, with buttons for the AOL main subject areas.

If your PC has a sound board or you're using a Mac, don't be surprised if your computer suddenly says "Welcome!" when you log in to AOL. If you have e-mail, it says "You have mail!" Try not to jump right out of your chair when you hear this message.

For more information about using your AOL account, see Chapter 17.

I'm outta here!

To get out of AOL, choose Sign Off⇨Sign Off from the menu (yes, it's a little redundant). The AOL program hangs up on your connection with the big AOL computer in the sky. Exit the program if you're done.

The next time you want to use AOL, double-click the AOL icon, fill in your screen name and password, and click the SIGN ON button or just press Enter. You're ready to surf the Net when you see the online Welcome window.

I Want My WebTV!

If you don't have a computer and for some reason don't want to buy one, you can get connected to the Internet in another way and reap some of (but not all) the benefits. It's called WebTV, the brand name of a system that includes both hardware and service. The hardware includes a box you connect to your television set, a remote control, and a remote keyboard (optional, but indispensable unless you are an extremely patient person); the service consists of an Internet connection for which you pay a monthly fee. After you connect the WebTV box to your TV and your telephone line — *voilà* — you're online. The box includes a computer, of course, but don't tell anybody. The computer basically runs one program, the WebTV program, and uses your TV as the monitor. WebTV became available in 1996, and, although it hasn't exactly caught on like wildfire yet, it may be right for you. Microsoft bought the company, so who knows what will happen. This section tells you how to get WebTV and connect it. Chapter 18 tells you in some detail how to use it and what its advantages and drawbacks are.

Getting started with WebTV

Before you buy WebTV, you should check to make sure that you can connect to the service through a local telephone number. If you have access to the Web already through a friend or work, you can go to the WebTV Web page, at `http://webtv.com`, to look up your local WebTV access number. Or, alternatively, if you already have an ISP (Internet service provider), you can use that connection, which WebTV calls OpenISP. This option reduces your monthly service charge by $10.

If you don't have a TV, don't buy WebTV unless you really want to buy a TV and can't admit that to yourself. Color is best, for the same reasons that having a color monitor on your computer is best — not only do things look snazzier in color but designers also use color to convey information.

To buy the WebTV equipment, go to a consumer electronics store and, while you're there, get a demonstration of the product. Because you have only a couple of options from which to choose, this process isn't quite as bad as picking out a new car. There are two versions of the box, the Classic for $99 or the Plus for $199. Plus offers some extra features such as on-screen TV schedule listings, and the monthly service is $25 rather than $20.

The next choice you have is whether to buy a keyboard for about $80. If you don't buy a keyboard, you can use the remote control to navigate your way around the screen and bring up a picture of a keyboard on-screen. You can then navigate around the keyboard and press a key when you land on it. This technique is not unlike the way that Gutenburg set type, a hideously painful way to operate the product, especially if you want to send e-mail or type URLs. Get the keyboard. Even if you can't type, you can hunt and peck infinitely faster than moving a selector across the grid of a keyboard image. (Some of us can't type properly either, despite many years — going back to the days of punched cards — of hanging around keyboards.) The keyboard is small and light, about the size of this book, and wireless. It communicates with the WebTV box by infrared light, just like all those remote controls sitting in your TV room. You can also use a regular $15 computer keyboard (it plugs into a socket in the back of the WebTV box), but then you have to buy an extension cable for the keyboard or sit close to the TV.

Because the WebTV box connects to your TV set by using RCA jacks, those cables with round things on the end that just push in, the box has to be close to the TV. If your TV isn't in a giant entertainment center unit that has plenty of room for more black boxes, put the box on the floor or on top of the TV. It has to be in the line of sight of the place (the couch) from which you want to use it. The hardware comes with a usable set of instructions that tell you how to connect it to your TV, either directly or through the VCR you already have connected. If you have any difficulty setting everything up, ask the teenager at the store where you bought the product for advice.

You have to connect your telephone line to the WebTV box. A phone jack splitter and phone cable come in the WebTV package. Find the nearest phone jack in your house, remove the phone cable from it, insert the splitter, and then put the phone cable back in. Then run the new phone cable from the other side of the splitter over to the WebTV box and plug it in around back. All you're doing is adding your WebTV to your phone system like an extension phone. When you're using WebTV, of course, you can't use the phone. While you're running the WebTV, you can easily disconnect from the Internet to make a phone call and then reconnect when you're done, just by pushing a button on your keyboard or remote control.

Full power, Scotty!

All right, you've connected all the wires, and now you're sitting on the couch (the best thing about WebTV) with the remote control and keyboard in front of you, the popcorn within easy reach, and no one in the house using the phone. What to do next? It's as easy as pie: Point your remote control in the general direction of your TV and push the green TV button and then the WEB button. This step turns on the power to everything. You may have to press the TV/Video button to get your TV set to listen to the box rather than to the television programs. When you see the WebTV logo and hear its soothing music, you're all set.

The first time you use the system, you go through a sign-up procedure with the folks at WebTV. Your WebTV connects to home base by dialing an 800 number. Then they ask you your name, address, credit card number, and so on, and find a local telephone number to call. (Without a keyboard, the sign-on phase takes a long time.) After you're registered, WebTV disconnects from the 800 number and calls the local number, and you're on your way.

You may want to call your phone company to confirm that the "local" number for WebTV is really local for you, before spending hours surfing the Net. They've been known to guess wrong. If there's no local number but you love WebTV anyway, try the OpenISP plan with a local ISP that really is a local call.

Part III
Web Mania

The 5th Wave   By Rich Tennant

It started as a wrap-around porch, and then Stuart found a section on medieval architecture on the Internet.

In this part . . .

No doubt about it, the Web's *the* happenin' place. For many people, the Web *is* the Internet. We explain what the Web is and how to get around. We give you great tips about how to actually find stuff you're looking for. We tell you about Web shopping so you can confidently spend your money online, and we've added a chapter about how to make a home page so that you too can "be on the Web."

Chapter 6

The Wild, Wonderful, Wacky Web

● ●

In This Chapter

▶ Hyper who?

▶ Understanding URLs

▶ Pointing, clicking, and other basic skills

▶ An introduction to Netscape, Internet Explorer, and other browsers

▶ Web surfing for the graphically challenged — life with Lynx

● ●

*P*eople talk about *the Web* today more than they talk about *the Net.* The World Wide Web and the Internet are not the same thing — the World Wide Web (which we call the Web because we're lazy typists) lives "on top of" the Internet. The Internet's network is at the core of the Web, although the Web itself is something different.

Okay, okay, so what is it already? The Web is, in some ways, sort of a cross between libraries, television, computer networks, and telephones — it's all of the above and none of the above.

The Web is a bunch of "pages" of information connected to each other around the globe. Each page can be a combination of text, pictures, audio clips, video clips, animations, and other stuff. (We're vague about naming the other stuff because they add new types of other stuff every day.) What makes Web pages interesting is that they contain *hyperlinks,* usually justs called *links* because the Net already has plenty of hype. Each link points to another Web page, and when you click a link, your *browser* fetches the page that the link connects to. (Stay calm — we talk about browsers in a couple of pages. For now, just think of your browser as the program that talks to the Web.)

Each page your browser gets for you can have more links that take you to other places. Pages can be linked to other pages anywhere in the world, so after you're on the Web, you can end up looking at pages from Singapore to Calgary, from Sydney to Buenos Aires, all faster than you can say "Jack's your uncle," usually. Give or take network delays, you're only seconds away from any site, anywhere in the world.

Where did the Web come from?

The World Wide Web was invented in 1989 at the European Particle Physics Lab in Geneva, Switzerland, an unlikely spot for a revolution in computing. The inventor is a British researcher named Tim Berners-Lee, who is now the director of the World Wide Web Consortium (W3) in Cambridge, Massachusetts, the organization that sets standards and loosely oversees the development of the Web. Tim is terrifically smart and hard-working and is the nicest guy you would ever want to meet. (Margy met him through Sunday school — is that wholesome or what?)

Tim invented *http* (*hypertext transport protocol*), the way Web browsers communicate with Web servers; *HTML* (*hypertext markup language*), the language in which Web pages are written; and *URLs* (*Uniform Resource Locators*), the codes used to identify Web pages and most other information on the Net. He envisioned the Web as a way for everyone to both publish and read information on the Net. Early Web browsers had editors that let you create Web pages almost as easily as you could read them.

For more information about the development of the Web and the work of the World Wide Web Consortium, visit its Web site, at `http://www.w3.org`.

Essentials of hypertext thought

If you can get a handle on the fundamental structure of the Web, you can use it better and think about all the other ways it can be used. *Hypertext* is a way of connecting information in ways that make it easy to find — in theory. Traditional libraries (both the kinds with books and the kinds in computers) organize information in an arbitrary way, such as alphabetical order or the Dewey decimal system. This order reflects nothing about the relationships among different pieces of information; it just reflects the limits of manual indexing. In the world of hypertext, information is organized in relationship to other information. The relationships between different pieces of information are, in fact, often much more valuable than the pieces themselves.

Hypertext can arrange the same set of information in multiple ways at the same time. A book in a conventional library can be on only one shelf at a time; a book about mental health, for example, is shelved under medicine or psychology, but not in both places at once. With hypertext, it's no problem to have links to the same document from both medical topics and psychological topics.

Suppose that you're interested in what influenced a particular historical person. Start by looking at her basic biographical information: where and when she was born, the names of her parents, her religion, and other basic stuff like that. Then you can expand on each fact by finding out what else was happening at that time in her part of the world, what was happening in other parts of the world, and what influence her religion may have had on her. You draw a picture by pulling together all these aspects and understanding their connections — a picture that's hard to draw from just lists of names and dates.

This system of interlinked documents is known as *hypertext*. Figure 6-1 shows a Web page (our Web page, in fact.) Each underlined phrase is a link to another Web page.

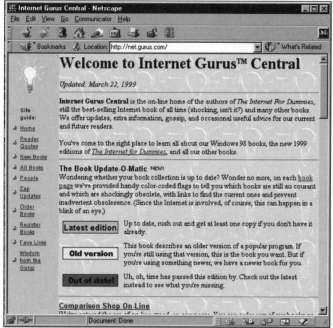

Figure 6-1: Underlined phrases on Web pages are links to other pages.

Hypertext, the buzzword that makes the Web go, is one of those simple ideas that turns out to have a much bigger effect than you would think. With a hypertext system, people can create connections among pieces of information that let you go directly to related information. As you draw connections among the pieces of information, you can begin to envision the web created by the links between the pieces. What's so remarkable about the Web is that it connects pieces of information from all around the *planet*, on different computers and in different databases, all pretty much seamlessly (a feat you would be hard-pressed to match with a card catalog in a brick-and-mortar library). We sometimes think of the Web as an extremely large but friendly alien centipede made of information.

The other important thing about the Web is that the information in it is searchable. For example, in about ten seconds, you can get a list of Web pages that contain the phrase *domestic poultry* or your name or the name of a book you want to find out about. You can follow links to see each page on the list, to find the information you want.

Hypertext: A reminiscence

John writes:

The term and concept of hypertext were invented around 1969 by Ted Nelson, a famous computer visionary who has been thinking about the relationship between computers and literature for at least 25 years now — starting back when most people would have considered it stupid to think that such a relationship could exist. Twenty years ago, he claimed that people would have computers in their pockets with leatherette cases and racing stripes. (I haven't seen any racing stripes yet, but otherwise he was dead-on.)

Back in 1970, Ted told me that we all would have little computers with inexpensive screens on our desks with superwhizzo graphical hypertext systems. "Naah," I said. "For hypertext, you want a mainframe with gobs of memory and a high-resolution screen." We were both right, of course, because what we have on our desks in 1999 are little computers that are faster than 1970s mainframes and that have more memory and better screens.

Various hypertext projects have come and gone over the years, including one at Brown University (of which Ted was a part) and one at the Stanford Research Institute (which was arguably the most influential project in computing history because it invented screen windows and mice).

Ted's own hypertext system, Project Xanadu, has been in the works for close to 20 years, under a variety of financing and management setups, with many of the same people slogging along and making it work. The project addresses many issues that other systems don't. In particular, Ted figured out how to pay authors for their work in a hypertext system, even when one document has pieces linked from others and the ensuing document consists almost entirely of a compendium of pieces of other documents. For a decade, I have been hearing every year that Xanadu, and now a smaller Xanadu Light, which takes advantage of a great deal of existing software, will hit the streets the next year. This year, I hope that they're right.

Margy adds:

Now that the World Wide Web has brought a limited version of hypertext to the masses, Ted is building a Xanadu system on the Web. Visit `http://www.xanadu.net` to see what he's up to!

Name That Page

Before you dive in and hit the Web (hmm, that metaphor needs work), you need one more basic concept. Every Web page has a name attached to it so that browsers, and you, can find it. Great figures in the world of software engineering named this name *URL*, or *Uniform Resource Locator*. Every Web page has an URL, a string of characters that begins with `http://` or `www`. Some people pronounce each letter ("U-R-L"), and some think that it's a word ("URL") — it's your choice. Now you know enough to go browsing. (For more entirely optional details about URLs, see the sidebar "*Duke of URL*.")

TECHNICAL STUFF

Duke of URL

Part of the plan of the World Wide Web is to link together all the information in the known universe, starting with all the stuff on the Internet and heading up from there. (This statement may be a slight exaggeration, but we don't think so.)

One of the keys to global domination is to give everything (at least everything that could be a Web resource) a name, and in particular a consistent name so that no matter what kind of thing a hypertext link refers to, a Web browser can find it and know what to do with it.

Look at this typical URL:

```
http://net.gurus.com/
     index.phtml
```

The first thing in a URL, the word before the colon, is the *scheme,* which describes the way a browser can get to the resource. Although ten schemes are defined, the most common by far is *HTTP,* the *hypertext transfer protocol* that is the Web's native transfer technique. (Don't confuse HTTP, which is the way pages are sent over the Net, with HTML, which is the way the pages are coded internally. We get to that in Chapter 7.)

Although the details of the rest of the URL depend on the scheme, most schemes use a consistent syntax. Following the colon are two slashes (always forward slashes, never reverse slashes) and the name of the host computer on which the resource lives; in this case, net.gurus.com. Then comes another slash and a *path,* which gives the name of the resource on that host; in this case, a file named index.phtml.

Web URLs allow a few other optional parts. They can include a *port number,* which specifies, roughly speaking, which of several programs running on that host should handle the request.

The port number goes after a colon after the host name, like this:

```
http://net.gurus.com:80/
     index.phtml
```

Because the standard http port number is 80, if that's the port you want (it usually is), you can leave it out.

Finally, a Web URL can have a *search part* at the end, following a question mark, like this:

```
http://net.gurus.com:80/
     index.phtml?plugh
```

Although not all pages can have search parts, in those that do, they tell the host, uh, what to search for. (You rarely type a search part yourself — they're often constructed for you from fill-in fields on Web pages.)

Three other useful URL schemes are mailto, ftp, and file. A mailto URL looks like this:

```
mailto:internet6@gurus.com
```

That is, it's an e-mail address. When you choose a mailto URL in Netscape, it pops up a window in which you can enter an e-mail message to the address in the URL. In Internet Explorer, clicking a mailto URL runs the Outlook Express program or whatever you've designated as your default mail program. (Outlook Express is described in Chapter 11.) Mailto URLs are most commonly used for sending comments to the owner of a page.

A URL that starts with ftp lets you download files from an FTP server on the Internet (see Chapter 12 for information about FTP servers). An ftp URL looks like this:

```
ftp://ftp.netscape5.com/
     navigator/3.0/mac/
     README.TXT
```

(continued)

(continued)

The part after the two slashes is the name of the FTP server (ftp.netscape5.com, in this case). The rest of the URL is the pathname of the file you want to download.

The file URL specifies a file on your computer. It looks like this:

```
file:///C|/www/index.htm
```

On a Windows or DOS computer, this line indicates a Web page stored in the file C:\www\index.htm. The colon turns into a vertical bar (because colons in URLs mean something else), and the reverse slashes turn into forward slashes. File URLs are useful mostly for looking at graphics files with .gif and .jpg filename extensions and for looking at a Web page you just wrote and stuck in a file on your disk.

Browsing Off

Now that you know all about the Web, you undoubtedly want to check it out for yourself. To do this, you need a *browser,* the software that goes and gets Web pages and displays them on your screen. Fortunately, if you have Internet access, you probably already have one. One probably came from your Internet service provider (ISP), and you installed it when you installed the rest of your Internet software. If you don't have a browser or want to get a copy of Netscape or Internet Explorer (most likely because you have one but want to try the other), see the section "Getting and Installing Netscape, Internet Explorer, or Opera," at the end of this chapter.

Now that the Web gets more press than the rest of the Internet put together, everyone and her uncle wants to write a Web browser. We discuss three of the most popular: Netscape, the world's most popular graphical browser; Internet Explorer, the Microsoft answer to Netscape; and Lynx, the text-only browser for the UNIX shell account crowd.

Older versions of America Online had a customized, not very good, browser, but now they use Internet Explorer. You can also install another browser if you want, as we explain in Chapter 17.

Browser Warfare

Are you sick of hearing about the war between Netscape, the "killer application" for the Internet, and Internet Explorer, the Microsoft attempt to kill off Netscape? This chapter shows you how to use both, as well as the #3 "we try harder" browser, Opera, which is smaller and faster than either of the big two. We don't take sides here because they all work okay, and they're similar enough that any reason to dislike one of them probably applies to the others.

If you have a text-only shell account, close your eyes and forget about all the pretty pictures. There is a very competent and fantastically fast text-only browser called Lynx, which works just fine over a text-only dial-up connection. Go to the section "Life with Lynx," later in this chapter.

Surfing with Netscape and Internet Explorer

When you start Netscape, you see a screen similar to the one that was shown in Figure 6-1. The Internet Explorer window looks like the one shown in Figure 6-2. Which page your browser displays depends on how it's set up; many providers arrange to have a browser display their home page; otherwise they tend to display the Netscape or Microsoft home page, respectively, until you choose a home page of your own.

At the top of the window are a bunch of buttons and the (Netscape) Location or (Internet Explorer) Address line, which contains the *Uniform Resource Locator,* or *URL,* for the current page. (Netscape sometimes labels this box Netsite for reasons that doubtless make sense to someone. Microsoft sometimes calls it Shortcut.) Remember that URLs are an important part of Web lore because they're the secret codes that name all the pages on the Web. For details, see the sidebar "Duke of URL," earlier in this chapter.

Figure 6-2:
Your typical
Web page,
using
Internet
Explorer.

Getting around

You need two very simple primary skills (if we can describe something as basic as a single mouse-click as a skill) to get going on the Web. One is to move from page to page on the Web, and the other is to jump directly to a page when you know its URL.

Moving from page to page is easy: Click any link that looks interesting. That's it. Underlined blue text and blue-bordered pictures are links. (Although links may be a color other than blue, depending on the look the Web page designer is going for, they're always underlined unless the page is the victim of a truly awful designer.) You can tell when you're pointing to a link because the mouse pointer changes to a little hand. If you're not sure whether something is a link, click it anyway because, if it's not, it doesn't hurt anything. Clicking outside a link selects the text you click, as in most other programs.

Backward, ho!

Web browsers remember the last few pages you visited, so if you click a link and decide that you're not so crazy about the new page, you can easily go back to the preceding one. To go back, click the Back button (its icon is an arrow pointing to the left, a pair of arrows in Opera) or press Alt+←.

All over the map

Some picture links are *image maps,* such as the big picture shown in the middle of Figure 6-3. In a regular link, it doesn't matter where you click; on an image map, it does. The image map in this figure is typical and has a bunch of obvious places you click for various types of information. (All the 1990 census data except private individual info is online on the Net, by the way, at www.census.gov.) Some image maps are actual maps — a map of the United States at the Census Bureau, for example, that shows you information about the state you click.

As you move the mouse cursor around a Web page, whenever you point at a link, the URL of the place it links to appears in small type at the bottom of the screen, or in a little box that "floats" over the mouse pointer. If the link is an image map, it shows the link followed by a question mark and two numbers that are the X and Y positions of where you are on the map. The numbers don't matter to you (it's up to the Web server to make sense of them); if you see a pair of numbers counting up and down when you move the mouse, however, you know that you're on an image map.

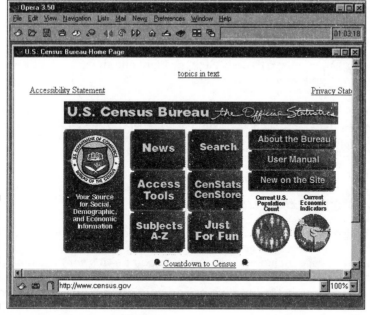

Going places

These days, everyone and his dog has a home page. A *home page* is the
main Web page for a person or organization. Chapter 10 shows you how
to make one for yourself and your dog. (For an example, check out
`users.aimnet.com/~carver/cindy.html`.) Companies are advertise their
home pages, and people send e-mail talking about cool sites. When you see a
URL you want to check out, here's what you do:

1. **Click in the Location or Address box, near the top of the Netscape or
   Internet Explorer window or the bottom of the Opera window.**

2. **Type the URL in the box.**

   The URL is something like `http://net.gurus.com/`.

3. **Press Enter.**

If you receive URLs in e-mail, Usenet news, or anywhere else on your Windows PC or Macintosh, you can use the standard cut-and-paste techniques
and avoid retyping:

1. **Highlight the URL in whichever program is showing it.**

2. **Press Ctrl+C (⌘+C on the Mac) to copy the info to the Clipboard.**

3. **Click in the Location or Address box to highlight whatever is in it.**

4. Press Ctrl+V (⌘+V on the Mac) to paste the URL into the box, and then press Enter.

Eudora and many other mail programs highlight any URLs in e-mail messages. All you have to do is click the highlighted link, and it'll switch to your browser and open the Web page.

You can leave the `http://` off the front of URLs when you type them in the Location or Address box. If you use Netscape, you can leave the `www` off the front and the `com` off the back — that is, rather than type **http://www. idgbooks.com,** you can just type **idgbooks.**

Where to start?

You find out more about how to find things on the Web in Chapter 8; for now, here's a good way to get started: Go to the Yahoo! page. (Yes, the name of the Web page includes an exclamation point — it's very excitable. But we'll leave it out for the rest of the book, because we find it annoying.) That is, type this URL in the Location or Address box and then press Enter:

```
http://www.yahoo.com
```

You go to the Yahoo page, a directory of millions of Web pages by topic. Just nose around, and you will find something interesting.

For updates to the very book you are holding, go to this URL:

```
http://net.gurus.com/update
```

Follow the links to the page about our books, and then select the pages for readers of *The Internet For Dummies,* 6th Edition. If we have any late-breaking news about the Internet or updates and corrections to this book, you can find them there. If you find mistakes in this book or have other comments, by the way, please send e-mail to us at `internet6@gurus.com`.

This page looks funny

Sometimes a Web page gets garbled on the way in or you interrupt it (by clicking the Stop button on the toolbar). You can tell your browser to get the information on the page again: In Netscape, click the Reload button or press Ctrl+R; in Internet Explorer, click the Refresh button or press F5. In Opera, click the Reload button or press F5.

Netscape and Internet Explorer are not in a big hurry

When Netscape announced Version 3.0, it publicized tests that showed that it was 200 percent faster than its rival program, Internet Explorer. Microsoft retaliated with studies and statistics of its own. Version 4.0 of both programs is still slow. This situation is not unlike a battle to claim the title of the world's slimmest hippopotamus — they're both big and slow.

The programs have two separate slowness problems. One is that fancy multimedia screens require a great deal of data, which means that they take a long time to transfer over any except the fastest networks. The other is that both programs are, to use a technical computer term, pigs. (They are not as piggish as some other Net browsers, though.)

A general rule says that you need a Pentium computer with 16 megabytes of RAM to get reasonable performance, and we can report from experience that if you run either program on a computer of that size, it still spends an awful lot of time swapping pieces of program back and forth from the disk. If you have a Pentium and 32 megabytes, they're reasonably but not breathtakingly fast. Opera, on the other hand, is pretty fast on any Windows system, although it can't do anything about the transfer time problem.

You can do a few things to speed up Netscape and Internet Explorer, which we address in Chapter 7. (That's a ploy to keep you reading.)

Get me outta here

Sooner or later, even the most dedicated Web surfer has to stop to eat or attend to other bodily needs. You leave your browser in the same way as you leave any other Mac or Windows program: by choosing File⇨Exit (File⇨Close for Windows Internet Explorer, we were surprised to notice) or pressing Alt+F4. In Windows 95 or Windows 98, you can also click the Close button in the upper-right corner of the window.

Getting and Installing Netscape, Internet Explorer, or Opera

With luck, Netscape or Internet Explorer is already installed on your computer. The two programs are so similar that if you have one of them, we suggest that you stick with it (for now, anyway). Without luck, you don't have either program, but they are, fortunately, not difficult to get and install.

Netscape Navigator (the real name of the program everyone calls Netscape) comes in several varieties: Windows 3.1 (the 16-bit version), Windows 95 (the 32-bit version), Mac, and versions for a bunch of UNIX workstations. Netscape also comes as part of a suite of programs called Netscape Communicator (we talk about the mail programs in Chapter 11). Netscape Navigator 4.0 includes a Web page editor, too, in case you want to create your own Web pages. (See Chapter 10 to find out how to create Web pages.)

Although Internet Explorer was originally available for only Windows 95, Microsoft now has versions for Windows 3.1, the Mac, and a few versions of UNIX.

Even if you already have a copy of Netscape or Internet Explorer, new versions come out every 20 minutes or so, and it's worth knowing how to upgrade because occasionally the new versions fix some bugs so that they're better than the old versions. The steps are relatively simple:

1. **Get a copy of the Netscape or Internet Explorer installation package on your computer.**

2. **Unpack the installation package.**

3. **Install the software.**

Because computers are involved, each of these steps is, naturally, a little more difficult than necessary.

Getting the package

Your Internet provider may have given you a copy of Netscape or Internet Explorer on a disk or CD. The installation package for most Internet providers includes a licensed version of Netscape or Internet Explorer right on the CD.

Because Internet Explorer comes as part of Windows 95 and Windows 98, you may already have it, but it may be an elderly version. Microsoft gives away Internet Explorer, so you may as well upgrade to the current version if you have an old one. (One can complain about many aspects of Internet Explorer, but not its price, unless you worry about software monopolies.)

You can also download any of these browsers from the Net. If you have access to any Web browser, try one of these Web sites:

✔ **TUCOWS (The Ultimate Collection of Internet Software):** http://www.tucows.com

✔ **The Consummate Winsock Applications page:** http://cws.internet.com

> ✔ **Netscape home page (for Netscape Navigator):** `http://home.netscape.com/download`
>
> ✔ **Microsoft home page (for Internet Explorer):** `http://www.microsoft.com/ie`
>
> ✔ **Opera Software (for Opera):** `http://www.operasoftware.com` (Opera is shareware; you should pay the $35 registration fee if you use it for more than 30 days.)

Use your Web browser to go to the page and then follow the instructions for finding and downloading the program. You may also want to consult Chapter 16 for more information about downloading files from the Internet.

Another option is to stroll into a software store and buy a boxed version of Netscape — you get a manual and the phone number for tech support, which you don't get when you download Netscape or install it from the Starter Kit edition of this book.

We're home — let's go

After you have the program, you have to install it. If you get Netscape or Internet Explorer on floppy disks or CD, follow the instructions that come with it. If you have the Netscape or Internet Explorer distribution file on your hard disk, follow these instructions (assuming that you use Windows 3.1 or Windows 95). Macintosh users, check the tips at the end of this section — installing on the Mac is even simpler.

To avoid excess user comprehension, the thing that Microsoft called a *directory* in MS-DOS and Windows 3.1 is called a *folder* in Windows 95 and Windows 98. We use the official newspeak term; if you're a Windows 3.1 user, however, pretend that we said *directory* wherever you read *folder*.

1. **The distribution file contains a program — run it.**

   The program begins installing Netscape, Internet Explorer, or Opera. First it extracts a bunch of files that it needs for the installation, and then it proceeds into the installation process.

2. **Follow the instructions on-screen.**

   Although the installation program asks a bunch of questions, the default answers for all of them are usually okay. If the Internet Explorer installation program asks whether you want to select optional components, choose <u>Y</u>es, and select the additional programs you want to install. (They may include Outlook Express, the Microsoft e-mail program; see Chapter 11 to find out how to use it.)

   The Internet Explorer installation program is actually just a "stub" that requires you to have your Net connection active when you run the program, because it goes out over the Net and fetches the rest of the program. The installation program is about 400 kilobytes, so you can download it in two or three minutes; after the installation starts, however, it has to download between 10 and 25 megabytes more, which takes a couple of hours. Consider starting the installation program and then going out for pizza (a lot of pizza).

When the Internet Explorer installation is done, you may have to restart your computer; if so, you see a message offering to restart it now. Click Yes unless you're in the middle of other work — then finish your work and restart your computer.

3. **Connect to your Internet provider or online service if you're not already online.**

The first thing your new browser wants to do is to display a Web page, so you had better be connected to the Internet.

4. **Try out your new browser.**

Click the attractive, new icon — the Netscape icon is labeled Netscape Navigator, which is the real name of the program, and the Internet Explorer icon goes by the intriguingly vague name The Internet. Opera calls itself (brace yourself, now) Opera.

The first time you run Netscape, you see a bunch of legal boilerplate stuff describing the license conditions for Netscape. If you can stand the conditions (many people can), click to indicate your acceptance. Netscape then starts up. It may want to connect to the Netscape Web page so that you can register your copy of Netscape — follow its instructions.

The first time you run Internet Explorer, it may run the Internet Connection Wizard, which offers to help you get connected to the Internet. If so, follow the instructions on-screen. If you already have an Internet connection that works, you have a chance to tell it so.

When you run Opera, it opens a nagging window to encourage you to register your copy. To use it without registering, click Evaluate. If you do use Opera regularly, do register it via its Web page at http://www.operasoftware.com.

Attention Mac users: The installation tips for a Mac are almost exactly the same. If you download your browser from the Net and you're lucky, the browser should arrive as an executable program in your download folder. Click it and follow its directions in order to install it. The program may arrive as a StuffIt file that self-extracts if you have StuffIt installed.

If you're upgrading from an older version of Netscape to a newer one, you can install the new version to replace the old one. When the installation program asks whether to replace netscape.ini, choose No to keep your existing Netscape settings.

Upgrade magic

After you install either Netscape or Internet Explorer, your software vendor would really, really, REALLY like you not to switch to a competing product. Toward this end, vendors have invented more or less automated schemes to upgrade from one version of their software to the next, and to help you figure out what needs upgrading in the first place.

For Netscape's "Smart Update," fire up Netscape, go to `http://home.netscape.com/download` and click Smart Update, and on the page that appears, click the Start Here to Begin button. You'll see a page like the one in Figure 6-4, noting what they have available and what you already have installed. Scroll down, click the stuff you want, choose a download location if needed (the default is fine if you're in the U.S.), and then click the Start Download button.

Netscape opens a small window listing what it's doing with detailed directions on what to click when. Follow the directions exactly (which can be a little confusing), and it downloads the new programs and installs them, one at a time. Some of the programs are large (new versions of Navigator and Communicator can be more than 10 megabytes), so the downloads may take a while.

For Microsoft's Windows Update (which includes Internet Explorer), click the Windows Update button that Microsoft has probably installed on your Start menu, or open Internet Explorer and go to `http://windowsupdate.microsoft.com`. Click Product Updates, and then when it asks whether it's

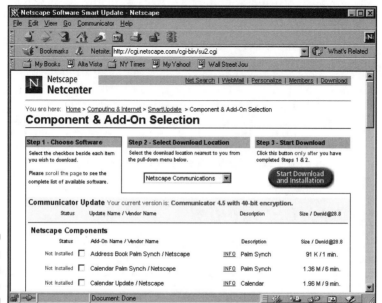

Figure 6-4: Netscape acts smart.

Okay to check what software is on your computer, click Yes. After quite a long delay, you see a Web page with suggested and available update software. Again, click the ones you want and then click the Download button, and it downloads and installs your new software. Microsoft's programs are even bigger than Netscape's, so the downloads can take a long time.

Opera doesn't have an automated upgrade system as such. To see what Opera has available, run the program and then on the menu, choose Lists⇨Opera Software⇨Download page.

Life with Lynx

The graphical browsers we've been discussing require PPP connections. What if you're stuck with a UNIX shell account? Those of you living a mouse-free existence can still do some serious Web surfing by using Lynx.

Because Lynx is a text-only browser, it can't do some things, such as show pictures, play audio and video clips, or display news-ticker-style moving messages at the bottom of your screen (a real advantage, in this last case). Within those limitations, though, it's a good program.

In fact, because Lynx *is* text-only, it's much faster than the graphics-based browsers, leaving you at least one thing to feel good about. And if you are sight-impaired, Lynx is definitely the way to go, because special programs can take Web page text and blow it up to huge sizes or read it aloud.

All UNIX shell providers should have Lynx available because it's free. To start it, you type **lynx** at the UNIX shell prompt. It starts up and displays a home page on-screen, as shown in Figure 6-5, which shows one of our friends' Web pages.

Because most text screens can't do underlining, the links are shown in reverse video. Bracketed text or the word [IMAGE] appears where a picture would be displayed. One link on the screen is *current* and is highlighted in a different color. (On our screen, it's yellow rather than white text, which doesn't show up on a black-and-white page. Use your imagination, or go get a yellow highlighting pen.) Lynx thoughtfully puts some help information on the bottom two lines, which makes it much easier to use.

Wandering around

Nearly all Lynx commands are single keystrokes. Pressing the ↑ and ↓ keys moves you from link to link on the current page. If the page fills more than one screen, the page scrolls as necessary. To move to the next screen of the current page, press the spacebar or press the plus and minus (+ and –) keys

```
                     TeamFlow - Team-based Process Flowcharting (p3 of 8)
         software products. Through an alliance, we also provide computer
         hardware, installation, and support in Northern Illinois.
       * Creative Learning Technologies uses TeamFlow's scheduling features
         to support Team-based project management for a variety of clients.
         TeamFlow is The Project Manager for the Rest of Us(TM).
       * Quality Management International uses TeamFlow to help their
         clients make ISO 9000 registration simple and certain.
       * R.T.Green & Associates is a group of experienced human resources
         professionals with broad range of accomplishments in the full
         spectrum of the Human Resources field. "Of the many productivity
         tools available we have tested, TeamFlow is the easiest to use and
         explain. Clients can see our processes and any discrete roles
         clearly laid out - the first time, every time."
       * Thousands of companies around the world use TeamFlow to help
         manage their business processes. Some of their stories and a
         listing of some of our customers are included here.
       _____

       What is TeamFlow?
       * TeamFlow is a powerful tool for team-based process management.
         TeamFlow is the only process flowcharter designed to implement the
         Deployment Flowcharting methodology invented by Dr. W. Edwards
       -more- http://www.teamflow.com/profiles.html
```

Figure 6-5:
Look, Ma,
no
pictures!

to move forward and backward a screen at a time.

You press the up- and down-arrow (↑ and ↓) keys to move from link to link, even when the links are next to each other on a line. For example, you may have a few lines on-screen, like this:

```
Famous philosophers:

[Moe] [Larry] [Curly] [Socrates]
```

If the highlight is on Larry, you press the ↑ key to go to Moe and press the ↓ key to go to Curly. The ← and → keys mean something else, as you will see in a second.

After you highlight a link you like, press the → key or Enter to follow that link. (Pressing → is the Lynx equivalent of clicking a link.) After Lynx fetches the new page, you can press the arrow keys to move around the new page. Pressing ← takes you back to the preceding page. You can press the ← key several times to go back several pages.

Lynx just can't do some things — most notably, image maps. Although it tells you that an image exists, because you can't see the image and you can't use a mouse, you have no way to click it. Fortunately, any sensible Web page that has an image map offers some other way to get to the places the image map would otherwise take you. The page has either a set of text links under the image or, in some cases, a link that says something like "Click here for a text-only version of this page." Lynx gives you a nice, clean, image-free page from which to work.

To go to a specific URL, press **g** for *go-to* and then type the URL on the line that Lynx provides, followed by pressing Enter.

Leaving Lynx

When you're finished with Lynx, press **q** to exit. Lynx asks whether you're sure that you want to quit; press **y**.

Is that all there is?

Of course not. Lynx is bristling with features, just like any other modern computer program. Just about every possible keystroke means something to Lynx (we discuss some of them in Chapter 7). The arrow keys and **g** and **q** are all you really need to get going.

Chapter 7

Wrangling with the Web

*1*f you know how to find your way around the Web, you are ready for some comparatively advanced features so that you can start to feel like a Web pro in no time. Remember that Netscape Navigator, Internet Explorer, Opera, and Lynx aren't the only browsers. If you're using something else, most of the features we cover here are probably also available to you. Try poking around. The best way to find out what you can do is by trying everything. If you have a manual or online Help resource, you may resort to reading it, of course, but, hey, why spoil all the fun?

Windows on the World

Windows and Mac browsers are known in the trade as *multithreaded* programs. What this term means in practice is that the program can do several things at a time and can display several pages at once. When we're pointing and clicking from one place to another, we like to open a bunch of windows so that we can see where we've been and go back to a previous page just by switching to another window. You can also arrange windows side by side, which is a good way to, say, compare prices for *The Internet For Dummies,* 6th Edition, at various online bookstores. (The difference may be small, but when you're buying 100 copies for everyone on your Christmas list, those pennies can add up. Oh, you weren't planning to do that? Drat.)

Wild window mania with Netscape and Internet Explorer

Netscape and Internet Explorer can have several Web browser windows open at a time. To open a link in a new window, click with the right mouse button and select Open in New Window on the menu that pops up. To close a window, click the little X box at the top right of the window frame, or press Alt+F4, the standard close-window shortcut. Macs don't have a right button, so hold down the button you do have to get the pop-up menu. You close all Mac windows the same way — by clicking the button at the top of the window. UNIX users with three-button mice can open a link in a new window by clicking the middle button.

You can also create a new window without following a link. Press Ctrl+N or choose File⇨New Web Browser (in Netscape 3.0) or File⇨New⇨Navigator Window (in Netscape 4.0) or File⇨Navigator Window (in Netscape 4.5) or File⇨New⇨Window (in Internet Explorer 4.0 or 5.0.) UNIX and Mac users should think "Alt" and "Apple" for "Ctrl" throughout this section.

Restrained, dignified window mania with Opera

Opera has what's known in Windows-ese as a Multiple Document Interface, which means that each page appears as a subwindow inside the main Opera window, just like what Word does with multiple document files. To open a link in a new window, right-click and select Get Link Document New Window. To close a window, press Ctrl+W or click the X in the top right of the document's window. To open a new window, press F2 or click the smoking cigarette icon (it's probably supposed to be a pencil and paper), and type the URL to open into the pop-up box that opens. Or to open an empty window, click the little piece of paper at the left end of the toolbar.

Short attention span tips

If you ask your browser to begin downloading a big file, it displays, most usefully, a small window in the corner of your screen. The Netscape and Opera versions of this window display a "thermometer" showing the download progress; Internet Explorer shows tiny pages flying from one folder to another. Although some people consider watching the thermometer grow or the pages fly enough entertainment (we do when we're tired enough), you can click back to the main browser window and continue surfing.

Doing two or three things at a time in your browser when you have a dial-up Net connection is not unlike squeezing blood from a turnip — only so much blood can be squeezed. In this case, the blood is the amount of data it can pump through your modem. A single download task can keep your modem close to 100 percent busy, and anything else you do shares the modem with the download process. When you do two things at a time, therefore, each one happens more slowly than it would by itself.

If one task is a big download and the other is perusing Web pages, everything usually works okay because you spend a fair amount of time looking at what the Web browser is displaying; the download can then run while you think. On the other hand, although browsers let you start two download tasks at a time (or a dozen, if you're so inclined), you have no reason to do more than one at a time because it's no faster to do them in parallel than one after another, and it can get confusing.

Lynx users are in a somewhat different situation because Lynx displays only one window at a time. In theory, you can run two copies of Lynx and switch back and forth; in practice, however, it's not worth the trouble. Because Lynx is running on your provider's system, it can take advantage of your provider's high-speed Net connection, and even large files load pretty quickly.

My Favorite Things

The Web really does have cool places to visit. Some you will want to visit over and over again. All the makers of fine browsers have, fortunately, provided a handy way for you to remember those spots and not have to write down those nasty URLs just to have to type them again later.

Although the name varies, the idea is simple: Your browser lets you mark a spot and then adds the URL to a list. Later, when you want to go back, you just go to your list and pick it out. Netscape calls these hot spots *bookmarks;* Internet Explorer calls them *favorites;* Opera calls them *hot lists.*

Bookmarks can be handled in two ways. One is to think of them as a menu so that you can choose individual bookmarks from the menu bar of your browser. The other is to think of them as a custom-built page of links so that you go to that page and then choose the link you want. Lynx takes the latter, custom-Web-page approach. Opera leans toward the menu approach. Netscape, a prime example of the Great Expanding Blob approach to software design, does both. Internet Explorer takes yet another tack: It adds your Web pages to a folder of favorite places to which you may want to return.

Marking Netscape

Netscape bookmarks lurk under the Bookmarks menu. To add a bookmark for a Web page displayed in Netscape 3.0, choose Bookmarks⇨Add Bookmark or press Ctrl+D. In Netscape 4.*x*, choose Communicator⇨ Bookmarks⇨Add Bookmark or press Ctrl+D. The bookmarks appear as entries on the Bookmarks menu (in Netscape 3.0) or on the menu that appears when you click the Bookmarks Quick File button, which is located to the left of the Location box (in Netscape 4.*x*). To go to one of the pages on your bookmark list, just choose its entry from this menu.

If you're like most users, your bookmark menu gets bigger and bigger and crawls down your screen and eventually ends up flopping down on the floor, which is both unattractive and unsanitary. Fortunately, you can smoosh (technical term) your menu into a more tractable form. Choose Bookmarks⇨ Go to Bookmarks (in Netscape 3.0) or Communicator⇨Bookmarks⇨ Edit Bookmarks (in Netscape 4.*x*), or press Ctrl+B (in either version) to display your Bookmarks window, as shown in Figure 7-1.

Because all these bookmarks are "live," you can go to any of them by clicking them. (You can leave this window open while you move around the Web in other browser windows.) You can also add separator lines and submenus to organize your bookmarks and make the individual menus less unwieldy. Submenus look like folders in the Bookmarks window.

Figure 7-1:
The
Netscape
Bookmarks
window
shows the
list of Web
pages you
want to
come
back to.

In the Bookmarks window in Netscape 4.*x*, choose File⇨New Separator to add a separator line and File⇨New Folder to add a new submenu. (Netscape asks you to type the name of the submenu before it creates the folder.) You can then drag the bookmarks, separators, and folders up and down to where you want them in the Bookmarks window. Drag an item to a folder to put it in that folder's submenu, and double-click a folder to display or hide that submenu. Because any changes you make in the Bookmarks window are reflected immediately on the Bookmarks menu, it's easy to fiddle with the bookmarks until you get something you like. Netscape folks preload your bookmark window with pages they'd like you to look at, but you can feel free to delete them if your tastes are different from theirs.

When you're done fooling with your bookmarks, choose File⇨Close or press Ctrl+W to close the Bookmarks window.

Netscape also has a cool feature that enables you to see which of the items on your bookmark list have been updated since you last looked at them. Open the Bookmarks window as described earlier in this section and then choose File⇨What's New (in Netscape 3.0) or View⇨Update Bookmarks (in Netscape 4.*x*) from the menu in the Bookmarks window. You see a little box asking which bookmarks you want to check. Click the Start Checking button. When Netscape is done checking the Web pages on your bookmarks list, it displays a message telling you how many have changed. The icons in the Bookmarks window reveal which pages have changed: The ones with little sparkles have new material, the ones with question marks are the ones Netscape isn't sure about, and the ones that look normal haven't changed.

Marking Internet Explorer

Internet Explorer uses a system similar to the one Netscape uses: You can add the current page to your Favorites folder and then look at and organize your Favorites folder. If you use Windows 95 or 98, however, this Favorites folder is shared with other programs on your computer. Other programs also can add things to your Favorites folder, so it's a jumble of Web pages, files, and other things.

To add the current page to your Favorites folder, choose Favorites⇨Add to Favorites from the menu. To see your Favorites folder, choose Favorites⇨ Organize Favorites or Open Favorites from the menu. Internet Explorer 4.0 and 5.0 also have a Favorites button on the toolbar that displays your list of Favorites down the left side of your Internet Explorer window.

Exactly how the Favorites folder works depends on which version of Internet Explorer you're running. The versions for Internet Explorer 4.0 and 5.0 for Windows 95/98 are shown in Figure 7-2 and 7-3. You can create subfolders in the Favorites folder so that you can store different types of files in different folders. (The Windows 3.1 version just lets you look at the

Favorites list — you can't reorganize it.) To create a folder, click the Create New Folder button in 4.0 (the button with the yellow folder with a little sparkle, near the upper-right corner of the window) or the Create Folder button in 5.0. To move an item in the Favorites window into a folder, click the item, click the Move or Move to Folder button, and select the folder to move it to. You can see the contents of a folder by double-clicking it. When you are done organizing your favorite items, click the Close button.

In Internet Explorer 5.0, you can make pages available when you're not connected to the Internet by clicking on the page in the Favorites window and then clicking the Make Available Offline box. Internet Explorer immediately fetches the page to your disk and refetches it from time to time when you're connected so that you can view the page when you click on it when you're offline.

Figure 7-2:
Internet Explorer 4.0 shows your favorites.

Figure 7-3:
Internet Explorer 5.0 shows your favorites, too.

If you make a lot of pages available offline, you'll find your browser spending a lot of time keeping them up-to-date. When you no longer need to browse a page offline, uncheck its Make Available Offline box or remove it from Favorites altogether.

The folders you create in the Organize Favorites window appear on your Favorites menu, and the items you put in the folders appear on submenus. To return to a Web page you've added to your Favorites folder, just choose it from the Favorites menu.

In Windows 95/98, the Favorites folder usually appears on your desktop or your Start menu. You can double-click the folder to open it and double-click an item to return to that item. If the item is a Web page, your browser fires up and (if you're connected to the Internet) displays the Web page.

Hot, hot, hot in Opera

Opera calls its bookmark list the *hot list.* You get to it from the Lists menu item, which comes preloaded with submenus and sub-submenus full of suggested pages (pretty good ones, in fact, including the Pacific Journal published in Fiji). You can add and update your own as well.

To open a page in the hot list, just select the Lists menu or the hot list icon that looks like a book, select the appropriate submenu, and select a page in the submenu. Opera opens the page in a new window. (Press Ctrl+W to close the window when done, same as always.)

To add the current page to the hot list, select the Lists menu or icon, select the appropriate submenu, and in that submenu, select Add Current Document Here. Opera pops up a window where you can enter a nickname to use in the menu and a description (both entirely optional) and then click OK to add it.

To edit the hot list, choose View➪Hotlist or press Ctrl+2, displaying a window like the one shown in Figure 7-4. The upper portion displays all the folders in the hot list; the lower portion contains the contents of the current folder. Click any folder in the upper part of the window to open that folder. To move an item from one folder to another, open the folder where it is now, and then click and drag the item into the new folder. If you right-click on any folder or item, you get a menu of useful operations, including Delete to get rid of an item and New➪Folder to create a new folder. While the hot list is open, you can double-click any item to open that item in a new window.

Press Ctrl+W or click the X icon at the top right of the border to close the hot list.

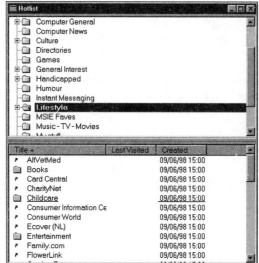

Marking Lynx

The Lynx bookmark scheme is a complete anticlimax compared to Netscape and Internet Explorer. It's controlled by two (count 'em — two) letters.

To add the current page to your bookmark list, press **a**. Lynx gives you the choice of adding a link to the page on-screen (**d** for document) or copying the highlighted link (**c** for current).

To look at (view) your current bookmark list, press **v**. When you're looking at your bookmark list, you move through it and choose links in the same way as you do on any other Web page. You can remove links from the bookmark page by pressing **r**.

If you're using Lynx on your own UNIX account, your bookmarks are saved in a file between Lynx sessions. On the other hand, if you're using telnet to connect to a Lynx system somewhere else, the bookmarks exist only through a single Lynx session, and they're discarded when you quit.

Speeding Things Up

Unless you have a high-speed dedicated connection rather than a normal dial-up account, you probably spend a great deal of time wishing that the process of getting to stuff on the Web was much faster. (John has a high-speed dedicated connection, and he spends a certain amount of time waiting for the Web anyway.) Here are a handful of tricks you can use to try to speed things up.

Where do we start?

In Netscape: When Netscape starts up, by default it loads the large and attractive Netscape home page chock full of irresistable offers (at least Netscape's owners at AOL hope they are). After one or two times, beautiful though the home page is, you will probably find that you can do without it. You can tell Netscape not to load any Web page when you start the program:

1. **Choose Options⇨General Preferences (in Netscape 3.0) or Edit⇨Preferences (in Netscape 4.x).**

    You see the Preferences dialog box.

2. **Click the Appearance tab (in Netscape 3.0) or the Navigator category (in Netscape 4.x).**

    In Netscape 3.0 under Startup, you see a setting called Browser Starts With. In Netscape 4.x, the setting is called Navigator Starts With.

3. **If you want to start with no Web page, click Blank Page. If you want to start with a page you specify, click Home Page, click in the box below it, and type the name of a page you would rather see (your provider's home page, for example).**

    In Netscape 4.x, you also have the option of starting where you left off last time, by clicking Last Page Visited.

4. **Click OK.**

In Internet Explorer: Internet Explorer 4.0 and 5.0 start by displaying the Microsoft home page or a Web page stored on your own hard disk, depending on which version of Internet Explorer you have. You can change that start page, or you can tell Internet Explorer to load a blank page. (Loading a home page from your disk is pretty fast, so we do that in preference to blank.) Follow these steps to change your start page:

1. **Display the Web page you want to use as your start page.**

    For example, you may want to start at the Yahoo page, described in Chapter 8, or Internet Gurus Central, at `http://net.gurus.com`.

2. **Choose View⇨Internet Options from the menu.**

    You see the Internet Options dialog box.

3. **Find the General tab along the top of the dialog box and click it.**

    You can set the addresses of several Web pages.

4. **In the Home Page section of the dialog box, click the Use Current button, or click the Use Blank button.**

    The URL of the current page appears in the Address box if you use the current page.

5. **Click OK.**

Choose a start page that doesn't have many pictures: By starting with a Web page that loads faster or with no start page, you don't have to wait long to start browsing.

In Opera: In Opera, the best bet is to display what you were looking at last time.

1. **Select Preferences⇨Generic.**

   You see the Generic Preferences box.

2. **Select Show Saved Windows and History.**

3. **Click OK.**

Switching to ugly mode

You can save a great deal of time by skipping the pictures when you're browsing the Web. True, the pages don't look as snazzy, but they load like the wind. If you decide that you want to see the missing pictures after all, you can still do so.

In Netscape: On the Netscape Options menu (in Netscape 3.0) or the Preferences dialog box (in Netscape 4.*x*, choose Edit⇨Preferences menu and then click the Advanced category), uncheck Auto Load Images. (For Netscape 3.0 users, choose Options or Edit⇨Preferences from the menu and look to see whether a check mark appears to the left of the Auto Load Images command. If it does, choose the command — this action removes the check mark. If no check mark is shown, *don't* choose the command — press Esc instead.) Turning Auto Load Images off tells Netscape to load only the text part of Web pages, which is small, and to hold off on the images, which are large. At every place on the page where an image should go, Netscape displays a box with three colored shapes. To see a particular image, click the three-shape box with the *right* mouse button and choose Load Image from the menu that appears.

In Internet Explorer: You can tell Internet Explorer 4.0 and 5.0 not to bother loading images by choosing View⇨Internet Options from the menu (Tools⇨Internet Options in 5.0), clicking the Advanced tab, and scrolling down to the Multimedia section. If a check mark or X appears in the Show Pictures box, click in the box to remove the check mark or X. Then click OK. Where pictures usually appear, you see a little box with three shapes in it. If you want to see a particular picture, right-click the little box and choose Show Picture from the menu that appears.

In Opera: You can tell Opera not to load images by choosing Preferences⇨Multimedia, and checking Do Not Load and Show Images. A good compromise is Show Loaded Images Only, which displays an image if it's already available but won't download new ones. You can turn image loading on and off in each individual window by clicking the little camera icon at the bottom left of the window.

Cold, hard cache

When Netscape or Internet Explorer retrieves a page you have asked to see, it stores the page on your disk. If you ask for the same page again five minutes later, the program doesn't have to retrieve the page again — it can reuse the copy it already has. If you tell the program not to load images, for example, you get a fair number of them anyway because they have already been downloaded.

The space your browser uses to store pages is called its *cache* (pronounced "cash" because it's French and gives your cache more *cachet*). The more space you tell your browser to use for its cache, the faster pages appear the second time you look at them.

In Netscape: To set the size of the Netscape cache, follow these steps:

1. **Choose Options⇨Network Preferences (in Netscape 3.0) or Edit⇨Preferences from the menu.**

   You see the Preferences dialog box.

2. **Click the Cache tab along the top of the dialog box (in Netscape 3.0) or double-click the Advanced category and click the Cache category (in Netscape 4.x).**

   The Disk Cache box shows the maximum size of the cache in kilobytes (K): We like to set Disk Cache to at least 1,024K (that is, 1MB). Set it to a higher number if you have a large hard disk with loads of free space — the more space your cache can occupy, the more often you can load a Web page quickly from the cache rather than slowly from the Net.

3. **Click OK.**

In Internet Explorer: To set the size of the Internet Explorer 4.0 or 5.0 cache, follow these steps:

1. **Choose View⇨Internet Options from the menu (Tools⇨Internet Options in 5.0).**

   You see the Internet Options dialog box.

2. **Click the General tab.**

3. **Click the Settings button in the Temporary Internet Files box.**

   You see the Settings dialog box, with information about the cache. (Many versions of Internet Explorer never call it a cache — guess they don't speak French.)

4. **Click the slider on the Amount of Disk Space to Use or Maximum Size line and move it to about 10 percent.**

   If you have tons of empty disk space, you can slide it rightward to 20 percent. If you're short on space, move it leftward to 1 or 2 percent.

5. **Click OK twice.**

In Opera: To set the size of the cache, follow these steps

1. **Choose Preferences⇨Cache from the menu.**

   You see the Cache Preferences dialog box.

2. **Set the sizes of the disk cache, documents cache, and images cache.**

   The default sizes are too small; try 5,000K for the disk cache and 1,000K apiece for the other two.

3. **Click OK.**

Some of us hardly ever exit from our browsers, which is probably not a good idea for our long-term mental stability. If you are one of us, however, remember that the pages your browser has cached aren't reloaded from the Web (they're taken from your disk) until you reload them. If you want to make sure that you're getting fresh pages, reload pages that you think may have changed since you last visited. Your browser is supposed to check whether a saved page has changed, but because the check sometimes doesn't work perfectly, an occasional Reload command for pages that change frequently, such as stock prices or the weather report, is advisable.

Getting the Big Picture

Browsers have so many buttons, icons, and boxes near the top of the window that not much space is left to display the Web page.

In Netscape: You can clear off a little more space in the Netscape window by using commands from the Options or View menu:

- To eliminate directory buttons (the bottommost row of buttons, just above the Web page area, that say "What's New?" and "What's Cool?"), choose Options⇨Show Directory Buttons. Netscape 4.0 eliminates these buttons permanently (a good move, in our opinion).

- To clear off the Location box, choose Options⇨Show Location (in Netscape 3.0) or View⇨Hide Location Toolbar (in Netscape 4.x). This action isn't such a good idea most of the time because the Location box shows you the URL of the page you're looking at and lets you type a new URL to go to.

✔ To say *sayonara* to the toolbar (the row of buttons just below the menu), choose <u>O</u>ptions⇨Show <u>T</u>oolbar (in Netscape 3.0) or <u>V</u>iew⇨Hide <u>N</u>avigation Toolbar (in Netscape 4.*x*). Most people use the Back button all the time, but you won't miss it if you remember that pressing Alt+← does the same thing.

To restore any of the things you just blew away, give the same command again. We never use the directory buttons and would rather keep the toolbar and Location box.

In Internet Explorer: You can reclaim screen real estate by giving these commands in Internet Explorer 4.0 or 5.0:

✔ To get rid of the toolbar (the row of buttons just below the menu), choose <u>V</u>iew⇨<u>T</u>oolbars⇨<u>S</u>tandard Buttons. Most buttons on the toolbar have keyboard equivalents, some of which we describe in this chapter.

✔ To suppress the Address bar and the Address box, choose <u>V</u>iew⇨<u>T</u>oolbars⇨<u>A</u>ddress Bar. This action isn't such a great idea because you need that Address box for typing URLs.

✔ To get rid of the status bar (the gray bar at the bottom of the Internet Explorer window), choose <u>V</u>iew⇨<u>S</u>tatus Bar.

Give the same command again to restore the item you got rid of. We prefer to keep these items on-screen most of the time, but your tastes may differ, and we have pretty big screens.

In Opera: The window's not as cluttered to start with, but you can unclutter it more.

✔ <u>V</u>iew⇨<u>B</u>utton bar⇨<u>O</u>ff turns off the buttons at the top of the window. They all have keyboard and menu equivalents anyway.

✔ <u>V</u>iew⇨<u>S</u>tatus bar⇨<u>O</u>ff removes the status bar at the bottom of the window, getting back a little more space.

✔ <u>V</u>iew⇨<u>P</u>rogress bar toggles the progress and status bar at the bottom of each window.

To see as much as possible of a browser window, maximize that window by clicking the maximize button near the top right of its border. This both makes the window the maximum size and removes the border around it. (This same trick works in any multi-document interface program, including Word and Excel.)

Filling In the Forms

Back in the Dark Ages of the Web (that is, in 1993), Web pages were just pages to look at. Because that wasn't anywhere near enough fun nor complicated enough, Web forms were invented. A *form* is sort of like a paper form, with fields you can fill out and then send in. Figure 7-5 shows a typical form.

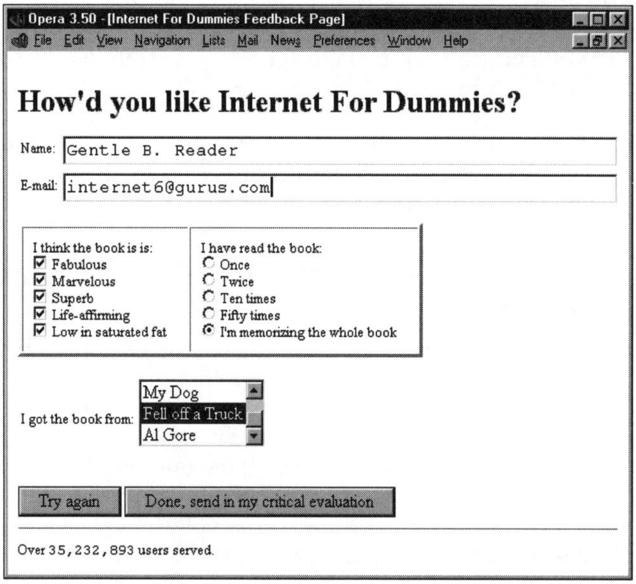

Figure 7-5:
Form-ally
speaking.

The top two lines in the form are fill-in text boxes in which you type, in this case, your name and e-mail address. Under that is a set of *check boxes,* in which you check whichever ones apply (all of them, we hope), and a set of *radio buttons,* which are similar to check boxes except that you can choose only one of them. Under that is a *list box,* in which you can choose one of the possibilities in the box. In most cases, more entries are available than can fit in the box, so you scroll them up and down. Although you can usually choose only one entry, some list boxes let you choose more.

At the bottom of the form are two buttons. The one on the left clears the form fields to their initial state and sends nothing, and the one on the right, known as the *Submit* button, sends the filled-out form back to the Web server for processing.

After the data is sent from the form back to the Web server, it's entirely up to the server how to interpret it.

Lynx handles forms just like other browsers do (one of the best Lynx features), as shown in Figure 7-6. You move from field to field on a Lynx form by pressing the ↑ and ↓ keys, the same as always. To submit a form, move to the Submit button (or whatever the button is labeled) and press Enter.

Figure 7-6:
Form-ally
speaking in
Lynx.

Some Web pages have *search items,* which are simplified one-line forms that let you type some text, usually interpreted as keywords for which to search. Depending on the browser, a Submit button may be displayed to the right of the text area, or you may just press Enter to send the search words to the server.

Save Me!

Frequently, you see something on a Web page that's worth saving for later. Sometimes it's a Web page full of interesting information or a picture or some other type of file. Fortunately, saving stuff is easy.

When you save a Web page, you have to decide whether to save only the text that appears or the entire HTML version of the page, with the format codes. (For a glimpse of HTML, see Chapter 10.) You can also save the pictures that appear on Web pages.

In Netscape, Internet Explorer, or Opera, choose File⇨Save As to save the current Web page in a file. You see the standard Save As dialog box, in which you specify the name to save the incoming file. Click in the Save As Type box to determine how to save the page: Choose Plain Text to save only the text of the page, with little notes where pictures occur. Choose HTML or HMTL Files to save the entire HTML file. Then click the Save or OK button.

To save an image you see on a Web page, right-click the image (click the image with your right mouse button). Choose Save Image As or Save Picture As from the menu that appears. When you see the Save As dialog box, move to the folder or directory in which you want to save the graphics file, type a filename in the File Name box, and click the Save or OK button.

A note about copyright: Contrary to popular belief, almost all Web pages, along with almost everything else on the Internet, are copyrighted by their authors. If you save a Web page or a picture from a Web page, you don't necessarily have permission to use it any way you want. Before you reuse the text or pictures in any way, send an e-mail message to the owner of the site. If an address doesn't appear on the page, write for permission to webmaster@`domain.com`, replacing `domain.com` with the domain name part of the URL of the Web page. For permission to use information on the `http://net.gurus.com/books.html` page, for example, write to webmaster@`gurus.com`.

Saving Lynx pages

Saving files in Lynx is a little more complicated but still not too difficult. How you do it depends on whether you want to save a page that Lynx knows how to display or to do something else.

Whenever Lynx saves something to disk, it saves it to your *provider's* disk. If you want it on your own PC, you have to download it yourself.

To save a page that Lynx can display, first move to the page so that it's displayed on-screen. Then press **d** for download. Lynx prompts you with the various ways it knows to save the page; usually, the only option is to save to disk, which lets you specify on your provider's system a filename in which to save it. Alternatively, you can press **p** for print, which gives you three options:

- ✔ Save to disk, just like **d** does.

- ✔ Mail to yourself, frequently the most convenient option.

- ✔ Print to screen. Turn on "screen capture" in the terminal program on your PC, which saves the contents of the page as it goes by on-screen.

Saving anything else in Lynx

Saving is the easiest part. If you choose a link that displays an image, program, or other sort of document Lynx can't handle, it stops and tells you that it can't display this link. You press **d** to download it to a local file, for which you specify the name, or **c** to cancel and forget that link.

The Dead-Tree Thing (Printing)

For about the first year that Web browsers existed, they all had print commands that didn't work. People finally figured out how to print Web pages, and now they all can do it.

To print a page from Netscape, Internet Explorer, or Opera, just click the Print button on the toolbar, press Ctrl+P, or choose File➪Print. Reformatting the page to print it can take awhile, so patience is a virtue. Fortunately, each browser displays a progress window to keep you apprised of how it's doing.

If the page you want to print uses frames, a technique that divides the window into subareas that can scroll and update separately, click in the part of the window you want to print before printing; otherwise, you're likely to get the outermost frame, which usually just has a title and some buttons.

Printing in Lynx is easy in principle: You press **p**. If you're dialed in to your provider, however, printing on your provider's computer doesn't do you much good, so Lynx gives you some options, the most useful of which are save to disk (so that you can download the Web page and print it locally) or e-mail the page to yourself (so that you can download and print it locally). Are you detecting a pattern here?

Getting Plugged In: Singing, Dancing, and Chatting with Your Browser

As Netscape has evolved from an unknown newcomer in the Web biz to the big gorilla on the block, it has gained a few new features. Lots and lots of features. Lots and lots and lots of features. Netscape already had about as many features as any single human could comprehend, but just in case someone somewhere understood the whole thing, you can now extend Netscape capabilities with *plug-ins,* or add-on programs that glue themselves to Netscape and add even more features.

Not to be outdone, each version of Internet Explorer tries to match the Netscape features. In addition to using plug-ins, you can also extend the already massive Internet Explorer capabilities by using things called *ActiveX* controls (formerly called OCX controls, but they changed the name when people started to figure out what they are), which are another type of add-on program. (Opera uses plug-ins like Netscape does.)

Web pages with pictures are old hat. Now, Web pages have to have pictures that sing and dance or ticker-style messages that move across the page or video clips. Every month, new types of information appear on the Web.

What's a Web browser to do with all these new kinds of information? Get the plug-in program that handles that kind of information and glue it onto Netscape or Internet Explorer. You *Star Trek* fans can think of plug-ins as parasitic life forms that attach themselves to your browser and enhance its intelligence.

A parade of plug-ins

Here are some useful plug-ins:

- **RealPlayer:** Plays sound files as you download them (other programs have to wait until the entire file has downloaded before beginning to play)

- **QuickTime:** Plays video files and VDOLive, which plays video files as you download them

- **Shockwave:** Plays both audio and video files as well as other types of animations

- **ichat:** Lets you use your Web browser to participate in online chats

- **Netscape Live3D, WIRL, Liquid Reality, and other VR plug-ins:** Let you move around inside 3-D "virtual reality" worlds on Web pages

How to use plug-ins with your browser

You can find Netscape or Opera plug-ins and Internet Explorer ActiveX controls at TUCOWS (http://www.tucows.com), the Consummate Winsock Applications page (http://cws.internet.com), the Netscape Web site (http://home.netscape.com), and other sources of software on the Web.

After you have downloaded a plug-in from the Net, run it (double-click its filename in My Computer, Windows Explorer, or File Manager) to install it. Depending on what the plug-in does, you follow different steps to try it out. Here are some examples:

- **RealPlayer:** Go to the http://www.realaudio.com Web page for a list of sites that handle RealAudio sound files. Our favorite site is the National Public Radio Web site (http://www.npr.org), where you can hear recent NPR radio stories.

- **ichat:** Go to the ichat Web site, at http://www.ichat.com, to join chats with other ichat users or to participate in Internet Relay Chat (IRC) conversations. (See Chapter 15 for more information about IRC.)

History? What history?

All three of the graphical browsers have a somewhat useful feature called History. Next to the box where you can type a URL, there's a little arrow that, when clicked, shows you a list of recently visited URLs. Some of our readers have asked us how to clear out that box, presumably because they meant to type www.disney.com but their fingers slipped and it came out www.hot-xxx-babes.com instead. (It could happen to anyone.) Because some of the requests sounded fairly urgent, here's the occasionally gruesome details about how to do it.

Netscape 4.5: Choose Edit⇨Preferences, select the Navigator category, and click the big Clear Location Bar button. Everything should be this easy.

Internet Explorer 4.0 and 5.0: Choose View⇨Internet Options or Tools⇨Internet Options, click the General tab, and click the Clear History button. Click Yes when it asks if you wanted to do that.

Netscape 4.0: This starts to get more complicated, because there's no button. The history's stored in a file called prefs.js, which is probably in the folder \Program Files\ Netscape\Users*yourname*. (If not, use the Start menu's Find⇨File to find it.) This file contains all of Netscape's preferences, and you can just delete it, but that will also make it forget all of your other settings, so it's better to edit it. Close all Netscape windows, start up Notepad or any other text editor you like, and open prefs.js. You'll see a bunch of lines in an obscure programming language (JavaScript, if you were wondering.) Some of those lines

have codes like browser.url_history .URL_1. Delete the lines with the, um, erroneous URLs. Then save and close the file, restart Netscape, and you're all set.

Netscape 3.0: The history is saved in the Windows registry, a black hole from which little data never escapes. It is possible to edit and delete registry entries, but if you do it wrong, you can screw up Windows so badly you'll have to reload it from scratch. So don't say we didn't warn you. Hmm, you're still here, you must be really desperate. Okay, close all Netscape windows, and then on the Windows Start menu, choose Run, and then type in **Regedit** and press Enter. The registry editor should start with a display in the left part of the window that looks sort of like the Windows Explorer folder tree. Double-click on HKEY_CURRENT_USER to see the subentries below it, and then double-click on Software, and then Netscape, and then Netscape Navigator, and then URL History. In the right window, you should see items from URL_1 to URL_10 listing the history. Click on each URL you want to get rid of to highlight it, and then press Delete. Regedit asks if you're sure; double-check to be sure you are and click Yes. Then choose Registry⇨Exit to leave Regedit and never, ever do that again.

Opera: Normally, the history is kept separately for each window, so closing the window gets rid of the history. Choose Preferences⇨ Generic and make sure Global History is *not* checked to be sure there's no extra history lurking around.

Chapter 8

Needles and Haystacks: Finding Stuff on the Net

"*O*kay, all this great stuff is out there on the Net. How do I find it?" That's an excellent question. Thanks for asking that question. Questions like that are what make this country strong and vibrant. We salute you and say, "Keep asking questions!" Next question, please.

Oh, you want an *answer* to your question. Fortunately, quite a bit of (technical term follows) stuff-finding stuff is on the Net. More particularly, indexes and directories of much of the interesting material are available on the Net.

The Net has different types of indexes and directories for different types of material. Because the indexes tend to be organized, unfortunately, by the type of Internet service they provide rather than by the nature of the material, you find Web resources in one place, e-mail resources in another place, and so on. You can search in dozens of hundreds of different ways, depending on what you're looking for and how you prefer to search. (John has remarked that his ideal restaurant has only one item on the menu, but that it's just what he wants. The Internet is about as far from that ideal as you can possibly imagine.)

TIP

Index, directory — what's the difference?

When we talk about a *directory,* we mean a listing like an encyclopedia or a library's card catalog (well, like the computer system that is replacing the card catalog). It has named categories with entries assigned to categories partly or entirely by human catalogers. You look things up by finding a category you want and seeing what it contains. In this book, we would think of the table of contents as a directory.

An *index,* on the other hand, simply collects all the items, extracts keywords from them (by taking all the words except for *the, and,* and the like), and makes a big list. You search the index by specifying some words that seem likely, and it finds all the entries that contain that word. The index in the back of this book is more like an index.

Each has its advantages and disadvantages. Directories are organized better, but indexes are larger. Directories use consistent terminology, while indexes use whatever terms the underlying Web pages used. Directories contain fewer useless pages, but indexes are updated more often.

Some overlap exists between indexes and directories — Yahoo, the best known Web page directory, lets you search by keyword, and many of the indexes divide their entries into general categories that let you limit the search.

To provide a smidgen of structure to this discussion, we describe several different sorts of searches:

- ✔ **Topics:** Places, things, ideas, companies — anything you want to find out more about
- ✔ **Built-in searches:** Topic searches that a browser does automatically, and why we're not thrilled about that
- ✔ **People:** Actual human beings whom you want to contact or spy on
- ✔ **Goods and services:** Stuff to buy, from mortgages to mouthwash

To find topics, we use the various online indexes and directories, such as Yahoo and AltaVista. To find people, however, we use directories of people, which are (fortunately) different from directories of Web pages. Wondering what we're talking about? Read on for an explanation!

Your Basic Search Strategy

When we're looking for topics on the Net, we always begin with one of the Web guides (indexes and directories) discussed in this section.

You use them all in more or less the same way:

1. **Start your Web browser, such as Netscape or Internet Explorer.**

2. **Pick a directory or index you like and tell your browser to go to the index or directory's home page.**

   We list the URLs (page names) of the home pages later in this section.

   After you get there, you can choose between two approaches.

3. **a. If a Search box is available, type some likely keywords in the box and click Search.**

   This is the "index" approach, to look for topic areas that match your keywords.

   After a perhaps long delay (the Web is pretty big), an index page is returned with links to pages that match your keywords. The list of links may be way too long to deal with — like 300,000 of them.

   or

   b. If you see a list of links to topic areas, click a topic area of interest.

   In the "directory" approach, you begin at a general topic and get more and more specific. Each page has links to pages that get more and more specific until they link to actual pages that are likely to be of interest.

4. **Adjust and repeat your search until you find something you like.**

   After some clicking around to get the hang of it, you find all sorts of good stuff.

You hear a great deal of talk around the Web about search engines. *Search engines* is a fancy way to say stuff-finding stuff. All the directories and indexes we're about to describe are in the broad category called search engines, so don't get upset by some high-falutin-sounding terms.

The lazy searcher's search page

You may feel a wee bit overwhelmed with all the search directories and indexes we discuss in this chapter. If it makes you feel any better, so do we.

To make a little sense of all this stuff, we made ourselves a search page that connects to all the directories and indexes we use so that we get one-stop searching. You can use it, too. Give it a try, at http://net.gurus.com/search.

In the not unlikely event that new search systems are created or some of the existing ones have moved or died, this page gives you our latest greatest list.

Search-a-Roo

So much for the theory of searching for stuff on the Net. Now for some practice. (Theory and practice are much further apart in practice than they are in theory.) We use our two favorite search systems for examples: Yahoo, which is a directory, and AltaVista, which is an index.

Yahoo-a-roo, our favorite directory

You can find stuff in Yahoo in two ways. (Yes, it's spelled with an exclamation point. Last year's fad was funny CapITallzaTion; this year's seems to be !funny? "¿¿"¿punc@@tuation! But henceforth we leave out the ! to avoid overexciting ourselves.) The easier way is just to click from category to category until you find something you like.

We start our Yahoo visit at its home page, at `http://www.yahoo.com` (at least the page name doesn't use an exclamation point), which looks like Figure 8-1. A whole bunch of categories and subcategories are listed. You can click any of them to see another page that has yet more subcategories and links to actual Web pages. You can click a link to a page if you see one you like or on a sub-subcategory, and so on.

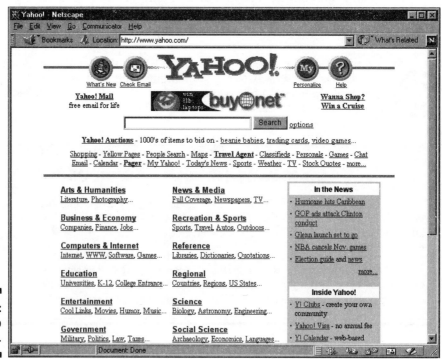

Figure 8-1: Ready to Yahoo.

At the top of each Yahoo page is the list of categories, subcategories, and so on, separated by colons, that lead to that page. If you want to back up a few levels and look at different subcategories, just click the place on that list to which you want to back up. After a little clicking up and down, it's second nature. Many pages appear in more than one place in the directory because they fall into more than one category. An advantage of a Web page directory over a card catalog in a library is that although a book can be in only one place on the shelf in the library, Web pages can have as many links referring to them as they want.

Although all the categories in the Yahoo list have plenty of subcategories under them, some have many more than others. If you're looking for a business-related page, it helps to know that Yahoo sticks just about everything commercial under the category Business and Economy, as shown in Figure 8-2. If we were looking for Internet For Dummies Central, for example (which we think people should look for several times a day, at least), we could click our way to it from the Yahoo home page by clicking Business and Economy and then, on that page, clicking Companies, then Books, then Computers, and then Internet; on that page, you link to pages with lots of Internet books, including ours.

If you know in general but not in detail what you're looking for, clicking up and down through the Yahoo directory pages is a good way to narrow your search and find pages of interest.

Figure 8-2:
A store-house of commercial information at Yahoo.

Searching through Yahoo

"Click on Business and Economy, and then, on that page, click Companies, then Books, then Computers, and then Internet? How the heck did they know which categories to click?" you're doubtless asking. We admit it. We cheated.

Yahoo also lets you search its index by keyword, which is the best way to use it if you have some idea of the title of the page you're looking for. Every Yahoo screen has near the top a search box in which you can type words you want to find in the Yahoo entry for pages of interest. For example, we typed `Internet dummies books`, clicked the Search button next to the type-in box, and got the answer shown in Figure 8-3, with one entry for our Web site and one book by Dan Gookin, who has written the occasional ...*For Dummies* book, as well.

Above each entry Yahoo finds, it reports the category in which it found the entry. Even if the entry isn't quite right, if you click the category, you find other related titles, and some of them may well do the trick.

Figure 8-3:
Zeroing in
on quality
literature.

If Yahoo finds hundreds of pages or categories, you should refine your search. One way to do that is to add extra words to make more specific what you're looking for. If you were looking for a key lime pie recipe (John sent out a good one on the Net about ten years ago) and you search for `baking`, you get 71 fairly random pages; if you search for `key lime pie`, however, you get two pages, one of which is on the Business and Economy: Companies: Food: Baked Goods: Pies page, which has links to lots of tasty pie recipes.

You can click Options, next to the Search button, to get to the slightly more advanced Yahoo search page. It lets you limit how far back you want to see pages (three years is the default), and you can tell it to look for either all the words or any of the words you typed.

Tons more at Yahoo

Although Yahoo is primarily a directory of resources available on the Web, it's now a "Web portal," which means that it has plenty of other databases available to encourage you to stick around inside Yahoo. Each has a link you can click just under the box in which you enter search terms:

- ✔ **Yellow Pages:** A business directory

- ✔ **People Search:** Finds addresses and phone numbers, like a white pages directory (see the "Finding People" section)

- ✔ **Maps:** Gets a more or less accurate map of a street address you type

- ✔ **Classifieds:** Lets you read and submit ads for automobiles, apartments, computers, and jobs

- ✔ **Personals:** Lets you read and submit ads for dates in all (and we mean *all*) combinations

- ✔ **Chat:** Gets you into online chat through the Web

- ✔ **Email:** Free Web-based e-mail service

- ✔ **TV:** Impressively complete TV and cable listings, by area

- ✔ **Travel:** A link to the Travelocity reservation system. (See `http://www.iecc.com/airline` for our opinions and suggestions about online travel services.)

- ✔ **My Yahoo:** A customized starting page just for you, with headlines, sports scores, and other news based on your preferences

- ✔ **Today's News, Stock Quotes, and Sports Scores:** News from Reuters

AltaVista-a-rista, our favorite index

Our favorite Web index, AltaVista has a little robot named Scooter that spends her time merrily visiting Web pages all over the Net and reporting back what she saw. AltaVista makes a humongous index of which words occurred in which pages; when you search AltaVista, it picks pages from the index that contain the words you asked for.

Because AltaVista is an index, not a directory, the good news is that it has about ten times as many pages as Yahoo; the bad news is that finding the one you want can be difficult. Regardless of what you ask for, you probably will get 15,000 pages on your first try, but the first pages AltaVista finds are usually the most relevant.

Using AltaVista, or any index, is an exercise in remote-control mind reading. You have to guess words that will appear on the pages you're looking for. Sometimes, that's easy — if you're looking for recipes for key lime pie, `key lime pie` is a good set of search words because you know the name of what you're looking for. On the other hand, if you have forgotten that the capital of Germany is Berlin, it's hard to tease a useful page out of AltaVista because you don't know what words to look for. (If you try `Germany capital`, you find info about investment banking.)

Now that we have you all discouraged, try some AltaVista searches. Direct your browser to `http://www.altavista.com`. You see a screen like the one shown in Figure 8-4.

Type some search terms, and AltaVista finds the pages that best match your terms. That's "best match," not "match" — if it can't match all the terms, it finds pages that match as well as possible. AltaVista ignores words that occur too often to be usable as index terms, both the obvious ones such as `and`, `the`, and `of` and terms such as `internet` and `mail`. These rules can sound somewhat discouraging, but in fact it's still not hard to tease useful results out of AltaVista. You just have to think up good search terms. Try that key lime pie example, by typing **key lime pie** and pressing the Search button. You get the response shown in Figure 8-5.

Your results will not look exactly like Figure 8-5 because AltaVista will have updated its database. Most of the pages it found do, in fact, have something to do with key lime pie — some have a pretty good recipe. (The first page is a hairdresser in Halifax, N.S., called "Key Lime Pie." Indexes are pretty dumb; you have to add the intelligence.) AltaVista found about 3,800 matches. Although that's probably more than you wanted to look at, you should at least look at the next couple of screens of matches if the first screen doesn't have what you want. At the bottom of the AltaVista screen are page numbers; click Next to go to the next page.

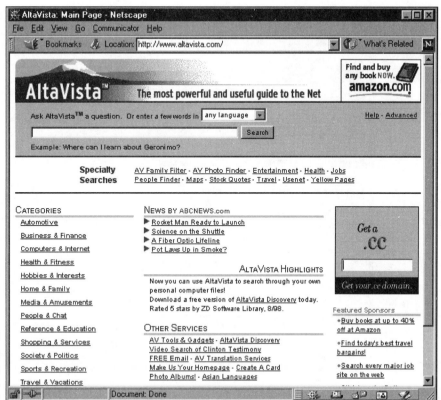

Figure 8-4:
AltaVista,
ready to roll.

Handy AltaVista targeting tips

AltaVista, unlike Yahoo, makes it easy to refine your search more exactly to target the pages you want to find. After each search, your search terms appear in a box at the top of the page so that you can change them and try again. Here are some tips on how you may want to change your terms:

- ✔ Type most search words in lowercase. Type proper names with a single capital letter, such as Elvis. Don't type any words in all capital letters.

- ✔ If two or more words should appear together, put quotes around them, as in "Elvis Presley". You should do that with the pie search ("key lime pie") because, after all, that is what the pie is called, although in this example, AltaVista is clever enough to realize that it's a common phrase and pretends you typed the quotes anyway.

- ✔ Use + and – to indicate words that must either appear or not appear, such as +Elvis +Costello –Presley if you're looking for the modern Elvis, not the classic one.

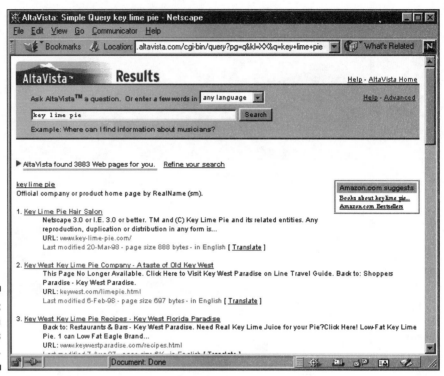

The number-one reason your searches don't find anything

Well, it may not be *your* number-one reason, but it's *our* number-one reason: One of the search words is spelled wrong. Check carefully. John notes that his fingers insist on typing "Interent," which doesn't find much other than Web pages from other people who can't spell. (Thanks to our friend Jean Armour Polly, for reminding us about this problem.)

TIP

The 404 blues

More often than we want to admit, when you click a link that Yahoo or one of its competitors found, rather than get the promised page, you get a message such as 404 Not Found. What did you do wrong? Nothing. Web pages come and go and move around with great velocity, and the various search systems do a lousy job, frankly, of cleaning out links to old, dead pages that have gone away.

The automated indexes, such as AltaVista, HotBot, and Lycos, are better in this regard than the manual directories, such as Yahoo.

The automated ones have software robots that revisit all the indexed pages every once in a while and note whether they still exist; even so, many lonely months can pass between robot visits, and a great deal can happen to a page in the meantime.

It's just part of life on the online frontier — the high-tech equivalent of riding your horse along the trail in the old West and noticing that there sure are a lot of bleached-white cattle skulls lying around.

AltaVista has a few other options that can be handy:

- ✔ Rather than search Web pages, you can search Usenet, the giant collection of Internet newsgroups (online discussion groups). Simply click the box that says Search the Web and flip to Search Usenet. If a topic has been discussed recently on Usenet, this technique is the best way to find the messages about that topic.

- ✔ You can limit your search to documents in a specific language. No sense in finding pages in a language you can't read, although AltaVista has a subsystem called Babelfish that can try, with mixed success, to translate pages from some other languages. Click the Translate link on a page in another language to try it.

Yahoo and more

A rather effective way to search the Web is to look in the Yahoo directory and then, if you don't find what you want, try an index. If you follow the "Go to Web Page Matches" link in Figure 8-3, which shows the result of a Yahoo search, you flip into an index not unlike AltaVista. (It's from Inktomi, the same people who provide the engine behind HotBot.) For our key lime pie example, you get a page with 20 links, at least 11 of which have pie recipes, the rest being places that will sell you ready-made pies. Here ends our survey of key lime pies. Just a minute while we run down to the kitchen and have another piece.

Who pays for all this stuff?

You may be wondering who pays for all these wonderful search systems. All except one of them are supported by advertising. On every page of Yahoo, Lycos, and most other search systems, you see lots and lots of ads. In theory, the advertising pays the costs. In reality, the independent advertising-supported search systems Excite, Infoseek, Lycos, and Yahoo have all lost pots of money. (In this case, a pot is sized in millions of bucks.) Fortunately for all of them, because they issued stock to the public at the height of the 1996 Internet investment craze, each has plenty of cash to burn up while they try to figure out how to turn a profit. WebCrawler belongs to AOL, which lost 500 pots in 1996–97, although it's hard to tell how much of that was the fault of WebCrawler. AOL and Yahoo have turned around and made money in the past year; the rest just keep burning it up.

The exception is AltaVista, originally a research project to see just how fast the Alpha line of workstations at Digital Equipment Corporation were. The new line turned out to be extremely fast, blowing the socks off most of the competition. Because DEC knew a good thing when it saw it, it turned AltaVista into a product line that it licenses to other search systems (such as Yahoo and CNET, Inc.) and that companies can use to create their own internal indexes. Some folks thought that DEC might issue stock in its AltaVista Internet Software division as well (if the Excite, Infoseek, Lycos, and Yahoo guys can raise all that money, you may as well get in on the party); they never did so, and DEC sold itself to Compaq, but AltaVista has cashed in on its popularity by accepting ads.

Some people think that a big "bubble" is occurring in the search biz and that we can expect more of the search systems to run out of money and shut down or merge with others. Visit http://net.gurus.com/search for the latest up- or down-dates.

We're from Your Browser, and We're Here to Help You

In 1998, Netscape and Microsoft both decided to crowbar their way into the search engine market. (Who? Us? Opinionated?) Starting with Netscape 4.06 and Internet Explorer 4.0, both will take you directly to their respective preferred search system if you give them half a chance. These search systems aren't awful, but unless you are the kind of person who turns on his TV and watches whatever is on the first channel you come to, you'll probably find that you prefer to choose your own search engine.

In both cases, you can type some keywords into the address bar where you'd normally type the URL of the Web page. The browser notices that what you typed doesn't look like a URL and sends it to a search engine instead. It displays the search result or, if there's only a single match, goes directly to the matching page.

That's okay as far as it goes, but remember that the page the browser finds is rarely the only possible match. There's some reason to believe that companies pay to get placed better, so you should search further if you have any doubt. Also keep in mind that when you do the search, your keywords are shipped off to Netscape or Microsoft, who presumably are keeping at least statistical logs of what people are looking at.

Netscape's Smart Browsing

Smart Browsing consists of two parts. The first is *Smart Keywords,* the keywords in the address box. You can type **goto** *word word* to jump to a Web site that those words suggest, or **search** *word word* to search for those words using Excite, yet another AltaVista-like search engine. If you don't type *search* or *goto,* Netscape assumes that you want goto if there's a close enough match; otherwise, it uses search.

The other feature, new in Netscape 4.06, is *What's Related.* There's a What's Related button to the right of the address box. When you click it, your browser sends your current URL to Netscape headquarters, which returns a menu of pages that seem to be on similar topics, based on pages that other people have visited in the past. We find What's Related kind of hit-and-miss, but if you're scratching your head, it's worth a click to see whether anything interesting is there.

Microsoft's Autosearch

Having said all those mean things, we now reveal that Microsoft links you to Yahoo, our favorite directory. In Internet Explorer 4.0, if you type keywords into the address box, Internet Explorer jumps to a simplified version of Yahoo and displays a list of matching pages.

Internet Explorer also has the Search Bar. If you click on the Search icon, the globe with the magnifying glass, a Search Bar subwindow appears to the left of your Explorer window with a small search engine page. In Internet Explorer 4.0, the page is for a specific search engine, usually AltaVista. If you prefer to use a different one, click the Choose a Search Engine button at the top of the window and pick one of the others.

In Internet Explorer 5.0, they've spiffed up the Search Bar. It has a bunch of buttons that let you choose one of several kinds of searches including Web pages, people, and companies. When you search for Web pages, the Search Assistant sends it off to one of the search engines, usually Hotbot. If you don't like what it finds, click the Next button at the top of the Search Bar window, and it'll try a different search engine. To start over with a new search, click New at the top of the Search Bar. You can customize what engines it uses and in what order by clicking the Customize icon, a little hammer and gear, at the top of the Search Bar.

This zillion-engine search can be a little overwhelming, but once you're used to it, it's nice. You remain firmly in control of what searches you do, and you can certainly do a lot of searching quickly until you find what you want.

More search magic

Microsoft and Netscape remain in frantic competition, so by the time you read this, there will doubtless be even more search features in each browser. Drop by our web site at `http://net.gurus.com/search` to find out what's new.

The Usual Suspects

After you have surfed around Yahoo and AltaVista for a while, you may want to check out the competition as well.

Excite and WebCrawler

```
http://www.excite.com
http://www.webcrawler.com
```

Excite is primarily an index, like AltaVista, with a "concept search," which is supposed to find relevant pages even if you don't type exactly the same words the pages use. We don't find that the Excite concept search helps much, but perhaps we were too wordy to start with. Excite also has sections with reviews of Web pages, city directories, white pages, and more.

WebCrawler is an automated indexer that crawls around the Web cataloging and indexing every page it comes across — again, sort of like AltaVista. It's a reasonable alternative to AltaVista. WebCrawler has been through a variety of owners, including AOL, but now belongs to Excite, although its data are different from Excite's.

Infoseek

```
http://www.infoseek.com
```

Infoseek is an index similar to AltaVista rather than a directory: You give it some keywords to look for, and it finds the pages that match the best. It also has a directory of useful Web pages. It can search the Web, Usenet, Reuters news, and a few other odds and ends. Infoseek is controlled by Disney; although we haven't yet seen any mouse ears, there's supposed to be a joint portal opening soon at `http://www.go.com`.

HotBot

http://www.hotbot.com

HotBot is yet another index, like AltaVista. It's affiliated with *Wired* magazine and uses — in classic *Wired* style — bright, clashing colors that make your head hurt. If you can deal with that (try sunglasses), it's not a bad index. It uses the Inktomi engine, the same as Yahoo's Web page search.

Lycos

http://www.lycos.com

Lycos is a largely automated index, sort of like AltaVista. It began as a project at Carnegie-Mellon University and has also gone commercial. It also has a directory called Top 5% of Web Sites. Although Lycos was one of the earliest Web search systems, at this point, honestly, AltaVista has a better index, and Yahoo has a better directory. Lycos also has headline news and local pages for some cities around the United States.

Northern Light

http://www.northernlight.com

This site contains an automated index of both the Web and its Special Collection, articles from various sources for which you must pay if you decide to read them. If you would rather stick with the (free) Web, you can choose to do so. The Northern Light searches also automatically categorize the pages they find, displaying a listing of "folders" you can choose among.

Other Web guides

Lots of other Web guides are available, including many specialized guides put together for particular interests (Femina, for example, is a feminist guide, at http://femina.cybergrrl.com).

Yahoo has a directory of other guides: Starting at the Yahoo page (http://www.yahoo.com), choose WWW (which appears under Computers and Internet) and then Searching the Web.

Finding Companies

The first way to search for companies is to search for the company name as a topic. If you're looking for the Egg Farm Dairy, for example, search for Egg Farm Dairy in Yahoo, AltaVista, or any of the other search systems. (You'll find it, too. We like the Muscoot cheese.) After you have done that, a few other places are worth checking for business-related info.

Hoovering in

`http://www.hoovers.com`

Company home pages vary in informativeness, but they often don't tell you much about the company itself. Hoover's is a business information company that has been publishing paper business directories for quite a while. Now it's on the Net as well. Its Web site offers free company capsules, stock prices, and other company info. If you sign up for its paid service, it offers considerably more. Even the free stuff is quite useful.

Ask EDGAR

`http://edgar.sec.gov (government)`
`http://www.edgar-online.com (private)`

The U.S. Securities and Exchange Commission (SEC), the people who regulate stock and bond markets, has a system called EDGAR that collects all the financial material that publicly traded companies have to file with the government. Although most of this stuff is dry and financial, if you can read financial statements, you can find all sorts of interesting information, such as Bill Gates' salary.

The government EDGAR site is run directly by the SEC, and the private site, EDGAR Online, is run by an independent company, Cybernet Data Systems, Inc. Although the two sites have pretty much the same information, the private site offers free, limited access and charges a modest price (about $5 per month) for more complete access and automatic e-mail updates when a company in which you're interested files EDGAR documents. Because EDGAR Online has partner arrangements with several other companies, including Hoover's, if you check on a company in Hoover's and then click the EDGAR link to get to EDGAR Online, you can often get documents not directly available from the EDGAR Online home page. If you use EDGAR Online often, however, pay the five bucks.

Lots of other business directories

Tons of business information is available on the Net. Here are a few places to begin.

Companies Online

    http://www.CompaniesOnline.com

Companies Online is a joint project between Dun & Bradstreet and Lycos. You enter the name of a company in which you're interested, and this site tells you about it.

Inc. magazine

    http://www.inc.com
    http://www.inc.com/500

Inc. magazine concentrates on small, fast-growing companies. Each year, its *Inc. 500* features the 500 companies it likes the best. Many hot little companies are listed here, with contact information.

Yellow Pages

    http://www.bigyellow.com
    http://yp.gte.net
    http://www.switchboard.com
    http://www.abii.com (Click American Yellow Pages.)

Quite a few yellow pages business directories, both national and local, are on the Net. The directories in this list are some of the national ones. We like Big Yellow the best (even though it's run by Bell Atlantic, which is otherwise not our favorite telephone company), but they're all worth a look. The American Yellow Pages even offers credit reports, although we can't vouch for its reliability.

Finding People

Finding people on the Net is surprisingly easy. It's so easy that, indeed, sometimes it's creepy. Two overlapping categories of people finders are available: those that look for people on the Net with e-mail and Web addresses and those that look for people in real life with phone numbers and street addresses.

In real life

The real-life directories are compiled mostly from telephone directories. If you haven't had a listed phone number in the past few years, you probably aren't in any of these directories.

On the Net

The process of finding e-mail and Web addresses is somewhat hit-and-miss. Because no online equivalent to the official phone book that the telephone company produces has ever existed, directories of e-mail addresses are collected from addresses used in Usenet messages, mailing lists, and other more or less public places on the Net. Because the different directories use different sources, if you don't find someone in one directory, you can try another. Remember that because the e-mail directories are incomplete, there's no substitute for calling someone up and asking, "What's your e-mail address?"

If you're wondering whether someone has a Web page, use AltaVista to search for his name. If you're wondering whether you're famous, use AltaVista to search for your own name and see how many people mention you or link to your Web pages.

Yahoo People Search (Four11)

`http://www.yahoo.com/search/people`

You can search for addresses and phone numbers and e-mail addresses. If you don't like your own listing, you can add, update, or delete it. This is the system formerly at `www.four11.com`.

American Directory Assistance

`http://www.abii.com`

Click American Directory Assistance.

This site is another white pages directory. After you have found the entry you want, you can ask for a graphical street map of the address.

WhoWhere

http://www.whowhere.lycos.com

WhoWhere is another e-mail address directory. Although Yahoo usually gives better results, some people are listed in WhoWhere who aren't listed in other places.

Canada 411

http://www.canada411.sympatico.ca

Canada 411 is a Canadian telephone book that is complete except for the boring provinces of Alberta and Saskatchewan, sponsored by most of the major Canadian telephone companies. Aussi disponible en français, eh? (***Note to residents of Alberta and Saskatchewan:*** Advise Telus and Saskatel to add their listings.)

Bigfoot

http://www.bigfoot.com

Bigfoot provides a way to search for people in addition to permanent, free e-mail addresses for life (it promises to forward mail from your Bigfoot address to your Internet account forever for free). ***Warning:*** Once you're listed in Bigfoot, there is no way whatsoever to remove your listing, even if it's wrong.

Mail, one more time

Mailing lists are another important resource. Most lists (but not all — check before you ask) welcome concrete, politely phrased questions related to the list's topic. See Chapter 13 to find more information about mailing lists, including how to look for lists of particular topics of interest to you.

The ten-minute challenge

Our friend Doug Hacker claims to be able to find the answer to any factual query on the Net in less than ten minutes. Carol challenged him to find a quote she vaguely knew from the liner notes of a Duke Ellington album, whose title she couldn't remember. He had the complete quote in about an hour but spent less than five minutes himself. How? He found a mailing list about Duke Ellington, subscribed, and asked the question. Several members replied in short order. The more time you spend finding your way around the Net, the more you know where to go for the information you need.

Getting the Goods

All the serious directories and indexes now put shopping information somewhere on their home pages to help get your credit card closer to the Web faster. Some are even sponsored by VISA. You can find department stores and catalogs from all over, offering every conceivable item (and some inconceivable items). We tell you all the do's, don'ts, and how-to's in Chapter 9.

Chapter 9
More Shopping, Less Dropping

▶ Why shop online?

▶ To charge it or not to charge it?

▶ Step-by-step shopping

▶ Where to find tickets, mutual funds, books, clothes, computers, and food online

*I*f, for some reason such as insomnia, you follow the computer trade press, you have heard far, far too much about online commerce. Surprisingly, much of the hype turns out to be true, and you can quite reasonably buy all sorts of stuff over the Net. We have bought lots of things online, from books to pants to plane tickets to stocks and mutual funds to computer parts to, uh, specialized personal products (don't read too much into that), and lived to tell the tale.

Shopping Online: Pros and Cons

Here are some reasons why we shop on the Net:

✔ Online stores are convenient, open all night, and don't mind if you window shop for a week before you buy something.

✔ Online stores can sometimes offer great prices and a better selection than brick-and-mortar stores.

✔ Two of the three authors of this book live in small rural towns; a lot of stuff just isn't available locally. (Trumansburg, N.Y., is a wonderful place, but you can't get a decent cup of coffee here.)

✔ Unlike malls, online stores don't have Muzak.

TIP

Net shopping's greatest hits

What should you buy online? Here are some good bets:

✔ **Books and CDs.** Online stores are fiercely competitive, and the prices can be impressively cheap.

✔ **Airplane tickets and other travel arrangements.** You can do better than all but the best travel agents.

✔ **Computers.** If you know what you want, online is usually cheaper and less hassle than a big computer store.

✔ **Stocks and mutual funds.** If you make your own investment decisions, online brokerage is much, much cheaper than a regular broker, $8 to $20 per trade rather than as much as $50 for discount or $100 for a full-service broker. Also, online brokers don't get annoyed if you check stock prices 47 times a day.

✔ **Anything you'd buy from a paper catalog.** Most catalog merchants have Web sites, usually with special offers not in the paper catalog. (They'd really like you to order over the Net, rather than talk to an expensive live operator at an 800 number.)

On the other hand, here are some reasons why we don't buy everything on the Net:

✔ You can't physically look at stuff before you buy it, and in most cases, you have to wait for it to be shipped to you. (We don't expect to buy milk and bananas online any time soon, although there's a service called Peapod that offers them.)

✔ We like our local stores and prefer to support them when we can.

✔ You can't flirt with the staff at a Web store.

The Credit Card Question

How do you pay for stuff that you buy online? Most often, with a credit card, the same way that you pay for anything else. Isn't it incredibly, awfully dangerous to give out your credit card number online, though? Well, no.

After several years of asking for reports of card numbers being stolen from the Net, we have yet to hear of one. It doesn't happen. For one thing, most online stores encrypt the message between your computer and the store's server (indicated in your Web browser by a lock or key icon in the bottom left corner of the window); for another, plucking the occasional credit card number from the gigabytes of traffic that flow every minute on the Net would be extremely difficult even without encryption.

When you use your plastic at a restaurant, you give your physical card with your physical signature to the server, who takes it to the back room, does something with it out of your sight, and then brings it back. Compared to that, the risk of sending your number to an online store is remote. A friend of ours used to run a restaurant and later ran an online store, and assures us that there's no comparison: The online store had none of the plastic problems the restaurant did.

If, after this harangue, you still don't want to send your plastic over the Net or you're one of the fiscally responsible holdouts who doesn't do plastic, most online stores are happy to have you call in your card number over the phone or send them a check.

Let's Go to the Store

Stores on the Web work in two general ways: with and without virtual "shopping carts." In stores without carts, you either order one item at a time or fill out a big order form with a check box for everything the store offers. In stores with carts, as you look at the items the store has for sale, you can add items to your cart and then visit the virtual checkout line when you're done and provide your payment and delivery information. Until you check out, you can add and remove items whenever you want, just like in the real world — except that you don't have to put unwanted items back on the shelf.

Simple shopping

For a simple example, we lead you through a shopping trip at the Great Tapes for Kids Web site, a small online store for children's videotapes, audiotapes, and books, run by one of us authors. (Us? Venal? Naah.) Start at the home page, `http://www.greattapes.com`, shown in Figure 9-1. It shows a featured item and has links to pages listing all the other books and tapes available.

Figure 9-1:
Welcome to
Great Tapes
for Kids.

When you know what you want, you click the Order Form icon on one of the Web pages to see a giant order form with a box for everything you could possibly want to order, as shown in Figure 9-2. (At large online stores, this method gets a little unwieldy.) As you continue through the form by pressing the cursor keys or clicking the scroll bar, you mark whatever it is you want to buy. At the bottom of the form, as shown in Figure 9-3, you enter the same stuff you would put on a paper order form. Most forms have a place for typing a credit card number; if you're not comfortable entering it there (we are, as we describe in the section "The Credit Card Question," earlier in this chapter), leave that blank — the store invariably has a way you can call the number in. Click the Send Order button, and your order is on its way.

You generally get an e-mail message confirming the details of your order and, frequently, e-mail updates if any problems or delays occur.

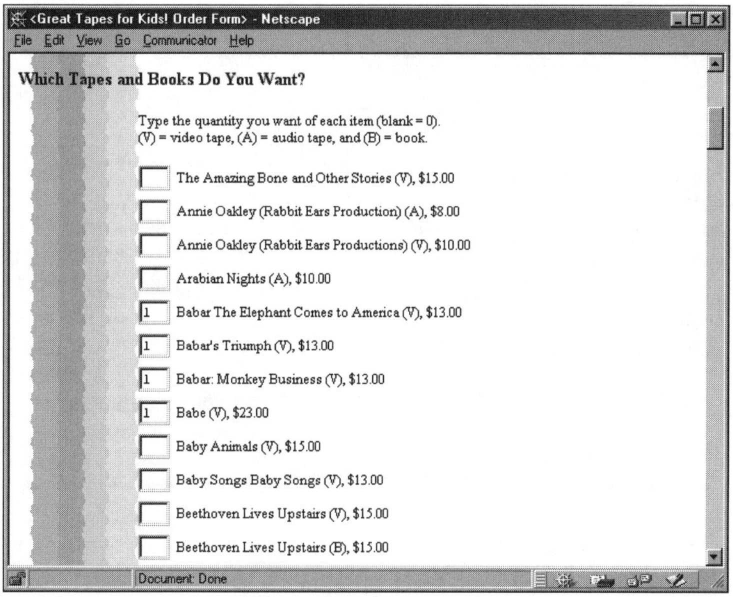
<Great Tapes for Kids! Order Form> - Netscape
File Edit View Go Communicator Help
Which Tapes and Books Do You Want?
Type the quantity you want of each item (blank = 0).
(V) = video tape, (A) = audio tape, and (B) = book.
The Amazing Bone and Other Stories (V), $15.00
Annie Oakley (Rabbit Ears Production) (A), $8.00
Annie Oakley (Rabbit Ears Productions) (V), $10.00
Arabian Nights (A), $10.00
1
Babar The Elephant Comes to America (V), $13.00
1
Babar's Triumph (V), $13.00
1
Babar: Monkey Business (V), $13.00
1
Babe (V), $23.00
Baby Animals (V), $15.00
Baby Songs Baby Songs (V), $13.00
Beethoven Lives Upstairs (V), $15.00
Beethoven Lives Upstairs (B), $15.00
Document: Done

Figure 9-2: Let's order some animal movies!

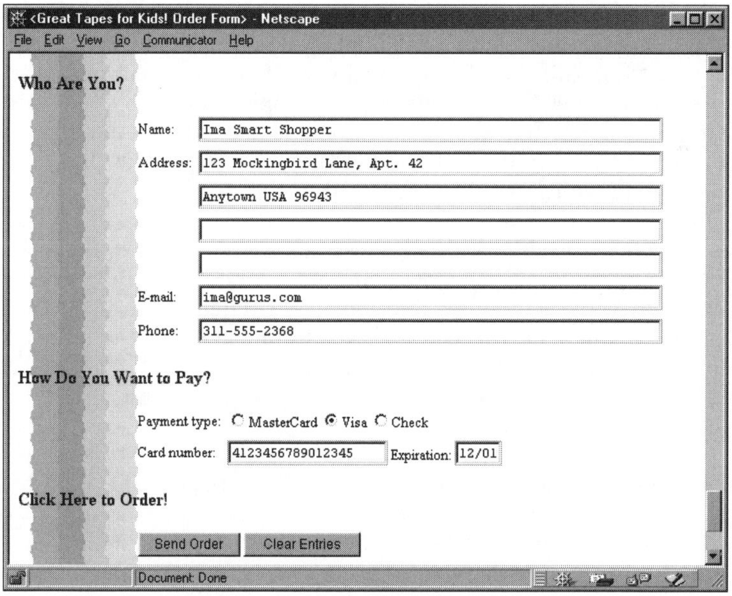
<Great Tapes for Kids! Order Form> - Netscape
File Edit View Go Communicator Help
Who Are You?
Name: Ima Smart Shopper
Address: 123 Mockingbird Lane, Apt. 42
Anytown USA 96943
E-mail: ima@gurus.com
Phone: 311-555-2368
How Do You Want to Pay?
Payment type: MasterCard Visa Check
Card number: 4123456789012345 Expiration: 12/01
Click Here to Order!
Send Order
Clear Entries
Document: Done

Figure 9-3: Those last crucial details.

Cookie alert

You may have heard horrible stories about things called *cookies* that Web sites reputedly use to spy on you, steal your data, ravage your computer, inject cellulite into your hips while you sleep, and otherwise make your life miserable. After extensive investigation, we have found that most cookies aren't all that bad; when you're shopping online, they can even be quite helpful.

A *cookie* is no more than a little chunk of text a Web site sends to a PC with a request (not a command) to send the cookie back during future visits to the same Web site. That's all it is. You can see the cookies now on file in your PC in a file called something like Cookies.txt. For online shopping, cookies let the Web server track your "shopping cart" of items you have selected but not yet bought, even if you log out and turn off your computer in the interim.

Fancy shopping

Although a simple store with a giant order form works okay for stores that don't have many different items in a catalog or businesses where you buy one thing at a time, this method is hopeless for stores with large catalogs. While writing this chapter, we decided that the Great Tapes order form had gotten hopelessly large, so we reprogrammed the Web site to provide a "shopping cart," also known as a book bag or any of a bunch of other metaphors, to help track the items people order. (We would do practically anything to avoid writing. It's an author thing.)

As you click your way around a site, you can toss items into your cart, adding and removing them as you want, by clicking a button labeled something like Add Item to Your Shopping Cart. Then, when you have the items you want, you visit the virtual checkout line and buy the items in your cart. Until you visit the checkout, you can always put back the items in your cart if you decide that you don't want them.

The cart-ized version of Great Tapes for Kids looks just like the old version, until you click the Order button on one of its pages. The giant order form is gone, and in its place is the Book and Tape Bag page, the interesting part of which is shown in Figure 9-4. It shows just the item we selected.

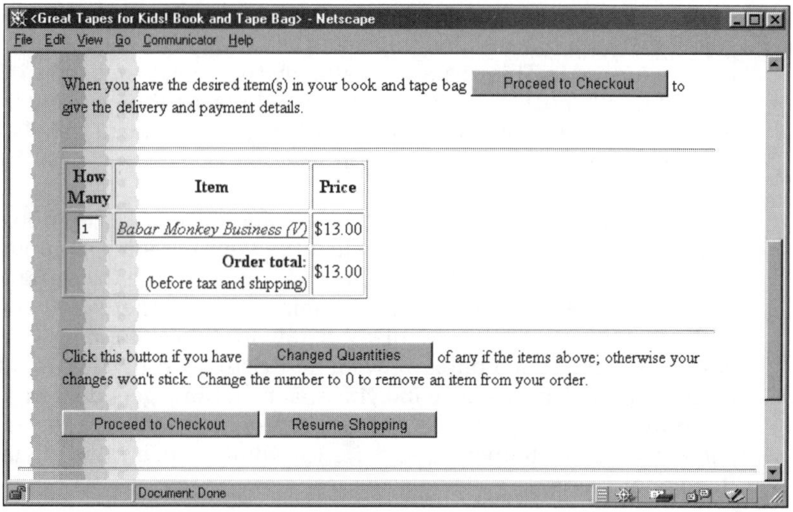

Figure 9-4:
An elephant
in the cart.

Suppose that one tape isn't enough for you because you have two nephews, so you click the Resume Shopping button, find another tape, and click Order again. Now both tapes are in your cart, as you can see in Figure 9-5. (Although this process looks totally obvious, the programming required to make it work correctly on a Web server is kind of tricky. Much as we would love to share the technical details, our editor regretfully informs us that we're short of space. Phoo.)

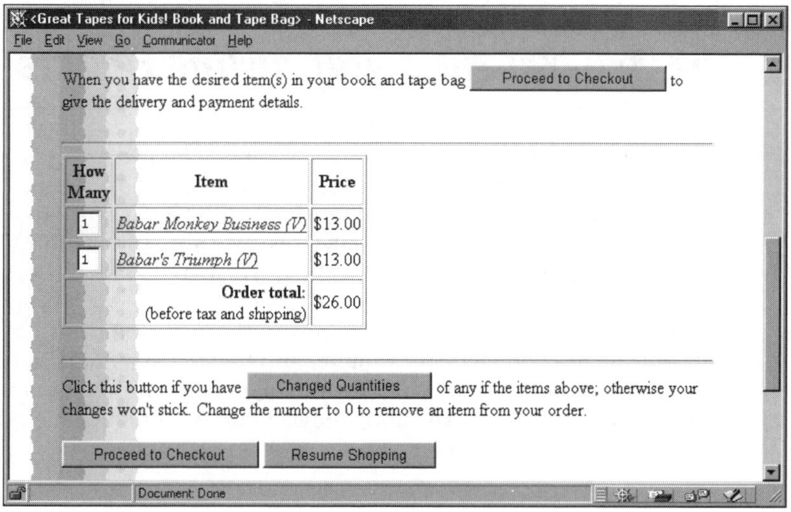

Figure 9-5:
Two
elephants
in the cart.

At this point, you can continue shopping, adjust the quantities (including adjusting down to zero anything you don't want), or go to the checkout to finish your order. This example is already too long, so just go to the checkout. It looks almost the same as the page that was shown in Figure 9-3, with the same places to put your name, address, and payment details, and a button you click to confirm your order.

Most virtual stores use a cookie (we talk about them in the "Cookie alert" sidebar, earlier in this chapter) to identify your personal shopping cart. The cookie lets you log out from the Internet, return to the Great Tapes Web site a day or two later, and find your shopping cart still there with your stuff in it. We find this process particularly handy for book shopping — every few days, we hear about a book we want and virtually throw it into our cart. (Throwing is okay, because in cyberspace, nothing gets dented.) Then, when we have enough books to make a decent order, we submit the order and pay a single shipping charge for the whole bunch rather than order them one at a time.

Up, Up, and Away

We buy lots of airline tickets online. Although the online travel sites aren't as good as really good travel agents, the sites are much better than bad travel agents. Even if you have a good agent, online sites let you look around to see what your options are before you get on the phone. We have also found some good travel agents who work via Web sites and e-mail.

The general theory of airline tickets

Four giant airline computer systems in the United States handle nearly all the airline reservations in the country. (They're known as CRSs, or computer reservations systems.) Although each airline has a "home" CRS, the systems are all interlinked so that you can, with few exceptions, buy tickets for any airline from any CRS. The systems are Sabre (home to American and US Airways), Apollo (home to United), Worldspan (home to Delta, Northwest, and TWA), and Amadeus (home to Continental). Many of the low-price start-up airlines don't participate in any of these systems but have their own Web sites where you can check flights and buy tickets. Southwest, the largest and oldest of the low-price airlines, doesn't participate but has an arrangement with Sabre, so Sabre shows Southwest flights even though none of the other three does.

In theory, all the systems show the same data; in practice, however, they get a little out of sync with each other. If you're looking for seats on a sold-out flight, an airline's home system is most likely to have that last, elusive seat. If you're looking for the lowest fare to somewhere, check all four systems because a fare that's marked as sold out on one system often mysteriously reappears on another system. Some categories of fares are visible only to travel agents and don't appear on any of the Web sites, particularly if you aren't staying over a weekend, so check with a good agent before buying. On the other hand, many airlines have available some special deals that are _only_ on their Web sites and that agents often don't know about. Confused? You should be. We were.

The confusion is even worse if you want to fly internationally. Official fares to most countries are set via a treaty organization called the IATA, so computer systems usually list only IATA fares for international flights. It's easy to find entirely legal "consolidator" tickets sold for considerably less than the official price, however, so an online or offline agent is extremely useful for getting the best price. The airlines also have some impressive online offers, most notably from Cathay Pacific, which once or twice a year runs an online auction for a plane full of tickets from the United States to Hong Kong, with the lowest winning bids often less than half the normal fare. In late 1997, Cathay Pacific had a remarkable online-only special of two round-trip tickets from the United States to Hong Kong and a week in a hotel for less than $1,000 (total, not per person).

Here's our distilled wisdom about buying tickets online:

✔ Check the online systems to see what flights are available and for an idea of the price ranges. Check more than one CRS.

✔ After you have found a likely airline, check that airline's site to see whether it has any special Web-only deals. If a low-fare airline flies the route, be sure to check that one too.

✔ Check with a travel agent to see whether he can beat the online price, and buy your tickets from the agent unless the online deal is better. Some agents give you a small discount if you make your reservations yourself, because the agent only has to issue the ticket and mail the receipt to you.

✔ For international tickets, do everything in this list and check both online and with your agent for consolidator tickets, particularly if you don't qualify for the lowest published fare.

More about online airlines

Because the online airline situation changes weekly, anything we print here would be out of date before you read it. One of the authors of this book is a plane nerd in his spare time; to get a current list of online CRSs, airline Web sites, Web specials, and online travel agents, visit his Web site at

```
http://www.iecc.com/airline
```

Pure Money

If you invest in mutual funds or the stock market (something that's difficult to avoid these days unless you anticipate dying at an early age), you can find a remarkable range of resources online. An enormous amount of stock information is also available, providing Net users with research resources as good as only professional analysts had a few years ago.

The most important thing to remember about all the online financial resources is that everyone has an ax to grind and wants to get paid somehow. In most cases, the situation is straightforward; for example, a mutual fund manager wants you to invest with her funds, and a stockbroker wants you to buy and sell stocks with him. Some other sites are less obvious: Some are supported by advertising, and others push other kinds of investments. Just keep a source's interests in mind when you're considering that source's advice.

Mutual funds

Mutual funds are definitely the investment of the 1990s. The world now has more mutual funds than it has stocks for the funds to buy. (Kind of makes you wonder, doesn't it?) Most fund managers have at least descriptions of the funds and prospectuses online, and many now provide online access so that you can check your account and move money from one fund to another within a fund group.

Well-known fund groups include

- **Fidelity Investments:** The 500-pound gorilla of mutual funds, specializes in actively managed funds (`http://www.fid-inv.com`)

- **Vanguard Group:** Specializes in low-cost and index funds (`http://www.vanguard.com`)

- **American Century:** Another broad group of funds (`http://www.americancentury.com`)

Many of the online brokers listed in the following section also let you buy and sell mutual funds, although it almost always costs less if you deal directly with a fund manager. Yahoo (`http://www.yahoo.com`) has a long list of funds and fund groups; click the Business and Economy option and then Finance and Investment and then Mutual Funds.

Stockbrokers

Most of the well-known full-service brokerage firms have jumped on the Web, along with a new generation of low-cost online brokers offering remarkably cheap stock trading. A trade that may cost $100 with a full-service firm can cost as little as $8 with a low-cost broker. The main difference is that the cheap firms don't offer investment advice and don't assign you to a specific broker. For people who do their own research and don't want advice from a broker, the low-cost firms work well. For people who do need some advice, the partial- or full-service firms often offer lower-cost trades online, and they let you get a complete view of your account whenever you want. The number of extra services the brokerages offer (such as retirement accounts, dividend reinvestment, and automatic transfers to and from your checking account) varies widely.

Online brokers include

- ✔ **Charles Schwab:** One of the oldest discount brokers (`http://www.schwab.com`)

- ✔ **Discover Brokerage Direct:** A low-cost, no-advice broker (`http://www.discoverbrokerage.com`)

- ✔ **Ameritrade:** A very low-cost, no-advice broker (`http://www.ameritrade.com`)

- ✔ **Smith Barney:** A full-service broker with online access to accounts and research info (`http://www.smithbarney.com`)

Most fund groups, including the ones listed above, have brokerage departments, which can be a good choice if you want to hold both individual stocks and funds.

Tracking your portfolio

Several services let you track your portfolio online. You enter the number of shares of each fund and stock you own, and at any time they tell you exactly how much they're worth and how much money you have lost today. Some of them send by e-mail a daily portfolio report, if you want. These reports are handy if you have mutual funds from more than one group or both funds and stocks. All the tracking services are either supported by advertising or run by a brokerage that hopes to get your trading business.

- ✔ **My Yahoo:** (`http://my.yahoo.com`) You can enter multiple portfolios and customize your screens with related company and general news reports. You can also get lots of company and industry news, including some access to sites that otherwise require paid subscriptions. Advertiser-supported and very comprehensive and easy to use.

- ✔ **My Snap:** (`http://my.snap.com`) Snap is a clone of Yahoo. Its portfolio features are similar to and arguably better than Yahoo's.

- ✔ **Reuters Moneynet:** (`http://www.moneynet.com`) Track portfolios and read Reuters news stories. Although a variety of premium services, such as real-time stock quotes, cost money, the free portfolio tracker isn't bad.

- ✔ **Microsoft Investor:** (`http://investor.msn.com`) Also has portfolios and lots of information. You can do quite a bit in the free area, but the site really, really wants you to subscribe for $9.95 per month for the advanced features. If you don't want the extra-cost stuff, the nagging to get you to subscribe gets really old, and we've found their portfolio calculations to be buggy.

Even More Places to Shop

Here are a few other places to shop that we have visited on the Web. We have even bought stuff from most of them.

Books and such

Although you can't (yet) flip through the books in an online bookstore, if you know what you want, you can get good deals.

Amazon.com

`http://www.amazon.com`

Amazon.com is one of online commerce's great success stories, springing up from nothing (if you call several million dollars of seed money nothing) to become one of the Net's biggest online stores. Amazon has an enormous catalog of books, music, and a growing variety of other junk, much of which can get to you in a few days. It also has an "affiliates" program in which other Web sites can refer you to their favorite books for sale at Amazon, creating sort of a virtual virtual bookstore. For an example, see our Web site, at `http://net.gurus.com`, where we venally have links to Amazon for every book we have written in case, because of an oversight, you don't already have them all. Amazon sells most books at less than list price; for users outside the United States, the prices are low enough that even with shipping they're usually cheaper than buying locally.

Books.com

http://www.books.com

Books.com is another large virtual online bookstore, a branch of Cendant (formerly CUC, formerly Comp-U-Card), the largest and oldest purveyor of online merchandise. They have very low prices, always beating Amazon and Barnes & Noble's prices if you click the Compare Prices button on a book's page, and a frequent-shopper program that's a good deal for people who buy a large number of books.

Computer Literacy Bookstore

http://www.clbooks.com

Computer Literacy is a specialty store for computer books, which it offers in great depth. It actually stocks almost everything in its catalog rather than getting all the books from wholesalers. If you really need something tomorrow, you can have it.

Clothes

This section points out a few familiar merchants with online stores. Directories such as Yahoo have hundreds of other stores both familiar and obscure.

Lands' End

http://www.landsend.com

Much of this catalog is online, and you can order anything you find in any of its individual printed catalogs, along with online-only discounted overstocks. It also has plenty of the folksy blather that encourages you to think of the company in terms of a few folks in the cornfields of Wisconsin rather than a corporate mail-order colossus. (It's both, actually.)

REI

http://www.rei.com

This large, outdoorwear co-op is headquartered in Seattle. (Members get a small rebate on purchases.) The whole catalog is online, and online orders get discounted shipping.

The Gap

http://www.gap.com

Although this site doesn't yet have the full line of stuff in the stores, for those of us who are of unusual vertical or horizontal dimension, it has jeans in sizes the stores don't stock, and the rotating 3-D pants are way cool.

Computers

When you're shopping for computer hardware online, be sure that a vendor you're considering has both a good return policy, in case you don't want the computer when it arrives, and a long warranty.

Dell Computer

`http://www.dell.com`

This site has an extensive catalog with online ordering and custom computer system configurations.

IBM

`http://www.ibm.com`

The world's largest computer company has what feels like the world's largest Web site with a great deal of information about both IBM products and more general computing topics.

IBM sells stuff online at `http://www.direct.ibm.com`. The online store sells everything from home PCs to printed manuals to mid-range business systems. We got as far as putting a $1.1 million AS/400 9406-650 in our cart, but then we chickened out. We did buy a nice manual for the 1965-era 360/67 for our historical collection. (At IBM, nothing seems to go out of print.)

Apple Computer

`http://store.apple.com`

The Apple site has lots of information about Apple products, and now it has online purchasing of systems and upgrades too.

Auctions and used stuff

`http://www.ebay.com` *(all sorts of stuff)*
`http://www.priceline.com` *(airline tickets)*
`http://www.netauction.com` *(computers)*
`http://www.uce.com` *(computers)*

You can participate in online auctions of everything from computers and computer parts to antiques to vacation packages. Online auctions are like any other kind of auction in at least one respect: If you know what you're looking for and know what it's worth, you can get some great values; if you don't, you can easily overpay for junk. When someone swiped our car phone handset, at eBay we found an exact replacement phone for $31, rather than the $150 the manufacturer charged for just the handset.

Many auctions, notably eBay, also allow you to list your own stuff for sale, which can be a way to get rid of some of your household clutter a little more discreetly than in a tag sale.

Food

Here are our two favorite online dairies. You have to try them both and compare.

Egg Farm Dairy

http://www.creamery.com

The best cheese in New York. Better than much of the cheese from France.

Cabot Creamery

http://www.cabotcheese.com

The best cheese in Vermont. Good bovine sound effects.

An online shopper's checklist

Here are some questions to keep in mind when you're shopping online. An astute shopper will notice that these are the same ones you keep in mind when you're shopping anywhere else.

✔ Are the descriptions clear enough to know what you're ordering?

✔ Are the prices competitive, both with other online stores and with mail-order and regular retail?

✔ Does the store have the products in stock, or does it offer a firm shipping date?

✔ Does the store have a good reputation?

✔ Can you return unsatisfactory goods?

The Shopping Update

Like everything else on the Net, shopping changes day by day as new businesses appear and old ones change. For the latest updates, see our update pages, at

`http://net.gurus.com/shopping`

Chapter 10

My First Home Page

In This Chapter

▶ Web page basics

▶ Up and humming

▶ Publish or perish

After a while, every Web user thinks about putting up a personal Web page. Although any Web site can consist of many Web pages, the main page of a site is generally known as its *home page*. People have home pages, companies have home pages, and groups of highly talented authors and speakers have home pages. (You can check out Carol's at `http://iecc.com/carol`, John's at `http://iecc.com/johnl`, Margy's at `http://www.gurus.com/margy`, and Internet Gurus Central at `http://net.gurus.com`.) If you're ready to have your own home page, you're in the right place.

Although creating a home page is not difficult, it may seem complicated for a new user. But if you can use a word processor such as Corel WordPerfect or Microsoft Word to type a letter, you can create at least a simple home page. (Indeed, you can use either of those two word processors to do so.)

Why you don't care (much) about HTML

Just so that you know what *HTML* is, in case someone asks, it stands for *hypertext markup language,* and it's the language native to the World Wide Web. Web pages are made up of text and pictures that are stuck together and formatted by using HTML codes. Fortunately, you have waited until now, when clever programs are available that let you create your pages and write the HTML codes for you automatically, so you don't have to write the codes yourself.

If you find you want to write a lot of Web pages, you should eventually learn some HTML. Although complex interactive pages require a fair amount of programming, the basics aren't all that complicated; the HTML for **complicated** is `<B>complicated</B>` (that's `<B>` for Bold type). In case you decide that you want to be in the Web-page creation business, entire books have been written about how to do it. Stick to recent titles because HTML is evolving at a furious pace, and the books become outdated in less than a year.

Creating a Web Page

All home pages are Web pages, although not all Web pages are home pages. We tell you how to make a Web page — whether it's a home page is up to you.

The big picture

The basic steps to creating a Web site are pretty simple:

1. **Write some Web pages.**

   One page is plenty to start with. You can use anything from Windows Notepad to a $10,000 Web-authoring system to create them. We discuss your options presently. Save the pages in files on your computer's disk.

2. **Publish them on your provider's system.**

   The rest of the world can't see Web pages in files on your disk. You have to copy them to your provider's system so that your provider's *Web server* can offer them to the world.

The usual way to publish your pages is to use FTP (which we discuss in more detail in Chapter 16) to upload them to your provider's system. You need to know these details to do so:

- ✔ **The name of the computer to which you upload your files.** This isn't always the same as the name of the Web server. At one of our local providers, for example, the Web server is `www.lightlink.com` but the FTP upload server is `ftp.lightlink.com`.

- ✔ **The username and password to use for FTP.** Usually this is the same as the name and password you use to connect in the first place and to pick up your e-mail.

- ✔ **The name of the folder on the server to which you upload the pages.** At Lightlink, it's `/www/`*username*.

- ✔ **The filename to use for your home page.** Usually this is `index.html` or `index.htm`. (You can call your Web pages anything you want, but this is the page that people see first.)

- ✔ **The URL where your pages will appear.** It's usually `http://`*`www.yourisp.com`*`/~`*username* or `http://www.`*yourisp*`.com/`*username*.

You can usually find this info on your provider's Web site or, in the worst case, you can call them or e-mail them and ask.

Picking your pen

The two general approaches to creating Web pages are the geek approach, in which you write all the HTML codes yourself, and the WYSIWYG approach, in which a program writes them for you. If you were an HTML geek, you wouldn't be reading this chapter, so we're not going to discuss that approach. The more normal approach is to use a WYSIWYG Web-page editor.

WYSIWYG, pronounced "wiz-ee-wig," stands for *w*hat *y*ou *s*ee *i*s *w*hat *y*ou *g*et. In the case of Web-page editors, it means that as you create your page, instead of seeing seriously unattractive HTML codes, you see what it will actually look like. HTML purists point out that WYSIWYG editors churn out less-than-elegant HTML code, but the pages they make generally look fine. If you are planning to create a large, complex Web site, WYSIWYG editors will run out of steam, but for a page or three, they're great.

Here are some of the better-known Web-page editors and where to find them:

- ✔ Claris Home Page: `http://www.claris.com`
- ✔ Netscape Composer, which is part of Netscape Communicator: `http://www.netscape.com`
- ✔ Microsoft FrontPage and FrontPage Express (FrontPage Express comes with Windows 98): `http://www.microsoft.com`

We like a lesser-known but just-fine-and-dandy freeware program called AOLpress, available at `http://www.AOLpress.com`, which, despite its name, works fine whether or not you're an AOL user. AOLpress also has *templates,* pages already set up so that all you have to do is fill in your information; *tutorials,* more step-by-step instructions in case ours aren't enough; and *clip art,* images you can add to your page.

Often the most convenient Web-page editor is your own word processor. Both Microsoft Word 97 and Corel WordPerfect 8 have capable Web-editing features built right in!

Getting started

A Web page is a file — just like a word-processing document or a spreadsheet. You begin by creating your Web pages directly on your hard disk. You can see how they look by telling your browser to view them from your hard disk. (Browsers are happy to accept filenames to display rather than URLs.)

Edit and view the pages until you have something you like, and then upload them to your ISP to impress the world.

Here's our step-by-step approach to using AOLpress. If you would rather use WordPerfect 8 or Microsoft Word 97, feel free, although the commands are a little different:

1. **Get a copy of AOLpress. If you would rather use your own word processor, skip this step.**

   Using your browser, go to `http://www.AOLpress.com`. You see the AOLpress home page. Click Download. Find the section that corresponds to the system you're using (Macintosh, Windows 3.1, Windows 95, Windows 98, or Windows NT). If you're using AOL, click AOL keyword AOLPRESS; otherwise, click Web and wait for AOLpress to download. After the download is completed, double-click the AOL installation program.

2. **Run AOLpress or your word processor.**

   AOLpress displays a big welcome screen. Actually, it displays a big welcome page. Because AOLpress is not only a Web-page tool but also a browser, when you wander in and around AOLpress, you're still visiting sites on the Web, which makes it easy to visit different sites and clip different items of interest. But we digress.

   At the top of your screen is the AOLpress toolbar. If you point to each icon with your mouse, AOLpress tells you what it's for. If, after you've looked around, things don't seem set up to work intuitively, we suggest that you double-click AOLpress Tutorial and use the online workbook to get started. If you're pigheaded, stick with us and we'll get you started, somewhat less graciously.

3. **To create a new Web page in AOLpress, choose File⇨New⇨New Page from the menu bar. In Word 97, choose File⇨New from the menu bar, click the Web Pages tab in the dialog box that appears, and choose a template (try the Web Page Wizard, which talks you through making a Web page in Word 97). In WordPerfect 8, Choose File⇨New to display the New dialog box. Choose WordPerfect Web Document from the list of possible document types, and click Create. WordPerfect displays the Internet Publisher window. If you already have a document that you want to convert to a Web page, choose the View⇨Web Page command from the menu and then save the document.**

   (Call the document `index.html` or `index.htm` if it's going to be your home page.) You're face-to-face with a big, empty page. Go ahead — make your page. Stuck for ideas and where to start? If you use

AOLpress, go to the AOLpress Welcome Page, click Templates, and check out the AOLpress ready-to-fill-in forms and coordinated artsy pages that help you set up your page so that it looks spiffy.

4. Save your work.

When you've done enough work that you wouldn't want to have to start over from scratch if your computer suddenly crashes, choose File➪Save from the menu bar. In principle, when you're done with your page, you save it, but dismal experience has taught us to save early, save often.

Creating your first Web page is as easy as 1-2-3. Choosing what you put on your page, however, is harder. What is the page for? Whom do you want to see it? Is it for you and your family and friends and potential friends across the world, or are you advertising your business online? If your page is a personal page, don't include your home address or phone number unless you want random people who see the page calling you up. If it's a business page, by all means, include your address and phone number. The content of your first page isn't all that important — we just want you to get the feel of putting it out there. You can always add to it and pretty it up, and you don't have to tell anybody about your site until you're happy with it.

Pictures to go

Most Web pages contain graphics of some sort. Each picture that appears on a Web page is stored in a separate file. AOLpress, Word, and WordPerfect let you add images. AOLpress even provides a fair number of images to use.

Picture formats

Pictures come in dozens of formats. Fortunately, only two picture formats, known as GIF and JPEG are in common use on the Web. Many lengthy . . . er, *free* and *frank* discussions have occurred on the Net concerning the relative merits of these two formats. John, who is an Official Graphics Format Expert, by virtue of having persuaded two otherwise reputable publishers to publish his books on the topic, suggests that photographs work better as JPEG, while clip art, icons, and cartoons are better as GIF. If in doubt, JPEG files are smaller and download faster.

If you have a picture in any other format, such as BMP or PCX, you must convert it to either GIF or JPEG before you can use it on a Web page. Check out the Consummate Winsock Applications page, at `http://cws.internet.com`, for some suggestions of graphics programs that can do conversions. We like Paint Shop Pro, a powerful shareware graphics program.

Where do pictures come from?

That's a good question. You can draw them by using a paint program or scan in photographs; unless you're a rather good artist or photographer, however, your graphics may not look as nice as you want.

Fortunately, you can find lots of sources of graphical material:

✔ Plenty of freeware, shareware, and commercial clip art is available on the Net. Yahoo has a long list of clip art sites, at `http://www.yahoo.com/Computers_and_Internet/Graphics/Clip_Art`.

✔ The king of the clip art sites is `http://www.arttoday.com`. There's a modest annual subscription fee, but they have hundreds of thousands of well-indexed pictures for download.

✔ If you see an image you want to use on a Web page, write to the page's owner and ask for permission to use it. More likely than not, the owner will let you use the image.

✔ Lots of regular old software programs totally unrelated to the Internet, such as paint and draw programs, presentation programs, and even word processors, come with clip art collections.

✔ You can buy CD-ROMs full of clip art, which tends to be of higher quality than the free stuff. These aren't all that expensive, particularly considering how many images fit on one CD-ROM.

Clip art, like any art, is protected by copyright laws. Whether it has already been used on a Web page or whether a copyright notice appears on or near the image doesn't matter. It's all copyrighted. If you use someone else's copyrighted art, you must get permission to do so. Whether your use is educational, personal, or noncommercial is irrelevant. If you fail to secure permission, you run the risk of anything from a crabby phone call from the owner's lawyer to winding up on the losing end of a lawsuit.

Most people are quite reasonable whenever you ask for permission to use something. If an image you want to use doesn't already come with blanket permission to use it, check with the owner before you decide to add it to your own Web page.

Linking to other pages

The *hyper* in hypertext is the thing that makes the Web so cool. A *hyperlink* (or just *link*) is the thing on the page that lets you "surf" the Web — go from page to page by just clicking the link. A Web page is hardly a page if it doesn't link somewhere else.

The immense richness of the Web comes from the links that Web page constructors have placed on their own pages. You want to contribute to this richness by including as many links to places you know of that the people who visit your page may also be interested in. Try to avoid including links to places that everyone already knows about and has in their address books. For example, the common Internet search engines and indexes are already well documented, so leave them off. If your home page mentions your interest in one of your hobbies, however, such as canoeing or volleyball or birding or your alma mater, include some links to related sites you know of that are interesting.

AOLpress, Word, and WordPerfect let you insert a URL and create the link for you. If you create multiple pages, you can put links among your pages; be sure to upload all the pages to ensure the links still work.

Good page design

After you have put together a basic Web page, use the tips in this section to avoid some mistakes that novice Websters often make.

Fonts and styles

Don't overformat your text with too many fonts, too much use of font colors, or emphasis with **bold,** *italics,* underlining, or some ***combination.*** Experienced designers sneeringly call it "ransom note" text. Blinking text universally annoys readers.

Background images

Tiled background images can be cool if they're subtle but make text utterly illegible as often as not. Black text on a solid white background (like the pages of this book) has stood the test of time for thousands of years.

Big images

Many Web pages are burdened with images that, although beautiful, take a long time to load — so long that many users may give up before the pages are completely loaded. Remember that not everyone has a computer or Internet connection as fast as yours.

Take a few steps to make your Web pages load more quickly. The main step, of course, is to limit the size of the images you use. A 20K (20,000 bytes big) image takes twice as long to load as a 10K image, which takes twice as long to load as a 5K image. You can estimate that images load at 1K per second (on a dial-up connection), so a 5K image loads in about 5 seconds, which is pretty fast; a 120K image takes 2 minutes to load, so that image had better be worth the wait.

Consider putting a small image on a page and give visitors an option (via a link) to load the full-size picture. We know that you're proud of your dog, and she deserves a place of honor on your home page, but not everyone visiting your site will wait excitedly for your puppy picture to download. (We hate it when they do that on the rug.)

In GIF files, images with fewer colors load faster than images with more colors. If you use a graphics editor to reduce a GIF from 256 colors to 32 or even 16 colors, often the appearance hardly changes, but the file shrinks dramatically. Set your graphics program to store the GIF file in *interlaced* format, which lets browsers display a blurry approximation of the image as it's downloading, to offer a hint of what's coming.

In JPEG files, you can adjust the "quality" level, with a lower quality making the file smaller. You can set the quality quite low with little effect on what appears on users' screens.

You can also take advantage of the *cache* that browsers use. The cache keeps copies of previously viewed pages and images. If any image on a page being downloaded is already in the browser's cache, that image isn't loaded again. When you use the same icon in several places on a page or on several pages visited in succession, the browser downloads the icon's file only once, and reuses the same image on all the pages. When creating your Web pages, try to use the same icons from one page to the next, to both give your pages a consistent style and speed up downloading.

Live and learn

If you're looking at other people's Web pages and come across one that's particularly neat, you can look at the source HTML for that page to see how the page was constructed. In Netscape 4.0, choose View⇨Page Source; in Netscape 3.0, choose View⇨Document Source; in Internet Explorer, choose View⇨Source, and in Opera choose View⇨Source.

Putting Your Page on the Web

After you've made some pages you're happy with (or happy enough with) and you're ready for other people to see them, you have to release your pages to the world. Although nearly every Internet service provider has a user Web server, no two providers handle the uploading process in quite the same way.

Assuming that you have the server details we discussed at the beginning of the chapter, here's what to do:

1. **Run your FTP program.**

   We use WS_FTP (described in Chapter 16), although any FTP program or even Netscape Navigator will do.

2. **Log in to your provider's upload server, using your own login and password.**

   In Netscape Navigator, type the location `ftp://` `username@ftp.gorgonzola.net` into the Location box (suitably adjusting both your username and the server name) and type your login password when it asks. Internet Explorer doesn't handle file uploads.

3. **Change to the directory (folder) where your Web home page belongs.**

   The name is usually something like /pub/elvis, /www/elvis, or /pub/ elvis/www (assuming that your username is *elvis*). In a Web browser, just click your way to the appropriate directory.

4. **Upload your Web page(s).**

   Use ASCII mode, not binary mode, for the Web pages because Web pages are stored as text files. Use binary mode when you're uploading graphics files. If you use Netscape Navigator, drag each file from Windows Explorer or File Manager into the Netscape window or choose File⇨Upload File.

After you've finished uploading, if your page on the server is called mypage.htm, its URL is something like

```
http://www.gorgonzola.net/~elvis/mypage.htm
```

Again, URLs vary by provider. Some providers don't follow the convention of putting a tilde (~) in front of the name.

You should generally call your home page, the one you want people to see first, index.html. If someone goes to your Web directory without specifying a filename, as `http://www.gorgonzola.net/~elvis`, a nearly universal convention is to display the page named index.html. If you don't have a page by that name, most Web servers construct a page with a directory listing of the pages in your Web directory. Although this listing is functional enough because it lets people go to any of your pages with one click, it's not cool.

Be sure to check out how your page looks after it's on the Web. Inspect it from someone else's computer, to make sure that it doesn't accidentally contain any references to graphics files stored on your own computer you forgot to upload. If you want to be compulsive, check how it looks from various browsers — Netscape, Internet Explorer, WebTV, and Lynx, to name a few.

Shortly after you upload your pages, you'll probably notice a glaring mistake. (We always do.) To update a page, edit the copy on your own computer and then upload it to your Internet provider, replacing the preceding version of the page. If you change some but not all of your pages, you don't have to upload pages that haven't changed.

Shout It Out!

After your page is online, you may want to get people to come and visit. Here are a few ways to publicize your site:

✔ Visit your favorite Web directories and indexes, such as Yahoo (`http://www.yahoo.com`) and AltaVista (`http://www.altavista.com`), and submit your URL (the name of your page) to add to their databases. They all have on their home pages an option for adding a new page. Automated indexes like AltaVista add pages promptly, but manually maintained directories like Yahoo may not accept them at all.

✔ Visit `http://www.submit-it.com`, a site that helps you submit your URL to a bunch of directories and indexes. You can get your site submitted to 20 popular searching sites for free or pay money if you want them to submit your URL to a much larger list.

✔ Find and visit other similar or related sites, and offer to exchange links between your site and theirs.

Getting lots of traffic to your site takes time. If your site offers something different that is of real interest to other folks, it can build a following of its own. A few homegrown sites that keep growing in popularity are Arnold Reinhold's Math in the Movies page, at `http://www.world.std.com/~reinhold/mathmovies.html`; Margy's Great Tapes for Kids site, at `http://www.greattapes.com`; and John's Airline Information On-Line on the Internet site, at `http://www.iecc.com/airline`. Just imagine what you can come up with!

Part IV
Essential Internet

The 5th Wave   By Rich Tennant

"QUICK KIDS! YOUR MOTHER'S FLAMING SOMEONE ON THE INTERNET!"

In this part . . .

1 f you're really going to use the Internet, you have to know the basics. We tell you all about electronic mail — how to send it and how to get it. We tell you all about electronic mailing lists so that you can meet people around the world. We've added new chapters about instant messages and chatting so that you can stay in touch with people around the world. We've rewritten our chapter about downloading files so that you can get things off the Net more easily. In addition to traditional Internet service providers, we cover the use of America Online and WebTV to do this stuff.

Chapter 11
Mailing Hither, Mailing Thither

● ●

In This Chapter

▶ Finding e-mail addresses

▶ Sending e-mail

▶ Receiving e-mail

▶ Following e-mail etiquette

● ●

*E*lectronic mail, or *e-mail,* is without a doubt the most popular Internet service, even though it's one of the oldest and (to some) most boring. Although e-mail doesn't get as much press as the World Wide Web, more people use it. Every system on the Net supports some sort of mail service, which means that if your computer — no matter what kind of computer you're using — has Internet access, you can send and receive mail.

Because e-mail, much more than any other Internet service, is connected to many non-Internet systems, you can exchange e-mail with lots of people who don't otherwise have access to the Internet, in addition to all the people who *are* on the Net. (See Chapter 20 for help in finding people's e-mail addresses.)

What's My Address?

Everyone with e-mail access to the Net has at least one *e-mail address,* which is the cyberspace equivalent of a postal address or a phone number. When you send e-mail, you enter the address or addresses of the recipients so that the computer knows where to send the message.

Before you do much mailing, you have to figure out your own e-mail address so that you can give it to people who want to get in touch with you. You also have to figure out some of their addresses so that you can write to them. (If you have no friends or plan to send only anonymous hate mail, you can skip this section.)

Internet mail addresses have two parts, separated by an @ (the *at* sign). The part before the @ is the *mailbox,* which is (roughly speaking) your personal name, and the part after that is the *domain,* usually the name of your Internet provider, such as aol.com or fltg.net.

The username part

The mailbox is usually your *username,* the name your provider assigns to your account. If you're lucky, you get to choose your username; in other cases, providers standardize their naming conventions, and you get what you get. Some usernames are just first names, just last names, initials, first name and last initial, first initial and last name, or anything else, including made-up names. Over the years, for example, John has had the usernames john, john1, jrl, jlevine, jlevine3 (must have been at least three jlevines there), and even q0246; Carol has been carol, carolb, cbaroudi, and carol377 (the provider threw in a random number); and Margy tries to stick with margy but has ended up with margy1 or 73727,2305 on occasion. A few systems assign names such as usd31516. Ugh.

For example, you can write to the President of the United States at president@whitehouse.gov. The President's mailbox is president, and the domain that stores his mailbox is whitehouse.gov — reasonable enough.

Back when e-mail users weren't as prevalent and most users of any particular system knew each other directly, figuring out who had what username wasn't all that difficult. These days, because that process is becoming much more of a problem, many organizations are creating consistent mailbox names for all users, most often by using the user's first and last names with a dot between them. In this type of scheme, your mailbox name may be something like elvis.presley@bluesuede.org, even though your username is something else. (If your name isn't Elvis Presley, adjust this example suitably. On the other hand, if your name *is* Elvis Presley, please contact us immediately. We know some people who are looking for you.)

Having several names for the same mailbox is no problem, so the new, longer, consistent names are invariably created in addition to — rather than instead of — the traditional short nicknames.

The domain name part

The domain name for Internet providers in the United States usually ends with three letters (called the *zone*) that give you a clue to what kind of place it is. *Commercial* organizations end with .com, which includes both providers such as America Online (AOL) and CompuServe and many companies that aren't public providers but that are commercial entities, such as amrcorp.com (AMR Corporation, better known as American Airlines), creamery.com (Egg Farm Dairy in New York state, which makes really good French-style soft cheeses), and iecc.com (the Invincible Electronic Calculator Company). Educational institutions end with .edu (such as yale.edu), networking organizations end with .net, U.S. government sites end with .gov, military sites end with .mil, and organizations that don't fall into any of those categories end with .org. Outside the United States, domains usually end with a country code, such as `.fr` for France or `.zm` for Zambia. Small businesses, local governments, and K-12 schools usually end with `.us` (such as John's community Web site at `www.trumansburg.ny.us`). See our Web site (at `http://net.gurus.com/countries`) for a listing of country codes.

In 1997, an international group proposed adding some extra generic domains like `.firm`, `.arts`, and `.web`. As of the end of 1998, the proposal was stalled in a twisty maze of international telecommunications politics, and it was anyone's guess when, if ever, it would emerge. We'll put any late-breaking updates at `http://net.gurus.com/domains`.

Putting it all together

Write your e-mail address in Table 11-1 and on the Cheat Sheet in the front of this book (then tear it out and tape it to the wall near your computer). Capitalization never matters in domains and rarely matters in mailbox names. To make it easy on your eyes, therefore, most of the domain and mailbox names in this book are shown in lowercase.

Table 11-1	Information Your E-Mail Program Needs to Know	
Information	*Description*	*Example*
Your e-mail address	Your username followed by an @ and the domain name.	`internet6@gurus.com`
Your e-mail password	The password for your e-mail mailbox (usually the same as the password for your account). Don't write it here! It's a secret!	`dum3my`
Your incoming (POP3) mail server	The name of the computer that receives your e-mail messages. (Get this name from your Internet provider.)	`mail.gurus.com`
Your outgoing (SMTP) mail server	The name of the computer that distributes your out-going mail to the rest of the Internet (often the same as the POP3 server).	`mail.gurus.com`

If you're sending a message to another user in your domain (the same machine or group of machines), you can leave out the domain part alto-gether when you type the address. If you and a friend both use AOL, for example, you can leave out the `@aol.com` part of the address when you're writing to each other.

If you don't know what your e-mail address is, try sending yourself a message, using your login name as the mailbox name. Then examine the return address on the message. Or you can send a message to Internet For Dummies Mail Central, at internet6@gurus.com, and a friendly robot will send back a message with your address. (While you're at it, tell us whether you like this book because we authors see that mail, too, and may also write back.) Chapter 20 has more suggestions for finding e-mail addresses.

My Mail Is Where?

If you're the sort of person who lies awake at night worrying about obscure questions, you may have realized that your computer can only receive e-mail while it's connected to the Internet. So, what happens to mail that people send during the 23 hours a day that you're engaged in real life?

When your mail arrives, unless you're one of the few whose computers have a permanent Internet connection, the mail doesn't get delivered to your computer automatically. Mail gets delivered instead to an *incoming mail server* (also known as a *POP3 server,* for Post Office Protocol), which holds onto the mail until you dial in and you run your mail program, which then picks up the mail. To send mail, your *mail* program has to take mail to the post office — your *outgoing mail server* (or *SMTP server,* for Simple Mail Transfer Protocol). It's sort of like having a post office box rather than home delivery — you have to pick it up at the post office and also deliver your outgoing mail there. (Strange but true: Margy and Carol, because they're normal, get their e-mail via a mail server and have their paper "snail" mail delivered to their homes; John, who's abnormal, has his e-mail delivered directly to his home computer but walks to the post office every day, often in the freezing drizzle, to get his regular mail.)

If you have a PPP account, your e-mail program has to be set up with the name of your incoming and outgoing mail servers. When your mail program picks up the mail, it sucks your mail from your provider's incoming mail server to your PC or Mac at top speed. After you download your mail to your own computer, you can disconnect and free up your phone. Then you can read and respond to your mail *offline* — meaning that the meter isn't running. When you're ready to send your responses or new messages, you can reconnect and transmit your outgoing mail to the outgoing mail server, again at top network speed.

Write the names of your incoming (POP3) and outgoing (SMTP) mail servers in Table 11-1 and on the Cheat Sheet (it's hanging on your wall, right?). If you don't know what to write, ask your provider. With luck, your mail program will have the server names set automatically, but when (note we don't say if) the setup gets messed up, you'll be glad you know what to restore the settings to.

If you use an online service like AOL or a UNIX shell account, the mail server is the same computer you connect to when you dial in (this statement is an oversimplification, but it's close enough) so that when you run your provider's e-mail program, your mail is right there for you to read, your provider can drop outgoing messages directly in the virtual mail chute, and no separate POP3 or SMTP server is involved.

Too Many E-Mail Programs

It's time for some hand-to-hand combat with your e-mail system. The bad news is that countless (so many that none of us felt up to the task of counting them) e-mail programs exist — programs that read and write electronic-mail messages. You have your freeware, you have your shareware and your commercial stuff, and stuff probably came with your computer, too. They all do more or less the same thing because they're all mail programs, after all.

Here's a quick rundown of e-mail programs:

- ✔ **Windows PC or Mac with a PPP Internet account:** The most widely used e-mail programs are Eudora (which we describe later in this chapter, in the section "Sending mail with Eudora") and Netscape (versions 2.0 and later). Eudora works pretty well, and one version (Eudora Light) is free. Microsoft offers Internet Mail with Internet Explorer 3.0. Windows 98 and Internet Explorer 4.0 and 5.0 come with Outlook Express, which has far too many flashy features but is usable. Pegasus is another excellent, free e-mail program for this type of Internet account, available from the Net. See Chapter 16 to find out how to get hold of Eudora, Pegasus, Netscape, Outlook Express, and Internet Mail from the Net.

- ✔ **UNIX shell accounts:** You almost certainly can use Pine (see the section "Sending mail with Pine" later in this chapter). If your Internet provider doesn't have Pine, demand it.

- ✔ **America Online (AOL):** The AOL package includes a built-in mail program which is the *only* mail program that AOL users can use. After reading this chapter, AOL users can turn to Chapter 17 for detailed instructions.

- ✔ **WebTV:** If you use this packaged Web connection, you also get an e-mail service. Chapter 18 has detailed instructions.

✔ **Microsoft Network (MSN):** MSN users use Microsoft Exchange, which comes with Windows 95; Microsoft Outlook, which comes with Microsoft Office 97; or Outlook Express, which comes with Internet Explorer 4.0/5.0 and Windows 98.

✔ **Free e-mail accounts:** At least one available service gives you free dial-up accounts for e-mail only. The price you pay is having advertisements appear on-screen as you read your messages. Juno Online is this type of service. (Call 800-654-JUNO to ask for a software disk.) If you use a service such as Juno, you have to use its e-mail software (otherwise, the advertisements aren't displayed).

✔ **Web-based mail:** A few systems offer free e-mail accounts that you can access through the Web. The best known are Hotmail at `http://www.hotmail.com` and Yahoo Mail at `http://mail.yahoo.com`.

If you're connected in some other way, you probably have a different mail program. For example, you may be using a PC in your company's local-area network that runs cc:Mail, Lotus Notes, or Microsoft Mail and has a mail-only link to the outside world. We don't describe local-area network mail programs here, but don't stop reading.

Regardless of which type of mail you're using, the basics of reading, sending, addressing, and filing mail work in pretty much the same way, so looking through this chapter is worth your time even if you're not using any of the mail programs we describe here.

Four Popular E-Mail Programs

After you understand what an e-mail program is supposed to do, it's much easier to figure out how to make a specific e-mail program do what you want. We've picked the four most popular e-mail programs to show you the ropes. For PPP users, we've picked Eudora, Netscape, and Microsoft Outlook Express. AOL and WebTV users should take a look at Chapters 17 and 18. For UNIX account users, we picked Pine.

✔ **Eudora:** This popular e-mail program runs under Microsoft Windows (3.1, 95, and 98) and on the Macintosh, and communicates with your mail server. Eudora is popular, for two reasons: It's easy to use, and it's cheap. You can get a limited version (Eudora Light) for free, and an enhanced commercial version (Eudora Pro) is available for as little as $29. The examples in this book use Eudora Light, and the professional version looks even better. See Chapter 16 to find out how to get either version. *Note:* A free mail service called eudoramail.com is run by the authors of Eudora but has nothing to do with the Eudora mail program.

✔ **Netscape:** Yes, this Netscape is the same one you meet in Chapter 6 while surfing the World Wide Web. All Netscape versions since 2.0 have an adequate if not superb mail program as well as a Web browser. The mail program runs on your own computer and communicates with your mail server. Although we strongly prefer Eudora, some people are stuck with Netscape, so we mention it here.

✔ **Outlook Express:** When Netscape began including an e-mail program with its browser, Microsoft felt compelled to follow suit. Windows 95 came with Microsoft Exchange; in Windows 98, however, Microsoft has introduced a new e-mail program — Outlook Express. When you get a copy of the Microsoft Web browser, Internet Explorer 4.0, you may get Outlook Express too. If not, you can download it from the Net (see Chapter 16).

✔ **Pine:** This rather nice mail program comes with a full-screen terminal interface. It's generally available from most UNIX shell providers because it's (no! wait! you guessed!) free. If you're using a UNIX shell system, Pine runs on your provider's computer, and you type commands at it by using a terminal program on your computer.

When you install Eudora, Netscape, or Outlook Express, you have to give the program the information in Table 11-1. When you first run these programs, they ask you various configuration questions. To tell these programs about your e-mail accounts later or to change your settings, choose Special⇨ Settings or Tools⇨Options (in Eudora), Edit⇨Preferences (in Netscape), or Tools⇨Accounts in Outlook Express.

Sending Mail Is Easy

Sending mail is easy enough that we show you a few examples rather than waste time explaining the theory.

Sending mail with Eudora

Here's how to run Eudora and send some mail:

1. **From your PC or Mac, start Eudora.**

   From Windows 3.1, start Eudora by double-clicking her Program Manager icon, which looks like an envelope. In Windows 95 and 98, her icon is on the desktop or on the Start⇨Programs menu. Mac users, click the Eudora icon. You should see an introductory "splash" window that goes away after a few seconds and then a window like the one shown in Figure 11-1. Exactly what's in the window varies depending on what you were looking at the last time you ran Eudora.

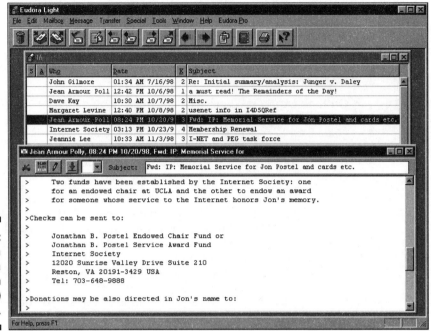

Figure 11-1:
Eudora
(Eudora
Light, in
this case)
says hello.

2. **To send a message, click the New message button (the button with the paper and pencil) on the toolbar, or choose Message⇨New message from the menu. (If you can remember shortcut keys, you can also press Ctrl+N.)**

   Eudora pops up a new message window, with spaces in which you type the address, subject, and text of a message.

3. **On the To line, type the recipient's address (internet6@gurus.com, for example).**

   For your first e-mail message, you may want to write to us (because we will send you back a message confirming what your e-mail address is) or to yourself (if you know what your e-mail address is).

4. **Press Tab to skip past the From line (which is already filled in) to the Subject line and then type a subject.**

   Make the subject line short and specific.

5. **Press Tab a few more times to skip the Cc: and Bcc: fields (or type the addresses of people who should get carbon copies and blind carbon copies of your message).**

The term *carbon copy* should be familiar to those of you who were born before 1960 and remember the ancient practice of putting sheets of carbon-coated paper between sheets of regular paper to make extra copies when using a typewriter. (Please don't ask us what a typewriter is.) In e-mail, a carbon copy is simply a copy of the message you send. All recipients, on both the To: and Cc: lines, see who's getting this message. *Blind carbon copies* are copies sent to people without putting their names on the message so that the other recipients can't tell. *You* can figure out why you may send a copy to someone but not want everyone to know that you sent it.

6. **Press Tab to move to the large area and then type your message.**

7. **To send the message, click the Send or Queue button in the upper-right corner of the message window (what the button says depends on how Eudora is set up).**

   If the button is marked Send, as soon as you click it, Eudora tries to send the message and puts up a little status window that contains incomprehensible status messages. If, on the other hand, the button is marked Queue, your message is stashed in your outbox, to be sent later.

   The usual reason to have a Queue button is that you have a dial-up PPP connection so that your computer isn't connected to the Net all the time. After you queue a few messages, you can send them all at one time.

8. **If your computer isn't already connected, dial up and connect to your provider.**

   You may be able to skip this step. Eudora tries to connect automatically when you send messages. (See Step 7.)

9. **Then switch back to Eudora and choose File⇨Send Queued Messages (Ctrl+T for the lazy) from the menu to transmit all the messages you have queued up.**

Even if you leave your computer connected while you write your mail messages, you may want to consider setting Eudora to queue the mail and not send it until you tell it to. (Choose Special⇨Settings or Tools⇨Options from the Eudora menu, click the Sending Mail category, and be sure that Immediate Send isn't checked.) That way, you get a few minutes after you write each message to ponder whether you really want to send it. Even though we have been using e-mail for over 20 years, we still throw away many of the messages we have written before we send them.

After you send a piece of e-mail, you have no way to cancel it!

The same idea, using Netscape

The steps for sending mail from Netscape are almost identical to those for sending mail from Eudora (you're doing the same thing, after all):

1. **Start Netscape.**

   The instructions from this point depend on whether you're using Netscape Version 3.0 or 4.0 or 4.5.

2. **Choose Window⇨Netscape Mail (in Netscape 3.0) or Communicator⇨Messenger Mailbox (in 4.0) or Communicator⇨Messenger (in 4.5).**

   This step opens the Netscape Mail or Inbox window. The first time you give the command, Netscape asks you for the password for your mailbox, which is usually the same as the password for your Internet account (refer to Table 11-1).

   If you see an error message about a POP3 mailbox, Netscape is complaining that it doesn't know the name of the computer on which your mail is stored. Click OK to make the error message go away. When you see the Netscape Mail or Inbox window, choose Options⇨Mail and News Preferences (in Netscape 3.0) or Edit⇨Preferences (in Netscape 4.0 or 4.5) from the menu, click the Servers or Mail Server tab along the top of the Preferences window that appears (in Netscape 3.0) or click Mail Server from the list on the left (in Netscape 4.0 and 4.5), and fill in the first three boxes you see. Type the name of your Internet provider's mail servers (most providers we know of use the same server for incoming and outgoing mail — refer to Table 11-1) and your username. Click OK.

   Netscape may try to retrieve any waiting mail; click Cancel or the red stop sign if you don't want it to bother. If you use Netscape 3.0, you see the Netscape Mail window, as shown in Figure 11-2; Netscape 4.0 users see the Inbox window, which looks similar.

3. **Click the To:Mail (in Netscape 3.0) or New Message (in Netscape 4.0/4.5) button on the icon bar.**

   Yet another window opens, the Message Composition window, with a blank message template.

   If Netscape complains that it doesn't know your e-mail address, click OK, choose Options⇨Mail and News Preferences (in Netscape 3.0) or Edit⇨Preferences (in Netscape 4.0/4.5), click the Identity tab, fill in the first three blanks, and click OK. Then click the To:Mail or New Msg button again.

4. **Fill in the recipient's address (or addresses) in the Mail To or To box, type the subject, and type the message.**

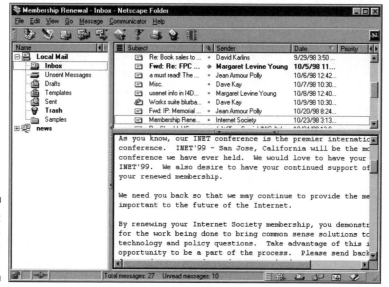

Figure 11-2:
Netscape
shows you
your e-mail.

5. **Click Send to send the message.**

The message wings its way to your Internet provider and on to the addressee.

Sending mail with Outlook Express

The first time you run Outlook Express, it asks you whether you want to sign up for an Internet account, set up an Internet connection to an existing account, or use a connection you've already set up. See Chapter 5 to find out how to set up a connection to an Internet account. Outlook Express can send and receive mail from more than one Internet account; choose Tools⇨Accounts to tell it about other accounts.

Here's how to send mail:

1. **Start Outlook Express. (You don't have to connect to your Internet provider — yet — but it's okay if you're already connected.)**

Click the Outlook Express icon, or choose it from the Start⇨Programs menu. The Outlook Express window, as shown in Figure 11-3, features a list of folders to the left, the contents of the current folder to the upper right, and the text of the current message to the lower right. (When you start the program, no folder or message is selected, so you don't see much.)

Figure 11-3:
The Outlook
Express
window is
divided into
three
sections,
showing a
list of
folders, a
list of
messages
in the
current
folder, and
the text
of the
selected
message.

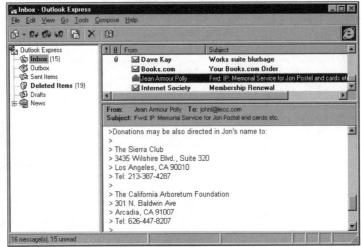

2. **Click the Inbox folder.**

   The first time you run the program, it may run the Internet Connection Wizard to ask you some questions about your e-mail account. Fill in the blanks to tell it your real name, your e-mail address, how to connect to your Internet account, and stuff like that. When it's done, you see the Inbox window again.

3. **Click the Compose Message or New Message button (the leftmost button on the toolbar), press Ctrl+N, or choose Compose⇨New Message (in 4.0) or Message⇨New Message (in 5.0) from the menu bar.**

   You see a New Message window, with boxes to fill in to address the message.

4. **In the To box, type the address to which to send the message and then press Tab.**

   Don't press Enter unless you want to add another line to the To box so that you can type an additional address to which to send the message.

5. **If you want to send a copy of the message to someone, type that person's address in the Cc box and then press Tab; in the Subject box, type a succinct summary of the message and then press Tab again.**

   The cursor should be blinking in the *message area,* the large empty box where the actual message goes.

6. **In the large empty box, type the text of the message.**

   After you type your message, you can press F7 to check your spelling.

7. **To send the message, click the Send button (the leftmost button) on the toolbar, press Alt+S (not Ctrl+S, for some strange reason), or choose File⇨Send Message from the menu.**

   Outlook Express sticks the message in your Outbox folder, waiting to be sent. If you're connected to your Internet provider, Outlook Express sends the message, and you can skip Steps 8 and 9.

8. **Connect to your Internet provider if you're not already.**

   To send the message, you have to climb on the Net.

9. **Click the Send and Receive button on the toolbar or choose Tools⇨ Send and Receive (in 4.0) or Tools⇨Send and Receive⇨Send All (in 5.0) from the menu.**

   Your message is on its way.

Sending mail with Pine

We presume that your UNIX shell provider has Pine all installed and ready to go (if not, call up and complain; the provider has no excuse not to have Pine available). This section tells you how to send a message.

If you have been using a PC with Windows or a Macintosh and have never experienced the utter thrill of computing without being able to point and click, you may — right this minute — be on the brink of a major trip into the past. Hide your mouse. It's of no use to you now. All the navigation you do requires you to use letters or arrow keys:

1. **Run Pine by typing** pine **and pressing Enter (or Return — same thing).**

   You see the Pine main menu, a list of commands that includes Compose Message.

2. **Press** c **to compose a new message.**

   Pine displays a nice, blank message, all ready for you to fill in.

3. **On the To line, type the address to which you want to send mail and then press Enter.**

   At the bottom of the screen, you see a bunch of options preceded by a funny-looking caret sign and a letter. The caret sign indicates the Ctrl key on your keyboard. To choose an option, press the Ctrl key and the letter of the option that interests you (such as Ctrl+G for ^G to get help).

4. **On the Cc: line, you can enter addresses of other people to whom you want to send a copy of this message.**

5. **Press Enter to get to the line labeled** Attchmnt.

   We don't know who came up with the idea that a good abbreviation can be constructed by heaving out all the vowels. This line is for *attachments* — files you want to send along with your message. You can enter the name of a file, even a file that contains stuff that isn't text, and Pine sends it along with your message. You can press Ctrl+T to choose from a list of existing files.

6. **Press Enter to get to the subject of your message, and then enter something descriptive about the content of your message.**

   Subject lines that say something like "A message from Fred" are somewhat less useful than something specific, such as "Re: Pizza dinner tomorrow (Sept. 26) at eight."

7. **Press Enter to get to the part you've been waiting for and enter your message.**

   The message can say anything you want, and it can be as long as you want. To let you enter the message text, Pine automatically runs the simple text editor Pico, which, with any luck, you already know how to use. If you don't know how to run Pico but you know how to run another UNIX editor, ask your Internet service provider to help you set up Pine to use the editor you do know how to run. (Some providers ask you when they configure your account.) You have to be able to stumble through some type of editor, so if you don't know any, starting with Pico is as good a place as any.

   Type the message. If you don't know how to use any editor features, just type your message. Press the arrow keys on the keyboard to move around if you need to make changes.

8. **When you finish, press Ctrl+X to save the message and return to Pine.**

   Pine asks whether you really want to send the message.

9. **Press y or Enter to send your message.**

   The Pine program responds with a cheery `[Sending mail....]` message, and you're all set.

Getting ANSI

If, when you're trying to run Pine on your UNIX shell account, you get a strange message that looks something like this:

```
Your terminal, of type "ansi,"
    is lacking functions needed
    to run pine.
```

You have to utter a magic spell before continuing. Type this line:

setenv TERM vt100

Or, if your provider's system doesn't grok that, type this line:

TERM=vt100 ; export TERM

Be sure to capitalize the commands exactly as you see here. Then try again. (You're giving it some hints about which kind of terminal your computer is pretending to be. Trust us — the details aren't worth knowing.)

Mail Coming Your Way

Once you begin sending e-mail (and in most cases even when you don't), you begin receiving it. The arrival of e-mail is always exciting, even when you get 200 messages a day.

Reading mail with Eudora

One seriously cool feature of Eudora is that you can do much of what you do with mail while you're not connected to your account and paying by the minute. On the other hand, when you really do want to check your mail, you have to be connected. Eudora can figure out that you're not connected and dial in for you (which, in our experience, doesn't always work).

If you don't have a full-time Net connection, follow these steps to get your mail:

1. **Make your Net connection, if you're not already connected.**

2. **Start up Eudora, if she's not already running.**

3. **If Eudora doesn't retrieve mail automatically, click the Check Mail button on the toolbar (the button with the check mark) or choose File⇨Check Mail (or press Ctrl+M) to retrieve your mail.**

   If you have a full-time Net connection, Eudora is probably set up to retrieve your mail automatically, in which case you only have to start Eudora and she gets your mail. (In addition, if you leave Eudora running, even hidden at the bottom of your screen as an icon, she automatically checks for new mail every once in a while.) Eudora 4.1 can even pick up mail in the background while you're reading or sending other messages.

   If you have mail on the Mac, Eudora blows a horn and shows you a cute picture of a mailman delivering a letter. If you don't have any mail, you don't get any sound effects, although you do get a nice picture of a letter with a big, red X through it. Windows users who have a sound card hear a little song (reminiscent of Mexican jumping beans in our opinion) to announce new mail.

   The mail appears in your inbox, a window that Eudora labels In, one line per message.

4. **To see a message, double-click the line or click the line and press Enter.**

   To stop looking at a message, double-click the box in the upper-left corner of the message window (the standard way to get rid of a window) or press Ctrl+W or Ctrl+F4.

Buttons at the top of the In window or at the top of your screen (depending on your version of Eudora) let you dispose of your mail. First, click (once) the message you want, to highlight it. Windows users can click the trash can button to discard the message or the printer icon to print it. Macintosh users can press Delete to delete it or choose File⇨Print to print it.

Although you can do much more to messages, which we discuss in Chapter 12, that's enough for now.

If you use Windows 95 or 98, you can tell Eudora 3.0 to connect to the Internet automagically when you tell it to send or fetch your mail. Choose Tools⇨Options from the menu, scroll the list of icons way down until you see the Advanced Network icon, and click the icon. Select the Automatically Dial and Hangup This Connection option, and choose your Dial-Up Networking connection from the list. Type your username in the box, click the Save Password option, and click OK.

Reading mail with Netscape

Reading mail with Netscape is similar to reading it with Eudora:

1. **Start Netscape and connect to your Internet provider.**

   The rest of these steps depend a little on whether you're running Netscape Version 3.0 or 4.0/4.5.

2. **In Netscape 3.0, choose Window⇨Netscape Mail or click the little envelope in the lower-right corner of the Netscape window. In Netscape 4.0 or 4.5, choose Communicator⇨Messenger Mailbox from the menu or click the Inbox icon in the lower-right corner of the Netscape window, the second of the four icons.**

   This step opens the Netscape Mail or Inbox window. Netscape may try to retrieve any waiting mail immediately; if it doesn't, click the Get Mail or Get Msg icon on the toolbar. Incoming mail is filed in your Inbox folder.

   Netscape 3.0: The upper-left part of the Netscape Mail window lists your mail folders (including Inbox and Sent — more folders are displayed later). The upper-right part lists the messages in the selected folder. The bottom part of the window displays the selected message.

   Netscape 4.0/4.5: The box just under the toolbar shows the current folder, the top half of the window shows a list of messages in that folder, and the bottom half of the window shows the text of the current message. The current folder is usually Inbox, which holds your incoming mail.

3. **In Netscape 3.0, click the Inbox icon in the list of folders. In Netscape 4.0/4.5, if the box just under the toolbar doesn't say Inbox, click in the box and choose Inbox from the list that appears.**

You see the subject lines for incoming mail. (In Netscape 3.0, the list appears in the upper-right part of the window.)

4. **Click each message to read it.**

The message displays in the bottom part of the Netscape window.

When you see the text of a message, you can click the Print, Delete, and other buttons to dispose of it. We discuss the other buttons in Chapter 12.

Reading mail with Outlook Express

If you have Microsoft Outlook Express, which comes with Internet Explorer 4 or 5 and Windows 98, here's how to get your mail:

1. **Run Outlook Express and connect to your Internet provider.**

2. **Click the Send and Receive button on the toolbar or choose Tools⇨ Send and Receive from the menu. In Outlook Express 5, select Send and Receive All.**

Outlook Express downloads your incoming mail on your computer and stashes the messages in your Inbox folder. See the list of folders on the left side of the Outlook Express window? You can choose which folder full of mail to look at. Right now, you should be looking at your Inbox.

The box in the upper-right part of the window lists the senders and subjects of messages in the Inbox. The box in the bottom right part of the window shows the text of the message you select.

Not such junky mail

Outlook Express 5 has an optional "junk mail filter" at Tools⇨Message Rules⇨Junk Mail that attempts to detect junk e-mail and stick it in a separate folder that you can discard. We recommend that you *not* use Microsoft's junk mail filter. Why? Because it has far too many false alarms. We tried it for a while and found nearly as much real mail, including some mail we'd have been really unhappy to lose, as junk mail in the "junk" folder. Microsoft won't say what its filtering rules are, but whatever they are, they don't match the junk mail we get.

In the Junk Mail window there's a tab labeled Block Senders in which you can list "blocked" addresses from which it should discard mail. So long as you have a firm handle on who your non-friends are, this works fine. It's particularly useful for deep-sixing those useless corporate memos and newsletters that self-impressed bureaucrats insist on sending to the entire company.

For more info on stopping junk e-mail once and for all, visit http://spam.abuse.net and http://www.cauce.org.

3. **Click a message header on the list of messages to see the text of the message at the bottom of the Outlook Express window. Or double-click the message header to see the message in a new, big window.**

   If you see a message in its own window, click the Close button, choose File⇨Close from the menu, or press Alt+F4 to get rid of the window.

You can delete, reply to, forward, or print a message after you have seen it. (Chapter 12 tells you how.)

Reading mail with Pine

When you log in to your shell account, you usually get a little message that says "You have new mail" if you do or "You have mail" if stuff you have already seen is hanging around. Depending on some obscure parameter, your mail gets checked periodically, and when you have new mail, you get the "You have new mail" message again.

Here are the steps to follow:

1. **Type the pine command.**

   The Pine main menu lets you choose from a variety of activities; if you have mail, the choice L (Folder List) is highlighted.

2. **Press Enter to see the list of folders you can choose from.**

   When you're just starting out, you don't have much to choose from, although that situation can change. Right now, you're interested in the folder labeled INBOX. INBOX should be highlighted. Press Enter to see your mail. Pine displays a list of messages.

3. **The message that is highlighted is the current message. To choose a different one, press the arrow keys or press P for the preceding message or N for the next message.**

   When you choose the message you want to read, press Enter. Pine displays your message.

   After reading a message, you have several choices about what to do with it. We talk in Chapter 12 about the details of deleting, forwarding, and filing messages.

4. **To read your next message, press N; to read the preceding message, press P; to return to the index of messages in the folder you're reading (in this case, INBOX), press I.**

5. **When you finish reading your mail, press Q to quit.**

   Pine asks you whether you really want to do that. (What — leave this fabulous program? It's so wonderful!) Reassure it by pressing **Y**.

A Few Words from the Etiquette Ladies

Sadly, the Great Ladies of Etiquette, such as Emily Post and Amy Vanderbilt, died before the invention of e-mail. Here's what they may have suggested about what to say and, more importantly, what *not* to say in electronic mail.

E-mail is a funny hybrid, something between a phone call (or voice mail) and a letter. On one hand, it's quick and usually informal; on the other hand, because e-mail is written rather than spoken, you don't see a person's facial expressions or hear her tone of voice.

A few words of advice:

- When you send a message, watch your tone of voice.

- Don't use all capital letters — it looks like you're SHOUTING.

- If someone sends you an incredibly obnoxious and offensive message, as likely as not it's a mistake or a joke gone awry. In particular, be on the lookout for failed sarcasm.

Flame off!

Pointless and excessive outrage in e-mail is so common that it has a name of its own: *flaming*. Don't flame. It makes you look like a jerk.

When you get a message so offensive that you just *have* to reply, stick it back in your electronic inbox for a while and wait until after lunch. Then, don't flame back. The sender probably didn't realize how the message would look. In about 20 years of using e-mail, we can testify that we have never, ever, regretted *not* sending an angry message (although we *have* regretted sending a few — ouch).

When you're sending mail, keep in mind that someone reading it will have no idea of what you *intended* to say — just what you *did* say. Subtle sarcasm and irony are almost impossible to use in e-mail and usually come across as annoying or dumb instead. (If you're an extremely superb writer, you can disregard this advice — but don't say that we didn't warn you.)

Another possibility to keep in the back of your mind is that forging e-mail return addresses is technically not difficult. If you get a totally off-the-wall message from someone that seems out of character for that person, somebody else may have forged it as a prank. (No, we don't tell you how to forge e-mail. How dumb do you think we are?)

Smile!

Sometimes it helps to put in a :-) (called a *smiley*), which means, "This is a joke." (Try leaning way over to the left if you don't see why it's a smile.) In some communities, notably CompuServe, <g> or <grin> serves the same purpose. Here's a typical example:

```
People who don't believe that we are all part of a warm,
           caring community who love and support each other
           are no better than rabid dogs and should be
           hunted down and shot. :-)
```

We feel that any joke that needs a smiley probably wasn't worth making, but tastes differ.

How Private Is E-Mail?

Relatively, but not totally. Any recipient of your mail may forward it to other people. Some mail addresses are really mailing lists that redistribute messages to many other people. Misrouted mail has landed in our internet6@gurus.com mailbox with details of our correspondents' lives and anatomy that they probably would rather we forget. (So we did.)

If you send mail from work or to someone at work, your mail is not private. You and your friend may work for companies of the highest integrity whose employees would never dream of reading private e-mail. When push comes to shove, however, and someone is accusing your company of leaking confidential information and the corporate lawyer says, "Examine the e-mail," someone reads all the e-mail. (This situation happened to a friend of ours who was none too pleased to find that all his intimate correspondence with his fiancée had been read.) E-mail you send and receive is stored on your disk, and most companies back up their disks regularly. Reading your e-mail is very easy for someone who really wants to, unless you encrypt it.

Hey, Ms. Postmaster

Every Internet host that can send or receive mail has a special mail address called postmaster that is guaranteed to get a message to the person responsible for that host. If you send mail to someone and get back strange failure messages, you can try sending a message to the postmaster. If king@bluesuede.org returns an error from bluesuede.org, for example, you may try a polite question to postmaster@bluesuede.org. Because the postmaster is usually an overworked volunteer system administrator, it is considered poor form to ask a postmaster for favors much greater than "Does so-and-so have a mailbox on this system?"

The general rule is not to send anything you wouldn't want to see posted next to the water cooler or perhaps scribbled next to a pay phone. The latest e-mail systems are beginning to include encryption features that make the privacy situation somewhat better so that anyone who doesn't know the keyword used to scramble a message can't decode it.

The most common tools for encrypted mail are known as S/MIME, PEM (privacy-enhanced mail), and PGP (pretty good privacy). PGP is one of the most widely used encryption programs, both in the United States and abroad. Many experts think that it's so strong that even the National Security Agency can't crack it. We don't know about that; if the NSA wants to read your mail, however, you have more complicated problems than we can help you solve. S/MIME is an emerging standard encryption system that Netscape and Outlook Express both support.

PGP is available for free on the Net. To find more information about privacy and security issues, including how to get started with PGP and S/MIME, point your Web browser to http://net.gurus.com/pgp.

To Whom Do I Write?

Now that you know how to use e-mail, you will want to send some messages. See Chapter 20 to find out how to find the e-mail address of someone you know. Chapter 13 tells you how to find other people to write to and how to get interesting information by e-mail.

TIP

BTW, what does IMHO mean?

E-mail users are often lazy typists, and many abbreviations are common. Here are some of the most widely used:

Abbreviation	What It Means	Abbreviation	What It Means
BTW	By the way	RTFM	Read the manual — you could have and should have looked it up yourself
IANAL	I am not a lawyer, (but . . .)		
IMHO	In my humble opinion	TIA	Thanks in advance
ROTFL	Rolling on the floor laughing	TLA	Three-letter acronym
RSN	Real soon now (vaporware)	YMMV	Your mileage may vary

Chapter 12

Putting Your Mail in Its Place

- -

In This Chapter

▶ Deleting mail

▶ Responding to mail

▶ Forwarding and filing mail

▶ Spotting and avoiding chain letters

▶ Sending and receiving exotic mail and mail attachments

▶ Exchanging mail with robots and fax machines

▶ Dealing with spam

- -

*O*kay, now that you know how to send and receive mail, you're ready for some tips and tricks to make you into a real mail aficionado. We describe Eudora, Netscape (Versions 3.0 and 4.0), Outlook Express, and Pine (see Chapter 11 for descriptions of these programs).

After you read an e-mail message, you can do a bunch of different things with it (much the same as with paper mail). Here are your usual choices:

- ✔ Throw it away.
- ✔ Reply to it.
- ✔ Forward it to other people.
- ✔ File it.

Unlike with paper mail, you can do any or all of these things to each message. If you don't tell your mail program what to do to a message, the message either stays in your mailbox for later perusal or sometimes — when you're using Pine, for example — gets saved to a read-messages folder.

If your mail program automatically saves messages in a read-messages, Sent, or Outbox folder, be sure to go through the folder every week or so, or else it becomes enormous and unmanageable.

Deleting Mail

When you first begin to get e-mail, the feeling is so exciting that just throwing the message away is difficult to imagine. Eventually, however, you *have* to know how to get rid of messages, or else your computer will run out of room. Start early. Delete often.

The physical act of throwing mail away is easy enough that you probably have figured out how to do it already. Using the Windows version of Eudora, you click a message and then click the trash can or press Ctrl+D. In the Macintosh version of Eudora, you can click the message and press Delete. If the message file is open, press ⌘+D or choose Delete from the Message menu. In Netscape (either the Netscape Navigator 3.0 Mail window or the Netscape 4.0 Messenger program) and Outlook Express, click the message and then the Delete button on the toolbar or press the Delete key. From Pine, press **D** for Delete.

You can often delete mail without even reading it. If you subscribe to mailing lists, certain topics may not interest you. After you see the subject line, you may want to delete the message without reading it. If you're the type of person who reads everything Ed McMahon sends to you, you may have problems managing junk e-mail, too. Consider getting professional help.

Back to You, Sam: Replying to Mail

You should know a couple of things about replying to mail. It's easy enough to do: In Eudora, choose Message⇨Reply or click the Reply button on the toolbar (a left-pointing blue arrow); in Netscape, click the Re:Mail icon on the toolbar or choose Message⇨Reply from the menu or press Ctrl+R; in Outlook Express, click the Reply to Author button on the toolbar or press Ctrl+R or choose Compose⇨Reply to Author (Message⇨Reply to Sender in 5.0); in Pine, press **R**.

Pay attention to two things in particular:

> ✔ To whom does the reply go? Look carefully at the To: line your mail program has filled out for you. Is that who you thought you were addressing? If the reply is addressed to a mailing list, did you really intend to post to that list, or is your message of a more personal nature that may be better addressed to the individual who sent the message? Did you mean to reply to a group? Are all the addresses that you think you're replying to included on the To: list? If the To: list isn't correct, you can move the cursor to it and edit it as necessary.

✔ Do you want to include the content of the message to which you're replying? Most e-mail programs begin your reply message with the content of the message to which you're replying. The Netscape toolbar has a Quote button you can click to stick the quoted text of the original message into your reply. We suggest that you begin by including it and then edit the text to just the relevant material. If you don't give some context to people who get a great deal of e-mail, your reply makes no sense. If you're answering a question, include the question in the response. You don't have to include the entire text, but give your reader a break. She may have read 50 messages since she sent you mail and may not have a clue what you're talking about unless you remind her.

When you reply to a message, most mail programs fill in the Subject field with the letters *Re:* (short for *regarding*) and the Subject field of the message to which you're replying.

Keeping track of your friends

After you begin using e-mail, you quickly find that keeping track of all your regular correspondents' e-mail addresses is a pain. Fortunately, every popular e-mail program provides an *address book* in which you can save your friends' addresses so that you can send mail to Mom, for example, and have it automatically addressed to chairman@exec.hq.giant-corp.com. You can also create address lists so that you can send mail to family, for example, and it goes to Mom, Dad, your brother, both sisters, and your dog, all of whom have separate e-mail addresses.

All address books let you do the same things: save the address from a message you have just read, use addresses you have saved, and edit your address book.

Netscape: Netscape has an adequate if uninspired address book. When you're reading a message, you can add the sender's address to your address book by choosing Message⇨ Add to Address Book (3.0 and 4.0) or Message⇨Add Sender to Address Book (4.5). Doing so pops up a window in which you can enter the nickname to use and then click OK to add the nickname to the address book. To use the address book when you're creating a message, click the Mail To: or Cc: button (in Netscape 3.0) or the Address button (in Netscape 4.0) in the message-creation window. Doing so pops up a window that lists the contents of your address book. Double-click the address or addresses you want and then click OK to continue composing your message. In Netscape 4.5, just start typing the name of someone in your address book; when Netscape recognizes a name, it displays the rest in faint type. Click the address book icon to the left of the name to accept the name Netscape found, or press Tab to see a list of names that match what you've typed so far and then double-click the one you want.

To edit your address book, choose Window⇨Address Book (in Netscape 3.0) or Communicator⇨Address Book (in Netscape 4.0/4.5). You can create a mailing list by choosing Item⇨Add List (in Netscape 3.0) or clicking the New List button (in Netscape 4.0), which creates an empty list, and then dragging existing addresses from the address book into the list or in 4.5, typing the addresses you want. (Yes, this means that in 3.0 and 4.0, you first have to put all the names for the list into the address book separately and then drag

(continued)

(continued)

them into the list. We said that the address book was uninspired.) In Netscape 3.0, the address book window is deliberately similar to the Netscape Navigator bookmark window: If you remember how to edit bookmarks, you edit the address book in the same way.

Eudora: Eudora has a good address book. If you're reading a message, choose Special⇨Make Address Book Entry (or press Ctrl+K). Eudora suggests using the person's real name as the nickname, which usually works fine. Then click OK.

To use the address book while you're composing a message, you can open the address book by choosing Tools⇨Address Book (Ctrl+L), click the nickname to use, and then click the To:, Cc:, or Bcc: button in the address book window to add the selected address to the message. Or use this shortcut: Type the first few letters of the nickname on the To: or Cc: line, enough to distinguish the nickname you want from any other nicknames, and press Ctrl+, (the Ctrl key plus a comma). Eudora finishes the nickname for you. To make a mailing list, open the address book by choosing Tools⇨Address Book (Ctrl+L), click New to create a new nickname, and then click in the Address(es) subwindow in the address book and type the addresses you want, one to a line. Alternatively, if you have received mail in your inbox from all the people you want to put on your list, you can Ctrl+click to highlight all

those messages in the inbox list and then press Ctrl+K to make a new address book entry, which is a list of all the authors of the selected messages.

Outlook Express: The process of copying a correspondent's address into the address book is easy but obscure: Double-click a message from your correspondent to open that message in its own window. Then right-click the person's name in the From line, and click the Add to Address Book button. You can edit the address book entry you're creating if you want, and then click OK. In 5.0, you can skip the first step and right-click the address in the list of messages in the mailbox.

To display and edit the Address book, click the Address Book or Addresses icon on the toolbar. After you manage to get some entries into your address book, you use them while you're creating a new message by clicking on the To: or Cc: line or the little icon that looks like a Rolodex card or a book. In the Select Recipients window that appears, double-click the address book entry or entries you want to use and then click OK. If you don't know someone's e-mail address, choose Edit⇨Find⇨People from the menu to display the Find People window; you can search in your own address book or in various Internet directories, such as Bigfoot and WhoWhere.

Hot Potatoes: Forwarding Mail

You can forward e-mail along to someone else. It's easy. It's cheap. Forwarding is one of e-mail's best features — and one of its worst. It's good because you can easily pass along messages to people who need to know about them. It's bad because you (not you personally, but, um, people around you — that's it) can just as easily send out floods of messages to recipients who would rather not read *another* press release from the local Ministry of Truth. You have to think a little about whether forwarding a message will actually enhance someone's quality of life.

What's usually called *forwarding* a message involves wrapping the message in a new message of your own, sort of like sticking Post-It notes all over a copy of it and mailing the copy and Post-Its to someone else.

Forwarding mail is almost as easy as replying to it. In Eudora, choose Message⇨Forward or click the icon of a red arrow pointing to the right; in Netscape, click the Forward icon on the toolbar or choose Message⇨ Forward from the menu or press Ctrl+L; in Outlook Express, click the Forward message button on the toolbar or press Ctrl+F or choose Compose⇨Forward; in Pine, press **F**. The mail program composes a message containing the text of the message you want to forward; all you have to do is address the message, add a few snappy comments, and send it.

✔ Eudora and Outlook Express provide the forwarded text in the message part of the window. Each line is preceded by the greater-than sign (>). You then get to edit the message and add your own comments. See the nearby sidebar "Fast forward" for tips about pruning forwarded mail.

✔ Netscape doesn't show you the text of the original message — you just have to trust the program to send the text along. (Netscape treats the message as an *attached file,* which we discuss later in this chapter.) The comments you type in the message box appear along with the text of the original message.

If you want Netscape to include the text of the original message in the usual way (with each line preceded by a >), choose the Message⇨Forward Quoted (Message⇨Forward As⇨Quoted in 4.5) command instead.

Sometimes, the mail you get may really have been intended for someone else. You probably will want to pass it along as is, without sticking the greater-than character at the beginning of every line, and you should leave the sender and reply-to information intact so that if the new recipient of the mail wants to respond, the response goes to the originator of the mail, not to you just because you passed it on. Some mail programs call this feature *remailing* or *bouncing,* the electronic version of scribbling another address on the outside of an envelope and dropping it back in the mailbox.

Eudora calls this process *redirecting;* you can redirect mail by choosing Message⇨Redirect from the menu or clicking the red-arrow-pointing-to-the-sky icon. Eudora sticks in a polite by-way-of notice to let the new reader know how the message found her. Pine uses B for Bounce; because Netscape and Outlook Express have no redirection, you have to forward messages instead.

Fast forward

Getting rid of the uninteresting parts is generally a good idea whenever you forward e-mail. The forwarded message often automatically includes all the glop in the meassage header, which almost none of is comprehensible — much less interesting — so get rid of it.

The tricky part is editing the text. If the message is short, a screenful or so, you probably should leave it alone:

```
>Is there a lot of demand for
    fruit pizza?

>

In answer to your question, I
    checked with our research
    department and found that
    the favorite pizza toppings
    in the 18-34 age group are
    pepperoni, sausage, ham,
    pineapple, olives, peppers,
    mushrooms, hamburger, and
    broccoli. I specifically
    asked about prunes, and
    they found no statistically
    significant response about
    them.
```

If the message is really long and only part of it is relevant, you should, as a courtesy to the reader, cut it down to the interesting part. We can tell you from experience that people pay much more attention to a concise, one-line e-mail message than they do to 12 pages of quoted stuff followed by a two-line question.

Sometimes it makes sense to edit material even more, particularly to emphasize one specific part. When you do so, of course, be sure not to edit to the point where you put words in the original author's mouth or garble the sense of the message, as in the following reply:

```
>In answer to your question, I
    checked with

>our research department and
    found that the

>favorite pizza toppings ...
    and they

>found no statistically sig-
    nificant

>response about them.
```

That's an excellent way to make new enemies. Sometimes, it makes sense to paraphrase a little — in that case, put the paraphrased part in square brackets, like this:

```
>[When asked about prunes on
    pizza, research]

>found no statistically sig-
    nificant response

>about them.
```

People disagree about whether paraphrasing to shorten quotes is a good idea. On one hand, if you do it well, it saves everyone time. On the other hand, if you do it badly and someone takes offense, you're in for a week of accusations and apologies that will wipe out whatever time you may have saved. The decision is up to you.

Cold Potatoes: Saving Mail

Saving e-mail for later reference is similar to putting potatoes in the fridge for later. (Don't knock it if you haven't tried it — day-old boiled potatoes are yummy with enough butter or sour cream.) Lots of your e-mail is worth saving, just as lots of your paper mail is worth saving. (Lots of it *isn't*, of course, but we cover that subject earlier in this chapter.)

You can save e-mail in a few different ways:

- ✔ Save it in a folder full of messages.
- ✔ Save it in a regular file.
- ✔ Print it and put it in a file cabinet with paper mail.

The easiest method usually is to stick messages in a folder (a folder is usually no more than a file full of messages with some sort of separator between each message).

People use two general approaches in filing mail: by sender and by topic. Whether you use one or the other or both is mostly a matter of taste. Some mail programs (such as Pine) help you file stuff by the sender's name. When you press S to save a message from your friend Fred, who has the username `fred@something.or.other`, Pine asks whether you want to put the message in a folder called `fred`. If some crazed system administrator has given him the username `z92lh8t@something.or.other`, make up names of your own.

For filing by topic, it's entirely up to you to come up with folder names. The most difficult part is coming up with memorable names. If you're not careful, you end up with four folders with slightly different names, each with a quarter of the messages about a particular topic. Try to come up with names that are obvious, and don't abbreviate. If the topic is accounting, call the folder `accounting` because if you abbreviate, you will never remember whether it's called `acctng`, `acct`, or `acntng`.

If you use Windows or a Mac, you can save all or part of a message by copying it into a text file or word-processing document. Select the text of the message by using your mouse. In Windows, press Ctrl+C (⌘+C on a Mac) or choose Edit⇨Copy to copy the text to the Clipboard. Switch to your word processor (or whatever program in which you want to copy the text) and press Ctrl+V (⌘+V on the Mac) or choose Edit⇨Paste to make the message appear where the cursor is.

Filing with Eudora

To file a message in Eudora, click the message and choose Transfer from the menu. The Transfer menu that appears lists all your mailboxes — all the choices you have for where to file your message. Choose the mailbox in which you want to stick your message. Poof — it's there.

The first time you try to file something, you may notice that you don't have anywhere to file it. Create a new mailbox in which to stick the message by choosing New from the Transfer menu. Every time you want to create a new file, choose New. Although you eventually have enough mailboxes to handle most of your mail, for a while you may feel as though you're choosing New all the time.

You can see all the messages in a folder by choosing Mailbox from the menu — a window appears listing all the messages in the folder.

If you want to save the message in a text file, click the message, choose File⇨Save As from the menu, move to the folder in which you want to save the message, type a filename, and click OK.

Filing with Netscape

In the Netscape 3.0 Mail window, you can save a message by clicking the message and choosing Message⇨Move from the menu. Then select the folder name from the list that appears. An easier way to move a message is to drag it from the list of messages to another folder in the list of folders. To make a new folder, choose File⇨New Folder from the menu.

In the Netscape 4.0 Inbox window, you can save a message in a folder by clicking the message, choosing Message⇨File message from the menu, and choosing the folder from the list that appears. In 4.5, right click on the message, choose Move to, and pick the desired folder on the submenu. To make a new folder, choose File⇨New Folder.

To save a message or several messages in a text file (in any version of Netscape), select the message or messages and choose File⇨Save As (File⇨Save As⇨File in 4.5) from the menu. Click in the Save as type box and choose Plain Text (*.txt) from the list that appears. Type a filename and click the Save button.

Filing with Outlook Express

To save a message in Outlook Express, you stick it in a folder. You start out with folders named Inbox, Deleted Items, Outbox, and Sent Items. To make a new folder, choose File⇨Folder⇨New Folder from the menu and give the folder a name. (Make one called Personal, just to give it a try.) The new folder appears on the list of folders on the left side of the Outlook Express window. Move messages into a folder by clicking a message header and dragging it over to the folder name or choosing Edit⇨Move to Folder from the menu. You can see the list of message headers for any folder by clicking the folder name.

You can save the text of a message in a text file by clicking the message and choosing File⇨Save As from the menu, clicking in the Save as type box and choosing Text Files (*.txt), typing a filename, and clicking the Save button.

Filing with Pine

To save a message in a folder, press **S** when you're looking at the message or when it's highlighted on your list of messages. To create a new folder, tell Pine to save a message to a folder that doesn't exist (yet). Pine asks whether you want to create the folder — press **Y** to do so.

Chain letters: Arrrrrggghhh!

One of the most obnoxious things you can do with e-mail is to pass around chain letters. Because all mail programs have forwarding commands, with only a few keystrokes you can send a chain letter along to hundreds of other people. Don't do it. Chain letters are cute for about two seconds, and then they're just annoying. After 20 years of using e-mail, we've *never* received a chain letter worth passing along. That's **NEVER**! (Please excuse the shouting.) So don't you pass them along either, okay?

A few chain letters just keep coming around and around, despite our best efforts to stamp them out.

The Good Times virus hoax: (Also known as Join the Crew and other names.) In late 1994, a chain letter appeared disguised as a warning that a horrible computer virus capable of erasing your hard disk was being spread by e-mail. The virus allegedly arrived in e-mail messages bearing the words *Good Times*. The chain letter, not the non-existent virus, spread rapidly throughout the Internet. Computer viruses are spread through infected programs that, after they are run, can have malicious effects. E-mail is stored as text — not as a program — that cannot cause damage to your disk unless you give specific commands to run a program. This chain letter shows up under various

names; regardless of the title, however, viruses don't spread by e-mail.

Dying boy wants greeting (or business) cards: Not anymore, he doesn't. A decade ago, an English boy named Craig Shergold was hospitalized with a serious brain tumor. Craig wanted to set the world's record for receiving the most greeting cards. Word got out, and Craig received millions of cards and eventually got into the *Guinness Book of World Records*. Then, U.S. TV billionaire John Kluge paid for Craig to fly to the United States for a successful operation. Craig is okay now and doesn't want any more cards. (You can read all about this story on page 24 of the July 29, 1990, edition of *The New York Times*.) Guinness is so sick of the whole business that it has closed the category — no more records for the most cards are accepted. To help dying children, give the two dollars that a card and stamp would cost to a children's welfare organization, such as UNICEF.

Make big bucks with a chain letter: These letters usually have the subject MAKE.MONEY.FAST, are signed by "Christopher Erickson" or Karen something, contain lots of testimonials from people who are now rolling in dough, and tell you to send $5 to the name at the top of the list, put your name at the bottom, and send the message to a zillion

(continued)

(continued)

other suckers. Some even say, "This isn't a chain letter" (you're supposedly helping to compile a mailing list or sending reports or something — your absolute guarantee that it's a chain letter). Don't even think about it. These chain letters are extremely illegal even when they say that they aren't, and, besides, they don't even work. (Why send any money? Why not just add your name and send it on? Heck, why not just replace all the names on the list with yours?) Think of them as gullibility viruses. Send a polite note to the sender's postmaster to encourage her to tell users not to send any more chain letters. If you don't believe that they're illegal, see the Postal Service Web site, at `http://www.usps.gov/websites/depart/inspect chainlet.htm`.

Send a copy of your child's birth certificate to a P.O. box in Minnesota and get a savings bond: Nobody seems to be quite sure how this one started, but it's completely untrue. If you send anything to the box, the post office sends it back because the box is closed.

Exotic Mail and Mail Attachments

Sooner or later, just plain, old, everyday e-mail isn't good enough for you. Someone's gonna send you a picture you just have to see, or you're gonna want to send something cool to your new best friend in Paris. To send stuff other than text through the mail, a message uses special file formats. Sometimes, the entire message is in a special format (such as MIME, which we talk about in a minute), and sometimes people *attach* things to their plain text mail. Attachments come in three flavors:

✔ **MIME:** Stands for *m*ultipurpose *I*nternet *m*ail extensions

✔ **Uuencoding:** A method of including information in e-mail; invented back in the days of UNIX-to-UNIX e-mail (hence the *uu* in the name)

✔ **BinHex:** Stands for *bin*ary-to-*hex*adecimal, as far as we can tell

The technical details of these three methods are totally uninteresting and irrelevant: What matters to you is that your e-mail program must be capable of attaching files by using at least one of these methods and capable of detaching incoming files that other people send you, preferably by using any of the three methods.

You can generally send a file as an e-mail attachment by using your regular mail program to compose a regular message and then giving a command to attach a file to the message. You send the message by using the program's usual commands.

When you receive a file that is attached to an e-mail message, your mail program is responsible for noticing the attached file and doing something intelligent with it. Most of the time, your mail program saves the attached file as a separate file in the folder or directory you specify. After the file has been saved, you can use it just like you use any other file.

For example, you can send these types of files as attachments:

- Pictures, in image files
- Word-processing documents
- Sounds, in audio files
- Movies, in video files
- Programs, in executable files
- Compressed files, such as ZIP files

See Chapter 21 for a description of the types of files you may encounter as attachments.

If you receive a message with an attachment that uses a method (MIME, uuencoding, or BinHex) that your mail program doesn't know about, the attached file shows up as a large message in your mailbox. If the attached file contains text, about half the kinds of tarted-up text are readable as is, give or take some ugly punctuation. If the attached file contains sound or pictures, on the other hand, reading the message is hopeless because it just contains binary digitized versions of the images and not any sort of text approximation.

If you get a picture or sound MIME message and your mail program doesn't automatically handle it, clunky but usable methods may exist for saving the message to a file and extracting the contents with separate programs. Consult your Internet service provider's help desk.

Eudora attachments

To attach a file to a message with Eudora, compose a message as usual. Then choose Message➪Attach File from the menu or click the Attach icon (a disk in front of a folder or, in newer versions of Eudora, a message clipped to an envelope) or press Ctrl+H. Eudora helps you choose the document you want to attach. Eudora Light (the freeware version of Eudora) always sends files as MIME attachments and can handle incoming files by using any of the three attachment methods.

If you drag a file from Windows Explorer, My Computer, or File Manager to Eudora, she attaches the file to the message you're writing. If you're not writing a message, she starts one for you.

When Eudora receives mail with attachments, she automatically saves them to your disk (in a directory you specify on the Options menu) and tells you where they are and what they're called.

Netscape attachments

In Netscape, you click the Attach button to attach a file to the message you're composing. Unlike most other mail programs, Netscape Navigator lets you attach any file or document you can describe with a *Universal Resource Locator,* or *URL* (the naming scheme used on the Web, as we explain in Chapter 6). Netscape Navigator gives you your choice of attaching a document, by default the last message or page you were looking at, or attaching a file — click Document or File. (Netscape 4.0/4.5 gives you even more choices.) If you attach a file, you can click the Browse button to choose the file to attach. When you have decided what to attach, click OK to attach the file to the outgoing message. Navigator attaches files by using MIME.

For incoming mail, Netscape displays any attachments that it knows how to display itself (Web pages and GIF and JPEG image files). For other types of attachments, it displays a little description of the file, which you can click. Netscape then runs an appropriate display program, if it knows of one, or asks you whether to save the attachment to a file or to configure a display program, which it then runs in order to display it. Netscape can handle all three attachment methods.

Outlook Express attachments

In Outlook Express, you attach a file to a message by choosing Insert⇨File Attachment from the menu while you're composing a message or click the paper-clip icon on the toolbar. Then select the file to attach. Send the message as usual.

When an incoming message contains an attachment, a paper-clip icon appears in the message on your list of incoming messages and in the message when you view it. Click the paper clip to see the filename — double-click to see the attachment.

Pine attachments

To attach stuff with Pine, you enter the filenames of whatever you want to attach, separated by commas. When you press Enter after you have entered your attachments, Pine goes and gets the file. If it can't find the file, the program enters it in your list of attachments anyway but tells you that it can't find the file, so pay careful attention. Pine attaches files by using MIME.

When Pine reads a message with attachments, it tells you which attachments you have and displays them if they're in a format it comprehends. Generally, what happens is that you save a file with a filename of your choosing and then read it by using other software. (Chapter 21 has info about just what type of file you may have received.) Pine can handle only MIME attachments directly. If you receive a uuencoded message (it starts with `begin filename 644` or something like that), press the vertical bar key (`|`) to tell Pine to feed your message to a program, and then type **uudecode**, the name of the UNIX program that decodes uuencoded messages. The file is stored in your home directory on your provider's system.

Hey, Mr. Robot

Not every mail address has an actual person behind it. Some are mailing lists (which we talk about in Chapter 13), and some are *robots,* programs that automatically reply to messages. Mail robots have become popular as a way to query databases and retrieve files because setting up a connection for e-mail is much easier than setting up one that handles the more standard file transfer. You send a message to the robot (usually referred to as a *mailbot* or *mail server*), it takes some action based on the contents of your message, and then the robot sends back a response. If you send a message to `internet6@gurus.com`, for example, you receive a response telling you your e-mail address.

The most common use for mail servers is to get on and off *mailing lists,* which we explore in gruesome detail in Chapter 13. Companies also often use the lists to send back canned responses to requests for information sent to `info@whatever.com`.

Your Own Personal Mail Manager

After you begin sending e-mail, you probably will find that you receive quite a bit of it, particularly if you put yourself on some mailing lists (see Chapter 13). Your incoming mail soon becomes a trickle, and then a stream, and then a torrent, and pretty soon you can't walk past your keyboard without getting soaking wet, metaphorically speaking.

Fortunately, most mail systems provide ways for you to manage the flow and avoid ruining your clothes (enough of this metaphor already). If most of your messages come from mailing lists, you should check to see whether the lists are available instead as *Usenet* newsgroups. (See the Web page at `http://net.gurus.com/usenet` for information about newsgroups.) Usenet newsreading programs generally enable you to look through messages and find the interesting ones more quickly than your mail program does and to automatically sort the messages so that you can quickly read or ignore an entire *thread* (conversation) of messages about a particular topic. Your system manager can usually arrange to make particularly chatty mailing lists look like Usenet newsgroups. At our site, we handle about 40 mailing lists that way.

Netscape 4.*x* users, Eudora Pro users, and, as of Version 3.0, Eudora Light users can create *filters* that can automatically check incoming messages against a list of senders and subjects and file them in appropriate folders. Outlook Express has the Inbox Assistant, which can sort your mail automatically. Some other mail programs have similar filtering features.

For example, you can create filters that tell your mail program, "Any message that comes from the POULTRY-L mailing list should be automatically filed in the Chickens folder." In Eudora 3.0, choose Tools⇨Filters to see a window that lists filters and lets you create, edit, and delete them. (The commercial version of Eudora — Eudora Pro — has even more flexible filters, so buy Eudora Pro if you use filters frequently.) In Netscape 4.0, choose Edit⇨Mail Filters (Edit⇨Message Filters in 4.5) from the menu to display the Mail Filters window, where you can see, create, edit, and delete filters. In Outlook Express, tell the Inbox Assistant how to sort your mail into folders by choosing Tools⇨Inbox Assistant (Tools⇨Message Rules⇨Mail in 5.0) from the menu.

All this automatic-sorting nonsense may seem like overkill, and if you get only five or ten messages a day, it is. After the mail really gets flowing, however, dealing with it takes much more of your time than it used to. Keep those automated tools in mind — if not for now, for later.

One-Click Surfing

Eudora (3.0 and later) turns all the URLs (Web site addresses) she finds in an e-mail message into links to the actual Web site. So do Netscape and Outlook Express. You no longer have to type these addresses into your browser. All you have to do is click the highlighted link in the e-mail message, and — poof — you're at the Web site.

Spam, Bacon, and Eggs

Pink tender morsel,
Glistening with salty gel.
What the hell is it?

— SPAM haiku, found on the Internet

More and more often, it seems, we get unsolicited e-mail from some organization or person we don't know. The word *spam* (not to be confused with SPAM, a meat-related product from Hormel) on the Internet now means thousands of copies of the same piece of unwanted e-mail, sent to either individual e-mail accounts or Usenet newsgroups. It's also known as "junk e-mail" or unsolicited commercial e-mail (UCE). The message usually consists of unsavory advertising for get-rich-quick schemes or even pornographic offers — something you may not want to see and something you definitely don't want your children to see. The message is *spam,* the practice is *spamming,* and the person sending the spam is a *spammer.*

Spam, unfortunately, is a major problem on the Internet because sleazy business entrepreneurs and occasional political lowlifes have decided that it's the ideal way to advertise. We get 50 spams a day (yes, really) and the number continues to increase.

Why call it spam?

The meat? Nobody knows. Oh, you mean the unwanted e-mail? It came from the Monty Python skit in which a group of Vikings sing the word *Spam* repeatedly in a march tempo, drowning out all other discourse.

Why is it so bad?

You may think that spam, like postal junk mail, is just a nuisance we have to live with. But it's worse than junk mail, in several ways. Spam costs you money. E-mail recipients pay much more than the sender does to deliver a message. Sending e-mail is cheap: A spammer can send thousands of messages an hour from a PC and a dial-up connection. After that, it costs you time to download, read (at least the subject line) and dispose of the mail. If spam volume continues to grow at its alarming pace, pretty soon e-mail will prove to be useless because the real e-mail is buried under the junk.

Not only do e-mail clients have to bear a cost, but all this volume of e-mail also strains the resources of the e-mail servers and the entire Internet. Internet service providers have to pass along the added costs to its users. America Online has been reported to estimate that more than one-quarter is spam, and many ISPs have told us that as much as $2 of the $20 monthly fee goes to handling and cleaning up after spam.

Spammers advertise stuff you'd never get in postal mail. It's generally fraudulent, dishonest, or pornographic. Many of the offers are for get-rich-quick schemes. No honest business would attempt to advertise by broadcasting on the Internet because of the immense bad publicity it would bring on itself.

Many spams include a line that instructs you how to get off their lists, something like "Send us a message with the word REMOVE in it." Why should you have to waste your time to get off the list? But don't bother, spammers' remove lists never work.

What can I do?

The Internet tries to be self-policing; and the community of people who make up the users and inventors of this marvelous medium don't want the Internet to fall under the control of short-sighted governments or gangsters. The Internet grew from a need for the easy and free flow of information, and everyone using it should strive to keep it that way.

Check out these Web sites for information about spam and how to fight it, technically, socially, and increasingly legally:

```
http://spam.abuse.net (a spam overview)
http://www.cauce.org (anti-spam laws)
http://www.abuse.net (a complaint forwarding service)
```

We believe that spam is fundamentally not a technical problem, and only non-technical, probably legal, solutions will work in the long run.

Chapter 13
Mail, Mail, the Gang's All Here

· ·

· ·

*N*ow that you know all about how to send and receive e-mail, only one thing stands between you and a rich, fulfilling, mail-blessed life: You don't know many people with whom you can exchange mail. Fortunately, you can get yourself on lots of mailing lists, which ensures that you arrive every morning to a mailbox with 400 new messages. (Maybe you should start out with only one or two lists.)

Are You Sure That This Isn't Junk Mail?

The point of a mailing list is simple. The list has its own special e-mail address, and anything someone sends to that address is sent to all the people on the list. Because these people in turn often respond to the messages, the result is a running conversation.

Different lists have different styles. Some are relatively formal, hewing closely to the official topic of the list. Others tend to go flying off into outer space, topicwise. You have to read them for a while to be able to tell which list works which way.

Mailing lists fall into three categories:

✔ **Discussion:** Every subscriber can post a message. These lists lead to freewheeling discussions and can include a certain number of off-topic messages.

✔ **Moderated:** A moderator reviews each message before it gets distributed. The moderator can stop unrelated, redundant, or clueless postings from wasting everyone's time.

> ✔ **Announcement-only:** Only the moderator posts messages. Announcement mailing lists work well for publishing an online newsletter, for example.

Getting On and Off Mailing Lists

The way you get on or off a mailing list is simple: You send an e-mail message. Two general schools of mailing-list management exist: the *manual* and the *automatic*. Manual management is the more traditional way: Your message is read by a human being who updates the files to put people on or take them off the list. The advantage of manual management is that you get personal service; the disadvantage is that the list maintainer may not get around to servicing you for quite a while if more pressing business (such as her real job) intervenes.

These days, lists are commonly maintained automatically, which saves human attention for times when things are fouled up. The most widely used automatic mailing managers are families of programs known as LISTSERV, Majordomo, and ListProc, which get their own sections later in this chapter.

Talking to a human being

To get on or off a manually managed list, you send a nice note to the human being who manages the list. Suppose that you want to join a list for fans of James Buchanan (the 15th President of the United States and the only one who never married, in case you slept through that part of history class), and the list's name is buchanan-lovers@gurus.com. The list manager's address is almost certainly buchanan-lovers-request@gurus.com. In other words, just add -request to the list's address to get the manager's address. Because the list is maintained by hand, your request to be added or dropped doesn't have to take any particular form, as long as it's polite. Please add me to the buchanan-lovers list does quite well. When you decide that you have had all the Buchanan you can stand, another message saying Please remove me from the buchanan-lovers list works equally well.

Messages to request addresses are read and handled by human beings who sometimes eat, sleep, and work regular jobs as well as maintain mailing lists. It can take a day or so to be added to or removed from a list, and, after you ask to be removed, you often get a few more messages before they remove you. If it takes longer than you want, be patient. *Don't* send cranky follow-ups — they just cheese off the list maintainer.

Subscribing from the Web

You can subscribe to a lot of mailing lists directly from Web sites. Generally you enter your e-mail address in a box on a Web page, click a Send or Subscribe button, and you're on the list. This is often more convenient than e-mailing a list manager.

But before you subscribe, be sure there is some way to get *off* the list, an option that some marketing-oriented outfits neglect to provide.

TIP

How to avoid looking like an idiot

Here's a handy tip: After you subscribe to a list, don't send anything to it until you have been reading it for a week. Trust us — the list has been getting along without your insights since it began, and it can get along without them for one more week.

You can learn what topics that people really discuss, the tone of the list, and so on. It also gives you a fair idea about which topics people are tired of. The classic newcomer gaffe is to subscribe to a list and immediately send a message asking a dumb question that isn't really germane to the topic and that was beaten to death three days earlier. Bide your time, and don't let this situation happen to you.

The number-two newcomer gaffe is to send a message directly to the list asking to subscribe or unsubscribe. This type of message should go to the list manager or to a LISTSERV, Majordomo, or ListProc address, where the list maintainer (human or robotic) can handle it, *not* to the list itself, where all the other subscribers can see that you screwed up.

To summarize: The first message you send, to join a list, should go to a something-request

or LISTSERV or majordomo or listproc address, *not* to the list itself. After you have joined the list and read it for a while, *then* you can send messages to the list.

Be sure to send plain text messages to mailing lists. Don't send "enriched" formatted messages, attachments, or anything other than text. Many e-mail programs don't handle non-text, and many people don't have the program they would need to open an attachment anyway. If you have a file you want to distribute on a mailing list, send a message inviting people interested in getting the file to e-mail you privately.

One last thing not to do: If you don't like what another person is posting (for example, some newbie is posting blank messages or "unsubscribe me" messages or is ranting interminably about a topic), don't waste everyone's time by posting a response on the list. The only thing stupider than a stupid posting is a response complaining about it. Instead, e-mail the person *privately* and tell him to stop, or e-mail the list manager and ask that person to intervene.

LISTSERV, the studly computer's mail manager

The BITNET network (a network of large computers, now mostly merged into the Internet) was set up so that the only thing it could do was ship files and messages from one system to another. As a result, BITNET users quickly developed lots and lots of mailing lists because no other convenient way, such as Usenet news, was available to stay in touch.

Because maintaining all those mailing lists was (and still is) a great deal of work, in order to manage the mailing lists, the BITNET crowd came up with a program called *LISTSERV,* which originally ran on great big IBM mainframe computers. (The IBM mainframe types have an inordinate fondness for eight-letter uppercase names, EVEN THOUGH TO MOST OF US, IT SEEMS LIKE SHOUTING.) Although only users on machines directly connected to BITNET could originally use LISTSERV, current versions have been improved so that anyone with an Internet address can use them. Indeed, LISTSERV has grown to the point that it is an all-singing, all-dancing mailing-list program with about 15 zillion features and options, almost none of which you care about.

Although LISTSERV is a little clunky to use, it has the huge advantage of being able to easily handle enormous mailing lists that contain thousands of members, something that makes many of the regular Internet mail programs choke. (LISTSERV can send mail to 1,000 addresses in about 5 minutes, for example, whereas that task would take the regular Internet `sendmail` program more like 1 hour.)

Urrp! Computers digest messages!

Some mailing lists are *digested.* No, they're not dripping with digital gastric juices — they're digested more in the sense of *Reader's Digest.* All the messages over a particular period (usually a day or two) are gathered into one big message with a table of contents added at the front. Many people find this method more convenient than getting messages separately, because you can easily look at all the messages on the topic at one time.

Some mail and newsreading programs give you the option of dividing digests back into the individual messages so that you can see them one at a time yet still grouped together. This option is sometimes known as *undigestifying,* or *exploding,* a digest. (First, it's digested, and then it explodes, sort of like a burrito.) Check the specifics of your particular mail program to see whether it has an option for digest-exploding.

You put yourself on and off a LISTSERV mailing list by sending an e-mail to LISTSERV@*some.machine.or.other*, where *some.machine.or.other* is the name of the particular machine on which the mailing list lives. This address — the address that includes "LISTSERV" as the username — is called the *administrative* address for the list. You send all administrative commands, like commands to get on or off the list, to the administrative address.

Because LISTSERV list managers are computer programs, they're rather simpleminded, and you have to speak to them clearly and distinctly, using standardized commands.

Suppose that you want to join a list called SNUFLE-L (LISTSERV mailing lists usually end with -L), which lives at bluesuede.org. To join, send to LISTSERV@bluesuede.org (the administrative address) a message that contains this line in the text of the message (not the subject line):

```
SUB SNUFLE-L Roger Sherman
```

You don't have to add a subject line or anything else to this message — it's better not to, so as not to confuse the LISTSERV program. SUB is short for subscribe, SNUFLE-L is the name of the list, and anything after that is supposed to be your real name. (You can put whatever you want there, but keep in mind that it shows up in the return address of anything you send to the list.) You don't have to tell LISTSERV your e-mail address, which it can read from the automatically generated headers at the top of your message.

Shortly afterward, you should get back a chatty, machine-generated welcoming message telling you that you have joined the list, along with a description of some commands you can use to fiddle with your mailing-list membership. Usually, this message includes a request to confirm that you received this message and that it was really you who wanted to subscribe. Follow the instructions by replying to this message with the single word *OK* in the body of the message. This helps lists ensure that they aren't mailing into the void. If you don't provide this confirmation, you don't get on the list.

Keep the chatty, informative welcome message that tells you about all the commands you can use when you're dealing with the list. For one thing, it tells you how to get *off* the mailing list if it's not to your liking. We have in our mail program a folder called Mailing Lists in which we store the welcome messages from all the mailing lists we join.

After you're subscribed, to send a message to this list, mail to the list name at the same machine — in this case, SNUFLE-L@bluesuede.org. This address is called the *list address* (creatively enough), and it's *only* for messages to be distributed to the entire list. Be sure to provide a descriptive `Subject:` for the multitudes who will benefit from your pearls of wisdom. Within a matter of minutes, people from all over the world will read your message.

To get off a list, you again write to `LISTSERV@some.machine.or.other`, this time sending this line in the text of the message (not the subject line):

```
SIGNOFF SNUFLE-L
```

or whatever the list name is. You don't have to give your name again because after you're off the list, LISTSERV has no more interest in you and forgets that you ever existed.

Some lists are more difficult than others to get on and off. Usually, you ask to get on a list, and you're on the list. In some cases, however, the list isn't open to all comers, and the human list owner screens requests to join the list, in which case you may get some messages from the list owner to discuss your request to join.

To contact the actual human being who runs a particular list, the mail address is `OWNER-` followed by the list name (`OWNER-SNUFLE-L`, for example). The owner can do all sorts of things to lists that mere mortals can't do. In particular, the owner can fix screwed-up names on the list or add a name that for some reason the automatic method doesn't handle. You have to appeal for manual intervention if your mail system doesn't put your correct network mail address on the `From:` line of your messages, as sometimes happens when your local mail system isn't set up quite right, or if your address changes.

Stupid LISTSERV tricks

The people who maintain the LISTSERV program have added so many bells and whistles to it that it would take an entire book to describe them all, but this isn't that book. Here are a few stupid LISTSERV tricks. For each of them, you send a message to `LISTSERV@some.machine.or.other` to talk to the LISTSERV program. You can send several commands in the same message if you want to do two or three tricks at one time:

✔ **Temporarily stop mail:** Sometimes, you're going to be away for a week or two, and you don't want to get a bunch of mailing-list mail in the meantime. Because you're planning to come back, though, you don't want to take yourself off all the lists either. To stop mail temporarily from the SNUFLE-L mailing list, send this message:

```
SET SNUFLE-L NOMAIL
```

The list stops sending you messages. To turn the mail back on, send this message:

```
SET SNUFLE-L MAIL
```

✔ **Get messages as a digest:** If you're getting a large number of messages from a list and would rather get them all at one time as a daily digest, send this message:

```
SET SNUFLE-L DIGEST
```

Although not all lists can be digested (again, think of burritos), the indigestible ones let you know and don't take offense. If you later want individual messages again:

```
SET SNUFLE-L NODIGEST
```

✔ **Find out who's on a list:** To find out who subscribes to a list, send this message:

```
REVIEW SNUFLE-L
```

Some lists can be reviewed only by people on the list and others not at all. Because some lists are enormous, be prepared to get back an enormous message listing thousands of subscribers.

✔ **Get or not get your own mail:** When you send mail to a LISTSERV list of which you're a member, the list usually sends you a copy of your own message to confirm that it got there okay. Some people find this process needlessly redundant. ("Your message has been sent. You will be receiving it shortly." Huh?) To avoid getting copies of your own messages, send this message:

```
SET SNUFLE-L NOACK
```

To resume getting copies of your own messages, send this one:

```
SET SNUFLE-L ACK
```

✔ **Get files:** Most LISTSERV servers have a library of files available, usually documents contributed by the mailing-list members. To find out which files are available, send

```
INDEX
```

To have LISTSERV send you a particular file by e-mail, send this message:

```
GET listname filename
```

where *listname* is the name of the list and *filename* is the name of a file from the INDEX command. For example, to get the article about Social Security number security from the LISTSERV that hosts the privacy forum, send this message:

```
GET privacy prc.ssn-10 to LISTSERV@vortex.com
```

✔ **Find out which lists are available:** To find out which LISTSERV mailing lists are available on a particular host, send this message:

```
LIST
```

Note: Keep in mind that just because a list exists doesn't necessarily mean that you can subscribe to it. It never hurts to try.

✔ **Get LISTSERV to do other things:** Lots of other commands lurk in LISTSERV, most of which apply only to people on IBM mainframes. If you're one of these people or if you're just nosy, send a message containing this line:

```
HELP
```

You receive a helpful response that lists other commands.

An excellent choice, Sir

The other widely used mailing-list manager is *Majordomo.* It started out as a LISTSERV wanna-be for workstations but has evolved into a system that works quite well. Because of its wanna-be origins, Majordomo commands are almost but (pretend to be surprised now) not quite the same as their LISTSERV equivalents.

The administrative address for Majordomo lists (the address to which you send commands), as you may expect, is majordomo@*some.machine.or .other*. Majordomo lists tend to have long and expressive names. One of our favorites is called explosive-cargo, a funny weekly column written by a guy in Boston who is in real life a computer technical writer. To subscribe, because the list is maintained on host world.std.com, send this message to Majordomo@world.std.com:

```
subscribe explosive-cargo
```

Unlike with LISTSERV, you *don't* put your real name in the subscribe command. Like LISTSERV, Majordomo will probably send back a confirmation question to make sure that it was you who wanted to subscribe. Read the confirmation message carefully and follow its instructions, since Majordomo's confirmations are more complicated than LISTSERV's.

To unsubscribe:

```
unsubscribe explosive-cargo
```

After you have subscribed, you can send a message to everyone on the mailing list by addressing it to the list address — _listname@some.machine.or.other._ (You can't post messages to explosive-cargo because it's an announcements-only list: Only the guy in Boston who runs it is allowed to post messages.)

Stupid Majordomo tricks

Not to be outdone by LISTSERV, Majordomo has its own set of not particularly useful commands (as with LISTSERV, you can send in a single message as many of these as you want):

- To find out which lists at a Majordomo system you're subscribed to:

```
which
```

- To find all the lists managed by a Majordomo system:

```
lists
```

- Majordomo also can keep files related to its lists. To find the names of the files for a particular list:

```
index name-of-list
```

- To tell Majordomo to send you one of the files by e-mail:

```
get name-of-list name-of-file
```

- To find out the rest of the goofy things Majordomo can do:

```
help
```

- If you want to contact the human manager of a Majordomo system because you can't get off a list you want to leave or otherwise have an insoluble problem, send a polite message to owner-majordomo@ hostname. Remember that because humans eat, sleep, and have real jobs, you may not get an answer for a day or two.

ListProc — third-place list manager

Although ListProc is not as widely used as LISTSERV and Majordomo, its popularity is increasing because it is easier to install than LISTSERV, cheaper, and almost as powerful.

To subscribe to a ListProc mailing list, you send this message to the administrative address for the list, `listproc@`*`some-computer`*:

```
subscribe listname yourname
```

To subscribe to the (hypothetical) `chickens` **mailing list at** `gurus.com`, **for** example, you send this message to `listproc@gurus.com`:

```
subscribe chickens George Washington
```

(assuming that you were named after the same person that the first President of the United States was).

To get off the mailing list, send this message to the same address:

```
signoff listname
```

You don't have to provide your name — the ListProc program should already know it.

After you have subscribed to the list, you can send messages to everyone on the list by addressing e-mail to the list address, *`listname`*`@`*`some-computer`* (`chickens@gurus.com`, **for example**).

To find out other things ListProc can do, send the message `help` to `listproc@`*`whatever`*, **where** *`whatever`* is the name of the computer on which the ListProc mailing list lives.

LISTSERV, ListProc, and Majordomo: They could have made them the same, but n-o-o-o-o

Because LISTSERV, ListProc, and Majordomo work in sort of the same way, even experienced mailing-list mavens get their commands confused. Here are the important differences:

✔ The address for LISTSERV is `LISTSERV@`*`hostname`*, the address for Majordomo is `majordomo@`*`hostname`*,

and the address for ListProc is `listproc@`*`hostname`*.

✔ To subscribe to a LISTSERV or ListProc list, send `sub` or `subscribe` followed by the list name followed by your real name. To subscribe to a Majordomo list, just send `subscribe` and the list name.

Sending messages to mailing lists

Okay, you're signed up on a mailing list. Now what? First, as we say a few pages back, wait a week or so to see what sort of messages arrive from the list — that way, you can get an idea of what you should or should not send to it. When you think that you have seen enough to avoid embarrassing yourself, try sending something in. That's easy: You mail a message to the list address, which is the same as the name of the list — buchanan-lovers@gurus.com or snufle-1@bluesuede.org or whatever. Keep in mind that because hundreds or thousands of people will be reading your pearls of wisdom, you should at least try to spell things correctly. (You may have thought that this advice is obvious, but you would be sadly mistaken.) On popular lists, you may begin to get back responses within a few minutes of sending a message.

Some lists encourage new subscribers to send in a message introducing themselves and saying briefly what their interests are. Others don't. Don't send anything until you have something to say.

After you watch the flow of messages on a list for a while, all this stuff becomes obvious.

Some mailing lists have rules about who is allowed to send messages, meaning that just because you're on the list doesn't automatically mean that any messages you send appear on the list. Some lists are *moderated:* Any message you send in gets sent to a human *moderator,* who decides what goes to the list and what doesn't. Although this process may sound sort of fascist, moderation can make a list about 50 times more interesting than it would be otherwise because a good moderator can filter out the boring and irrelevant messages and keep the list on track. Indeed, the people who complain the loudest about moderator censorship are usually the ones whose messages most urgently need to be filtered out.

Another rule that sometimes causes trouble is that many lists allow messages to be sent only from people whose addresses appear on the list. This rule becomes a pain if your mailing address changes. Suppose that you get a well-organized new mail administrator and that your official e-mail address changes from jj@shamu.pol.bluesuede.org to John.Jay@bluesuede.org, although your old address still works. You may find that some lists begin *bouncing* your messages (sending them back to you rather than to the list) because they don't understand that John.Jay@bluesuede.org, the name under which you now send messages, is the same as jj@shamu.pol.bluesuede.org, the name under which you originally subscribed to the list. Worse, LISTSERV doesn't let you take yourself off the list, for the same reason. To resolve this mess, you have to write to the human list managers of any lists in which this problem arises and ask them to fix the problem by hand.

Boing!

Computer accounts are created and deleted often enough and mail addresses change often enough that a large list always contains, at any given moment, some addresses that are no longer valid. If you send a message to the list, your message is forwarded to these invalid addresses, and a return message reporting the bad addresses is generated for each of them. Mailing-list managers (both human and computer) normally try to deflect the error messages so that they go to the list owner, who can do something about them, rather than to you. As often as not, however, a persistently dumb mail system sends one of these failure messages directly to you. Just ignore it because you can't do anything about it.

The Fine Points of Replying to Mailing-List Messages

Often, you receive an interesting message from a list and want to respond to it. When you send your answer, does it go *just* to the person who sent the original message, or does it go to the *entire list?* It depends, mostly on how the list owner set up the software that handles the list. About half the list owners set things up so that replies automatically go to just the person who sent the original message, on the theory that your response is likely to be of interest only to the original author. The other half set things up so that replies go to the entire list, on the theory that the list is a running public discussion. In messages coming from the list, the mailing-list software automatically sets the Reply-To: header line to the address to which replies should be sent.

Fortunately, you're in charge. When you start to create a reply, your mail program should show you the address to which it's replying. If you don't like the address it's using, change the address. Check the To: and Cc: fields to make sure that you're sending your message where you want.

While you're fixing the recipient's address, you may also want to fix the Subject: line. After a few rounds of replies to replies to replies, the topic of discussion often wanders away from the original topic, and it's a good idea to change the subject to better describe what is really under discussion.

Mailing lists versus Usenet news versus Web pages

Some mailing lists are "gatewayed" to Usenet newsgroups (see our Web site), which means that all the messages you would receive if you subscribed to the mailing list appear as items in the newsgroup and vice versa. Most gateways are two-way: Anything you mail to the list shows up also in the newsgroup, and anything you post as a news item also goes to the list. A few are one-way, usually because of sloppy gateway management, and many of them are moderated, which means that you have to mail any items to the human moderator, who filters out inappropriate messages. An increasing number of mailing lists are also available as Web pages, where you can search through both current messages and the list's archives of old messages.

Whether you get a particular list as mail or news is largely a matter of personal taste. The advantages of receiving lists as mail are that mail items tend to arrive faster than news items do (usually by only a few hours); mail items stick around until you explicitly delete them whereas news is deleted automatically after a few days; and some mail programs are more flexible than the newsreading programs. The advantages of receiving news are that items are collected in a newsgroup rather than mixed in with your mail; items are automatically deleted unless you save them, avoiding mailbox bloat if you don't read and clean up your mail every day; and news programs usually do a better job than mail programs of collecting threads of related messages so that you can read them in order.

If you don't care which way you get your stuff, get it as news because the load on both your local computer and the network in general is considerably lower that way.

Some Interesting Lists

Thousands of lists reside on the Internet — so many, in fact, that entire *books* have been written that just enumerate all the *lists*. To get you started, this section presents some lists we find interesting in addition to short descriptions of what they are. These addresses change relatively frequently, and we keep finding new and interesting lists. For our latest list of lists, check out our Web update, at http://net.gurus.com/lists. For a complete list of lists — thousands exist — check out one of the mailing list directory sites, such as the Liszt (bad pun) site, at http://www.liszt.com.

If you don't have access to the Web, send e-mail to lists@gurus.com, and we'll send you back our current list. If you have a favorite list you want to share, send us mail at list-suggestions@gurus.com.

Each list in our list of lists is accompanied by at least one of the following codes, describing what kind of list it is:

- ✔ **Manual:** Manually maintained list. To get on or off or to contact the human who maintains the list, write to *whatever-request@sitename*. In the text of your e-mail, state what you want. A human being handles these requests.

- ✔ **LISTSERV:** A LISTSERV-type list. To get on or off, send e-mail to *listserv@sitename*. In the body of the message, use the LISTSERV commands detailed earlier in this chapter, as shown in this example:

```
sub LISTNAME yourname
signoff LISTNAME
```

  To contact the relevant human, send mail to *owner-whatever@ sitename*.

- ✔ **Majordomo:** A Majordomo list. To get on or off, send a "subscribe" or "unsubscribe" message to *Majordomo@sitename* asking to subscribe to the list name we give, as shown in this example:

```
subscribe listname
unsubscribe listname
```

- ✔ **ListProc:** A ListProc list. To get on or off, send a "subscribe" or "signoff" message to *listproc@sitename* asking to subscribe to the list name we give. Put your name after the list name, as shown in this example:

```
sub listname yourname
signoff listname
```

- ✔ **Moderated:** Moderated list. Messages are filtered by the human list owner (moderator).

- ✔ **News:** The list is also available as Usenet news, which is usually the better way to receive it (see the preceding sidebar, "Mailing lists versus Usenet news versus Web pages"). Although nearly all BITNET lists are also available as a special type of newsgroup, this list marks only lists available as regular news.

- ✔ **Digest:** Messages normally arrive as a digest rather than one at a time.

Risks Digest
Majordomo@csl.sri.com
Majordomo (list name risks) moderated, news, digest

This forum discusses risks to the public in computers and related systems. It covers the risks of modern technology, particularly of computer technology (lots of great war stories).

Privacy Forum Digest
LISTSERV@vortex.com
LISTSERV (list name PRIVACY) moderated

This running discussion of privacy in the computer age has lots of creepy reports about people and organizations you would never expect were snooping on you (ambulance drivers, for example).

Tourism Discussions
LISTSERV@VM.EGE.EDU.TR
LISTSERV (list name TRAVEL-L)

The TRAVEL-L list covers travel and tourism, airlines, guidebooks, places to stay — you name it. Because participants come from all over the world (the system host is in France), you get lots of tips you would never get locally.

The Jazz Lover's List
LISTSERV@brownvm.brown.edu
LISTSERV (list name JAZZ-L)

This friendly, laid-back, ongoing discussion makes no claim to staying on-topic but rather to creating a salon-type atmosphere in which "like-minded, intelligent people from diverse backgrounds" can make real connections.

Liberal Judaism
Listproc@shamash.org
Listproc (list name MLJ) moderated, digest

Nonjudgmental discussions of liberal Judaism (including Reform, Reconstructionist, conservative, and secular humanist), issues, practices, opinions, and beliefs take place here. Include your real first and last name in your request — such as `subscribe MLJ yourfirstname yourlastname`.

Kideo children's video
majordomo@gurus.com
Majordomo (list name kideo)

All about videos for children, suggestions, opinions, discussions. Run by one of the authors of this book, whose kids watch a lot of videos. Please, no Disney.

Chapter 14

Attention, Dick Tracy

● ●

In This Chapter

▶ Instant messages with ICQ

▶ Instant messages with AOL

▶ Lots of other instants

● ●

*I*nternet e-mail is pretty fast, usually arriving in less than a minute. But sometimes, that's just not fast enough. A new generation of *instant message* systems let you pop up a message on someone's screen in a matter of seconds. They also have *buddy lists* that watch to see when one of your buddies comes online so you know the instant you can instantiate an instant message to them. (Excuse us, this gives us a headache, just a moment while we get some instant coffee. Ahh, that's better.)

The good thing about instant messages is that you can stay in touch with people as fast as talking to them on the phone. The bad thing about them is that they also offer an unparalleled range of ways to annoy people. The AOL Instant Messenger, discussed later in this chapter, has about two features to send and receive messages, and about 12 features to reject, denounce, erase, and otherwise deal with unwanted messages. (This may say more about AOL users than the technology, of course.)

Which instant message system should I use?

Since the goal of all these systems is to stay in touch with your friends, use whichever one they use. If you're not sure who your friends are, AOL Instant Messenger is a good bet because it's easy to set up and automatically works with any AOL user, since it's the same system that AOL uses internally.

If you're really message-mad, you can run more than one system at the same time. While we were writing this chapter, we had ICQ, AOL Instant Messenger, and Yahoo Pager all running at once, which was an awful lot of blinking and flashing, but it did work.

ICQ

ICQ (which is supposed to sound like "I Seek You") is the current king of the instant messages. ICQ has about a quadrillion different features and options, but basically, you download and install ICQ, and set it up to get an eight-digit ICQ#, sort of like a phone number, that identifies you. Then you identify some buddies and start sending them instant messages and chatting with them.

As of late 1998, all the distributed ICQ software is officially "beta," that is, it may stop working at some point, they may change the rules, ask people to pay, or something. But with 20 million registered users, they aren't likely to make changes that will throw all those users off.

Installing ICQ

First, you have to get a copy of the ICQ software and install it on your computer. Unless you already have a copy (from a friend or a CD-ROM), visit the ICQ home page at `http://www.icq.com`, a page that, if there were an Academy Award for the Most Baffling and Cluttered Home Page, would be a shoo-in for a lifetime achievement award. Squint hard at the page and look near the upper-left corner for a blob called *Download.* Click that and you'll see a much more reasonable page on which there's an area for new users with links to versions for various kinds of computers. Click the link that applies to you and follow the links to the `Download.com` Web site where there is a green-and-white arrow that will, at long last, download the ICQ program. (The program is not all that big: Downloading it may take less time than all the rigmarole to find the download page.) Follow the instructions to install and start ICQ. After you install the software, you see a window similar to Figure 14-1, inviting you to get a new ICQ#.

Figure 14-1:
ICQ
Registration
Wizard,
ready to go.

The Registration Wizard invites you to enter lots of personal information, including e-mail address, name, nickname, city, age, phone number, home page, and more. Unless you're the kind of person who welcomes phone calls from strangers at odd hours of the night, we suggest you limit it to e-mail and name. You also have to choose a password to protect your number; all of the other options you can leave alone. When you're done, the ICQ program starts, with a small window on your screen, Figure 14-2.

Normally, ICQ runs all the time you're online. Minimize it using the standard minimize button, and it'll change the icon in the Windows toolbar and tell you over your computer's speakers when someone's trying to contact you.

Figure 14-2:
ICQ, ready
to go.

Getting buddy-buddy

Well, now you're set up with ICQ. Where are your friends? Click the bar in the ICQ window marked Add/Find Users and then click Main Search to find the Contact List Wizard, shown in Figure 14-3.

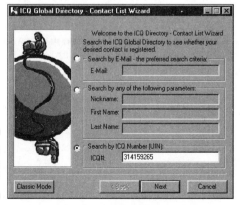

Figure 14-3:
Who ya
gonna call?

The best ways to search for someone are by ICQ# if you know it, or e-mail address. (We've found name and nickname searches to be unreliable.) If ICQ finds a match for the e-mail address or number, it displays the match(es). Click the one you want (if more than one match is displayed), click Next to add that person to your contact list. Normally you can add the contact immediately, but some ICQ users have set their accounts with a privacy option. In that case you need their permission, in which case ICQ pops up a window, Figure 14-4, in which you can type a note to plead your case.

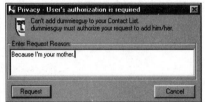

Figure 14-4:
Talk to me,
please.

If ICQ can't find a match, it offers to send the victim, uh, friend an e-mail extolling the wonders of ICQ and encouraging your friend to sign up. Use your discretion, please.

Once you add a person to your buddies list, the ICQ window displays a bar with the buddy's nickname. You can adjust your buddies list at any time — there's no need to identify everyone right away. To add more people, click the Add/Find Users bar again. To delete a person, click on the nickname and select Delete from the menu.

Flashing away

Once you have your buddies list set up, sending and receiving messages is easy.

When you receive a message from a person or from the ICQ system, the appropriate bar in the ICQ window flashes. Click the bar to see the message.

To send someone a message, click his bar and select Message from the menu. If the person is online, you can send a message right away. If not, ICQ offers to save a message until your friend shows up.

Chatting away

If you want to have an online conversation rather than just send a single message, click your buddy's name and select ICQ chat. Assuming that your friend is online, ICQ asks you to enter a short message to send to your friend saying why you want to chat.

At the receiving end, the sender's bar in the ICQ window flashes and ICQ says "Incoming chat request." Double-click the flashing bar to see the request message, and either click Accept to start chatting or click Decline to blow the sender off (you get your choice of excuses).

After both ends agree to chat, ICQ opens a chat window. The first time, ICQ asks how to arrange the window; accept its suggestion of split screen. Now each person can type and see what the other is typing. When you're done, just close the chat window.

Unless you are a very fast typist or your friend lives in Mongolia, the most effective thing to type is "What's your phone number?" and call the person on the phone.

The other 999.999 billion ICQ features

As well as messages and chats, ICQ can do a lot of other stuff:

- ✔ You can send files to and receive files from your buddies. The files go directly from one person's computer to the other, so it's pretty fast. But it should go without saying that you should never accept files from people you don't know; files can contain programs with viruses, offensive pictures, or other undesirable material.

- ✔ You can join group chats on various topics. Click Add/Find Users and look at some of the chat options.

- ✔ If you're really bored, you can send messages to randomly selected people. (This also means that randomly selected people may send you messages.)

- ✔ In Advanced Mode, you can set up profiles, adjust your status to tell people whether you want to be interrupted, send e-mail, try to place Internet phone calls, and otherwise engage in many time-consuming communication activities. The ICQ Web site has extensive documentation on all of this.

AOL Instant Messenger

AOL Instant Messenger (AIM for short) is a lot less fancy than ICQ. All it does is let you type messages back and forth. But it's easier to set up than ICQ, and enables you to talk directly to AOL users.

Setting up Instant Messenger

If you're an AOL user, you're already set up for instant messages. If not, you have to install the AIM program.

AOL, being the hyper-aggressive marketing organization it is, has arranged for AIM to be bundled in with a lot of other packages. In particular, if you have a copy of Netscape 4.5, you probably have AIM already. If you don't have it, visit http://www.newaol.com/aim, click the download button for your computer, and save the downloaded file somewhere on your computer. (C:\Windows\Temp is an okay place if you don't have another folder that you use for downloads.) Then run the downloaded program to install AIM. Normally, AIM runs in the background whenever you're online.

The first time you use AIM, you have to select a screen name, as shown in the left part of Figure 14-5. Click Sign On, and AIM asks whether you want to use an existing AOL screen name or select a new one. Just this once AIM starts your Web browser and displays a Web page; either enter your existing AOL screen name or choose a name (being creative so as not to collide with one of the 14,000,000 names already in use) and password, and enter your e-mail address. AOL, refreshingly, doesn't want any more personal information. The e-mail address you give has to be real: AOL sends a confirmation message to that address, and you must reply or your screen name is deleted.

After you sign up, enter your screen name and password into AIM and click Sign On. If you want to use AIM every time you're online, check the Save password and Auto-login boxes before signing on, and AIM will sign you on automatically in the future.

AIM for Internet users

First you create your buddy list, and then you can send messages.

In the AIM window, as in the right part of Figure 14-5, click the List Setup tab. You may want to make the window wider to make the tab visible. AOL provides three groups: Buddies, Family, and Co-Workers. To add a buddy, click the group to which you want to add it, click the Add Buddy button, and enter the buddy's screen name. If you know the e-mail address but not the screen name, click the Menu button and select Find a buddy⇨By e-mail address. Doing so starts a wizard that looks for that address and helps you add any screen names that match.

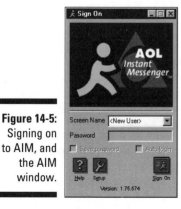

Figure 14-5:
Signing on
to AIM, and
the AIM
window.

After you select your buddies, click the Online tab. AIM displays the buddies who are currently online.

To send a message to someone, double-click the buddy's name to open a message window, type the message, and click the Send button. AIM pops up a window on the recipient's machine, and you and your buddy can type back and forth. When done, close the message window.

AIM for AOL users

AOL has buddy lists and instant messages included. You need only set them up and start messaging.

Go to keyword BUDDYLIST to set up your buddy list. You see the same three groups: Buddies, Family, and Co-Workers. Click one of the groups and then click the Edit button to edit the group. Type the screen name of each buddy and click the Add Buddy button. When you're done, click Save. Note that you can enter screen names of either AOL users or of Internet AIM users interchangeably.

To use your buddy list, go to keyword BUDDYVIEW, which shows a window similar to the AIM window. Double-click the buddy to whom you want to send a message, and AIM opens a message window. Type the message, click Send, and you can type back and forth with the other person. Click Cancel when you are done.

Incoming messages pop up a window on your screen. Click Respond to accept the message and start a conversation, or Cancel to reject it. After the conversation, click Cancel to close the window.

Buzz off

AOL evidently has a lot of ill-mannered users, because AIM has an elaborate system for warning and blocking users you don't like.

For Internet users, the AIM window has Warn and Block buttons. Click the Warn button if you get a message that you find moderately annoying to send a warning to the sender. With enough warnings (about five), a user is blocked from sending instant messages for a while. If you find a sender to be totally meretricious, click Block to refuse all messages from that person. You can further adjust who is able to send messages and who isn't via the Controls window; click Menu⇨Options⇨Edit Preferences and then the Controls tab. You can limit messages to people on your buddies list, permit specific people, or block specific people. You can also add or delete people from your block list.

For AOL users, go to BUDDYLIST and click Privacy Preferences. You can permit or block specific users, block all Internet AIM users, or block all users.

Dozens of Other Message and Paging Systems

Instant messages are very trendy, so there are plenty of other options for instant messages. Keep in mind that on each system you can only send messages to other people on the same system, so the situation is sort of like the telephone industry in the early 1900s, with many competing companies stringing wires, but no two companies connected together. (If you're wondering why there isn't a system on the Internet that connects everyone, there is. It's called e-mail. See Chapters 11, 12, and 13.)

- **Yahoo Pager.** Go to `http://www.yahoo.com` and click Pager in the list of subareas near the top of the screen. The Yahoo pager works as a Java applet in your Web browser, which means that it works on systems such as UNiX that have Web browsers but no ICQ or AIM program available.

- **Infoseek Instant Messaging.** Yet another instant message system. Visit `http://www.infoseek.com` and click the tiny Instant Messaging link at the bottom of the page to go to the software download page.

✔ **UNIX talk.** UNIX systems have had a simple but functional message system called "talk" for many years. (The system is actually called ntalk for New Talk, new as of about 1981.) All UNIX and Linux systems have a talk command, and freeware Wintalk (for Windows, from `http://www.elf.com/elf/wintalk`) and shareware Talk (for Mac, available at `http://www.tucows.com`) are available, too. The system is pretty basic, but if you have friends on UNIX workstations, it's the way to send them a message.

TIP

Some fairly obvious rules of messaging conduct

Sending someone an instant message is the online equivalent of walking up to someone on the street and starting a conversation. If it's someone you know, it's one thing; if not, it's usually an intrusion.

Unless you have a compelling reason, don't send instant messages to people you don't know who haven't invited you to do so. (ICQ's random message feature is the most likely such invitation.) Don't say anything that you wouldn't say in an analogous situation on the street. If someone's set her ICQ status to "urgent messages only," save your non-urgent messages for later or send them as e-mail.

For some reason, AOL is plagued with childish users who now and then send rude instant messages to strangers or unwilling acquaintances, which is why AIM has its Warn and Block buttons. Not only is it rude to do that, it's silly, since AOL has chat rooms full of people eager to converse on all sorts of topics, rude or otherwise.

Chapter 15

Let's Get Together and Chat

E-mail is swell, but for some people it's just not conversational enough. Do the recipients of your witty and insightful messages neglect to answer for hours or maybe even days (what? — they have something better to do?) while you sit around looking at your empty mailbox? Maybe online chat is for you.

Online chat lets you communicate instantly with another person anywhere who is logged on to the Net, by typing messages back and forth to each other. It's much faster than regular mail and considerably faster than e-mail. And you can chat with several people at one time. Unlike instant messages (covered in Chapter 14), chatting enables you to have a conversation, not just send quick notes back and forth.

Look Who's Chatting

Online chat is similar to talking on an old-fashioned party line or CB radio. In the infancy of the telephone system, people usually shared their phone line with other families, especially in rural America, where the cost of stringing telephone lines was expensive. Everyone on the party line could join in any conversation, offering hours of nosy fun for people with nothing better to do (of whom there were a lot)! Today, people often arrange conference calls to have several people all talk together.

Chatting is similar to a conference call except that rather than talk, you type on your keyboard what you want to say and read on-screen what other people are saying. Although all the people participating in the chat can be typing at one time, each person's contribution is presented on-screen in order of its receipt, identified by the name of the person who typed it. After you type what you want to say, it appears on the screen of general conversation and is identified by your screen name.

You can chat in two main ways:

- ✔ *Channels,* which resemble an ongoing conference call with a bunch of people. After you join a channel, you can read on-screen what people are saying and then add your own comments just by typing them and pressing Enter.
- ✔ *Direct connection,* which is a private conversation between you and another person connected to a chat system.

Who are those guys?

The people who are chatting at any particular time are organized into groups referred to as *rooms,* or *channels.* Which groups are available when you begin to chat depends on how you're connected to the Internet. If you use America Online, or AOL (where the groups are called rooms), you chat with other AOL users. WebTV users have WebTV's Chat City. Users with PPP accounts talk to other people using the Internet's IRC (Internet Relay Chat) system — see "Chatting via IRC" at the end of this chapter.

Each channel has a name; with luck, the name is an indication of what the chatters there are talking about or what they have in common. Some channels have names such as #chat, and the people there are probably just being sociable.

Who am I?

No matter which chat facility you're using, you should know that most people select a *screen name,* or *nickname,* to use before they join a group. Other members of the group know you by your screen name, a temporary name often chosen to be unique, colorful, or clever and used as a mask. The choice of a screen name is good for only the duration of a chat session. If you join a group and have a nice chat with someone named DrNo, the next time you see that name, you have no guarantee that it's the same person. This anonymity can make chatting a place to be careful. On the other hand, one of the attractions of chatting is meeting new and interesting people. Many warm and wonderful friendships have evolved from a chance meeting in a chat room.

When you join a group and begin chatting, you see the screen names of the people who are already there and a window in which the current conversation goes flying by. If the group is friendly, somebody usually sends you a welcome message because everyone is notified when you join the group.

As in real life, a room full of strangers can have people you don't like much. Because it's possible to be fairly anonymous on the Internet, some people act boorish, vulgar, or crude. So you should be careful (to put it mildly!) about letting your children chat unsupervised. When you're new to chat, you may accidentally visit some disgusting places, although you'll find out how to avoid them and find rooms that have useful, friendly, and supportive conversations.

Your First Chat Room

Your first time in a chat room can seem stupid or daunting. Here are some of the things you can do to get through your first encounters:

✔ Remember that when you enter a chat room, a conversation is probably already in progress. You don't know what went on before you arrived.

✔ Wait a minute or two to see a page full of exchanges so that you can understand some of the context before you start writing.

✔ Start by following the comments of a single screen name. Then follow the people that person mentions or who reply to that person.

✔ After you can follow one thread, try picking up another. It takes practice to get the hang of it.

✔ AOL and some IRC programs can highlight the messages from selected people. This can make things easier to follow.

✔ You can also indicate people to ignore. Messages from these chatters no longer appear on your screen, though other members' replies to them do appear.

✔ Scroll up to see older messages if you have to, and remember that after you have scrolled up, no new messages appear until you scroll back down.

Figure 15-1 shows a chat in progress. Fritz is asking a German group about a phrase.

Figure 15-1:
English chat
in progress
in the
#german_chat
room.

```
#german_chat [+tnl 45]: NEUE HOMEPAGE!!! http://193.17...
                                          @NoRegret2
                                          @X
                                          fl¥eR3Ø3
                                          fritz
*** Now talking in #german_chat          michael_g
<fritz> hi.  Can I ask a question in      QFrankgb
   English?                               woermi
<woermi> ja
<NoRegret2> sure
<NoRegret2> but we answer in german ;)
<fritz> I remember from a long ago
   time, the phrase "Rostkartoffeln
   Uerhaltnis".  Is that accurate?
```

Online etiquette

Chatting etiquette is not that much different from e-mail etiquette, and common sense is your best guide. Here are some additional chatting tips:

✔ The first rule of chatting is not to hurt anyone. A real person with real feelings is at the other end of the computer chat connection.

✔ The second rule is to be cautious. You really have no idea who the other person is. See "Safety first," later in this chapter.

✔ Read messages for a while to figure out what is happening before sending a message to a chat group. (Reading without saying anything is known as *lurking.* When you finally venture to say something, you're *de-lurking.*)

✔ Keep your messages short and to the point.

✔ Don't insult people, and don't use foul language.

✔ Create a profile with selected information about yourself. Most chat systems have provisions for creating profiles (personal information) that other members can access. Don't give out your last name, phone number, or address. We think that extra caution is necessary for kids: Insist that kids not enter their ages, hometowns, schools nor last names, phone numbers, or addresses.

✔ Although you don't have to tell everything about yourself in your profile, what you do say should be truthful.

✔ If you want to talk to someone in private, send him or her a message saying hi, who you are, and what you want.

✔ If the tone of conversation in one chat room offends you, try another. As in real life, you may run into more people out there you *don't* want to meet than people you *do.*

For more information about the history and art of meeting people online, see Philippe Le Roux's chapter, "Virtual Intimacy — Tales from Minitel and More" on our Web site at http://net.gurus.com/leroux.phtml.

Safety first

Here are some guidelines for conducting safe and healthy chats:

✔ Many people in chat groups lie about their occupations, ages, localities, and, yes, even genders. Some think that they're just being cute, some are exploring their own fantasies, and some are really sick.

✔ Be careful about revealing information that enables someone to find you personally — such as where you live or work or your phone number. This information includes your last name, phone number, mailing address, and schools your kids attend.

✔ Never give your password to anyone. No one should ever ask you for it. If someone does, don't respond, but do tell your service provider about the request. (We once received a message saying, "There's been a serious threat to security, and we need your password to help determine the problem." If you ever get a message like that — anytime you're online — it's a fake.)

✔ If your chat service offers profiles and a person without a profile wants to chat with you, be extra cautious.

✔ If you're a child, never, ever meet someone without your parents. Do not give out personal information about yourself or any member of your family, even when you're offered some sort of prize for filling out a form.

✔ If your children use chat, realize that others may try to meet them. Review the guidelines in this list with your kids before they log on.

If you choose to meet an online friend in person, use at least the same caution that you would use in meeting someone through a newspaper ad:

✔ Don't arrange a meeting until you have talked to a person a number of times, including conversations at length by telephone over the course of days or weeks.

✔ Meet in a well-lit public place.

✔ Bring a friend along, if you can. If not, at least let someone know what you're doing and agree to call that person at a certain time (for example, a half-hour) after the planned meeting time.

✔ Arrange to stay in a hotel if you travel a long distance to meet someone. Don't commit yourself to staying at that person's home.

Chat abbreviations and smileys

Many chat abbreviations are the same as those used in e-mail, as described in Chapter 11. Because chat is live, however, some are unique. We've also listed some common *emoticons* (sometimes called smileys) — funky combinations of punctuation used to depict the emotional inflection of the sender. (If at first you don't see what they are, try tilting your head down to the left.) Table 15-1 shows you a short list of chat abbreviations and emoticons:

Table 15-1	Chat Shorthand
Abbreviation	*What It Means*
AFK	Away from keyboard
A/S/L	Age/sex/location (response may be 35/f/LA)
BAK	Back at keyboard
BBIAF	Be back in a flash
BBL	Be back later
BRB	Be right back
BTW	By the way
GMTA	Great minds think alike
IM	Instant message
IMHO	In my humble opinion
IMNSHO	In my not so humble opinion
J/K	Just kidding
LTNS	Long time no see
LOL	Laughing out loud
M4M	Men seeking other men
NP	No problem
ROTFL	Rolling on the floor laughing
RTFM	Read the manual
TOS	Terms of service (the AOL member contract)
TTFN	Ta-ta for now!
WAV	A sound file
WB	Welcome back
WTG	Way to go!
:D	A smile or big grin
:) or :-)	A smile
;)	A wink
{{{{bob}}}}	A hug for Bob
:(or :-(	Frown
:'(	Crying
:~~(	Crying
0:)	Angel

Abbreviation	What It Means
}:>	Devil
:P	Sticking out tongue
:P~~	Drooling
***	Kisses
<——	Action marker (<——eating pizza, for example)

In addition to the abbreviations in the table, chatters sometimes use simple shorthand abbreviations, as in "If u cn rd ths u r rdy 4 chat."

Trouble city

Some people act badly online while hiding behind the anonymity that chat provides. You have four good options and one bad option when this situation happens:

- ✔ Go to another chat room. Some rooms are just nasty. You don't have to hang around.

- ✔ Pay no attention to the troublemaker, and just converse with the other folks.

- ✔ Make offenders disappear from your screen. On AOL, double-click the jerk's screen name in the room list and then click the Ignore box. On CompuServe, you can add people to your "Prohibited List" — a list of people whose comments you will never see. Choose Access⇨ Preferences from the menu bar and then choose the Chat tab to get to the list.

- ✔ Complain to the individual's service provider. This technique is most effective on the value-added services. See "Calling the AOL cops," later in this chapter.

- ✔ (The bad option.) Respond in kind, which just gives the offender the attention he (it's usually a he) wants and may get *you* kicked off your service.

Let's Chat

Starting to chat on the commercial online providers, such as AOL, is easy because chat service is one of their major attractions. In this section, we first cover chatting with this type of provider, and then we discuss chatting using *Internet Relay Chat (IRC)*, the Internet's chat service.

AOL users can participate in IRC too, as well as in AOL's own chat service.

Chatting on AOL

When you chat on AOL, you have a conversation with other AOL users. This feature, one of the most popular at AOL, may be why AOL is the largest value-added provider. Only AOL members can participate in the AOL chat rooms; the groups accessible to IRC networks are not available as AOL chat rooms.

You get started chatting in America Online 4.0 by clicking the People icon on the toolbar and choosing People Connection or by typing the keyword CHAT. Then click the Chat Now icon.

You're then in an AOL "lobby room." You see two windows, a larger one in which conversation is taking place and a smaller one that lists the people (screen names) in this room. If you're one of those people who just has to say something when you enter a crowded room, type something in the bottom area of the conversation window and click Send. In a few seconds, your comment is displayed in the window.

AOL limits the number of people in a room to 23, so when a room is full and a new user wants to join in, a new (similar) room is automatically created.

Look who's here

If you want to know something about the other occupants of the room, double-click one of their names in the window labeled "people here." A little box pops up that enables you to do one of several things:

- **Ignore:** If you check this box, no messages from this user are displayed on-screen. This technique is one way to stop receiving messages from annoying people.

- **Get Profile:** Click this button to retrieve the profile of this user. A *profile* is a list of information a user has supplied about herself. You have no guarantee that a profile has any true facts in it.

- **Send Message:** Click to send an instant mail message to this user. It's sort of like whispering in his ear. If someone sends you such a message (an Instant Message or IM), that message appears in a small window. You can ignore it or respond with a message of your own. The two of you can keep a running conversation going as long as you want.

"Who am I, and what am I doing here?"

You're identified by your screen name, the name you used when you signed on to the service. Many people use, for privacy reasons, a different screen name when they're chatting. AOL lets each account use as many as five different screen names, as long as no other AOL user is already using it.

One of the screen names is the master screen name, which can never be changed. If you want to add or change other screen names, you must log on to AOL under the master screen name. After you've established other screen names and passwords, you can log on to AOL by using the alternative name. Each screen name has a separate mailbox. You can use screen names for either different family members or different personalities: for example, your business self and your private self.

To set your profile, the information that other users can see about you when you're chatting, click the Member Directory button under the People Here window or go to keyword PROFILE. A box is displayed in which you can search the AOL membership list for names you may know. In this window is a button labeled My Profile. If you click this button, you can set or modify all your own profile settings.

Other public rooms

You probably won't find much conversation of interest in the lobby room you were thrown into when you joined the chatters. Pressing the Find a Chat button shows you the Find a Chat window with a list of the public chat rooms that are available. Two windows are displayed; the left one shows the room categories. When you double-click a category, the right window shows the room names in that category along with the number of current occupants in that room.

The room categories are mostly self-explanatory:

- **Town Square:** Rooms with a restaurant, bar, or coffeehouse flavor
- **Art & Entertainment:** Hollywood, music, book, and trivia themes
- **Friends:** People who like to talk
- **Life:** All sorts of lifestyles and age groups
- **News, Sports, Finance:** What you would expect
- **Places:** Major metropolitan areas
- **Romance:** Boy meets girl, in all combinations
- **Special Interests:** Hobbies, pets, cars, and religion
- **Countries:** Germany, United Kingdom, Canada, France, and Japan

Figure 15-2 shows a chat taking place in the Boston room. Everything you type in the little box at the bottom, next to the Send button, is part of the conversation. You can either press the Enter key after typing your message or click Send. When you want to leave a room, click List Chats, find another room, and join it. Or you can close the window of the chat room to get out of the AOL People Connection.

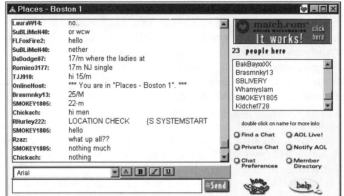

Figure 15-2:
Chatting in
the Boston
room.

Member rooms

In the Find a Chat window, click the button labeled "member chats" and the list of rooms switches over to the member rooms. Anyone can create a member room, and so can you, by clicking the Start Your Own Chat button. These rooms have the same categories as the public rooms — they're usually silly, serious, or kinky.

Private chats

The names of private rooms, unlike public or member rooms, are not revealed. To join one, you have to know its name; that is, someone must invite you to join. When you click the Enter a Private Chat button in the Find a Chat window, you're asked to name the room that you want to join. If it doesn't exist, one is created, and you're the sole occupant.

Private rooms enable people to talk more intimately — there's little danger of a stranger popping in. Two (or more) people can agree to create a private room and meet there. Private rooms have a somewhat sleazy reputation: If you get invited to one, you should be careful about guarding your privacy. Remember that what the other persons are saying about themselves may not be true.

Calling the AOL cops

Another button under the "people here" window is labeled Notify AOL. If you think that someone is violating the AOL terms of service (TOS) by asking you for your password or credit card number, using abusive language, or otherwise behaving badly, you can and should report them to AOL. When you press the Notify AOL button, a window pops up to help you gather all the information you want to report: the chat category and room you were in, the offensive chat dialog pasted into a window, and the offender's screen name, for example. You can then send the report to AOL, and it promises to look at it within 48 hours.

Because of this policing and the power of AOL to terminate (permanently) the accounts of people who play without the rules, the AOL chat rooms have a deserved reputation for safety and for being a good place to play. That AOL has so many subscribers who like chat means that you have a good chance of finding a chat room that meets your needs.

Chatting via WebTV

Chapter 18 tells you how to navigate around the WebTV pages. WebTV offers easy access to chat rooms from the WebTV home page. Along the left edge of the home page are several buttons in a stack, called a *sidebar*. Click the Community button in the stack and then the selection labeled Chat to display the list of rooms. WebTV offers a small list of rooms called Chat City. The rooms New2TalkCity and New2Internet are good places to start. Alternatively, you can click Go To in the sidebar to connect to any IRC server and room, as long as you know their names.

To enter a chat room from the Chat City page, click the room name. The upper-right corner of the screen displays the room's conversation, and the left side of the screen has a new sidebar. In the box below the conversation window you can enter your contribution to the conversation. Click Send or press Enter on your keyboard to send your comment to the room.

As other people enter and leave the room, you see notes in italics in the conversation window. You can find out who else is in the room by typing /whois in the box. WebTV lists the current occupants directly in the conversation window.

You leave a room by going to the sidebar to return to the Chat page or to a previous page.

Whisper in my ear

While you're in a chat room, you can send a private message by clicking Whisper in the sidebar. A new window pops up with a list of all the people in the room. You select the person or persons you want to receive your private message and then type the message. When you send it, the message appears in the conversation window, and the recipient is indicated in parentheses:

KoolKatz (to Ignez): Do you like Muenster?

Restricting chatting

When you set up sub-accounts from your WebTV master account, you can restrict the sub-account from using the chat facilities. If you're a parent, this restriction may make sense when you're setting up accounts for your children. Because each account can have its own password, it's easy to keep your children from using the master account.

Chatting via IRC

IRC (Internet Relay Chat) is available from most Internet providers as well as from AOL. To use IRC, you have to install an IRC client program on your computer. An IRC client (or just *IRC program*) is another Internet program, like your Web browser or e-mail program, and freeware and shareware programs are available for you to download from the Net. If you use Windows, use a Winsock-compatible program; if you use a Mac, use a MacTCP-compatible program.

Two of the best shareware IRC programs are the following:

- ✔ **mIRC** for Windows
- ✔ **Ircle** for the Macintosh

You can find these IRC programs, along with others, at shareware Web sites, such as TUCOWS (`http://www.tucows.com`), or at the mIRC home page (`http://www.mirc.co.uk`) and the Ircle home page (`http://www.amug.org/~ircle`).

The information in Chapter 16 can help you download and install the IRC client program. For more detailed information about setting up mIRC, point your browser to `http://www.mirc.com`. You can also find a great deal of useful information about IRC there.

Although most of our examples are from mIRC, Ircle is very similar. You can read the Ircle Help file by choosing Help from the Apple menu.

Check with your Internet provider for any additional information you may need to use IRC. If you have a direct link to the Internet, ask your system administrator whether the link supports IRC.

Firing up IRC

To start chatting using IRC, start up your IRC program. If you're using a PPP account, double-click the program's icon. From a UNIX shell Internet provider that offers IRC, type **ircii** or **irc** at the UNIX prompt.

Getting connected

To use IRC, your IRC client program has to connect to an *IRC server* — an Internet host computer that serves as a switchboard for IRC conversations. Although dozens of IRC servers are available, many are full most of the time and may refuse your connection. You may have to try several servers, or the same one dozens of times, before you can connect.

When you're choosing a server, pick one that's geographically close to you (to minimize response lag, as explained in the following sidebar, "Lags and netsplits") and on the IRC network you want.

To connect to a server:

✔ In mIRC, choose File⇨Setup (or press Alt+E) to display the mIRC Setup window, and then click the IRC Servers tab. When you start mIRC, it gives the Setup command for you automatically, so you see the mIRC Setup window right away. Double-click a server on the list to attempt to connect to it.

✔ In Ircle, choose File⇨Preferences⇨Startup. Select a server and then choose File⇨Save Preferences.

At peak times, the servers can be extremely busy. If at first you don't connect, try, try again.

Choosing a network

IRC servers are organized into networks. Although servers within each network talk to each other, servers on one IRC network don't connect to servers on other networks. Someone on EFnet can't talk to someone on Undernet, for example.

The four biggest networks and their home pages are shown in this list (in descending order):

✔ **EFnet:** http://www.irchelp.org

It's the original network of servers and has the most users.

✔ **Undernet:** http://www.undernet.org

✔ **IRCnet:** http://www.funet.fi/~irc

✔ **DALNet:** http://www.dal.net

Most people on IRC eventually develop a preference for one network. It's usually the one where their friends hang out.

Lots of smaller IRC networks exist. Here are some, with the addresses of Web pages that have more information about them:

✔ **Kidsworld:** http://www.kidsworld.org

✔ **StarLink:** http://www.starlink.org

If you use mIRC, you can find a list of servers it knows about by choosing File⇨Setup (or pressing Alt+E) and clicking the tab labeled IRC Servers. Because each server entry notes its network and location, you can easily choose one near you.

Commanding your IRC

You control what is happening during your chat session by typing IRC commands. All IRC commands start with the slash character (/). You can type IRC commands in upper- or lowercase or a mixture — IRC doesn't care. If you use the mIRC client program, many commands are available directly from the menu or by clicking or double-clicking items you see in the mIRC window.

If anyone ever tells you to type in IRC any commands you don't understand, *don't do it — ever.* You can unwittingly give away control of your IRC program and even your computer account to another person. (No, we don't tell you the commands!)

The most important command for you to know gets you out of IRC:

```
/quit
```

The second most important command gives you an online summary of the various IRC commands:

```
/help
```

Here are a few of the most useful IRC commands:

- ✔ **/admin *server*:** Displays information about a server.

- ✔ **/away:** Tells IRC that you will be away for a while. You don't have to leave this type of message; if you do, however, it's displayed to anyone who wants to talk to you.

- ✔ **/clear:** Clears your screen.

- ✔ **/join: *channel*:** Joins a channel. See "Group chat" later in this chapter.

- ✔ **/leave:** Leaves a channel. Typing /part does the same thing.

- ✔ **/me:** Sends a message that describes what you're doing and is used to punctuate your conversation with a description of gestures. If you're Mandrake, for example, and type /me gestures hypnotically, other users see *Mandrake gestures hypnotically on-screen.

- ✔ **/topic *whatwearetalkingabout*:** Sets the topic message for the current channel.

- ✔ **/who *channel*:** Lists all the people on *channel*. If you type /who *, you see displayed the names of the people on the channel you're on.

- ✔ **/whois *name*:** Lists some information about the user *name*. You can use your own name to see what other users can see about you.

- ✔ **/nick *newname*:** Changes your name to newname.

- ✔ **/ping *#channelname*:** Gives information about the lag (delay) between you and everyone on that channel.

✔ **/msg** *name message:* Sends a private message to *name* (only *name* can see it).

Remember: Lines that start with a slash are commands to the IRC program; everything else you type is conversation and gets put in the chat box.

If you use mIRC or Ircle, you can achieve most of the same effects controlled by IRC commands by choosing commands from the menu bar or clicking icons on the toolbar. These IRC commands work too, however, and some IRC programs don't have menu bar or toolbar equivalents.

Group chat

The most popular way to use IRC is through *channels.* Most channels have names that start with the # character. Channel names are not case-sensitive. Numbered channels also exist (when you type a channel number, you don't use the # character).

Thousands of IRC channels are available. You can find an annotated list of some of the best by visiting http://www.funet.fi/~irc/channels.html. Each channel listed there has its own linked home page that tells you much more about what that channel offers.

To find out how to see a list of channels, see the section "Channel surfing," later in this chapter.

Good channels to know about include the following:

✔ **#irchelp:** A place to ask questions about IRC

(Read the FAQ, which answers the most common questions, first: See the section "Getting more info," later in this chapter.)

✔ **#newbies:** All your IRC questions answered

✔ **#21plus: and #30plus:** Age-appropriate meeting places

✔ **#41plus:** A more mature channel (with many people on it younger than 41)

✔ **#teens:** For teenagers — chill and chat

✔ **#hottub:** A "rougher" meeting place

✔ **#macintosh:** Meeting place for Mac users

✔ **#windows95:** Meeting place for Windows users

✔ **#chat:** A friendly chat channel

✔ **#mirc:** A help channel for mIRC users

You can also try typing # followed by the name of a country or major city.

Channeling

You join a channel by typing the following line:

```
/join #channelname
```

To join the #dummies channel, for example, you type /join #dummies and press Enter. Don't forget the / before the command or the # before the channel name.

In mIRC, you can click the Channels Folder icon on the toolbar and then double-click one of the channels listed.

In Ircle, choose Command⇨Join from the menu.

After you join a channel, everything you type that doesn't start with a slash (/) appears on the screen of everyone on that channel after you press Enter. The text of your messages is preceded by your nickname.

In mIRC, you can join several channels at a time. Each channel has its own window, with a list of the participants on the right side and the conversation on the left and with a box at the bottom in which you type your messages.

You leave a channel by typing

```
/leave
```

In mIRC, you can leave a channel by simply closing the window for that channel. In Ircle, choose Commands⇨Part from the menu.

Lags and netsplits

Two phenomena, lags and netsplits, are the bane of an IRCer's existence. A *lag* is the delay between the time you type a message and when it appears on other people's screens. Lags foul up conversations. Sometimes, one group of people on a channel are lagged while another group is not, and the first group's messages appear after delays of several minutes. You can check on the amount of time a message takes to get from you to another person and back again by typing the command **/ping nickname**.

A *netsplit* breaks the connection between IRC servers — the network of connected IRC servers gets split into two smaller networks. A netsplit looks like a bunch of people suddenly leaving your channel and then reappearing en masse sometime later. Although all the people who are connected to the IRC servers in one half of the network can chat among themselves, they can't communicate with the people connected to the IRC servers in the other half. Eventually (after minutes or hours), the two networks reconnect and the netsplit is over.

Channel surfing

To see available channels in mIRC, click the List channels icon on the toolbar. If you're looking for a particular channel name, type in the Match text box the text you're looking for. If you want to see channels with at least several people on them (rather than the hundreds of channels with one bored, lonely, or lascivious person waiting), type a number in the Min box. Then click Get List. Because the list of channels can be extremely long, you may have to wait a few minutes for the list to be displayed. If you want to see the channels listed in your Channels folder (the list of channels you visit frequently), click the Channels folder icon instead.

In any IRC program, you can find out all the public and private channels by typing the following command:

```
/list
```

Figure 15-3 shows an mIRC window after a /list command has been given. The window shows the channel name, number of current chatters, and the channel topic.

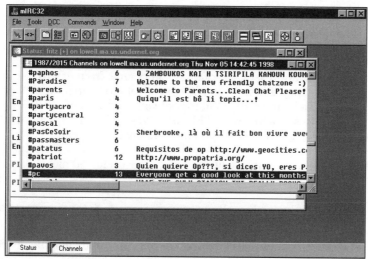

Figure 15-3:
A heap o' channels to choose from!

In Ircle, you choose Commands⇔List from the menu.

Before typing **/list** to see all of the available channels, type the following line:

```
/set hold_mode on
```

This phrase keeps the names from flying by so fast on-screen that you can't read them. Don't forget to type /set hold_mode off after you finish reading the list.

You can also limit the number of channels listed by typing

```
/list -min 8
```

Only channels with at least eight people on them are listed when you type this phrase.

In the listing, Pub indicates a public channel. You may see Prv, which means a private channel. The @ sign indicates a channel operator *(chanop)*, who is in charge of managing the goings-on of the channel.

Picking a nickname

Everyone using IRC needs a *nickname*. This name is unique within the network: No two people connected to the same IRC network can use the same nickname at the same time. If you attempt to connect to a network and your chosen nickname is already in use, you cannot join a channel. The name can be the same as the username in your e-mail address, although most people pick a different name. To choose a nickname, type the following command:

```
/NICK thenameyouwant
```

Nicknames can be as long as nine characters. Because common names will already be in use, obviously, you have to choose something distinctive.

Unlike e-mail addresses, nicknames can change from day to day. Whoever claims a nickname first on an IRC server gets to keep it for as long as she is logged in. Nicknames are good for only a single session on IRC. If you chatted with someone named ElvisPres yesterday and then run into someone named ElvisPres today, you have no guarantee that it's the same person.

If you use Ircle or mIRC, you can tell it your preferred nickname so that it doesn't ask you each time you run it:

- ✔ In Ircle, choose File➪Preferences➪Startup. Enter your name and then choose File➪Save Preferences.
- ✔ In mIRC, choose File➪Setup or press Alt+E and click the IRC Servers tab. mIRC lets you specify an alternative nickname also in case the first one is in use when you start.

To find out more about the person behind a nickname, type the following command:

```
/whois nickname
```

The two ways to find someone's nickname are to see it on a channel or to have another user reveal it to you.

Just between us

To send a message to someone whose nickname you know, type the following line:

```
/msg nickname whatyouwanttosay
```

This method becomes tiresome, however, for more than one or two lines of text. You can instead start a longer conversation by typing this line:

```
/query nickname
```

Now, whenever you type something that doesn't start with /, it appears on *nickname*'s screen, preceded by your nickname, immediately after you press Enter.

Your "private" conversation can go through many IRC servers, often in different countries, and the operators of any of these servers can log all your messages.

A more private way to chat is via Direct Client Connections, or DCC. You don't have to be on the same channel as the person you want to talk to; you just have to know the person's nickname. You type this line (assuming that you want to talk to Shirley):

```
/dcc chat shirley
```

When someone tries to start a DCC chat with you, mIRC asks whether you want to chat with the other person. If you click Yes, mIRC opens a window for the discussion. Your DCC chat window is just like a minichannel, with only two people in it.

You can also use DCC commands to send files to other people. For example, you can send a picture of yourself to a person you have just met. If someone offers to send you a file, however, consider declining unless you know the person. Unsolicited files can be unbelievably rude and disgusting, as well as dangerous because they may be infected with a virus.

Operating your own channel

Each channel has its own channel operator, or *chanop,* who can control, to some extent, what happens on that channel. In the list of nicknames on a channel, operators' nicknames are preceded by an at-sign (@). You can start your own channel and automatically become its chanop by typing this line:

```
/join #unusedchannelname
```

As with nicknames, whoever asks for a channel name first gets it. You can keep the name for as long as you're logged on as the chanop. You can let other people be chanops for your channel — just make sure that they're people you can trust. A channel exists as long as anyone is on it; when the last person leaves, the channel winks out of existence.

As chanop, you get to use special commands. The main one is /kick, which kicks someone off your channel, at least for the three seconds until he rejoins the channel. Kicking someone off is a thrill (although a rather small one), sort of like finding a penny on the sidewalk. People usually get kicked off channels for being rude or by sending so many garbage messages that they make the channel unusable.

Server operators manage entire servers and can kick unruly users off a server permanently.

Channel types

The following three types of channels are available in IRC:

- ✔ **Public:** Everyone can see them, and everyone can join.
- ✔ **Private:** Although everyone can see them, you can join them only by invitation.
- ✔ **Secret:** They don't show up by typing the /list command, and you can join them only by invitation.

If you're on a private or secret channel, you can invite someone else to join by typing the following:

```
/invite nickname
```

If you get an invitation from someone on a private or secret channel and want to join, you just type the following:

```
/join #invite
```

Reporting bad guys

Compared to AOL, IRC is a lawless frontier. Few rules, if any, exist. If things get really bad, you can try to find out an offender's e-mail address by using the /whois command. If you type the command

```
/whois nickname
```

you will receive a bundle of information about that person, including, perhaps, his e-mail address — say it's badguy@gurus.com. You can then send an e-mail complaint to postmaster at the same host name; in this example, postmaster@gurus.com. Don't expect much help, however.

What about CompuServe?

CompuServe practically invented online chat with its CB simulator in the 1970s and 1980s. But a series of bad decisions in the 1990s reduced CompuServe from the dominant online service to a weak also-ran, ending with it being sold to AOL.

CB simulator still works if you're a CompuServe member. We discuss it on our Web site at `http://net.gurus.com/irc`; click on CompuServe in the Table of Contents box.

Chapter 16

Swiping Files, Why and How

● ●

In This Chapter

▶ Why download?

▶ Using your Web browser to swipe files

▶ Finding out about FTP

▶ Using WS_FTP to swipe files

▶ Installing software you've swiped from the Net

● ●

*T*he Internet is chock full of computers, and those computers are chock full of files. What's in those files? Programs, pictures, sounds, movies, documents, spreadsheets, recipes, *Anne of Green Gables* (the entire book), you name it. Some of the computers are set up so that you can copy some of the files they contain to your own computer. That's only about 0.0001 percent of the total files on the Net, but it's still an awful lot of files with a lot of very useful stuff, most of it for free. In this chapter, we tell you how to find some of those files and how to copy and use them. For a list of the types of files you may want to download and what to do with them after you have them, see Chapter 21. As a free added bonus, we also tell you how to copy files from your own computer to another computer, most often a Web page you've just made to a *server* that makes it available to the rest of the Net.

Downloading means copying files from a computer Up There on the Internet "down" to your computer on your desk. *Uploading* is the reverse — copying a file from your computer "up" to a computer on the Internet.

You probably won't be surprised to hear that there are at least two different ways to download and upload files. *HTTP* is the HyperText Transfer Protocol that your Web browser uses to retrieve Web pages, which turns out to be just as good at retrieving any other kind of file. *FTP* stands for File Transfer Protocol, an older but still very popular way that computers transfer files across the Internet. FTP both downloads and uploads. HTTP in principle does both but in practice mostly downloads. You can also transfer files by using e-mail attachments to other e-mail users, but we don't discuss that here; see Chapter 12.

Getting Files over the Web

Getting files over the Web is simplicity itself. You probably have been doing it for ages and didn't even know. Every Web page, every icon or image on a Web page, every ornate Web background is a file. Every time you click a link or type a URL to go to a Web page, you're getting at least one file. (If it's a page with many graphics, you're getting many files, one per picture. Regardless of how many files it is, your Web browser manages the space it uses for automatically downloaded files so that it won't fill up your disk.)

Getting the picture

To download a picture over the Web, first display the picture in your Web browser. When you see on a Web page a picture that you want to save on your hard disk, right-click the picture. From the menu that appears, choose Save Image As or Save Picture As. Tell your browser where to save the picture. That's all it takes!

Graphics files have special filename extensions that identify what graphics format the file is in. When you download a picture, you can change the name of the file, but *don't* change the extension. See Chapter 21 for details.

Just because a picture is now stored on your hard disk doesn't mean that you own it. Most pictures on Web pages are copyrighted. Unless a picture comes from a site that specifically offers pictures as reusable "clip art," you have to get permission to use the picture for commercial purposes or even to upload it to your own noncommercial Web page.

Getting with the program

Downloading a program file over the Web is also easy — you click a link to it, frequently a link that says either "Download" or the name of the program. Your Web browser stops and asks you what to do with the file. If it's a program (a Windows EXE file or the like) or a ZIP file, the most reasonable thing for your browser to do is to save it to disk so that you can run it or unzip it later. If it's a ZIP file and you have WinZip (mentioned later in this chapter) installed, you can also tell the browser to run WinZip directly; we find that method less handy than it might seem.

If you're interested in downloading an Internet program, for example, you may go to TUCOWS, The Ultimate Collection of Windows Software, at http://www.tucows.com. After you're at the site, click links to choose a site near you, choose the operating system you use (Windows 3.1, Windows 95 or Windows 98, or the Mac), and choose the type of programs you want to download. TUCOWS displays a Web page like the one shown in Figure 16-1,

Try Now button

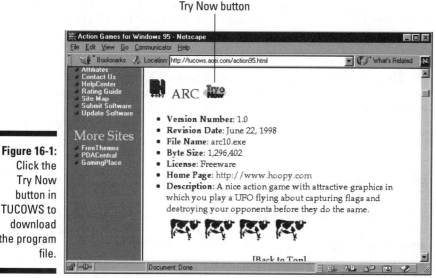

Figure 16-1:
Click the
Try Now
button in
TUCOWS to
download
the program
file.

with a list of programs available for downloading. To download a program file, just click the name of the program or the Try Now button.

To make absolutely sure that your browser downloads a file for which you have a Web link to the disk, rather than try to run it, display it, or otherwise get clever, hold down the Shift key while you click the link.

Getting other files

To download other types of files — sound files, video files, whatever — you follow the same steps as for downloading a program. Find a Web page that contains a link to the file you want. Then click the link for the file you want and tell your browser where to store it.

How FTP Works

Being able to download files from the Web is great, but not all files are available over the Web. You need FTP — File Transfer Protocol.

Transferring a file via FTP requires two participants: an *FTP client program* and an *FTP server program.* The FTP client is the program that we, the Joe Six-Pack Users of the world, run on our computers. The FTP server is the program that runs on the huge mainframe somewhere (or, these days, likely as not, on a PC under someone's desk) and stores tens of thousands of files.

The FTP server holds an online library of files. The FTP client can *upload* (send) files to the FTP server or, more commonly, *download* (receive) files from the FTP server.

Thousands of publicly accessible FTP servers exist; they store millions of files. Many of the files are freeware or shareware programs. Some FTP servers are so popular that they can't handle the number of file requests they receive. When FTP servers are inundated, other FTP servers, called *mirrors,* which have copies of the same files, are set up to handle the over-flow traffic.

Hello, this is anonymous

To use an FTP server, you have to log in with a username and password. What happens if you don't have an account on the FTP server machine? No problem, if it's a publicly accessible FTP server. You log in as `anonymous` and type your e-mail address as your password. Voilà! You have access to lots of files! This method of using public FTP servers is called *anonymous FTP.* There's nothing sleazy about it; public FTP sites expect you to use anonymous FTP to download files.

When is a file not a file?

When it's a text file. The FTP definition specifies six different types of files, of which only two types are useful: ASCII and binary. An *ASCII* file is a plain text file; a *binary* file is anything else. FTP has two modes: ASCII and binary (the latter also called *image* mode), to transfer the two types of files. When you transfer an ASCII file between different types of computers that store text files differently, ASCII mode automatically adjusts the file during the transfer so that the file is a valid text file when it's stored on the receiving end. (Because Macs, Windows, and UNIX all have slightly different conven-tions for storing text files, this automatic conversion can save a great deal of hassle.) A binary file is left alone and transferred verbatim.

Note that a document from Microsoft Word, WordPerfect, or other word processing program is *not* a text file for FTP purposes because the file contains non-text formatting codes. Text here means plain unadorned text, like you'd view with Simpletext on a Mac or Notepad on a Windows machine.

Getting your FTP client

If you want to get files by FTP, you need an FTP client program. Luckily, you have several excellent ways to do so:

A few anonymous FTP tips

Some FTP servers limit the number of anonymous users or the times of day that anonymous FTP is allowed. You may be refused access, but don't gripe about it — no law says that the owner of the system has to provide any access at all.

Don't store *(upload)* files on the FTP server unless the owner invites you to do so. A directory called INCOMING or something similar is sometimes available in which you can put stuff.

Some FTP servers allow anonymous FTP only from host computers that have names. That is, if you try to FTP anonymously from a host that has a number but no name, these hosts don't let you in. This problem occurs most often with PPP dial-up accounts, which, because they generally offer no services that are useful to other people, don't always have names assigned. If you have this problem, complain to your provider, who can fix it easily.

✔ **Use your Web browser.** Most browsers can handle anonymous FTP for downloading files (no anonymous uploading — you probably didn't want to do that anyway). See the next section, "Your Web Browser Is an FTP Client, Too."

✔ **With a PPP account, you can use a Winsock or MacTCP FTP program.** The most popular freeware FTP program that's Winsock-compatible is WS_FTP, and you find out how to use it in this chapter (in the section "Hard-Core FTP-ing By Using WS_FTP"). If you have a Mac, you can use a shareware program called Fetch. These programs can handle both the uploading and downloading of files by using both anonymous FTP or private accounts on an FTP server.

✔ **If you use America Online (AOL), it's easy to get files via anonymous FTP.** Use the keyword **ftp**. See the section in Chapter 17 about grabbing files from FTP servers.

Your Web Browser Is an FTP Client, Too

To get your Web browser to transfer files by using FTP, you use a special kind of URL: an FTP URL. (Too many TLAs — Three-Letter Acronyms.) Usually, browsers are smart enough to tell which files are ASCII and which are binary. You don't have to worry about it.

The URL of FTP

When you've used your Web browser as a Web browser, you have probably typed URLs that begin with *http*, the abbreviation for the way that browsers talk with Web servers (Hypertext Transport Protocol, if you must know). To tell your Web browser to log in to an FTP server, you tell it a different kind of URL — an FTP URL. An FTP server's URL looks like this:

```
ftp://servername/directoryname/filename
```

You can leave out the directory name and filename, if you like, to get the top-level directory of that FTP server. For example, the URL of the Microsoft FTP server (at `ftp.microsoft.com`) is

```
ftp://ftp.microsoft.com/
```

This URL has no filename part: If you omit the filename, the server displays the top-level directory to which you have access.

Browsing with an FTP URL

No matter which Web browser you use, you follow the same general steps to retrieve files via FTP:

1. **Run the Web browser as usual.**

2. **To tell your browser to load the URL of the FTP server, type the FTP URL in the Address, URL, or Netsite box just below the toolbar, and then press Enter.**

   The browser logs in to the FTP server and displays its home directory, as shown in Figure 16-2. Each file and directory in the current directory appear as a link. Depending on the Web browser you use, the format may differ from the one shown in this figure.

Hey, it's me!

Most Web browsers can handle more than just anonymous FTP; they can FTP files from sites on which you have to have an account. To download a file from a password-protected FTP server, assuming that you have an account on the server, you can include your account name by typing the account name followed by an at-sign (@) immediately before the FTP server name. If your account name is `elvis`, for example, you type a URL like this:

```
ftp://elvis@ftp.gurus.com
```

When it logs in to the server, your browser asks you to type your password, which on your provider's system is probably the same password it uses when you first connect.

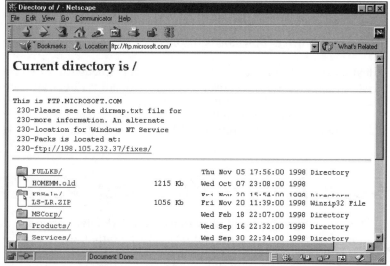

Figure 16-2:
Netscape
Navigator
can act as
your FTP
program.

3. **Move to the directory that contains the file you want, by clicking the directory name.**

   When you click a directory name, you move to that directory, and your browser displays its contents.

4. **Download the file you want by clicking its filename.**

   If you download a text file or another file that your browser knows how to display, the browser displays it after it downloads. If you click the filename readme.txt, for example, the browser displays the text file. If you want to save the file after you look at it, choose File⇨Save As from the menu and tell your browser the filename to use.

   If you download a file that your browser doesn't know how to display, such as a program, it usually asks what to do. (Figure 16-3 shows the message that Netscape displays.)

Figure 16-3:
Netscape
Navigator
doesn't
know what
to do with
the file you
want to
download.

5. **If your browser asks what to do with the file, tell it to save the file, and choose the directory and filename in which to save it.**

Your browser downloads the file.

If you use a Web browser other than Netscape Navigator or Internet Explorer, the browser may download files differently. Check your browser's documentation to find out how to save files that are downloaded. Or just try it — click the filename of a file that looks interesting and see what happens. If you don't like what happens, try holding the Shift key and clicking again.

Hard-Core FTP-ing By Using WS_FTP

The basic steps that you follow to use your FTP client program, no matter which program you use, are more complicated than using a browser:

1. **If you use a UNIX shell provider and you want to upload files to an FTP server, first upload them from your own computer to the provider's computer.**

2. **Log in to the FTP server by using your FTP client program.**

3. **Move to the directory on the server that contains the files you want to download, or move to the directory to which you want to upload files.**

4. **Tell the program which type of files (ASCII or binary) you will be moving.**

5. **Download or upload the files.**

6. **Log off the FTP server.**

7. **If you use a UNIX shell provider and you downloaded files from an FTP server, download them to your own computer from the provider's computer.**

If you use a PPP account, you can use any Winsock (for Windows users) or MacTCP (for Mac users) FTP client program. Many good freeware and shareware FTP programs are available right off the Internet. Our favorites are WS_FTP for Windows and Fetch for the Mac. This section describes how to use WS_FTP.

Handy features of WS_FTP include

- ✔ Scrollable and selectable windows for the names of local and remote files and directories
- ✔ Clickable buttons for such common operations as connecting and setting binary mode

FTP-ing Web pages

If you maintain a Web site, you use FTP to transfer from your computer to the Web server the Web pages that you create or edit. You can use WS_FTP or another FTP program to transfer the pages, although you have to keep track of which Web pages you created, changed, or deleted on your computer and remember to do the same on the Web server computer. The larger your Web site grows, the bigger headache you have.

There's a better way: Use an FTP program designed just for maintaining Web sites. Margy uses NetLoad, a nifty program that can compare the files (by checking file sizes and dates) on your computer and on your Web site to see which files need to be uploaded or deleted. One click of a button, and NetLoad transfers all the necessary files. You can get NetLoad, or one of a number of similar programs, from TUCOWS (at http://www.tucows.com) on the Net.

> ✔ Connection profiles, which save the host name, login name, password, and remote host directory of your favorite FTP sites; comes with a bunch of useful profiles already set

Getting WS_FTP

Our favorite Winsock FTP program is called WS_FTP. The freeware version, WS_FTP LE, for Limited Edition, is available by (what else!) FTP from a variety of places, including its "home," the United States Military Academy. (Doubtless there's a connection between FTP and our national security.) Because we get a little better service from a mirror site, that's what we encourage you to use:

1. **In My Computer or Windows Explorer (in Windows 95 or Windows 98) or File Manager (in Windows 3.1), make a folder (directory) in which to put WS_FTP.**

2. **Use your Web browser to go to The Ultimate Collection of Winsock Software (TUCOWS), at http://www.tucows.com. Click the mirror site closest to you and then click Windows 95 (or Windows 98) or Windows 3.1. Then click the link for FTP programs.**

   You see a long list of freeware and shareware FTP clients. Cool!

3. **Scroll down to WS_FTP LE and click the program name. Tell your browser to store the file in the folder you created in Step 1.**

   Your browser downloads the file. It's time to install it.

4. **Unzip the Ws_ftple.zip file.**

We give you instructions later in this chapter for unzipping a file. You end up with a bunch of files, including the install program, which is named Inst.exe (Windows 3.1) or Inst32.exe (Windows 95 or Windows NT).

5. **Run the installation program.**

The installation program asks a bunch of questions, such as whether you agree to the terms for noncommercial use (if you're a home user, you probably do), which directories to use, and which version of the program to use. In each case, the suggested answer is fine.

You're ready to FTP by using WS_FTP!

Dialing for files

Here's how to use the WS_FTP program to swipe files from or put files on an FTP server:

1. **Run the WS_FTP program by double-clicking its icon.**

You see the FTP Client Connect To dialog box, as shown in Figure 16-4. This dialog box lets you enter information about the FTP server that you want to connect to. After you have entered this information, WS_FTP saves it so that you can easily connect to the saved FTP server again.

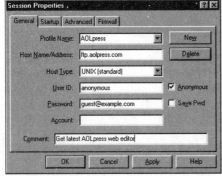

Figure 16-4:
Which FTP
server do
you want to
talk to?

2. **In the Profile Name box, enter the name you want to use for this FTP server.**

If you want to FTP to `rtfm.mit.edu`, for example, which contains FAQs for all the Usenet newsgroups, you might enter **Usenet FAQ Central**.

3. **In the Host Name box, enter the name of the FTP server.**

This name can be a regula r Internet name (such as `oak.oakland.edu`, another useful FTP server) or a numeric address.

4. **Leave the Host Type box set to auto-detect.**

   This step tells WS_FTP to guess which operating system the FTP server is using.

5. **If you really have a username on the FTP server, enter your username and password in the User ID and Password boxes.**

   Otherwise, click the Anonymous FTP box. WS_FTP asks for your e-mail address, which it uses as your password (the usual thing to do when you FTP anonymously).

6. **Enter your address and click OK.**

   WS_FTP fills in the User ID and Password boxes for you.

   If you want WS_FTP to store the password in the Password box rather than ask you for it every time you connect to the FTP server, click the Save Password box so that it contains an X.

   Leave the Account box blank, unless you have your own username on the FTP server and you know which account to enter.

7. **Click the Startup tab and then in the Remote Dir box, enter the directory in which you want to look on the FTP server.**

   Alternatively, you can leave this box blank and look around on your own.

8. **In the Local Dir box, enter on your own PC the directory in which you want to store downloaded files.**

9. **Click the OK button to save this information.**

10. **Click OK.**

    WS_FTP tries to connect to the FTP server.

"It won't speak to me!"

If you have a problem connecting to the FTP server, messages appear in the two-line box at the bottom of the WS_FTP window. You can scroll the little window up and down to see what happened. For example, `rtfm.mit.edu` is frequently overloaded and doesn't let you log on. When this situation happens, some helpful messages are displayed about other FTP sites that may have the information you want. You can see these messages in this box.

To see the messages the FTP server sent, double-click them. WS_FTP opens a big window so that you can see them better. To close the window, click the Close button. Frequently the FTP server will send messages explaining access policies or other useful information.

Do you copy?

After you're connected to the FTP server, you see the WS_FTP window, as shown in Figure 16-5. (Some versions of WS_FTP arrange the window a little differently.) WS_FTP displays information about the files on your own computer on the left side of the window (labeled Local System) and the directories and files on the FTP server on the right side (labeled Remote System). On each side are buttons that enable you to change directories (ChgDir), and make directories (MkDir), view files, and so on. Naturally, you don't have permission to delete or change anything on most FTP servers, so don't even try.

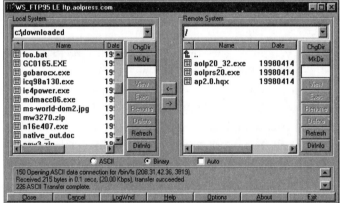

Figure 16-5:
Prepare to
receive
some files!

To move from directory to directory on the FTP server, choose directory names from the list box. Or you can click the ChgDir button and enter the full pathname of the directory to go to.

Here's how to copy a file:

1. **Choose ASCII or Binary by clicking the buttons at the bottom of the window.**

   For files that consist entirely of text (like HTML files), choose ASCII. For anything else (like graphics files), choose Binary.

2. **Choose the file you want on the FTP server.**

3. **Choose the directory to put it in on your own computer.**

4. **Click the left-pointing arrow button in the middle of the window.**

   WS_FTP downloads the file. For large files, this step can take some time; WS_FTP displays your progress as a percentage completed.

For Mac users

It's not that we want you to feel slighted by the in-depth coverage of WS_FTP. Things on the Mac are a little simpler, and we have a tight page budget.

When it comes to FTP, we like the excellent shareware program Fetch, by Jim Mathews. The problem, of course, is figuring out how to get it before you have FTP. Using your handy browser software, go to

```
http://www.dartmouth.edu/
    pages/softdev/fetch.html
```

where you can find complete information about Fetch and instructions for downloading.

Fetch gives you a choice between downloading files as raw data and MacBinary. The *MacBinary* format combines the parts *(forks)* of Macintosh files into one file so that they can travel together when they're being FTP'd. Use MacBinary for Mac-specific stuff that only other Macs can understand, such as Macintosh software. When you download Mac software from a Mac software archive, for example, use MacBinary. Don't use MacBinary for text files, graphics files, and other non-Mac-specific stuff. MacBinary-formatted files usually have the filename extension .bin.

Hang up!

To disconnect from the FTP server after you're finished, click the Close button at the bottom of the WS_FTP window.

Connecting again

To call someone else, click the Connect button. You see the FTP Client Connect To window again. Fill in different information and click OK to make the connection.

To call an FTP server you have called before, click Connect. In the FTP Client Connect To window, click the arrow button to the right of the Profile Name box. You see a list of the configurations you've entered — choose one and then click OK.

How to foul up your files in FTP

The most common error that inexperienced Internet users make (and *experienced* users, for that matter) is transferring a file in the wrong mode. If you transfer a text file in binary mode from a UNIX system to an MS-DOS or Macintosh system, the file looks something like this (on a DOS machine):

Patience is a virtue

The Internet is pretty fast, although not infinitely so. When you're copying stuff between two computers on the same local network, information can move at about 200,000 characters per second. When the two machines are separated by a great deal of intervening Internet, the speed drops — often to 1,000 characters per second or fewer. If you're copying a file that's 500,000 characters long (the size of your typical inspirational GIF image), it takes only a few seconds over a local network, although it can take several minutes over a long-haul connection.

It's often comforting to look at the directory listing before retrieving a file so that you know how big the file is and can have an idea of how long the copy will take. Because programs get inexorably larger, even with faster modems, patience remains as the key to successful downloading.

```
This file
        should have been
                copied in
                        ASCII mode.
```

On a Mac, the entire file looks like it's on one line. When you look at the file with a text editor on a UNIX system, you see strange ^M symbols at the end of every line. You don't necessarily have to retransfer the file. Many networking packages come with programs that do ex post facto conversion from one format to the other.

If, on the other hand, you copy something in ASCII mode that isn't a text file, it gets scrambled. Compressed files don't decompress; executable files don't execute (or they crash or hang the machine); images look unimaginably bad. When a file is corrupted, the first thing you should suspect is the wrong mode in FTP.

If you're FTP-ing (Is that a verb? It is now!) files between two computers of the same type, such as from one Windows system to another, you can and should make all your transfers in binary mode. Because a text file or a nontext file doesn't require any conversion, binary mode does the right thing.

About Face!

Okay, now you know how to retrieve files from other computers. How about copying the other way? If you write your own Web pages and want to upload them to your Internet provider's computer, here's how you do it: FTP them to the provider's Web server.

Uploading with your browser

In Netscape Navigator and Internet Explorer 4.0 or later, you can log in to the Web server as yourself by using an FTP URL, like this:

```
ftp://yourid@www.yourprovider.com/
```

Use your login ID rather than *yourid* and the name of your provider's Web server, which most likely is www followed by the provider's name but may also be something like ftp.www.fargle.net. (Ask your provider whether this info is in the sign-up packet it gave you.)

The browser asks for your password; use the same one you use when you dial in. If this password works, you see your home Web directory listed on-screen. If you want to upload files to a different directory, click that directory's name so that you see that directory.

After you have the directory you want on-screen, just drag the file to upload from any other program (such as File Manager or Windows Explorer) into the browser window. Poof! (It may be a slow poof, depending on how big the file is.) In Netscape, you can also choose File⇨Upload File from the menu if you find dragging to be a drag.

Uploading with WS_FTP

In WS_FTP, log in as we just described in the preceding section, using your login ID and password. After you have the local and remote directories you want in their respective windows in WS_FTP, just click the local file you want to upload, and then click the arrow button pointing to the remote window.

If you're uploading a Web page to a Web server, be sure to upload the page itself (in ASCII mode because the HTML file that contains the Web page is a text file), along with any graphics files that contain pictures that appear on the page (in binary mode).

Other FTP Shenanigans

If you use WS_FTP or another FTP client program (rather than a Web browser), a bunch of other file-manipulation commands are sometimes useful. In particular, you can delete and rename files on both your computer and (if permissions allow) the remote computer to which you're connected.

In WS_FTP, click a file of interest and then click the Delete or Rename buttons to delete and rename it. WS_FTP asks for confirmation for deleting and asks you to type the new name if you're renaming. If the remote system doesn't let you delete or rename stuff, you don't find out until after you try to do so.

If you plan to do much file deleting, directory creating, and the like, using WS_FTP can be cumbersome. Instead, log in to the other system by using a telnet terminal program to do your work by using the usual local commands (usually UNIX commands).

For information about where to find out more about telnet and other UNIX commands, turn to our Web site, at `http://net.gurus.com/telnet`.

It's Not Just a File — It's Software

Using FTP, you can download freeware and shareware programs and install and use them. You need a few well-chosen software tools, including a program to uncompress compressed files. (Useful little programs like this one are called *utilities* in the jargon.)

Installing FTP'd software usually requires three steps:

1. **Using FTP, download the file that contains the software.**

2. **If the software isn't in a self-installing file, it's usually in a compressed format, so uncompress it.**

3. **Run the installation program that comes with it, or at least create an icon for the program.**

The first part of this chapter describes how to do Step 1, the FTP part. The rest of this chapter describes Steps 2 and 3: uncompressing and installing. Here goes!

Decompressing and unzipping

Most software on FTP servers is in a compressed format, to save both storage space on the server and transmission time when you download the file. An increasing amount of software is self-installing — the file is a program that does the necessary uncompressing and installing. Self-installing Windows files end with .exe, and non-self-installing compressed files end with .zip.

If a file is compressed, you need a program to deal with it. Files with the file extension .zip identify compressed files (these files are called, amazingly, *ZIP files*). Programs with names such as PKZIP, PKUNZIP, and UNZIP have been around for years for DOS users to zip and unzip files. Although UNZIP and its brethren work fine, they're DOS programs and not really convenient to use from Windows. It's annoying to use the MS-DOS icon every time you want to run one. Luckily, someone (a guy named Nico Mak) wrote a nice little Windows program called WinZip that can both unzip and zip things for you, directly from Windows. Mac users can get a program named unzip.

 If you already have WinZip (which is also available through the mail or from various shareware outlets), skip this entire section. If you have and love PKZIP and PKUNZIP or UNZIP and don't mind running them from DOS, you too can skip the section. You can get a Windows version of PKUNZIP, which isn't as nice as WinZip, although some people like it. It works fine.

 To get WinZip on the Web, go to `http://www.winzip.com`, a page full of pictures of outer-space-type blobs. Click the blob marked Download Evaluation to get to the download page. On that page, download either the Windows 3.1 or Windows 95/98 version, as appropriate.

To install WinZip:

1. **Run winzip31.exe or winzip70.exe.**

   That's the program you just downloaded.

2. **Follow the installation instructions that WinZip gives you.**

   Although you have a bunch of options, you can accept the suggested defaults for all of them.

Mac users say StuffIt

Mac users can download an unzip program from `ftp.uu.net` in the /pub/ archiving/zip/MAC directory or from `ftp.doc.ic.ac.uk` in the /packages/ zip/MAC directory or from `quest.jpl.nasa.gov` in the /pub/MAC directory. The file that contains the unzip program is called something like unz530x.hqx. (The exact name depends on the latest version number.)

More popular than zip and unzip for the Mac crowd is a shareware program, by Raymond Lau, known as StuffIt. StuffIt comes in many flavors, including a commercially available version called StuffIt Deluxe. StuffIt files of all varieties generally end with the extension .sit.

For decompression, you can use the freeware programs UnStuffIt and StuffIt Expander.

Running WinZip

Give it a try! Double-click that icon! WinZip looks like Figure 16-6.

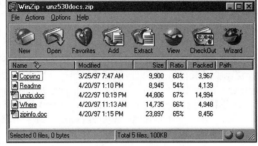

Figure 16-6:
WinZip is
ready to
deal with
your ZIP
files.

To open a ZIP file (which the WinZip folks call an *archive*), click the Open button and choose the directory and filename for the ZIP file. Poof! WinZip displays a list of the files in the archive, with their dates and sizes.

Unzip it!

Sounds suggestive, we know, although it's not as much fun as it sounds. If you want to use a file from a ZIP file, after you have opened the ZIP file, you *extract* it — that is, you ask WinZip to uncompress it and store it in a new file.

To extract a file:

1. **Choose it from the list of files.**

   You can choose a group of files that are listed together by clicking the first one and then Shift+clicking the last one. To select an additional file, Ctrl+click it.

2. **Click the Extract button.**

   A dialog box asks in which directory you want to put the file and whether you want to extract all the files in the archive or just the one you selected.

3. **Select the directory in which to store the unzipped files.**

4. **Click OK.**

   WinZip unzips the file. The ZIP file is unchanged, and now you have the uncompressed file (or files) also.

Zipped out?

Although WinZip can do a bunch of other things too, such as add files to a ZIP file and create your own ZIP file, you don't have to know how to perform these tasks in order to swipe software from the Net, so we skip them. (We bet that you can figure them out just by looking at the buttons on the WinZip toolbar.)

Now that you know how to unzip software that you get from the Internet, you're ready for the next topic: safe software.

Scanning for viruses

We all know that you practice safe software: You check every new program you get to make sure that it doesn't contain any hidden software viruses that may display obnoxious messages or trash your hard disk. If that's true of you, you can skip this section.

For the rest of you, it's a good idea to run a virus-scanning program. You never know what naughty piece of code you may otherwise unwittingly FTP to your defenseless computer!

If you use Windows 3.1 with DOS 6.2, you have a somewhat out-of-date virus checker built right in to File Manager. Here's how to run the virus checker:

1. **Run File Manager.**

2. **Choose Tools⇨Antivirus from the menu.**

   You see the Microsoft Anti-Virus window, shown in Figure 16-7.

3. **Choose a disk drive, by clicking it in the Drives box.**

4. **Click the Detect and Clean button.**

   If you're scanning a large hard disk for viruses, this step can take several minutes.

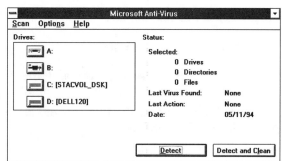

Figure 16-7:
Evict those
viruses!

It's a good idea to run a virus checker after you have obtained and run any new piece of software. Although the FTP servers on the Internet make every effort to keep their software archives virus-free, nobody is perfect. Don't get caught by some prankster's idea of a joke!

If you use WinZip, you can configure it to run your virus checker before you even unzip the ZIP file containing a program. Choose Options⇨Program Locations from the menu and type in the Scan program box the pathname of your virus checker program.

Although Windows 95 and Windows 98 don't come with a virus checker, several commercial ones are available, including the McAfee VirusScan program, which you can download from the McAfee Web site, at `http://www.mcafee.com`.

Installing the program

After you have downloaded the software and unzipped it (if it's a ZIP file), the program is ready to install. To install the program, double-click its name in Windows Explorer, My Computer, or File Manager. If it's an installation program, it installs the program. In the process, the installation program probably creates an icon for the program. In Windows 95 or Windows 98, it may also add the program to your Start menu.

Some programs don't come with an installation program — you just get the program itself. To make the program easy to run, you need an icon for it. Here's how to make one in Windows 3.1:

1. **Open both Program Manager and File Manager and arrange the screen so that you can see the program group in which you want to put the icon (in Program Manager) and the program name (in File Manager).**

2. **Drag the program name from File Manager into Program Manager, and place it in the program group where you want it.**

   You see a new icon in the program group.

To run your new program, you can just double-click the icon. Cool!

In Windows 95 and Windows 98, follow these steps:

1. **Run either My Computer or Windows Explorer, and select the program file (the file with the extension .exe, or occasionally .com).**

2. **Use your right mouse button to drag the filename out on the desktop or into an open folder on the desktop.**

   An icon for the program appears.

Configuring the program

Now you can run the program by double-clicking its icon. Hooray!

You may have to tell the program, however, about your Internet address or your computer or who knows what before it can do its job. Refer to the text files, if any, that came with the program or choose Help from the program's menu bar to get more information about how to configure and run your new program.

Where Is It?

"The world of FTP sounds fine and dandy," you may say, "but what's out there, and where can I find it?" One of the best places to find software is to look at `http://www.tucows.com`. It has a great collection of FTP sites grouped by platform and category of program.

Also look at Chapter 8 and visit our online favorite software page, with our current updated list of greatest hits:

`http://net.gurus.com/software`

Chapter 17

Can Ten Million Users All Be Wrong? It's AOL!

● ●

In This Chapter

▶ Using America Online

● ●

Can ten million users really be wrong? Sure they can. But if you're brand-new to the world of computers as well as to the world of the Internet, you may find using America Online easier than starting off with a traditional Internet service provider. Also, if you're interested in online chatting, AOL is the world capital of chat. (In his book *Burn Rate,* Michael Wolff claims that AOL's success is primarily due to naughty online chat. He may well be right, although there are certainly plenty of other things to do on AOL.)

This chapter tells you how to use e-mail, the World Wide Web, and FTP from AOL. Because chatting is extremely popular all over the Net, it has its own chapter, Chapter 15. You probably want to read through Chapters 6 through 13 that describe e-mail and the World Wide Web — all the conceptual information there applies to you too. In this chapter, we give you the specifics for using AOL.

Hello, America Online

If you've decided to join the AOL ranks, we tell you how to sign up and then install AOL and connect to it in Chapter 5. After you have AOL running, how do you do all those Internet tricks? We take you on a tour of AOL features using Version 4.0 of the AOL software.

When AOL has successfully connected, you see the Welcome window, as shown in Figure 17-1. The row of icons under the menu is called the toolbar, or Flashbar. Some Flashbar buttons display their own little menus when you

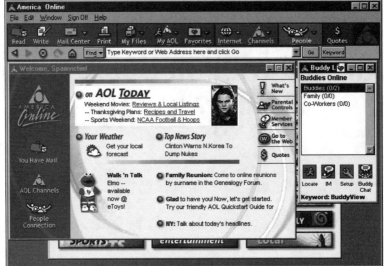

Figure 17-1:
AOL
welcomes
you, and
you have
mail!

click them. Below the Flashbar is yet another row of buttons with the Keyword box in the middle of the row.

One way to get around in AOL is to "go to" a keyword: You either click in the Keyword box (the long box below the Flashbar, between the Keyword and Go buttons) or type Ctrl+K, and then type one of the AOL keywords. In the rest of this section about AOL, we just say "go to **keyword**."

Using E-Mail from AOL

The first thing to do is send mail to all your friends to let them know that you have successfully installed AOL and tell them your e-mail address. You can send messages to other AOL members and to folks on the Internet.

Your Internet mail address is your screen name (omitting any spaces) plus @aol.com. You screen name is the user name you use when you log on. If your screen name is John Smith, for example, your Internet address is JohnSmith@aol.com.

"Do I have mail?"

Every time you connect to AOL, it tells you whether you have mail. The leftmost icon on the Flashbar is a little mailbox, and in the lower-left corner of the Welcome window you see a similar mailbox with some writing nearby. If the little red flag is *up,* you have mail. The message says "You Have Mail," just in case you're from a part of the world where mailboxes don't have little red flags. If your computer has speakers, a voice may also say "You have mail!" — try not to jump right out of your seat when you hear it.

Reading your mail

You probably *do* have mail, in fact, because every new member gets a nice note from the president of AOL and because AOL members tend to get mountains of junk mail, much more than people with other types of accounts. To read your unread mail, follow these steps:

1. **Click any mailbox you can find.**

   It's the Read New Mail icon. Alternatively, you can click the Mail Center icon on the Flashbar and choose Read Mail from the menu that appears or press Ctrl+R. You see the New Mail window.

   In the New Mail window, each line on the list describes one incoming mail message with the date it was sent, the sender's e-mail address, and the subject.

2. **To read a message, double-click it or highlight it on the list and then either click Read or press Enter.**

   You see the text of your message in another cute little window.

3. **To reply to the message, click the Reply button. Type the text of your message in the box in the lower part of the window that appears. Then click the Send or the Send Later button.**

4. **To forward the message to someone else, click the Forward button. Fill in the e-mail address to which you want to forward the message. You can add a message to go along with the original message too, by typing it in the large message area box. Then click Send Now (if you're online) or Send Later (if not).**

   If you get annoying or unwanted mail from another AOL member, forward it to TOSspam, a special mailbox at AOL set up to investigate junk e-mail.

5. **To see the next message, click the Next button; to see the preceding message, click the Prev button.**

6. **When you finish, double-click the little AOL icon in the upper-left corner of each window you're finished with. (In Windows 95, click the Close button, which is the X button in the upper-right corner.)**

It's not always a good idea to respond to messages right away. You may have to get some information or cool off after reading the brainless message some jerk sent you.

Saving a message on your PC

If you get a message on AOL that you want to save someplace other than the AOL Personal Filing Cabinet, display it on-screen as described in the preceding section, "Reading your mail." Then choose File⇨Save from the menu bar or press Ctrl+S. AOL lets you choose the directory and filename in which to save the file on your computer. When you click OK, the e-mail message is saved as a text file. Nice and easy!

Composing a new message

You don't have to reply to other messages — you can begin an exchange of messages, assuming that you know the e-mail address of the person to whom you want to write:

1. **Click the Write button — the second icon from the left on the Flashbar, the picture of a pencil and paper.**

   Alternatively, you can click the Mail Center icon on the Flashbar and choose Write Mail from the menu that appears, or you can press Ctrl+M. You see the Write Mail dialog box, shown in Figure 17-2.

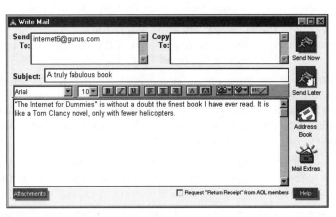

Figure 17-2: Send a message to anyone with an AOL or Internet account.

2. **Enter the recipient's address in the Send To box.**

   For AOL members, just enter the screen name. For others on the Net, type the entire Internet address.

3. **In the Copy To box, enter the addresses of anyone to whom you want to send a copy.**

   You don't have to send a copy to yourself — AOL keeps copies of mail you have sent.

4. Enter a brief subject line in the Subject box.

You have to enter a subject — AOL doesn't let a message leave home without it.

5. In the box with no name, type the text of your message.

Don't press the Tab key, because it moves your cursor from one box to the next in the dialog box. You can press Enter, though, to begin a new paragraph. If you're sending a message to another AOL user, you can use the buttons above the text box to add underlining, italics, color, and other whizzo formatting to your message. Don't bother formatting messages to the Internet, however, because the formatting doesn't work on non-AOL e-mail programs.

6. When you like what you see, click the Send Now or the Send Later button.

AOL confirms that the mail is winging on its way.

7. Click OK.

Attaching a file to your message

If you want to send a file from your computer to someone as an e-mail message, AOL makes this process easy. When you're writing the message, click the Attachments button. You see the Attachments dialog box, which lets you choose any file from your PC. Click Attach, select a file, and click OK.

AOL attaches the file by using MIME, a method that most other e-mail programs can deal with. (It's still a good idea to ask first before sending attachments, to make sure that the recipient has the necessary program to read the file you want to send.)

Keeping an address book

Of course, you can't remember all your online friends' Internet addresses; AOL provides you with an address book to keep track of them. It's rather primitive by other mail program standards, but serviceable.

Adding names to your book

To add new entries in your book, click the Mail Center icon on the Flashbar and choose Address Book from the menu that appears. (While you're composing a message, click the Address Book icon.) The Address Book window shows your current address book contents.

Click the New Person button to create a new entry and then fill out the first name, last name, and e-mail address of the person to whom you want to write. You can create an entry for a group of people (your special friends, for example) by clicking the New Group button instead. Give the group a name, such as Cabal, and then list in the Addresses box their mail addresses separated by commas.

Using the black book

When you compose a message, you can bring up the address book by clicking its icon on the left of the Write Mail window. In the Address Book window, select the person you want to write to and click the Send To button. To send the person a copy of the message, click Copy To or (for a blind copy) Blind Copy. After you have put addresses in the message, you can remove them by ordinary methods.

"What if I get an attachment?"

Sometimes, when people send you e-mail, they send along an attachment. If you don't know the person who sent you the message, do not download the attachment, in case it contains a virus or an offensive picture or document.

The name of the attached file is noted in the message as well as its size and estimated time to download. Two extra buttons are at the bottom of the message window: Download File and Download Later. The attachment is not in your computer until you download it from AOL Central. If you choose to

Stop the junk mail!

America Online users get more junk e-mail messages than users of any other online system. Most of the messages are for fraudulent (in our opinion) get-rich-quick schemes and offers to advertise *your* product by e-mail to millions of people who are just as unenthusiastic about getting those types of messages as you are.

As you can imagine, AOL has gotten many complaints about the level of junk mail, especially from users who have to pay by the hour to read it. (Even with the new flat rates, some people still pay by the minute for phone calls.)

The folks at AOL have been fighting the junk e-mailers for some time, including trying to block their messages, and have fought several court battles with the online spammers. Because many junk e-mail messages have forged return addresses, however, it isn't always easy to trace or block them. What's an e-mail reader to do?

Go to the keyword **mail controls**, that's what. For each screen name on your account, you can block all incoming e-mail, e-mail from sites you select, or only e-mail attachments.

download the file immediately, you get a chance to choose the folder to save it in. If you choose Download Later, the file gets added to the Download Manager list of tasks to do. You can call up the file by clicking My Files on the Flashbar and choosing Download Manager; it can get all your attachments at one time.

Going Offline

You can work *offline* with AOL; that is, you can disconnect from AOL and read your downloaded e-mail or compose new messages or replies. You may want to work offline to avoid tying up your phone line and give some other AOL-deprived individual a shot at getting connected. In fact, when you first run the AOL program, you're not online yet; you can minimize the sign-on window and start composing messages or reading old ones. All the features of AOL that you cannot access because you're not connected are grayed out so that you can't use any features that require you to be online. If you're online and want to go offline without exiting AOL, choose Sign Off⇨Sign Off from the menu bar.

To the Net

AOL has organized its Internet services in one dialog box so that they're easy to find. To get at the AOL Internet services, click the Internet button on the Welcome window or click Internet on the Flashbar and choose Internet Connection from the menu that appears. Alternatively, you can go to keyword **internet**. You see the Internet Connection window, shown in Figure 17-3.

Figure 17-3:
The Internet Connection window, with buttons for the World Wide Web, Usenet newsgroups, and more.

The Internet Connection window has the following icons you can use:

- **Go to the Web:** Lets you browse the Web
- **NetFind, Timesavers, Find a Business:** Several icons that take you directly to the AOL search engines
- **Newsgroups:** Read Usenet newsgroups
- **Internet Extras:** Takes you to another window with more AOL Internet services: FTP, Help, Gopher, Software, and Personal Publisher

When you finish using the Internet Connection, double-click the little AOL icon in the upper-left corner of its window to close the window.

Web Browsing from AOL

The AOL software includes a built-in Web browser, so it's easy to find out how to use it. You can save the addresses of Web pages in your Favorite Places list. You can have a Web browser window open at the same time that other AOL windows are open.

The Web browser requires that you use AOL software Version 2.5 or higher. If you don't yet have AOL Version 4.0, you should download it — the built-in Web browser is much better than earlier versions. Go to keyword **upgrade** and follow the directions on-screen. The good news is that it's easy and that AOL doesn't charge you for the connect-time while you're downloading the Web browser program. The bad news is that it takes a while (several minutes to a half-hour, depending on your modem speed) to download the program.

Starting the Web browser

Here are two ways to start the AOL Web browser:

- Choose Internet Connection from the main menu (or go to keyword **internet**) and then click the Go to the Web button. Unless you configured your AOL browser differently, this method brings you to the AOL home page.
- Click in the keyword box (just below the Flashbar, between the Find and Go buttons), type the URL of the Web page you want to see (rather than a keyword) and press Enter or click Go.

To use the browser, click any picture that has a blue border or any button or any text that appears underlined. (Chapters 6 through 8 tell you how to find information on the World Wide Web.)

Protecting your kids

In Chapter 3, we talk about the need for parents to be involved with their kids' online experience. Because you're using AOL, you may want to take advantage of its parental controls. If kids use your AOL account, you can create a separate screen name for each kid and control what each kid can do on AOL; go to keyword **parental controls**.

Creating your own Web page

Although it's fun to look at Web pages that other people have created, what about making your own? AOL lets you create your own *home page* (a page about you).

Go to keyword **my home page**, which takes you to the Personal Publisher window. Follow the instructions to create your own home page on the Web. AOL uses a Web-authoring tool called Personal Publisher II that generates HTML 3.2 with some Netscape extensions. AOL gives you two megabytes of space to save your Web pages, at the URL `http://members.aol.com/screenname`. Read Chapter 10 for help in writing your first home page.

Grabbing Files from FTP Servers

AOL lets you download files from FTP servers on the Internet. AOL can do anonymous FTP, in which you connect to an FTP server that you don't have an account on, or FTP-ing, in which you do have an account. To use the AOL FTP service, you have to know which file you want to download, which FTP server has it, and which directory the file is in. For information about FTP, see Chapter 16.

Most people now download software via the Web. Links on Web pages may be FTP links — that is, you click a link to start downloading a file.

If you need to use FTP directly, here's how to download a file:

1. **Click in the keyword box (or press Ctrl+K), type ftp, and click Go.**

   You see the FTP–File Transfer Protocol window.

2. **Click the Go To FTP button.**

   The Anonymous FTP dialog box appears.

3. **If the FTP server that has the file you want is listed, select it and click Connect. If not, click Other Site, type the Internet name of the FTP server, and click Connect.**

   When you have connected to the FTP server of your choice, AOL may display an informational message about it — click OK when you have read it. Then you see a list of the contents of the current directory on the FTP server.

4. **To move to the directory that contains the file you want, double-click the directory names.**

   AOL shows little file-folder icons by directory names and little sheet-of-paper icons by filenames. For files, look at the size of each file (in bytes, or characters) — the larger the file, the longer it takes to download.

5. **To download a file to your computer, choose the file and click Download Now.**

   The Download Manager dialog box appears, asking where to put the file on your computer.

6. **Choose the directory in which you want to put the file on your own computer and edit the filename. Then click OK.**

   AOL downloads the file to your computer's disk. Depending on the size of the file and the speed of your modem, this step can take seconds, minutes, or hours.

7. **Close dialog boxes in AOL when you're finished.**

   You can even close dialog boxes while AOL is transferring the file.

   If you have an account on the FTP server (and therefore have access to files not available to the public), use the Other Site button and click the button named Ask for login name and password.

   Some FTP servers are extremely busy, and you may not be able to connect. Try again during off-hours or try another server. AOL keeps copies of most or all of the files on some of the busiest servers, to alleviate the traffic jams online.

Using AOL as an Internet Account

It's a tough decision, choosing between a commercial online service, such as America Online, and an Internet account. Although America Online has lots of AOL-only information, an Internet PPP account lets you use all that snazzy, new Winsock software, such as Netscape Navigator. What's a cybernaut to do?

Now you don't have to choose — you can have it all. AOL has created a special version of the Winsock.dll program that all Winsock programs use to talk to PPP accounts. (See Chapter 5 for an explanation of Winsock and PPP accounts.) Using the AOL Winsock.dll program, your Winsock programs talk to your AOL account.

Confused? So were we. Here's how it works: When you run the AOL program, it checks to see whether a Winsock.dll is loaded in your computer's memory. If it isn't, AOL loads its own Winsock.dll. Either way, you're now ready to run Winsock software. (Older versions of AOL software require you to download and install the Winsock.dll program yourself.) Users of Windows 95 and 98 already have a Winsock.dll, so they don't need to do a thing.

Getting Winsock-compatible programs

Lots of freeware and shareware Winsock software is available from AOL and from the World Wide Web. Here are places to look for Winsock programs:

✔ Go to Winsock Central in AOL (keyword **winsock**) and click the Software Library button. You see a list of Winsock programs that AOL promises work with its Winsock software.

✔ Look at the TUCOWS (The Ultimate Collection Of Windows Software) Web site at this Web address:

```
http://www.tucows.com
```

Click on United States and then Virginia to choose a server. (Regardless of where you are, AOL connects from headquarters in Virginia.) You see an extensive list of Winsock programs. Click the type of program you want, Web browsers or newsreaders, for example, and you see names, descriptions, and even reviews of the programs. Click the Location section of the program description to download the program.

Using a Winsock program

Suppose that you want to use Netscape Navigator rather than the AOL Web browser. Assuming that you're running a new version of the AOL software that includes a Winsock.dll and you have downloaded the Netscape Navigator program (or bought a commercial version), here's all you have to do:

1. **Run it.**

   That's it. That's all you do. To be specific, run AOL and log in to your account. Then run Netscape Navigator (or any other Winsock-compatible program). It works, using your AOL account as its connection to the

Internet. The Winsock application will run in its own window, even though it's sharing AOL's connection to the world.

When you finish, exit from your program. Then log off from AOL.

For more information about where to get nifty Winsock programs that you may want to use, see Chapter 16.

Doing Other Things

Because America Online offers tons of information that has nothing to do with the Internet, after you sign up, you may as well check it out. The Computing and Software channel (department) lets you exchange messages with others about the software you use or download shareware. The Reference channel offers all kinds of online reference materials, including the Library of Congress database of books, *Compton's Encyclopedia,* and *Webster's Dictionary of Computer Terms.* The Kids Only channel has fun and educational stuff for kids, including games, homework help, and AOL-supervised chat rooms. The Travel channel lets you make and check your own airline reservations.

Connecting to AOL via your Internet account

If you have an existing Internet account, you can use AOL via the Internet. This technique is really useful if no AOL access number is available in your local calling area, or your computer is already directly connected to the Net via a fast network at school or work or a cable modem — connect to your local Internet account and then connect to AOL over that account.

Start up the AOL software, but *don't* connect yet. Go to the Edit Location menu and change the Network setting to TCP/IP. It doesn't matter what the telephone number is set to because AOL doesn't dial it. Connect to your Internet provider in the usual way and, after that connection is made, connect to AOL. AOL connects via your Internet provider as just another Winsock program, and you can start any other Internet programs you want and

click back and forth between AOL and the other programs. When you're finished with AOL, disconnect from AOL and then disconnect from your Internet provider. When you use AOL this way, it's running as a Winsock program, and you can run other Winsock programs at the same time if you want.

If your Internet provider charges by the hour, you probably don't want to connect this way because you'll pay its hourly charges; otherwise, it can be the best way to go because your provider may provide a faster connection than your local AOL access number; rural customers may not even have a local AOL dial-in. AOL has a special "bring your own access" price of $9.95 per month if you always connect via an Internet account instead of dialing into AOL.

It can be hard to *cancel* an AOL account if you decide that you don't want it. You may have to make several phone calls and let your credit card company know that you refuse any additional charges from AOL. One time, one of us canceled over the phone, sent a certified letter, and AOL *still* charged us for months afterward.

Chapter 18

Not Just "I Love Lucy," It's WebTV

Chapter 5 introduces WebTV and tells you where you can get one and how to connect it. In this section, we tell you what to do with it.

On Your Mark, Get Set, Click

We make the bold assumption that if you've chosen WebTV as your Wway of getting on the Net, you already know how to use a remote control. The WebTV remote has a few special functions. The green buttons at the top turn on the power to your TV and WebTV. Turn on your TV first and then press the TV/Video button at the top to select video mode (you see the word *Video* on the screen). Then power up WebTV. The "thermometer bar" is there to let you know that something is happening. We hope you find it reassuring.

After you're connected, press the up and down arrows on the remote to select the account you want to use (assuming that you have more than one account), and then press the Special button (in the middle of all the arrows) to activate your selection. Pressing this button is equivalent to clicking with the mouse button or pressing the Return or Enter key on a computer keyboard. To help you tell what's what as you move up or down on the screen, WebTV draws an orange border around the portion of the screen that is "active." You can always use the arrow keys to move the active area left, right, up, or down. If you try to move off the screen, you hear a little "thunk" noise. In the following sections, whenever we say *select an icon or a button on the screen,* we mean that you navigate the orange border to the correct place and then press the Special button on the remote or Enter on the keyboard.

You can buy WebTV without a keyboard, although we don't think that's a good idea. Without a keyboard, you have to pull up an image of a keyboard and use the remote to select each letter you want to type — the '90s equivalent of setting type nineteenth century style, by picking individual metal letters out of a type case. (At least one of your authors actually did that. It was fun for about the first 20 minutes.) You can get the remote keyboard from WebTV for $70 or buy a computer keyboard for about $15 and plug it in to the back of the WebTV terminal. If you like your couch, buy the remote keyboard.

Getting E-Mail on Your WebTV

Until you tell someone, nobody, except for the folks at WebTV, will know your e-mail address. If you want to get mail, spread the word.

Your e-mail address is *accountname*@webtv.net. (Replace *accountname* with your WebTV account name.) You can prove that this statement is true and make sure that your mail is working by sending a message to our robot at internet6@gurus.com. You can tell us what you think of WebTV and what you think of this book because we peek over the robot's shoulder and read its mail, too.

Reading your mail

When you sign on to WebTV, you get a nice letter from the president of WebTV. If you have unread messages, the Mail icon on the Home Page shows an envelope sticking out of the mailbox. To read your mail, select the Mail icon. Your mail is always kept at WebTV Central. The WebTV

Watch those phone bills

When you first sign up for WebTV, your WebTV box calls an 800 number at WebTV headquarters and looks up local access numbers that you can call for free. At least, that's what it tries to do. We've heard at least one report where it guessed wrong and a large phone bill arrived at the end of the month.

To see which phone numbers WebTV is using, visit WebTV's home page by pressing Goto and then typing **www.webtv.net** and pressing Return. Select the small "local access" link at the left side of the page and then enter your area code and the first three digits of your own phone number. WebTV shows you the numbers it's dialing. If any of those numbers are not a local call for you, call WebTV on the phone and see if it can straighten the problem out before you run up a huge phone bill.

All in the family

When you first sign up with WebTV, you create a master account (the one that gets the bill for the service). From this account, you can create other accounts, each of which can have its own password and receive its own e-mail. You can bar sub-accounts from using e-mail or chatting.

You can set up sub-accounts to use Internet screening programs to protect your kids. Choose from two screening levels: SurfWatch, which restricts access to pages it considers inappropriate, and Kid friendly, which allows access to only approved pages.

e-mail program displays a list of the messages you have, showing whom the message is from along with the subject of the message and the date received. Messages you have not read yet are highlighted. To read a message, select it.

When you select a message to read, the body of the message is retrieved from WebTV Central, and a new table of options appears on the left. You can discard, save, reply to, or forward the message. Or you can move to the next or preceding message or return to the List of Messages page.

WebTV keeps four folders of messages: current messages, saved messages, sent messages, and discarded messages. Messages you discard are kept for a week before they are permanently erased.

To see if new mail has arrived, press the Mail button on the keyboard, or press Home on the remote and select the mailbox.

Sending mail

To send mail, select the Mail icon. Then choose Write to begin writing your message. Be sure to fill in the To and Subject lines. To use the address book, press the Select button while you're in the To or CC fields. The address book opens, and you can select an entry from the book.

Select the Send button in the lower-right corner to mail your message. Watch WebTV stuff an envelope into a mailbox and slam the mailbox door shut. Klunk.

Where's the Web in WebTV?

To get to a Web site from WebTV, press the GoTo button on your keyboard, or the Options button on your remote control, and GoTo on the panel of choices that slides onto your screen. Another panel slides in with a place to type an address, already started with **http://**. Type the URL and press the Go To button. (Don't know what a URL is? Read Chapter 6.)

To search for something special, click the Search button on the WebTV home page. It takes you to the Infoseek search system (the same one that the rest of the world finds at http://www.infoseek.com).

Use the Explore button on the WebTV home page to select from a list of topics, such as Economy and Sports.

Traditionally designed Web pages look a little different on WebTV from what they look like on a computer. On your WebTV, you may have to scroll to see a whole page. Links are highlighted with an orange border, and you can move from link to link by pressing the arrow keys on your remote. Press the Select button to follow a link.

Keep pointers to your favorite Web sites by pressing Save on the options panel.

Chatting on WebTV

Like every other Internet provider, WebTV provides online chat. On the WebTV home page, select Community. On the Community page, select Chat.

WebTV's chat is provided by a service called Talk City, which any Internet user can get to via http://www.talkcity.com. You can join any of the chats that WebTV's chat page suggests, or you can go directly to http://www.talkcity.com and choose from a larger set of chats there.

On normal Internet accounts, Talk City has a fancy Java-based talk program that requires Netscape or Internet Explorer, but it recognizes when you're connecting from WebTV and automatically uses WebTV's simpler but adequate chat scheme. Either way, it's the same set of chats, and WebTV users can chat with anyone else.

Although in theory you can chat without a keyboard, it's hard to imagine anyone patient enough to do it (and other chatters willing to wait while you pick the letters out of the virtual type case.)

Part V
The Part of Tens

The 5th Wave   By Rich Tennant

"IT'S JUST UNTIL WE GET BACK UP ON THE INTERNET."

In this part . . .

Because some things just don't fit anywhere else in this book, we've grouped them into lists. By the strangest coincidence, exactly *ten* facts happen to be in each list. (*Note to the literal-minded:* You may have to cut off or glue on some fingers to make your version of ten match up with ours. Perhaps it would be easier just to take our word for it.)

Chapter 19

Ten Frequently Asked Questions

In This Chapter

▶ Answers to some general Internet questions

▶ Our opinions about computers, providers, and other favorite things

*W*e get lots of questions in our e-mail every day. We've picked some common questions to answer in the hope that the answers can help you.

If you have more than ten remaining questions after you read this book, surf to our Web site, at `http://net.gurus.com`, where we tell you where to find hundreds of answers.

"Why can't you just give me step-by-step instructions?"

We get this question by e-mail all the time: Other ...*For Dummies* books give detailed, step-by-step instructions, although this book can be vague.

Two reasons spring to mind. One is that we don't know what kind of computer you use or what programs you use We've tried to give you lots of general background so that you have a good idea about how the Internet works, in addition to specific instructions wherever possible for the most commonly used systems. Our Web site, lists books and other Web sites with more specific instructions for many systems and programs.

The other reason is that the programs change continually. Since the last edition of this book, all the programs we describe have been updated. By the time you read this chapter, even newer versions may appear and may work a little differently from the way we describe. We hope you learn enough from reading this book to help you negotiate the inconsistencies you're bound to run into as you find out how to use the Net.

If you're using Windows 98, you might check our *The Internet For Windows 98 For Dummies* (published by IDG Books Worldwide), which does have steps for many of the Internet programs that come with Windows 98.

"Are the Internet and the World Wide Web the same thing?"

Nope. The Internet started out in 1969 and is a network of networks. The World Wide Web, born in 1989, is a system of interconnected Web pages that you can access via the Internet. In the past couple of years, the Web has become the most common way of using the Internet, and more and more, Web browsers include traditional Internet technology. For example, you can send and receive e-mail from Netscape Navigator, and you can find Usenet newsgroups at `http://www.dejanews.com`. On the other hand, you can find plenty of things other than the Web on the Net, such as instant message systems, multi-user games, and plain old e-mail.

"What's the difference between a browser and a search engine?"

A *browser* is the software program that lets your computer show you pages on the World Wide Web. The most commonly used browsers are Netscape Navigator and Internet Explorer. A *search engine* (or directory or index) helps you find pages (on the Web) about specific topics of interest to you. Netscape and Internet Explorer are browsers, programs you install on your own computer. AltaVista, Yahoo, Lycos, Excite, and a host of other search engines are Web sites that can help you find stuff on the Web. Think of the browser as the telephone and the search engine as the phone book.

"Should I buy WebTV?"

Maybe, if you don't own a computer. Visit a consumer electronics store and get a demonstration. If e-mail and Web surfing are all you want to do on the Internet, WebTV may be adequate. WebTV is certainly cheap, and it does get you on the Net for about $100 plus $75 for a remote keyboard and $20 per month to actually connect (assuming that you already own a TV and a telephone); if you use WebTV much, however, you will soon pine for a real computer with a real screen. See Chapter 18 for details about WebTV.

"Can I change my e-mail address?"

It depends. (Don't you hate it when we say that?) On most systems, you can't just change your e-mail address. Your e-mail address is usually your username on your provider's system. Most Internet providers let you choose any username you want, as long as it's not already taken. If you want to be called SnickerDoodles, that's okay with the provider, and your e-mail address may be something like `snickerdoodles@furdle.net`.

Later, when it occurs to you that SnickerDoodles will not look real great on your business card, you may want to change your e-mail address. If you're using a small, local provider, you can probably call up and ask politely, and the company will grumble and change the name. If the company doesn't change it, or if you like being SnickerDoodles to your friends, you can usually get a mail alias for a small extra charge.

No law says that each address corresponds to exactly one mailbox, and having several *aliases,* or mail addresses that put all the mail in one mailbox, is a common practice. Although John's true mailbox name is john1, for example, mail addressed to john, john1, jlevine, and a couple of other misspellings all are aliased to john1 so that the mail is delivered automatically.

Ask your provider whether it will give you a mail alias. Most will — it's just a line in a file full of mailing addresses. After the provider does that, you can set your return address (in Eudora, for example) to the alias so that your address is, as far as anyone can tell, your new alias.

CompuServe and Prodigy Classic assign you an arbitrary username, which is your mail address by default. Both let you get a reasonable mail alias too; call them and ask how you do it.

If your provider can't or won't give you a mail alias, you can check out some third-party e-mail alias services. One is PoBox, which likens itself to a post-office-box service. It gives you, for a modest fee, any addresses you want at pobox.com, which it then forwards to your true mail address. Contact PoBox at http://www.pobox.com, or you can send a message to info@pobox.com. Zillions of Web sites including Yahoo and Hotmail also offer free, Web-based mail addresses. Visit http://mail.yahoo.com and http://www.hotmail.com.

America Online (AOL) is a special case because its users can change their e-mail addresses with wild abandon at a moment's notice. When you sign up for AOL, you choose a screen name, which is your username and e-mail address. Each AOL user can choose as many as four extra screen names, ostensibly for other family members, and can change them at any time. The good news is that AOL users can have any addresses they want (as long as they don't conflict with any of the 14 million AOL addresses already assigned); the bad news is that it's practically impossible to tell who's sending any particular piece of mail from AOL. WebTV uses the same scheme as AOL and allows as many as five extra accounts.

"How can I get a file from my word processor into e-mail?"

It depends. (Oops, we said it again.) Do you want to send the contents in just plain text or do you want to send them in pretty, formatted text — what some people call *rich text*. It depends too on to whom you are sending the file and what that person is able to receive.

Everyone can always read plain text, and, if that's all you need, the process is easy. Use simple copy and paste commands, either from the Edit menu in your word-processor and e-mail programs or by pressing Ctrl+C (⌘+C on the Mac) and Ctrl+V (⌘+V). Select and copy the text of the document in your word processor and then paste it into your e-mail message.

If you and your recipient both use e-mail programs that support rich text, you can include rich text in your message. But be sure before you do, or the result will be very different from what you intend — what you think is going to look beautiful will be filled with illegible formatting codes.

If both your e-mail program and that of your recipient can handle attachments and your recipient uses the same word-processing software as you do, you can attach the word-processing file to your e-mail message. (See Chapter 12 for details.)

"Is it safe to use my credit card on the net?"

Everyone's idea of what is safe is different. Some people say that using a credit card is a lousy idea — period. Others think that the Net is full of people trying to steal credit card numbers and in no case should you ever send your card number across the Net. We think that the risks of online credit card use have been overblown. See Chapter 9, in which we address this topic in detail.

"How important is this Internet stuff?"

Darned important. We're writing this same book for the sixth time in five years. We're here to tell you that ignoring the Internet is not an option anymore. Yeah, you may get away with not knowing about it for a little while longer; if you're in school, in business, or looking for a job, however, you're doing yourself a big disservice. Catch on now. It's really not that tough.

"What's the best Internet provider?"

If all you want is e-mail and access to the World Wide Web, almost any account will do, although the price ranges vary widely, and how easy it is to get started may be the deciding factor for you. If you have never, ever used a computer in your life and get frustrated easily, we recommend choosing a service that puts a great deal of effort into making your life easier. Look at the services with access numbers that are a local call from where you are. Assuming there's more than one, find out how much help is available from your provider. Talking to someone from a provider before you begin and asking your online friends how they like its services can give you valuable insight into which one is best for you. These days, the biggest difference between providers isn't technical — it's the level of service. Don't waste time with one that doesn't offer good service.

We generally prefer small local providers who have live people in the same town as you and who know the local conditions. (One local provider, for example, run by our friend Homer, can tell you based on where in town you live how good your phone line is and how fast a connection you'll be able to get. AOL may be open all night, but it sure can't do that.)

For information on how to find an Internet provider with local numbers near you, look at `http://net.gurus.com/isp`, where we have links to ISP directories.

"How can I make money on the Net?"

We can't remember exactly how many trillions of dollars of business opportunity the Internet represents according to the people who claim to know about these things. We do see that businesses rely on communication. As a new medium of communication, the doors of the Internet are being flung open for new ways of doing business.

We recommend that, rather than try to figure out how to make money in the Internet business, you spend time getting to know the Net extensively — by checking out newsgroups and mailing lists in addition to exploring the World Wide Web. The more you see, the more you can think about organic ways in which your business can use the Net.

We have found that the best way to make money on the Net is to write books about it! If we weren't authors we probably would look at business-to-business commerce, either online services or Net-related "real world" business services, as the candidates.

This should go without saying, but anyone who tells you that you can make big bucks on the Net without working hard and being creative and determined is lying to you. It's no different from the rest of the world.

"What type of computer should I buy to use the Internet?"

You can guess what we're going to say, right? "It depends." For many people, the Internet is the first good reason they have for buying a computer. Which type of computer you buy depends on how you expect to use it.

You don't *absolutely have to have* a computer to use the Internet. You can get a WebTV instead (see "Should I buy WebTV?," earlier in this chapter, for details). But if you think you're gonna buy a computer eventually, and you can afford to do it now, keep reading.

If you want to buy a computer to use the Internet, buy a new computer or, at worst, one that's no more than a year old. New computers come with Internet software already installed and are often under $1,000. By the time you add whatever you need to an old computer, you will probably spend just as much money, invest more time, and get something not as good.

If you're purchasing a new computer primarily to surf the Net, you can buy a reasonably fast computer — a Pentium with a color monitor — for between $1,000 and $1,500. The World Wide Web is a colorful place; to get the real effect, you have to see it in color.

Pardon our limited vision — we tend to talk about only two categories of computers: Macintoshes and IBM PC clones. Which one is for you? Either is okay, they both work. Our advice: Buy what your friends have so that you can ask them for help.

When you're talking to other people and asking them what to buy, talk to people who do the same kinds of things you do, not just people who have computers. When you evaluate price, don't forget the value of your own time spent learning how to set up and use a computer and its software programs and your own nature when it comes to mechanical devices.

Incidentally, if you have some other type of computer, such as an Amiga or other "niche" machine (boy, are we going to hear from Amiga users about that one), try to track down a local users' group and find out which type of Internet software is available for your machine. More likely than not, someone will have something cheap or free you can use.

"What's your favorite Web page?"

It's http://net.gurus.com, of course. We never said that we aren't vain. You can find links to some of our other favorite pages, of course, as well as all sorts of useful Internet information that wouldn't fit into this book.)

Chapter 20

Ten Ways to Find E-Mail Addresses

As you probably have figured out, one teensy detail is keeping you from sending e-mail to all your friends: You don't know their addresses. In this chapter, you find out lots of different ways to look for addresses. We save you the trouble of reading the rest of this chapter by starting out with the easiest, most reliable way to find out people's e-mail addresses:

> Call them on the phone and ask them.

Pretty low-tech, huh? For some reason, this technique seems to be absolutely the last thing people want to do (see the nearby sidebar, "Top ten reasons not to call someone to get an e-mail address"). Try it first. If you know or can find out the phone number, this method is much easier than any of the others.

Search for People on the Web

The world is changing. Perhaps your friend has created a home page. Use your favorite Web directory or index to search by using your friend's name in quotes (" ") as the keyword for your search. If your friend does have a home page, an e-mail address is probably somewhere on the page.

Whaddaya mean you don't know your own address?

It happens frequently — usually because a friend is using a private e-mail system that has a gateway to the outside world that provides instructions for how to send messages to the outside but no hint about how outsiders send stuff in. The solution is, fortunately, usually easy: Tell your friend to send you a message. All messages have return addresses, and all except the absolute cruddiest of mail gateways put on a usable return address. Don't be surprised if the address has a great deal of strange punctuation. After a message makes it through a few gateways, you always seem to end up with things like this:

"blurch::John.C.Calhoun"%farp@slimemail.com

If you type the strange address back in, it usually works, so don't worry about it.

You can find out your own address this way by sending a message to our ever vigilant mail robot, at `internet6@gurus.com`, which sends you back a note telling you, among other things, what the return address in your message was. (Because the human authors also see those messages, feel free to add a few words telling us whether you like the book, what you'd like us to improve the next time we update it, and what Internet software you use.)

Top ten reasons not to call someone to get an e-mail address

✔ You want to surprise a long-lost friend.

✔ You want to surprise a long-lost *ex*-friend who owes you a large amount of money and thinks that she has given you the slip.

✔ You or your friend don't speak English. (Actually happens — many Internauts are outside the United States.)

✔ You or your friend don't speak at all. (Actually happens — networks offer a uniquely friendly place for most people with handicaps because nobody knows or cares about the handicaps.)

✔ It's 3 a.m. and you need to send a message right now or else you'll never get to sleep.

✔ You don't know the phone number, and because of an unfortunate childhood experience, you have a deathly fear of calling directory assistance.

✔ The phone takes only quarters; nobody around can break your $100 bill.

✔ Your company has installed a new phone system, no one has figured out how to use it, and, no matter what you dial, you always end up with Dial-a-Prayer.

✔ You inadvertently spilled an entire can of soda into the phone and can't wait for it to dry out to make the call.

✔ You called yesterday, didn't write down the answer, and forgot it. Oops.

Hey, Ms. Postmaster

Sometimes, you have a pretty good idea of what machine someone uses, but you don't know its name. In that case, you can try writing to the postmaster. Every *domain,* the part of the address after @ (the at-sign) that can receive Internet mail has the e-mail address postmaster, which contacts someone responsible for that machine. If you're pretty sure that your friend uses my.bluesuede.org, you can try asking postmaster@my.bluesuede.org (politely, of course) what the address is. (We assume that, for some reason, you can't just call your friend and ask for the e-mail address.)

Although most postmasters are overworked system administrators who don't mind an occasional polite question, you shouldn't expect any big favors. Keep in mind that the larger the mail domain, the less likely that the postmaster knows all the users personally. Don't write to postmaster@ibm.com to try to find someone's e-mail address at IBM. (Fortunately, for people who want to find correspondents in the Blue Zone, IBM has an online directory — see the following sidebar, "Okay, how do I find people at big companies?")

The postmaster is also the appropriate place to write when you're having trouble with mail to or from a site. If your messages to someone are coming back with a cryptic error message that suggests that the mail system is fouled up or if you're receiving a flood of mechanically generated junk mail from a deranged automatic mail server (see Chapter 13), the postmaster at the relevant site is the one to write.

Search for People in Newsgroups

If your friend participates in any Usenet newsgroups (online discussions), you can use AltaVista to search Usenet (rather than the Web) or check out the Web page at http://www.dejanews.com. Remember that although your friend may not use his full name or anything resembling his name, it's worth a try.

For a description of Usenet newsgroups, see http://net.gurus.com/usenet.

Online Directories

Wouldn't it be cool if some online directory listed everybody's e-mail address? Maybe, but the Internet doesn't have one. For one thing, nothing says that somebody's e-mail address has any connection to her name. For another, not everybody wants everybody else to know his e-mail address. Although lots of directories in progress are attempting to accumulate e-mail addresses, none of them is complete, and many work only if people voluntarily list themselves with the service.

This situation reiterates, of course, our point that the best way to find someone's e-mail address is to ask. When that method isn't an option, this section presents some other routes to try. Some of the directories you can use to find people provide an e-mail address if it's known. Although we talk about these directories in Chapter 8, it's worth pointing out here which ones purport to find e-mail addresses.

Yahoo People Search

Chapter 8 tells you all about Yahoo People Search, formerly called the Four11 directory service. Go to `http://people.yahoo.com` and try its e-mail search. If you want other people to find you, this is a good place to list yourself.

WhoWhere?

Go to `http://www.whowhere.lycos.com`, enter the name of the person you want to find, and click the WhoWhere FIND button. Look up yourself, and find your long-lost relatives.

Bigfoot

Go to `http://www.bigfoot.com` to search for e-mail addresses or phone numbers. They have "yellow pages" too. **Warning:** Unlike all the other directories, Bigfoot refuses to delete listings, so think twice about adding yourself if you're not already there.

InterNIC

In Chapter 8, where we tell you how to find people, we also tell you about InterNIC. The short version is to go to `http://www.internic.net/wp/whois.html`, enter in the search string the name of the person you want to find, and press the Search button. If you're looking for someone who runs an Internet computer, domain, or network, InterNIC is a good place to look; otherwise, don't bother.

Online services directories

Both America Online and CompuServe have member directories. If you don't have an account with either of them but you know someone who does, you can ask your acquaintance to look up someone's address for you.

Okay, how do I find people at big companies?

We thought that you would never ask. IBM has a mail server that lets you look up people's names. Send a message to `nic@vnet.ibm.com` that contains a line like this:

    whois Watson, T

The response lists any users with e-mail addresses whose names match. Although almost all IBM employees have internal e-mail addresses, only a fraction can receive mail from the outside, and you can see only those addresses. (Makes sense — no point in telling you about mail addresses you can't use.)

Many other companies have a straightforward addressing system that gives everyone at the company an alias, such as `Firstname.Lastname`. This technique works at AT&T, and mailing to the following address finds someone reliably:

    Theodore.Vail@att.com

This technique also works at Sun Microsystems (`sun.com`). It's always worth a try because the worst that can happen is that you get your message back as undeliverable. If several people have the same name, you usually get a mechanical response telling you how to figure out which of them you want and what the correct address is.

Alumni directories

Colleges and universities are creating Web sites to help promote themselves, and many are choosing to list some sort of alumni directory. Check your alma mater, and see whether it has a place for you to list yourself, your e-mail address, or your home page. Carol just got e-mail from the local chapter of her alumni organization. It could happen to you.

Compatible Mail System — an Oxymoron?

A zillion different networks are spliced into the Internet in one way or another. With many of them, you can barely tell that it's a different network. Because most UNIX systems, for example, have arranged to register standard Internet addresses, you can send mail to them in the same way as you send mail to any other Internet mailbox.

Many other mail systems are also out there, and several of them are in fact connected to the Internet. Because most of the connections seem to have been assembled with spit and baling wire, however, you have to type something strange to get the mail through. In this section, we talk about how to send mail to the most popular systems.

X.400: We're from the government, and we're here to help you

A great deal of international mail uses the somewhat unpleasant X.400 addressing system, defined by the international phone bureaucrats at the International Telecommunications Union in Switzerland.

An X.400 address isn't just a name and a domain: It's a bunch of attributes. Although the official specification goes on for dozens, if not hundreds, of pages, we spare you the detail (which would have been fascinating, you can be sure, if we had had the space) and report on the minimum. The attributes that are usually of interest and the codes used to represent them are shown in the following list:

Surname (S): Recipient's last name

Given name (G): Recipient's first name

Initials (I): First or middle initial (or initials)

Generational Qualifier (GQ or Q): Jr. or III, for example (these folks think of everything)

Administration Domain Name (ADMD or A): More or less the name of the mail system

Private Domain Name (PRMD or P): More or less the name of a private system reached via a public ADMD

Organization (O): The organization with which the recipient is affiliated, which may or may not have anything to do with the ADMD or PRMD

Country (C): A two-letter country code (see the list on our Web site, at http://net.gurus.com/countries)

Domain-Defined Attribute (DD or DDA): Any magic code that identifies the recipient, such as username or account number

You encode these attributes in an address, using / (a slash) to separate them and writing each attribute as the code, an equal sign, and the value. Is that clear? (No? Can't imagine why.)

Here's a concrete example: Suppose that your friend uses the Sprint Sprintmail service (formerly known as Telemail, the ADMD), which has an X.400 connection to the Internet. Your friend's name is Samuel Tilden, he's in the United States, and he's with Tammany Hall. His attributes are

G: Samuel

S: Tilden

O: TammanyHall

C: US

Because the Internet domain for the gateway is `sprint.com`, the address is

```
/G=Samuel/S=Tilden/O=TammanyHall/C=US/ADMD=TELEMAIL/
     @sprint.com
```

We're not making up this syntax. Sorry. Notice that a slash appears at the beginning of the address and just before the @. The order of the slash-separated chunks doesn't matter.

Exactly which attributes you need for a particular address varies all over the place. Because some domains connect to only a single country and ADMD, you don't use those attributes with those domains. Others (such as Sprintmail) connect to many, so you need both. It's a mess. You have to find out for each X.400 system which attributes it needs. In theory, redundant attributes shouldn't hurt; in practice, who knows?

One minor simplification applies to the hopefully common case in which the only attribute necessary is the recipient's actual name. If the user's name is Rutherford B. Hayes, the full attribute form is

```
/G=Rutherford/I=B/S=Hayes/@gateway
```

Instead, you can write

```
Rutherford.B.Hayes@gateway
```

Pretty advanced, eh? You can leave out the given name or the initial, if you want. You can hope that most X.400 addresses can be written this way, but you are probably doomed to disappointment.

In most cases, the easiest way to figure out someone's X.400 address is to have your correspondent send you a message and see what the `From:` line says. Failing that, you have to experiment.

X.500: We're from the government, and we're back

An official white pages directory-service model to look up people's e-mail addresses called X.500 is brought to us by the same people who brought us X.400. Not surprisingly, considering who defined it, X.500 organizes its data like a shelf full of phone books (or, in a large X.500 system, like a library of shelves organized by country). For any particular person, you have to tell X.500 in which book or books to look.

Another fact: If you're in one country, country A, and you want the phone number of someone in country B, the official ITU-T directory-assistance procedure is to connect you to someone in country A in a room full of old phone books from all over the world, in which they attempt to find the appropriate country B phone book and look up the person. If they can't find the number — because their country B phone books are all 15 years old and your friend moved 12 years ago, for example — tough. The scheme traditionally used in the United States, in which they connect you to an actual directory operator in country B who is likely to have current phone numbers, is in complete violation of standards. We feel that a moment of breathless admiration is appropriate for people who can invent standards like that.

Note: It looks like X.500 will be widely used, for two reasons: It is somewhat more usable than X.400, and no other competing candidates exist. (You get one guess about which is the more important reason.)

You can search a variety of X.500 directories via the World Wide Web. To get started, point your browser at `http://nic.nasa.gov:8888`.

A Parade of Mail Systems

This section presents a short (well, *pretty* short) list of major mail and online systems connected to the Internet and instructions for how to send mail to people on that system.

America Online

An AOL user's mail address is his *screen name*. To send mail to a user whose screen name is Spam Victim, for example, you type

```
spamvictim@aol.com
```

If the screen name has spaces, leave them out.

Some AOL users prefer their "stage name," such as `dickhmr@aol.com`. If you can't find your friend on AOL after trying the obvious, call your friend and ask. AOL makes the process of changing your screen name extremely easy; because a single user can have several screen names, AOL addresses change frequently.

For more information about using AOL, see Chapter 17.

AT&T Mail

AT&T Mail users have arbitrary usernames. To send mail to a user whose username is `blivet`, for example, you type

```
blivet@attmail.com
```

Note: AT&T Mail provides gateways to some companies' internal mail systems. In these cases, you may have an address like this:

```
argle!bargle!google@foocorp.attmail.com
```

CompuServe

CompuServe is a large online service. For ancient, historical reasons, CompuServe usernames are pairs of *octal* (base eight) numbers, usually beginning with the digit 7 for users in the United States and 10 for users overseas. If a user's number is 712345,6701, for example, her address is

```
712345.6701@compuserve.com
```

Note: The address uses a *period,* not a comma, because Internet addresses cannot contain commas. Although some users now also have regular-looking addresses, such as `johnsmith@compuserve.com`, their old, numeric addresses still work.

Because CompuServe used to charge its users for *incoming* Internet mail, many users have set their accounts to refuse mail from the Net.

Delphi

Delphi is an online service from the same people who run BIX, although the services are separate. Delphi usernames are arbitrary strings, most often the first initial and last name of the user. To send mail to user `support`, for example, you type

```
support@delphi.com
```

FIDONET

FIDONET is an extremely large, worldwide BBS network. On FIDONET, people are identified by their names, and each individual BBS (called a *node*) has a three- or four-part number in the form 1:2/3 or 1:2/3.4. To send a message to Grover Cleveland at node 1:2/3.4, you type

```
grover.cleveland@p4.f3.n2.z1.fidonet.org
```

If a node has a three-part name, such as 1:2/3, you type

```
grover.cleveland@f3.n2.z1.fidonet.org
```

Note: Many FIDO systems no longer accept incoming Internet mail because of the recent glut of junk e-mail. Too bad.

Internet service providers

Because each Internet service provider (ISP) has its own domain name, you need to ask your provider what its domain name is. A subscriber's address is the username followed by a @ and the ISP's domain name. For example, if your username were zac and your ISP's domain name were sover.net, your e-mail address would be zac@sover.net.

Microsoft Network

Microsoft Network (MSN) is a commercial online service run by the software giant Microsoft.

If your account name is Bill Gates (for example), your Internet e-mail address is

```
BillGates@msn.com
```

Many MSN users seem to have addresses like BillGates@ classic.msn.com, which as far as we can tell are equivalent to the non-classic variety.

Prodigy

Prodigy is a large online system that lost many millions of dollars while it was run by IBM and Sears. They sold it in 1996, and now it's losing someone else's money.

Prodigy is now two almost unrelated services. Prodigy Classic, which lives at `prodigy.com`, gives users arbitrary usernames, such as `KS8GN3`. Send mail to them at

```
KS8GN3@prodigy.com
```

Prodigy Internet, at `prodigy.net`, is a conventional Internet provider. If a user's name is `jqadams`, the address is

```
jqadams@prodigy.net
```

UUCP

UUCP is an old and cruddy mail system still used by many UNIX systems because (how did you guess?) it's free. UUCP addresses consist of a system name and a username, which are both short, arbitrary strings. The system here at Internet For Dummies Central, for example, used to have a UUCP address — `iecc` — in addition to its normal Internet address, so you could address mail to `iecc!internet6`. (The `!` is pronounced "bang," and it's called a *bang path address*.) Multihop UUCP addresses also exist: `world!iecc!internet6` says to send the message first to the machine called `world`, which could send it to `iecc`, where the address is `internet6`. (Think of it as the e-mail version of "Whisper Down the Lane.") UUCP addresses are written relative to an Internet host that also talks UUCP, so an address would look like this:

```
world!iecc!internet6@uunet.uu.net
```

(Because we have a real Internet connection now and gave up on UUCP, you actually send your message to `internet6@gurus.com`.) If you think that UUCP addresses are ugly and confusing, you're not alone.

Because UUNET Communications is a large outfit that, among other things, brings e-mail to the UUCP-speaking masses, it's the Internet system most often seen with UUCP addresses. Most UUNET customers also have regular Internet addresses that internally are turned into the ugly UUCP addresses. If you know the Internet address, use it rather than the UUCP address.

WebTV

WebTV is the new Internet access device that lets you use your TV and telephone for Internet access. Users have a username (such as couchpotato) that they select when they sign up, and their e-mail address is just something like couchpotato@webtv.net. See Chapter 18.

Chapter 21

Ten Types of Files and What to Do with Them

*N*ow that you know how to use the Web and FTP and how to download, you probably have already retrieved zillions of files (or maybe three or four). When you look at them with your word processor or text editor, however, you may notice that they're garbage. In this chapter, we describe the various types of files on the Net and how to tell what they are and what to do with them.

How Many Kinds of Files Are There?

Hundreds, at least. Fortunately, they fall into five general categories:

  ✔ **Text:** Files that contain text, believe it or not.

  ✔ **Executable:** Files you can execute, or run; in other words, programs.

  ✔ **Compressed:** Archives, ZIP files, SIT files, and other compressed files.

  ✔ **Graphics, audio, and video:** Files that contain pictures and sounds encoded in computer-readable form. Graphics files on Web pages are usually in GIF or JPEG format. Audio files can be in WAV (Windows audio), RAM (RealAudio), or other formats. Video files contain digitized movies.

  ✔ **Data:** Any other type of file.

This chapter describes all five types in more detail.

Macs are different, too

Macintosh files, regardless of what's in them, usually come in two or three chunks, one of which is the data file. Although you don't see the chunks on your own Macintosh, you do see them if you try to upload them to a non-Mac server on the Net. In the Macintosh world, the three files are all pieces of one file and are referred to as *forks* — the data fork, the resource fork, and the information fork.

When you upload from a Macintosh what you think is one file, it often appears as three separate files with the extensions DATA, RESC, and INFO appended to the filename. Various schemes exist (described in the section "Packing It In" later in this chapter) to glue the forks back together for transportation over the Net.

The name of a file — in particular, its *extension* (the end of the name after the period) — gives you a clue about the type of file it is. Although the person who names the file usually tries to be consistent and follow the conventions for naming files, file naming isn't a sure thing. In the old days of DOS, filenames always had an extension at the end of as many as three characters, and the period could be used only to separate the extension. Because UNIX and later versions of Windows allow the period character to be any part of the filename, hard rules about extensions no longer exist. Nevertheless, old habits cling, and computer people still use conventional extensions to help in giving files a name that conveys something about their content. Windows uses the extension to tell what program to use to open a file, so you may sometimes have to rename a file to an extension that will persuade Windows to use the right program.

Just Plain Text

Text files contain readable text without any word-processor-style formatting codes. (What did you expect?) Sometimes, the text is human-readable text, such as the manuscript for this book, which we typed into text files the first time we wrote it. Sometimes, the text is source code for computer programs in languages such as C or Pascal. Occasionally, the text is data for programs. PostScript printer data is a particular kind of text file, discussed in the sidebar "It's a program that draws a picture" later in this chapter.

On PCs, text files usually have the file extension .txt. You can look at these files by using Notepad in Windows 3.1, WordPad in Windows 95 or 98, or any word processor. Read text files on a Macintosh with SimpleText or any word processor.

We don't have much to say about text files — you know them when you see them. As mentioned in Chapter 16, because the way text is stored varies from one system to another, you should FTP text files in ASCII mode to convert them automatically to your local format. That is, if you're using an FTP program, choose the ASCII rather than Binary option when you're downloading files; if you're using a Web browser, never mind. The reason is that, historically, different systems have had trouble agreeing what character should be used to separate the lines of text. (We know that you're thinking, "Why can't we all just get along?") Should the character be a carriage return? A line-feed? A newline? A carriage return followed by a newline? Your browser knows what's best for you.

A few text documents are really archives or non-text files in drag. See the discussions of uuencoded files in Chapter 16.

Any Last Requests before We Execute You?

Executable files are actual programs you can run on a computer. Executable programs are particularly common in archives of stuff for PCs and Macs. Some executable programs are also available on the Net for other kinds of computers, such as various workstations. Any single executable file runs on only a particular type of computer: A Mac executable file is useless on a Windows machine and vice versa.

It's a program that draws a picture

If you encounter a text file that starts out something like the following, you have a PostScript file:

```
%!PS-Adobe-2.0
%%Title: Some Random Document
%%CreationDate: Fri Jan 15
    1999
/pl transform 0.1 sub round
    0.1 add exch
  0.1 sub round 0.1 add exch
    itransform bind def
```

A PostScript file is a program in the PostScript computer language that describes a printed document. (PostScript is called a *page-description language.*) Unless you're a world-class PostScript weenie, the only sensible thing to do with this type of file is to run the program and see the document. The normal way to do that is to send the whole thing to a PostScript printer. Programs called PostScript *viewers,* such as *GNU Ghostscript,* can read your PostScript file and display it on-screen (so that you can see how it would look if you printed it) or convert it into a format your non-PostScript printer can use.

The most common executable programs are for DOS and Windows. These files have filenames such as Foog.exe, Foog.com, or (sometimes in Windows) Foog.dll. You run them in the same way as you run any other DOS or Windows program: Double-click its filename in File Manager in Windows 3.1 or in My Computer or Windows Explorer in Windows 95 and 98.

Some chance always exists that any new PC or Mac program may be infected with a computer virus. (Because of the different ways in which the systems work, UNIX programs are much less likely to carry viruses.) Stuff from well-run software archives is unlikely to be infected; if you run an unknown program from a random place, however, you deserve whatever you get.

Executable programs for workstations don't have easily recognizable filenames, although any file whose filename contains a dot is unlikely to be executable. Even though almost every kind of workstation runs UNIX, the executables are not interchangeable. Code for a SPARC, for example, doesn't work on an IBM RS/6000 or vice versa. Several different versions of UNIX run on 386 PCs, with different executable formats. Newer versions of PC UNIX generally run executables from older versions but not vice versa.

Packing It In

Many software packages require bunches of related files. To make it easier to send such a package around, you can glom the files together into a single file known as an *archive.* (Yes, archive also refers to a host from which you can FTP stuff. Sorry. In this chapter, at least, archive means *a multifile file.*) After you retrieve an archive, you use an *unarchiving program* to extract the original files.

Some files are also *compressed,* which means that they're encoded in a special way that takes up less space but that can be decoded only by the corresponding *uncompressor.* Most files you retrieve by anonymous FTP are compressed because compressed files use less disk space and take less time to transfer over the Net. In the PC world, archiving and compression usually happen together by using utilities such as WinZip to create *ZIP files.* In the Mac world, the StuffIt program is popular. In the workstation world, however, the two procedures — compression and archiving — are usually done separately: The programs *tar* and *cpio* do the archiving, and the programs *compress* and *gzip* do the compressing.

If you retrieve many files from the Net, you have to learn how to uncompress stuff. The four main compression schemes are

- ✓ ZIP
- ✓ compress

⊩ ✔ gzip

⊩ ✔ StuffIt

ZIPping it up

The most widely used compression and archiving programs for Windows and DOS are the shareware programs WinZip and PKZIP. Zipped files all end with the extension .zip.

Windows users can use the excellent shareware WinZip program, mentioned in Chapter 16. It not only handles ZIP files but also knows how to extract the contents of most of the other types of compressed files you run into on the Net.

DOS users can use the original shareware PKZIP and PKUNZIP programs to create and extract zip files.

Compatible UNIX zipping and unzipping programs called *zip* and *unzip* (the authors are creative programmers but not creative namers) are available at ftp.uu.net and elsewhere. For situations in which the shareware nature of PKUNZIP is a problem, a DOS version of UNIX unzip is available, although it's only about half as fast as PKUNZIP.

Many ZIP files you encounter on the Net are *self-extracting,* which means that the ZIP file is packaged with an unzipping program; even if you don't already have an unzipper, you just run the archive and it extracts its contents. (PKZIP and WinZip are distributed in this way.) Because self-extracting archives are programs, they have the extension *.exe* rather than *.zip.* If you *do* have an unzipper already, use it to extract the files; tell it to open the archive in the same way as you would open any other archive. This process ensures that the archive contains what it says it does and also lets you use the WinZip installation-assist feature. Although the self-extracting feature works on only DOS and Windows, self-extracting ZIP files are still ZIP files, and you can extract their contents anyway if you have an unzip program for your computer.

Compression classic

Back in 1975, a programmer named Terry Welch published a paper about a swell, new compression scheme he had just invented. A couple of UNIX programmers implemented it as the program *compress,* and it quickly became the standard compression program on UNIX systems. Although better compressors are available now, compress is still the standard.

You can easily recognize a compressed program because its name ends with Z. On PCs, compressed files often have names ending with Z, such as

Blurfle.taz. A UNIX-compatible version of compress is available in the SIMTEL archive, in the directory /msdos/compress as comp430d.zip; it's easier, however, for Windows users to use WinZip.

It's patently obvious

Something that the people who wrote compress didn't realize is that Welch not only published the scheme that compress uses but also patented it. (Two other guys at IBM, named Miller and Wegman, independently invented the same scheme at the same time and also got a patent on it, something that's not supposed to happen because only the first person to invent something is allowed to patent it. The patents are definitely there, though.) UNISYS, which employs Welch, has said from time to time that it may someday begin to collect royalties from the use of compress. It has done so for other things that use the same compression scheme (notably, CompuServe GIF files) but never compress.

So the Free Software Foundation, which runs the GNU free software project, wrote *gzip,* which uses 100 percent nonpatented algorithms. Files that are *gzip*-ped use the filename extension .gz and can also be decompressed by WinZip.

Just StuffIt!

The favorite Macintosh compression and archiving program is a shareware program written by Raymond Lau and known as StuffIt. StuffIt comes in many flavors, including a commercially available version called StuffIt Deluxe. StuffIt files of all varieties generally use the filename extension .sit.

For decompression, you can use the freeware programs UnStuffIt, StuffIt Expander, or DropStuff with Expander Enhancer, widely available for Macs.

Other archivers

Dozens of other compressing archivers are out there, with names such as LHARC, ZOO, and ARC. DOS and Mac users can find unarchivers for all of them in the SIMTEL repository. The only other one that's widely used is the Japanese LHA because it compresses well and is free. Look for LHA213, the most recent version.

In the Archives

Two different UNIX archive programs are *tar* and *cpio*. They were written at about the same time by people at two different branches of Bell Laboratories in different parts of New Jersey. They both do about the same thing; they're just different.

An important difference between UNIX-type archives and ZIP files is that UNIX archives usually contain subdirectories; ZIP files rarely do. You should always look at a UNIX archive's table of contents (the list of files it contains) before extracting the files so that you know where the files will end up.

The name *tar* stands for *t*ape *ar*chive. Although tar was designed to put archives of files on old reel-to-reel tapes, it writes to any medium. Files archived by tar usually have the filename extension .tar, and the frequent combination of tar archiving followed by compress compression creates the extension .tar.Z or .taz. Windows users can, as usual, unscramble either with WinZip.

Cpio files are difficult to handle if your computer is not running on a UNIX system. If someone gives you a cpio file, give it back and ask him to re-archive it in a more tractable format.

For the Artistically Inclined

A large and growing fraction of all the bits flying around the Internet is made up of increasingly high-quality digitized pictures. About 99.44 percent of the pictures are purely for fun, games, and worse. We're sure that you're in the 0.56 percent of users who need the pictures for work, so here's a roundup of picture formats.

The most commonly used graphics formats on the Net are GIF, JPEG, and PNG. You almost never find GIF or JPEG image files compressed or archived. The reason is that these formats already do a pretty fair job of compression internally, so compress, zip, and the like don't help any.

I could GIF a . . .

The most widely used format on the Internet is the CompuServe *GIF* (Graphics Interchange Format). This format is well matched to the capabilities of a typical PC computer screen — no more than 256 different colors in a picture and usually 640 x 480, 1024 x 768, or some other familiar PC screen resolution. Two versions of GIF exist: *GIF87* and *GIF89*. The differences are small enough that almost every program that can read GIF can read either version equally well. Because GIF is well standardized, you never have problems with files written by one program being unreadable by another. GIF files have the extension *.gif.*

Dozens of commercial and shareware programs on PCs and Macs can read and write GIF files. Netscape and Internet Explorer can display them as well; just choose Open from the File menu.

PNG-a-ding

GIF files use the same patented compression as the UNIX compress program, and in 1995, UNISYS began collecting royalties from CompuServe and anyone else it could find who sells software that uses the patented technique. As a result, a group of Net graphics users came up with a patent-free replacement for GIF called PNG (with the extension *.png*). We expect to see GIF fade away eventually and PNG replace it. PNG handles the same kinds of images that GIF does, and most programs that can handle GIF are being updated for PNG.

The eyes have it

A few years back, a bunch of digital photography experts got together and decided that a.) it was time to have an official standard format for digitized photographs and b.) none of the existing formats was good enough. They formed the *Joint Photographic Experts Group (JPEG),* and after extended negotiation, the JPEG format was born. JPEG is designed specifically to store digitized, full-color or black-and-white photographs, not computer-generated cartoons or anything else. As a result, JPEG does a fantastic job of storing photos and a lousy job of storing anything else.

A JPEG version of a photo is about one-fourth the size of its corresponding GIF file. (JPEG files can be *any* size because the format allows a trade-off between size versus quality when the file is created.) The main disadvantage of JPEG is that it's considerably slower to decode than GIF; the files are so much smaller, however, that JPEG is worth the time. Most programs that can display GIF files, including Netscape and Internet Explorer, now also handle JPEG. JPEG files usually have filenames with the extension .jpeg or .jpg.

Some people occasionally claim that JPEG pictures don't look anywhere near as good as GIF pictures do. What is true is that if you make a 256-color GIF file from a full-color photograph and then translate that GIF file into a JPEG file, it doesn't look good. So don't do that. For the finest in photographic quality, demand full-color JPEGs.

A few words from the vice squad

We bet that you're wondering whether any public online archives contain, er, exotic photography but you're too embarrassed to ask. Well, we'll tell you — there isn't much of it. Nothing in any public FTP archive is any raunchier than fashion photos from *Redbook* or *Sports Illustrated.*

That's for two reasons. One is political. The companies and universities that fund most of the free public sites on the Internet are not interested in being accused of being pornographers or in filling up their expensive disks with pictures that have nothing to do with any legitimate work. (At one university archive, when the *Playboy* pictures went away, they were replaced by a note which said that if you could explain why you needed them for your academic research, they would put them back.)

The other reason is practical. From time to time, someone makes his (almost always *his,* by the way) private collection of R- or X-rated pictures available for anonymous FTP. Within

5 minutes, 1,000 sweaty-palmed undergraduates try to FTP in, and that corner of the Internet grinds to a halt. After another five minutes, out of sheer self-preservation, the pictures go away. (If you don't believe us, see *Sex For Dummies,* published by IDG Books Worldwide, Inc, in which Dr. Ruth Westheimer says the same thing.)

If someone you know is in desperate need of these types of works of art (not you, of course, but, er, someone down the hall needs them for sociology research — that's it), you might direct him to look at the sites http://www.playboy.com and http://www.penthousemag.com, which usually contain a few of the milder pictures from the current issues of the magazines.

Plenty of sites on the Web *do* show you porn if you give them a credit card number to pay for it. We're cheap, so we have never looked to see what they offer.

A trip to the movies

As networks get faster and disks get bigger, people are starting to store entire digitized movies (still rather *short* ones, at this point). The standard movie format is called *Moving Picture Experts Group (MPEG).* MPEG was designed by a committee down the hall from the JPEG committee and — practically unprecedented in the history of standards efforts — was designed based on earlier work.

MPEG viewers are found in the same places as JPEG viewers. You need a reasonably fast workstation or a top-of-the-line power-user PC to display MPEG movies in anything close to real time.

A few other competing movie formats are also used — notably, Shockwave and Apple QuickTime — and appear on Web pages. You can get Web browser plug-ins that run the movies for you. For Netscape plug-ins, visit http://home.netscape.com/plugins. For Internet Explorer add-ons, visit http://www.microsoft.com/msdownload/default.asp and click Internet Explorer under Windows Update. You can also check for other sources at our Web site, at http://net.gurus.com/software.

Let a hundred formats blossom

Many other graphics-file formats are in use, although GIF and JPEG are by far the most popular ones on the Internet. Other formats you run into include

- ✔ **PCX:** This DOS format (with extension *.pcx*) is used by many paint programs — it's also okay for low-resolution photos.

- ✔ **TIFF:** This enormously complicated format (with extension *.tiff* or *.tif*) has hundreds of options — so many that a TIFF file written by one program often can't be read by another.

- ✔ **TARGA:** (With extension *.tga* on PCs.) This format is a common one for scanned, full-color photos. In Internet archives, TARGA is now supplanted by the much more compact JPEG.

- ✔ **PICT:** This format (with extension *.pict*) is common on Macintoshes because the Mac has built-in support for it.

- ✔ **BMP:** This Windows bitmap format (with extension *.bmp*) is not used much on the Net because BMP files tend to be larger than they need to be.

Sound Off!

Audio files — files that contain digitized sound — can be found all over the Web. If you like to listen to National Public Radio news, for example, but can't get around to listening when it's on, you can listen to major news stories from the NPR Web page (at `http://www.npr.org`) at any time — totally cool. We also like some of the live concerts and radio stations at `http://www.audionet.com`.

You can listen to sounds from the Web in two ways:

- ✔ **Download an entire audio file, and then play it.** This method has the advantage that you can play the file as many times as you want without downloading it again. Downloading an audio file can take quite a while, however.

- ✔ **Play the audio file *as you download it* so that you don't have to wait for the whole file to arrive before starting to hear it.** This method involves *streaming audio.* Although the quality isn't as good, most sound on the Net isn't worth waiting to download, anyway.

Nonstreaming audio files have extensions such as *.wav, .mp3, .au,* and *.aif.* MPLAYER, which comes with most versions of Windows, can play WAV files. You can download sound players from many online software archives (see `http://net.gurus.com/software` to find out where to download sound players and plug-ins). The latest Web browsers have built-in sound players, too.

The most popular system for playing streaming audio files is RealAudio, and files in its format have the extension *.ra* or *.ram*. To play RealAudio files, you need the RealPlayer plug-in, which you can download from `http://www.real.com` or from software archives such as TUCOWS (`http://www.tucows.com`). The RealAudio player also handles RealVideo, which has small, blurry moving pictures to go with your sound.

None of the Above

Some files don't fit any of the descriptions mentioned in this chapter. For example, you occasionally find formatted word-processor files to be used with programs such as WordPerfect and Microsoft Word. If you encounter one of these files and don't have access to the matching word-processor program, you can usually load the files into a text editor, in which you see the text in the file intermingled with nonprinting junk that represents formatting information. In a pinch, you can edit out the junk to recover the text. Before you resort to that method, however, try loading them with whatever word processor you have. Most word-processing software can recognize a competitor's format and makes a valiant effort to convert the format to something usable by you so that you aren't tempted to buy the other product. For the particular case of Microsoft Word, the company gives away a free program for Windows that displays and prints Word documents. It's at

```
http://officeupdate.microsoft.com/
```

Scroll down to the Word section of the page and find the viewer for your version of Windows.

The most commonly used text-processing program on the Net remains the elderly but serviceable TeX, invented to help typeset scientific books. TeX takes as its input plain text files with formatting commands in text form, something like this:

```
\begin{quote}
Your mother wears army boots.
\end{quote}
```

If you want to know more about TeX, you can begin by pointing your browser to `http://www.tug.org`. Free versions of TeX are available for most computers. Another, even more elderly, text processor called *troff* (pronounced "tee-roff," and we used it to write the first edition of this book, so don't make too many smart-alecky comments) is also in moderately wide use. In fact, free versions of troff are available for UNIX and Linux.

Chapter 22

Ten Ways to Avoid Looking Like a Klutz

● ●

In This Chapter

▶ Tips for suave, sophisticated Net usage

▶ Some bonehead moves not to make

● ●

Gosh, using the Internet is exciting. And gosh, it offers many ways to make a fool of yourself — heaven forbid that you should act like a *clueless newbie*. In this chapter, we round up the usual suspects of unfortunate moves so that you can be the coolest Web surfer on your block.

Read before you write

The moment you get your new Internet account, you may have an overwhelming urge to begin sending out lots of messages right away. *Don't do it!* Read mailing lists, Web pages, and other Net resources for a while before you send anything out. You will figure out where best to send your messages, which makes it both more likely that you will contact people who are interested in what you say and less likely that you will annoy people by bothering them with irrelevancies by sending something to an inappropriate place. If you see a FAQ (Frequently Asked Questions) section, read it to see whether your question has already been answered.

Netiquette matters

On the Net, you are what you type. The messages you send are the only way that 99 percent of the people you meet on the Net will know you.

Speling counts

Many Net users feel that because Net messages are short and informal, spelling and grammar don't count. Some even think that strange spelling makes them E133T K00L D00DZ. If you feel that wey, theirs' not much wee can do abowt it. We think that a sloppy, misspelled message is like a big grease stain on your shirt — your friends will know that it's you, but people who don't know you will conclude that you don't know how to dress yourself.

Many mail programs have spell checkers. Eudora Pro (the commercial version of Eudora) checks your spelling after you click the dictionary icon (the *ABC* one) on the toolbar or choose Edit⇨Check Spelling from the menu; in Netscape 4.0/4.5, which also comes with a spell checker, you choose Tools⇨Check Spelling from the menu. In Outlook Express, you can elect, via the Options menu, to have your outgoing messages checked or choose Tools⇨Spelling to check any message in progress. In Pine, you check your spelling by pressing Ctrl+T. Although spell checkers aren't perfect, at least they ensure that your messages consist of 100 percent genuine words.

DO NOT SEND YOUR ENTIRE MESSAGE IN CAPITAL LETTERS. This technique comes across as shouting and is likely to get you some snappy comments suggesting that you do something about the stuck Shift key on your keyboard. Now and then we get mail from someone who says, "i dont use capital letters or punctuation its too much work." Uh-huh.

If you don't have anything to say, don't say it

Avoid trying to sound smart. When you do, the result is usually its opposite. One day on the mailing list TRAVEL-L someone asked for information about some travel destination. Then came the edifying comment "Sorry, Bud, Can't Help You." Well, duh. We hoped that people who don't know anything could keep their mouths shut, but we were wrong. Each message you post to a list goes to the entire list. Each list member is there on a voluntary basis. Like us, they often have conflicts about mailing-list subscriptions. Does the good content of the list outweigh the noise and inanity? The more inanity, the more sensible subscribers will leave and the list will deteriorate. If you're going to participate, find a constructive way to do so.

Keep your hands to yourself

Another stupidity we witnessed involved someone subscribing his arch enemy to a list against his wishes. Okay, folks. This is not kindergarten. When you start to abuse public lists, they go private. Lists that are unmoderated turn moderated. Moderated lists become "by invitation only." Although some lists thrive on juvenile behavior, it's not welcome on most lists.

Subscription inscription (and defection)

Signing up for a mailing list is a cool thing. We tell you all about how to do it in Chapter 13. Still, however (or maybe this advice is just for people who aren't reading our book), a classic way to look like a klutz is to send to the list itself a message asking to be added to or taken off a list, where all the people on the list have to read it, but it doesn't actually get the sender subscribed or taken off. Subscribe and unsubscribe requests go to the list server program in a particular format or, in the case of lists that are not automated, to the list owner.

Read the rules

When you first subscribe to a mailing list, you usually get back a long message about how this particular list operates and how to unsubscribe if you want. Read this message. Save this message. Before you go telling other people on the list how to behave, read the rules again. Some officious newbie, newly subscribed to JAZZ-L, began flaming the list and complaining about the off-topic threads. JAZZ-L encourages this kind of discussion — it says so right in the introduction to the list. Can't say as how she made herself really welcome with that move.

Edit yourself

When you're posting to a mailing list, remember that your audience is the entire world, made up of people of all ethnicities and races speaking different languages and representing different cultures. Work hard to represent yourself and your culture well. Avoid name-calling and disparaging comments about other peoples and places. Read several times through whatever you intend to post before you send it. We have seen inadvertent typos change the intended meaning of a message to its complete opposite.

Discretion is the better part

Sooner or later, you see something that cries out for a cheap shot. Sooner or later, someone sends you something you shouldn't have seen and you want to pass it on. Don't do it. Resist cheap shots and proliferating malice. The Net has plenty of jerks — don't be another one. (See the suggestion later in this chapter about what to do when you're tempted to flame.) Be tolerant of newbies — you were once one yourself.

Keep it private

Okay, someone makes a mistake, such as sending to the entire mailing list a message that says "subscribe" or posting a message that says, "Gee, I don't know!" in response to a request for help with a newsgroup. Yes, it's true, someone made a dumb move. Don't compound it, however, by posting additional messages complaining about it. Either delete the message and forget about it or respond privately, by e-mail addressed only to the person, not to the mailing list. The entire mailing list probably doesn't want to hear your advice to the person who blew it. For example, you can send a private e-mail message saying, "In the future, send subscription and unsubscription messages to `eggplants-request`, not to `eggplants`, okay?" or "This is a list about domestic laying hens, so could you post your message about cats somewhere else?"

Signing off

All mail programs let you have a *signature,* a file that gets added to the end of each mail or news message you send. The signature is supposed to contain something to identify you. Snappy quotes quickly became common, to add that personal touch. Here's John's signature, for example:

```
Regards,
John Levine, johnl@iecc.com, Primary Perpetrator of "The
        Internet For Dummies,"
Information Superhighwayman wanna-be, http://iecc.com/
        johnl, Sewer Commissioner
```

(Yes, he really is the sewer commissioner. Tours! Free samples!) Some people's signatures get way out of hand, going on for 100 lines of "ASCII art," long quotations, extensive disclaimers, and other allegedly interesting stuff. Although this type of signature may seem cute the first time or two, it quickly gets tedious and marks you as a total newbie.

Keep your signature to four lines or fewer. All the experienced Net users do.

Don't get attached

Attachments are a useful way to send files by e-mail. But they work only if the person on the receiving end has a program that can read the files you are sending. For example, if you send a WordPerfect document to someone who doesn't have a word-processing program, the file is unreadable. Ditto for graphics files, sound files, and other files you may want to send around. Indeed, some older mail systems can't handle attachments at all. Ask *first* before sending an attachment.

Flame off!

For some reason, it's easy to get VERY, VERY UPSET ABOUT SOMETHING SOMEONE SAYS ON THE NET. (See, it happens even to us.) Sometimes it's something you find on the Web, and sometimes it's personal e-mail. You may be tempted to shoot a message right back telling that person what a doofus he is. Guess what? He will almost certainly shoot back. This type of over-stated outrage is so common that it has its own name: *flaming.* Now and then, it's fun if you're certain that the recipient will take it in good humor, but it's always unnecessary. For one thing, e-mail messages always come across as crabbier than the author intended; for another, crabbing back will hardly make the person more reasonable. A technique we often find helpful is to write the strongest, crabbiest response possible, full of biting wit and skewering each point in turn. Then we throw it away rather than send it.

Antisocial mail

Although we mention this subject in Chapters 11 and 12, it's worth mentioning here, too: There are a few kinds of messages you should never, ever send. Most are not illegal (at least not in most places), but your mailbox will quickly fill with displeased responses, and your provider will soon cancel your account.

The chain gang

Sending a chain letter on the Net is easy: Just click the Forward button, type a few names, and send your letter off. It's a lousy idea. We have never, ever gotten a chain letter that was worth passing along. A bunch of classic chain letters have been circulating around the Net for a decade (see Chapter 12 for details about the boy who doesn't want cards, the phantom good-times virus, the nonexistent modem tax, the overpriced recipe that isn't, and a way that you won't make money fast). Regardless of where they come from, even if they seem to be for a good cause, please just throw them away.

Some of the online chain letters started as paper letters. We once got a paper version of the Make Money Fast chain letter from Guam. We did the same thing with it that we do with computer chain letters — into the trash.

Spammity spam, horrible spam

One of the least pleasant online innovations in recent years is *spamming,* or sending the same message — usually selling something that was rather dubious in the first place — to as many e-mail addresses or Usenet groups as possible. This practice is annoying, illegal in some places, and the spammer is usually liable for her provider's costs in cleaning it up. Spamming is also ineffective because automatic systems identify and cancel most Usenet spams within minutes after they occur, an increasing number of providers offer e-mail filtering, and most recipients including us presume that anything advertised by spam must be fraudulent. For more information about this topic, see Chapter 12.

Don't be a pig

Unbelievable amounts of material are on the Net: programs, documents, pictures, megabyte after megabyte of swell stuff — all free for the taking. You can download it all. Don't. Go ahead and take whatever you're likely to use, but don't download entire directories full of stuff or leave your computer online for hours at a time "just in case."

Your Internet provider sets its charges based on the resources a typical user uses. A single user can use a substantial fraction of the provider's Net connection by sucking down files continuously for hours at a time. Providers typically "overcommit" their Net connection by a factor of three or so. That is, if every user tried to transfer data at full speed at the same time, it would require three times as fast a connection as the provider has. Because real users transfer for a while and then read what's on-screen for a while, sharing the connection among all the users works out okay. (The provider is not cheating you by using this method; it's a sensible way to provide access at a reasonable cost. Although you can get guaranteed connection performance if you want it, the price is horrifying.) If users begin using several more connections than the provider budgeted for, prices will go up.

Hang up, already!

This advice applies particularly to providers who offer unlimited connect-time per month. Don't leave your computer connected if you're not using it. Most Net software packages have a time-out feature that hangs up if no data is transferred to or from the Net for a specified period. We leave ours set to 15 minutes on our dial-up connections; otherwise, other users get a busy signal when they try to connect.

Audio and video pigs

Internet Phone and the like present a particular problem on the Net because they put a much, much heavier load on both the local provider and the Net in general than do other Internet services. When you're transferring voice information over the Net, you're pumping data through as fast as your connection will let you. Video connections are even worse: When sites with fast Net connections begin sending video programs around to each other, the entire Net slows down.

For the moment, few enough people are using Internet Phone that it hasn't become a big problem. If it becomes popular enough, providers will have to provide "no phone" and "phone" accounts, with the latter costing much more, to keep reasonable access for all their users.

Cybercafé etiquette

Cybercafés are new, and our parents never had the opportunity to teach us the ins and outs. As experienced Internet users, however, we have a few tips to help you ease your way into the scene and not embarrass yourself.

No gawking over other people's shoulders

Okay, we understand that you're curious — that's why you're here, to find out about this stuff. Great. Cool. Rent some time, and get some help. Don't stand over other people's shoulders reading their screen. It's rude.

Clean up after yourself

We mean not just the trash around your computer but also the trash you probably left *on* the computer. Many folks don't seem to be aware that most mailer programs keep copies of messages that are sent. If you don't want someone to read your mail, make sure that you find the sent-message folder and delete your mail. Then take the next step and empty the trash. We have found all kinds of interesting goodies we're sure that the sender wouldn't have wanted to share.

Don't order stuff from a public PC

Normally, we think that ordering stuff over the Web or by e-mail is perfectly safe — much safer than handing your credit card to some waiter you've never met! Some shopping sites store information about you, however (including your mailing address and payment info), in a file on your computer. This arrangement works perfectly when you are ordering from your own computer — you don't have to type all that info when you visit the site the next time to place an order. When you order stuff at a cybercafé, however, this personal information may be stored on the cybercafé's computer instead. Better not chance it.

Some Web wisdom

Most Internet providers let you put your own private pages up on the World Wide Web. (Chapter 10 helps you get your Web page going.) Again, because what you put on your Web page is all that most people will know about you, this section provides a few suggestions.

Small is beautiful, Part I

Most people who look at your Web page are connected by using a dial-up line and a modem, which means that big pictures take a long time to load. If your home page contains a full-page picture that takes $12^1/_2$ minutes to load, you may as well have hung out a Keep Out sign. Keep the pictures small enough so that the page loads in a reasonable amount of time. If you have a huge picture that you think is wonderful, put a small "thumbnail" version of it on your home page and make it a link to the full picture for people with the time and interest to look at the big version.

Small is beautiful, Part II

Small pages that fit on a screen or two work better than large pages. Small pages are easier to read, and they load faster. If you have 12 screens full of stuff to put on your Web page, break up your page into five or six separate pages with links among them. A well-designed set of small pages makes finding stuff easier than does one big page because the links can direct readers to what they want to find.

If we want the White House, we know where to find it

No Web page (or set of Web pages, as we just suggested) is complete without some links to the author's other favorite pages. For some reason, every new user's Web page used to have a link to `http://www.whitehouse.gov` and maybe to Yahoo, Netscape, and a few other sites that every Net user already knows about. Cool Web sites give you links to interesting pages you *don't* already know about.

Let a hundred viewers blossom

Whenever you create a new Web page, look at it with as many Web browsers as possible. Yes, most people use some version of Netscape or Internet Explorer, but Prodigy and AOL users (over 10 million possible visitors to your site) use the browsers that come with those services, and users with dial-up shell connections use the text-only browser Lynx. Take a look at your pages to make sure that they're at least legible regardless of which browser people are using.

Don't be dumb

Don't put information on your Web page that you don't want everyone in the world to know. In particular, don't include your home address and phone number. We know at least one person who received an unexpected phone call from someone she met on the Net and wasn't too pleased about it. Why would Net users need this information, anyway? They can send you e-mail!

Appendix

About the CD

•••

*I*n this appendix, we tell you how to install and get more information about the programs on *The Internet For Dummies,* 6th Edition Starter Kit CD-ROM.

We first provide brief descriptions of each program. We then explain how to run and use the CD-ROM's Installer to copy the programs to your hard disk. Finally, we provide more details about each program, such as installation and usage tips and pointers for where to get additional information.

The program lists are organized into two groups: software for Microsoft Windows (Windows 95, Windows 98, and Windows 3.1) and software for the Macintosh. Within each group, the programs are listed alphabetically.

The Windows programs on the CD-ROM are

- ✔ **Acrobat Reader:** A free program that lets you view and print Portable Document Format, or PDF, files.

- ✔ **Eudora Light:** An excellent, free electronic-mail program that lets you send and receive e-mail messages over the Internet.

- ✔ **Free Agent:** An excellent, free newsgroup reader (or *newsreader*) program that lets you participate in thousands of online discussions over the Internet.

- ✔ **HotDog:** A shareware program that enables you to create your own World Wide Web pages without having to become an HTML programming whiz.

- ✔ **Internet Explorer:** The Web browser from Microsoft as well as related Internet utility programs (for Windows 3.1, 95, and NT only).

- ✔ **MindSpring:** Software to sign you up for an Internet account with MindSpring, an Internet service provider (ISP) available locally for many cities in the continental United States, as well as a large set of Internet software.

- ✔ **mIRC:** A shareware Internet Relay Chat, or IRC, program that lets you interact live with a group of people on the Internet via your keyboard.

- ✔ **Netscape Communicator:** The Web browser from Netscape, along with related programs for mail, news, and Web-page editing.

- ✔ **Paint Shop Pro:** A shareware graphics program you can use to view virtually any image you're likely to encounter on the Web. It also lets you create and edit images and convert them into different file formats, which is useful if you want to make your own Web pages.

- ✔ **WinZip:** An invaluable shareware utility you can use to compress and decompress files.

- ✔ **WS_FTP LE:** A free (for noncommercial use) File Transfer Protocol, or FTP, program you can use to copy files between your PC and a computer on the Internet.

The Macintosh programs on the CD-ROM are

- ✔ **Acrobat Reader:** A free program that lets you view and print Portable Document Format, or PDF, files.

- ✔ **Anarchie:** A free (for noncommercial use) File Transfer Protocol, or FTP, program you can use to copy files between your Macintosh and a computer on the Internet.

- ✔ **BBEdit Lite:** A freeware program that enables you to create your own World Wide Web pages without having to become an HTML programming whiz.

- ✔ **Eudora Light:** An excellent, free electronic-mail program that lets you send and receive e-mail messages over the Internet.

- ✔ **FreePPP:** A freeware PPP program that provides the foundation a Macintosh needs to get connected to the Internet.

- ✔ **GraphicConverter:** A shareware graphics program you can use to view virtually any image you're likely to encounter on the Web. It also lets you convert images from one file format to another, which is useful if you want to make your own Web pages.

- ✔ **Internet Explorer:** The Web browser from Microsoft, as well as related Internet utility programs.

- ✔ **InterNews:** A shareware newsgroup reader (or *newsreader*) program that lets you participate in thousands of online discussions over the Internet.

- ✔ **Ircle:** A shareware Internet Relay Chat, or IRC, program that lets you interact live with a group of people on the Internet via your keyboard.

- ✔ **MindSpring:** Software to sign you up for an Internet account with MindSpring, an Internet service provider (ISP) available locally for many cities in the continental United States.

- ✔ **NCSA Telnet:** A shareware program that lets you log on to other computers as a terminal via a slightly old-fashioned method called telnet.

- ✔ **Netscape Communicator:** The Web browser from Netscape, along with related programs for mail, news, and Web-page editing.

- ✔ **StuffIt Expander and DropStuff with Expander Enhancer:** Invaluable shareware decompression utilities you can use to make compressed files useable again.

A few words about shareware: Shareware programs are available to you for an evaluation period (typically, anywhere from 30 to 90 days). If you decide that you like a shareware program and want to keep using it, you're expected to send a registration fee to its author or publisher, which entitles you to technical support and notifications about new versions. (It also makes you feel good.)

Because most shareware operates on an honor system, the programs continue working even if you don't register them. It's a good idea, however, to support the shareware concept and encourage the continued production of quality, low-cost software by sending in your payment for the programs you use.

If you don't know the letter of your PC's CD-ROM drive: Most PCs assign the letter D to a CD-ROM drive. Here's how to find out which letter your CD-ROM drive uses:

- ✔ If you use Windows 95 or Windows 98, double-click the My Computer icon on your desktop. A window appears that lists all your drives, including your CD-ROM drive (which is usually represented by a shiny disk icon), and shows you the letter of each drive. When you're done examining the My Computer display, exit by clicking the window's Close button in its upper-right corner or choosing File⇨Close from its menu.

- ✔ If you use Windows 3.1, double-click the File Manager icon in Program Manager. In the File Manager window, you see a row of disk icons. The CD-ROM drive is the one with the little CD-ROM sticking out of it.

- ✔ If you use a Macintosh, you don't have to worry about it; simply double-click the icon on your desktop that looks like a CD and is named Internet For Dummies.

Late-breaking news: If we have any up-to-the-minute news about the programs on this CD-ROM, we put it on our Web site, at `http://net.gurus.com` (click the link about Books, then the title of this book, and then the Update link).

System Requirements

Make sure that your computer meets the minimum system requirements listed below. If your computer doesn't match up to most of these requirements, you may have problems using the contents of the CD.

- A PC with a 486 or faster processor, or a Mac OS computer with a 68030 or faster processor.

- Microsoft Windows 3.1 or later, or Mac OS system software 7.5 or later.

- At least 8MB of total RAM installed on your computer if it's running Windows 3.1, at least 16MB for Windows 95 or 98 or a Mac.

- At least 130MB of hard drive space available to install all the software from this CD. (You need less space if you don't install every program.)

- A CD-ROM drive.

- A monitor capable of displaying at least 256 colors or grayscale.

- A modem with a speed of at least 14,400 bps, preferably 33,000 or 56,000.

If you need more information on the basics, check out *PCs For Dummies,* 6th Edition, by Dan Gookin; *Macs For Dummies,* 6th Edition, by David Pogue; *Windows 95 For Dummies,* 2nd Edition, by Andy Rathbone; *Windows 98 For Dummies,* by Andy Rathbone; or *Windows 3.11 For Dummies,* 4th Edition, by Andy Rathbone (all published by IDG Books Worldwide, Inc.).

Installing the Programs from Microsoft Windows

If you are using a PC running any flavor of Microsoft Windows, follow these steps to install any of the programs from *The Internet For Dummies,* 6th Edition Starter Kit CD-ROM:

1. **Insert the CD-ROM into your CD-ROM drive. Be careful to touch only the edges of the CD-ROM.**

   If your CD-ROM drive requires a caddy (a protective plastic holder), insert the CD-ROM into an empty caddy and then place the caddy into your drive; otherwise, simply insert the CD-ROM directly into the holder provided by your drive. In either case, be sure to insert the CD-ROM with its printed side up.

2. **If you use Windows 95 or Windows 98, click the Start button (located in the bottom-left corner of your screen) and choose the Run option. If you're using Windows 3.1, choose File from the menu in Program Manager and then choose Run.**

3. **In the Run dialog box that appears, type** d:\setup **(the letter d, a colon (:), a backslash (\), and the word** *setup***). If your CD-ROM drive isn't drive D, type the letter appropriate for your drive rather than d.**

   If you're not sure which letter to type, see the paragraphs that begin "If you don't know the letter of your PC's CD-ROM drive," earlier in this appendix.

4. **Press Enter or click OK.**

   In a few moments, you see a License Agreement.

5. **Read the IDG Books Worldwide, Inc., agreement to see if you can stand its terms. When you're ready, click the Accept button. (After you click Accept, you'll never be bothered by the License Agreement again, but if you don't click Accept, you can't use the Installer program, although you can use the individual programs.)**

   After you click Accept, an opening screen appears.

6. **Admire the attractive screen and then click anywhere to continue.**

   A menu displays three software categories: Connecting, for programs that get you connected to the Net; Communicating, for programs that let you interact on the Net; and Working Offline, for programs that help you deal with files you've downloaded from the Net. This menu is the Installer's *main menu* (so named because all your other selections stem from this initial menu).

7. **Click a category in which you're interested.**

   A submenu displays the particular programs grouped under the category you selected.

8. **Click a program in which you're interested.**

   A description of the program appears. Notice that in addition to an Install button, the screen displays Go Back and Exit buttons.

9. **If you want to copy the program to your hard disk, click the Install button. (Otherwise, skip to Step 11.)**

   After you click Install, installation for the program you selected begins.

10. **Follow the prompts that appear on-screen to complete the installation of the program.**

Although some installations of a more complicated nature have to restart your computer, don't worry. If this happens, the programs' installation screen might come back, or the program may simply be ready to run. Look for it on your Start menu or in a Program Group. If you want to install more software, start the CD installer program up again, like you did in Step 2, and pick up where you left off.

11. **Click the Go Back button to return to previous menus and explore the other contents of the CD-ROM.**

    Because the Go Back button is available on every screen (except the first one), you can always use it to retrace your steps to the main menu.

12. **When you're done examining all the options you're interested in and installing all the programs you want, click the Exit button.**

    The Installer program closes. You can now start using the new software you've installed on your hard disk.

To run the Installer program again: If you've exited the Installer program and then want to run it again while *The Internet For Dummies,* 6th Edition Starter Kit CD-ROM is still in your drive, simply return to Step 2 of the preceding list of steps.

To examine *The Internet For Dummies* CD-ROM's contents: You can use the *Internet For Dummies* Installer program to install all the software on your CD-ROM. If you're simply curious about the CD-ROM, however, you can examine its contents after you exit the Installer. If you're using Windows 95 or Windows 98, open a Windows Explorer window (as opposed to a My Computer window) and double-click the CD-ROM's icon. If you're using Windows 3.1, double-click the CD-ROM's icon in File Manager. If you're using a Macintosh, double-click the Internet For Dummies folder that looks like a CD on your desktop.

Installing the Programs from a Macintosh

To install the items from the CD to your Mac hard drive, follow these steps:

1. **Insert the CD into your computer's CD-ROM drive.**

   In a moment, an icon representing the CD you just inserted appears on your Mac desktop. Chances are, the icon looks like a CD-ROM.

2. **Double-click the CD icon to show the CD's contents.**

3. **Double-click the License Agreement icon.**

   This is the End-User License that you are agreeing to by using the CD. You should look it over at least once to see if you can accept its terms.

4. **Double-click the Read Me First icon.**

   This text file contains information about the CD's programs and any last-minute instructions you need to know about installing the programs on the CD that we don't cover in this appendix.

5. **Most programs come with installer programs; to install these programs, you simply open the program's folder on the CD and double-click the icon with the word "Install" or "Installer."**

   To install some programs, just drag the program's folder from the CD window and drop it on your hard drive icon.

   After you install the programs you want, you can eject the CD. Carefully place it back in the plastic jacket of the book for safekeeping.

Windows Programs

Acrobat Reader

Acrobat Reader 3.0, from Adobe Systems, is a free program that lets you view and print Portable Document Format, or PDF, files. The PDF format is used by many programs you find on the Internet for storing documentation, because it supports the use of such stylish elements as assorted fonts and colorful graphics (as opposed to plain text, or ASCII, which doesn't allow for any special effects in a document).

For example, a document on the CD-ROM is the manual for Eudora Light. That document, a PDF file, requires you to use the Acrobat Reader program to view or print it.

To install Acrobat Reader, follow Steps 1 through 6 in the section "Installing the Programs from Microsoft Windows," near the beginning of this appendix. When you see the main menu, click the Working Offline category, click the Acrobat Reader option, click the Install button appropriate for your version of Windows, and follow the prompts that appear on-screen to complete the installation.

You can now run Acrobat Reader at any time by opening your Windows 95 or Windows 98 Acrobat Reader folder (which, if you accepted the installer's suggestion, is named Acrobat3\Reader) or your Windows 3.1 Acrobat Reader program group and then double-clicking a program icon named AcroRd32 or Acroread. If you use Windows 95 or Windows 98, you can click the Start button, choose Programs and then Adobe Acrobat, and then click the Acrobat Reader 3.0 icon.

To find out more about using Acrobat Reader, choose Reader Online Guide from the Help menu. You can also get more information by visiting the Adobe Systems Web site at http://www.adobe.com.

Eudora Light

Eudora Light 3.0.6, from QualComm, Inc., is a free, powerful electronic-mail program. If you have an Internet e-mail account, you can use Eudora Light to send e-mail to and receive e-mail from any of the tens of millions of other people around the world who are connected to the Net. In addition to text messages, Eudora Light lets you attach files to e-mail, so you can use it to transmit electronic pictures, sound clips, or any other kind of data stored in files.

To install Eudora Light, follow Steps 1 through 6 in the section "Installing the Programs from Microsoft Windows," near the beginning of this appendix. When you see the main menu, choose the Communicating category and then the Eudora Light option, click the Install button, and follow the prompts that appear on-screen to complete the installation of the version of Eudora appropriate for your version of Windows.

To run the program, double-click the Eudora Light icon in its folder or Program group. If you use Windows 95 or Windows 98, you can click the Start button, choose Programs, and click the Eudora Light icon.

For information about how to use Eudora Light (and its even more powerful commercial relative, Eudora Pro), see Chapters 11 and 12. You can also find out more about Eudora Light by choosing options from its Help menu and by visiting its Web site at http://www.eudora.com.

Free Agent

Free Agent 1.11, from Forté, Inc., is a free Windows program that lets you read and participate in ongoing group discussions that take place on the Internet via Usenet newsgroups. Tens of thousands of newsgroups exist, devoted to virtually every topic under the sun, ranging from knitting to high finance and from dating to decoding DNA, and Free Agent is one of the best programs available for accessing them. Among the great features of Free Agent is its capability to let you read newsgroup articles offline, which could conceivably save you Internet connection charges and phone charges.

To install Free Agent, follow Steps 1 through 6 in the section "Installing the Programs from Microsoft Windows," near the beginning of this appendix. When you see the main menu, choose the Communicating category and then the Free Agent option, click the Install button appropriate for your version of Windows, and follow the prompts that appear on-screen to complete the installation.

To run Free Agent, double-click the Agent icon in its folder or program group. If you use Windows 95 or Windows 98, you can click the Start button, choose Programs, and click the Agent icon.

For information about how to use Free Agent (and its commercial version, Agent), see our Web site, at http://net.gurus.com/news. You can also find out more about Free Agent by choosing Contents from its Help menu to launch its online manual and by visiting the Free Agent Web site at http://www.forteinc.com/agent/freagent.htm.

HotDog

HotDog, from Sausage Software, is a powerful but easy-to-use Windows shareware program that helps you create Web pages. The Windows 95 or Windows 98 version is HotDog Professional 5.

To install HotDog, follow Steps 1 through 6 in the section "Installing the Programs from Microsoft Windows," near the beginning of this appendix. When you see the main menu, choose the Communicating category and then the Hot Dog Web Editor option, click the Install button appropriate for your version of Windows, and follow the prompts that appear on-screen to complete the installation.

To run the program, click the Start button, click Programs, click HotDog Professional 5, and then click the HotDog icon.

When the program starts, it gives you several ways to get help, including tutorials. For more information about HotDog, visit the witty program's Web site at http://www.sausage.com.

Internet Explorer

Internet Explorer 4.0, from Microsoft, is one of the best-known Web browsers available. Chapters 6 and 7 describe in some detail how to use it. In addition to the browser, this package includes other Internet tools from Microsoft: Outlook Express, a mail and news reading program; FrontPage, a Web page publishing program; Microsoft Chat, a chat program; and others. *Note:* The CD-ROM version is available for only Windows 95. If you have a version of

Windows 95 or 98 that already includes Internet Explorer, *don't* install the CD-ROM version. Instead, go to the Microsoft Web site at `http://www.microsoft.com/windows/ie/download/windows.htm` and see what updates are available to fix errors and security problems in the version you have.

To install Internet Explorer, follow Steps 1 through 6 in the section "Installing the Programs from Microsoft Windows," near the beginning of this appendix. When you see the main menu, choose the Communicating category and then the Internet Explorer option, click the Install button, and follow the prompts that appear on-screen to complete the installation.

You are given a choice of installing only the browser or the browser and other components. Choose whichever option that you think is best (and for which you have room on your disk). If you choose not to install some parts at this time, you can go back later and get the pieces you missed.

To run Internet Explorer, click the Start button, choose Programs and then Internet Explorer, and then click the Internet Explorer icon or double-click the Internet Explorer icon on the desktop.

You can find information about Internet Explorer and other Microsoft Internet programs at its Web site at `http://www.microsoft.com/ie`.

MindSpring

MindSpring is an Internet service provider (ISP) that has local telephone access from most areas of the continental United States. The software provided by MindSpring on the CD-ROM includes PipeLine+ (Version 2.70), an easy-to-use interface to the Internet programs you will want to use, as well as a large selection of the Internet client programs.

Before you sign up for an account with MindSpring, check whether it's accessible from your location as a local telephone call. If you have access to the Web, you can check the MindSpring Web site, at `http://www.mindspring.com`, or call 1-888-677-7464 to speak to a customer representative.

MindSpring has several plans you can choose from, depending on how much time you need to spend connected. The least expensive plan (at the time this book was written) is $6.95 per month for five hours of connect time plus $2 per hour for every extra hour. The most expensive plan is for $26.95 per month with unlimited connect time. While you're on the phone with MindSpring to ask about local phone numbers, check to see whether its pricing has changed.

The programs that come with the MindSpring package are

- ✔ **Eudora Light:** A freeware e-mail program by Qualcomm.
- ✔ **Internet Explorer:** The Microsoft Web browser licensed by MindSpring. The version for Windows 3.1 comes with IE 3.0 (widely agreed to be out of date, unfortunately), but the version for 95 and 98 comes with IE 4.0.
- ✔ **Free Agent:** A freeware newsreader by Forté.
- ✔ **WS_FTP:** A freeware FTP client by John A. Junod.
- ✔ **mIRC:** A shareware IRC client by Khaled Mardam-Bey.
- ✔ **EWAN/Telnet:** A terminal emulator.
- ✔ **WinZip:** A file compression and decompression utility.
- ✔ **LView Pro:** A shareware graphics viewer by Haddad Loureiro.

Some of these programs are on the CD-ROM as separate programs. In most cases, they are more recent versions, so you may want to install them rather than the versions from MindSpring.

To install the MindSpring programs, follow Steps 1 through 6 in the section "Installing the Programs from Microsoft Windows" near the beginning of this appendix. On the main menu, choose the Connecting category and then the MindSpring option, click the Install button appropriate for your version of Windows, and follow the prompts that appear on-screen to complete the installation.

The installation program asks whether you want to make a New or Custom installation. A New installation installs all the programs in the preceding list; a Custom installation enables you to pick the ones you want. The installation program prompts you for all the information necessary to open an account with MindSpring, including a credit card number. The program checks your modem, dials an 800 number to register you, and returns with your password and other groovy information.

The MindSpring installation reboots your computer. Make sure that you're not running any other applications while you're installing it.

To run the MindSpring program in Windows 95 or Windows 98, press the Start button, and then choose Programs and then MindSpring Pipeline+. The program called the Access Panel dials your ISP and lets you run any of the programs you installed with MindSpring.

A full manual of the MindSpring software is on the CD-ROM, in a file called MindSpring/Manual/manual.doc. You can get help and current information about MindSpring at its Web site at http://www.mindspring.com.

mIRC

mIRC 5.41 is a shareware Windows program from its author, Khaled Mardam-Bey. mIRC lets you participate in Internet Relay Chat (IRC), a worldwide system that enables you to receive messages over the Internet within seconds of when other people type them, and vice versa. Chapter 15 has detailed instructions for using IRC.

To install mIRC, follow Steps 1 through 6 in the section "Installing the Programs from Microsoft Windows" near the beginning of this appendix. When you see the main menu, choose the Communicating category and then the mIRC option, click the Install button appropriate for your version of Windows, and follow the prompts that appear on-screen to complete the installation.

To run mIRC, double-click the mIRC icon in its folder or program group. If you use Windows 95 or Windows 98, you can click the Start button, choose Programs and then mIRC v5.41, and click the mIRC32 icon.

For more information about mIRC, click its Introduction button in the first window that appears. You can get additional information after you're past the opening window by pressing F1, clicking a Help button that looks like a life preserver, or choosing the Contents option from the Help menu. The mIRC home page is a good source of information too; you can reach it at http://www.mirc.co.uk.

Netscape Communicator

Netscape Communicator, from Netscape Communications, is one of the best-known Web browsers available. Chapters 6 and 7 describe in detail how to use this powerful tool. *The Internet For Dummies,* 6th Edition Starter Kit CD-ROM installs Netscape Communicator 4.5 for Windows 95 or 98 and Version 4.07 for Windows 3.1.

To install Netscape Communicator, follow Steps 1 through 6 in the section "Installing the Programs from Microsoft Windows" near the beginning of this appendix. When you see the main menu, choose the Communicating category and then the Netscape Communicator option, click the Install button, and follow the prompts that appear on-screen to complete the installation.

To run Netscape Navigator, double-click the program's icon in its folder or program group. If you use Windows 95 or Windows 98, you can click the Start button, choose Programs and then Netscape Communicator, and choose Netscape Navigator. You can find information about Netscape Navigator from its Help menu or at its Web site at http://home.netscape.com.

Paint Shop Pro

Paint Shop Pro, from JASC, Inc., is a multipurpose graphics tool for Windows. This superb shareware program lets you view images in virtually any graphics format you're likely to encounter on the Internet. In addition, it lets you edit and crop images, convert images from one file format to another, and even create pictures from scratch, which all can be useful in helping to create your own World Wide Web pages. _The Internet For Dummies,_ 6th Edition Starter Kit CD-ROM installs Paint Shop Pro Version 5 for Windows 95 or 98 and Version 3.11 for Windows 3.1.

To install Paint Shop Pro, follow Steps 1 through 6 in the section "Installing the Programs from Microsoft Windows" near the beginning of this appendix. When you see the main menu, choose the Working Offline category and then the Paint Shop Pro option, click the Install button appropriate for your version of Windows, and follow the prompts that appear on-screen to complete the installation.

To run Paint Shop Pro, double-click the program's icon in its folder or program group. If you use Windows 95 or Windows 98, you can click the Start button, choose Programs and then Paint Shop Pro, and click the Paint Shop Pro 5 icon.

For more information about Paint Shop Pro, click the floating question mark icon on the program's toolbar or choose Help Topics from its Help menu. Also, visit the program's Web site at `http://www.jasc.com/psp.html`.

WinZip

WinZip 7, from Nico Mak Computing, is an invaluable file compression and decompression Windows shareware utility. Many files you find on the Internet are _compressed,_ or shrunken in size via special programming tricks, both to save storage space and to cut down on the amount of time they require to be downloaded. You may also occasionally receive compressed files (ZIP files) as e-mail attachments. After you have a compressed file on your hard disk, you can use WinZip to decompress it and make it useable again.

To install WinZip, follow Steps 1 through 6 in the section "Installing the Programs from Microsoft Windows" near the beginning of this appendix. When you see the main menu, choose the Working Offline category and then the WinZip option, click the Install button appropriate for your version of Windows, and follow the prompts that appear on-screen to complete the installation.

To run WinZip, double-click the WinZip icon from its folder or program group. If you use Windows 95 or Windows 98, you can click the Start button, choose Programs and then WinZip, and click the WinZip 7 32-bit icon.

The first time you launch WinZip, it displays a bunch of messages and configuration questions. When you're asked whether you want the program to operate in WinZip Wizard or WinZip Classic mode, we recommend that you choose WinZip Classic, which we consider easier to use. After you've answered all the questions, WinZip is ready to go.

For information about using WinZip, see Chapters 16 and 20 or choose the Contents option from the program's Help menu or double-click the program's Online Manual icon in its folder. To find out even more about WinZip, visit the program's Web site at http://www.winzip.com.

WS_FTP LE

WS_FTP LE 4.6, from Ipswitch, Inc., is a free (for noncommercial use) Windows File Transfer Protocol (FTP) program you can use to copy files between your PC and a computer on the Net. FTP programs were more useful before the World Wide Web took hold and made finding and down-loading files a snap. FTP programs are still handy, however, for activities not supported by the Web, such as uploading your own files and Web pages.

To install WS_FTP LE, follow Steps 1 through 6 in the section "Installing the Programs from Microsoft Windows" When you see the main menu, choose the Communicating category and then the WS_FTP LE option, click the Install button appropriate for your version of Windows, and follow the prompts that appear on-screen to complete the installation.

To run the program, double-click the WS_FTP icon in its folder or program group. If you use Windows 95 or Windows 98, you can click the Start button, choose Programs and then Ws_ftp, and click WS_FTP95 LE.

For information about using WS_FTP LE, see Chapter 16. You can also find out more by clicking the Help button from the program's main window or Session Profile dialog box or by double-clicking the WS_FTP Help icon from the WS_FTP folder; you can also visit the WS_FTP LE Web site at http://www.ipswitch.com.

Macintosh Programs

Acrobat Reader

Acrobat Reader 3.0, from Adobe Systems, is a free program that lets you view and print Portable Document Format, or PDF, files. The PDF format is used by many programs you find on the Internet for storing documentation, because it supports the use of such stylish elements as assorted fonts and colorful graphics (as opposed to plain text, or ASCII, which doesn't allow for any special effects in a document).

For example, the manual for Eudora Light on the CD-ROM is a PDF file that requires you to use the Acrobat Reader program to view or print it.

To install Acrobat Reader, follow the steps in the section "Installing the Programs from a Macintosh," near the beginning of this appendix. When you see the main window, choose the Working Offline folder and then the Acrobat Reader folder. Open the Reader folder first and then double-click the Reader 3.01 Installer icon. Follow the prompts that appear on-screen to complete the installation. If you would like to add the capability to search for specific words or phrases in PDF documents to your version of Acrobat Reader, open the Search folder and double-click the Search Installer icon.

You can now run Acrobat Reader at any time by double-clicking the Acrobat Reader 3.0 icon. If you want to view the manual for Eudora Light, for example, after you have installed the program, open the Eudora folder and double-click the file with the Acrobat Reader icon.

To find out more about using Acrobat Reader, view the Acrobat.pdf file that was installed in the same folder as the program. You can also get more information by visiting the Adobe Systems Web site at `http://www.adobe.com`.

Anarchie

Anarchie 3.0, from Stairways Shareware, is a Macintosh shareware File Transfer Protocol (FTP) program you can use to find files on the Net and to copy files between your Mac and a computer on the Net. FTP programs were more useful before the World Wide Web took hold and made finding and downloading files a snap. FTP programs are still handy, however, for activities not supported by the Web, such as uploading your own files and Web pages.

To install Anarchie, follow the steps in the section "Installing the Programs from a Macintosh," near the beginning of this appendix. When you see the main window, choose the Communicating folder and then double-click the Anarchie Installer icon. Follow the prompts that appear on-screen to complete the installation. After the installation is finished, you can run the program by double-clicking the Anarchie icon in its folder.

To use Anarchie to find a file on the Internet, first choose File from the menu, and then choose either the MacSearch option (for a Macintosh file) or the Archie option (for any file). Type part of the name of the file you want and then click the Find It button. If a matching list of files is displayed, double-click the one you're after; the file is then downloaded to your hard disk. After the file is saved, if it turns out that it's compressed, use StuffIt Expander (which is also on *The Internet For Dummies,* 6th Edition Starter Kit CD-ROM) to decompress the file and make it useable.

For more information about downloading and uploading files, see Chapter 16; for more information about Anarchie, visit its Web site at `http://www.share.com/peterlewis/anarchie`.

BBEdit Lite

BBEdit Lite 4.1, from Bare Bones Software, Inc., is a Macintosh freeware program that helps you create Web pages. Chapter 10 tells you all about how to do that. We also include a demo of BBEdit 5.0, the not-free version of BBEdit Lite, for you to check out.

To install BBEdit Lite, follow the steps in the section "Installing the Programs from a Macintosh," near the beginning of this appendix. When you see the main window, choose the Communicating folder. Click and drag the BBEdit Lite 4.1 folder and drop it on your hard drive icon. You can run the program by double-clicking the BBEdit Lite 4.1 icon in its folder.

If you'd like to install the BBEdit 5.0 Demo, open the Connecting folder and double-click the Install BBEdit 5.0 Demo icon. Follow the prompts that appear on-screen to complete the installation. After the installation is finished, you can run the program by double-clicking the BBEdit icon in its folder. With this demo, you will not be able to save anything you create.

For more information about BBEdit Lite, visit the program's Web site at `http://www.barebones.com/free/free.html`.

Eudora Light

Eudora Light 3.1, from QualComm, Inc., is a free, powerful electronic-mail program. If you have an Internet e-mail account, you can use Eudora Light to send e-mail to and receive e-mail from any of the tens of millions of other people around the world who are connected to the Net. In addition to text messages, Eudora Light lets you attach files to e-mail, so you can use it to transmit electronic pictures, sound clips, or any other kind of data stored in files.

To install Eudora Light, follow the steps in the section "Installing the Programs from a Macintosh," near the beginning of this appendix. When you see the main window, choose the Communicating folder. Double-click the Eudora Light 3.1.3 Installer icon and follow the prompts that appear on-screen to complete the installation. After the installation is finished, you can run the program by double-clicking the Eudora icon in its folder.

To run the program, double-click the Eudora Light 3.1 icon in its folder. For information about how to use Eudora Light (and its even more powerful commercial version, Eudora Pro), see Chapters 11 and 12. You can also find out more about Eudora Light by choosing options from its Help menu and by visiting its Web site at `http://www.eudora.com.`

FreePPP

FreePPP 2.6.2, from Rockstar Studios, is free Macintosh software that provides the foundation TCP/IP software your computer needs to get connected to the Internet. This type of software is usually provided automatically when you sign up with an Internet provider. (The FreePPP program, for example, is bundled with the MindSpring sign-up kit for the Macintosh that's included on *The Internet For Dummies,* 6th Edition Starter Kit CD-ROM.) If you're not satisfied with the TCP/IP software you have, however, you can try using the excellent FreePPP instead.

To install FreePPP, follow the steps in the section "Installing the Programs from a Macintosh," near the beginning of this appendix. When you see the main window, choose the Connecting folder and then the FreePPP 2.6 Installer folder. Double-click the Install FreePPP 2.6.2 icon and then follow the prompts that appear on-screen to complete the installation. After the installation is finished, you can setup FreePPP by double-clicking the FreePPP Setup icon in the FreePPP Software folder.

For more information about FreePPP and TCP/IP software, see Part II and visit the program's Web site at `http://www.rockstar.com/ppp.shtml.`

GraphicConverter

GraphicConverter 3.4.1, by shareware author Thorsten Lemke, is a Macintosh program that lets you view images in virtually any graphics format you're likely to encounter on the Internet. It lets you convert the most common Windows, DOS, Amiga, and Atari computer images to

Macintosh formats and vice versa; and it provides a rich set of image-editing options. The latter two features are especially useful if you're interested in creating your own Web pages.

To install GraphicConverter, follow the steps in the section "Installing the Programs from a Macintosh," near the beginning of this appendix. When you see the main window, choose the Working Offline folder and then double-click the GraphicConverter Installer icon. Follow the prompts that appear on-screen to complete the installation. After the installation is finished, you can run GraphicConverter by double-clicking the GraphicConverter icon in the GraphicConverter 3.4.1 (US) folder.

For more information about GraphicConverter, double-click the Documentation icon in the program's folder, or visit the Web site at www.lemkesoft.de.

Internet Explorer

Internet Explorer 4.0, from Microsoft, is one of the best-known Web browsers available. Chapters 6 and 7 describe in some detail how to use it. In addition to the browser, this package includes other Internet tools from Microsoft: Outlook Express, a mail and news reading program.

To install Internet Explorer, follow the steps in the section "Installing the Programs from a Macintosh," near the beginning of this appendix. When you see the main window, open the Communicating folder and then the Internet Explorer folder. Double-click the Installer icon that is correct for your computer and follow the prompts that appear on-screen to complete the installation.

To run Internet Explorer, click its icon on your desktop.

You can find information about Internet Explorer and other Microsoft Internet programs at its Web site at http://www.microsoft.com/ie.

InterNews

InterNews 2.0.2, from Moonrise Software, is a shareware Macintosh program that lets you read and participate in ongoing group discussions that take place over the Internet via Usenet newsgroups. Tens of thousands of newsgroups exist, devoted to virtually every topic under the sun, ranging from knitting to high finance and from dating to decoding DNA. InterNews is one of the best Mac programs available for accessing them. Among this program's charms is that it's trim and quick — it doesn't require a great deal of memory or a superfast Mac to operate effectively. In addition, because it's highly customizable, you can tailor it to your tastes.

To install InterNews, follow the steps in the section "Installing the Programs from a Macintosh," near the beginning of this appendix. When you see the main window, open the Communicating folder and then double-click the InterNews 2.0.2 FAT.sea icon. Follow the prompts that appear on-screen to complete the installation. After the installation is finished, you can run the program by double-clicking the InterNews icon in its folder.

To run InterNews, double-click the program's icon in its folder.

To find out more about newsgroups, see our Web site at http://net.gurus.com/news. For more information about InterNews, visit the program's Web site at http://www.dartmouth.edu/~moonrise.

Ircle

Ircle 3.0.1 is a Macintosh shareware program from MacResponse that lets you participate in Internet Relay Chat (IRC), a worldwide system that enables you to receive messages over the Internet within seconds of when other people type them and vice versa. For a detailed discussion of IRC and chatting, read Chapter 15.

To install Ircle, follow the steps in the section "Installing the Programs from a Macintosh," near the beginning of this appendix. When you see the main window, open the Communicating folder and click and drag the Ircle 3.0.3 US folder to your hard drive icon. To run Ircle, double-click on its icon.

For more information about Ircle, choose the Help option from the program's Apple menu, and visit the Ircle Web site at http://www.ircle.com.

MindSpring

MindSpring is an Internet service provider (ISP) that has local telephone access from most areas of the continental United States. The software provided by MindSpring on the CD-ROM includes PipeLine+ (Version 2.70), an easy-to-use interface to the Internet programs you will want to use, as well as a large selection of the actual Internet client programs.

Before you sign up for an account with MindSpring, you may want to check whether it's available from your location as a local telephone call. If you have access to the Web, you can check its Web site, at `http://www.mindspring.com`, or you can call 1-888-677-7464 to speak to a customer representative.

MindSpring has several plans you can choose from, depending on how much time you need to spend connected. The least expensive plan (at the time this book was written) is $6.95 per month for five hours of connect time plus $2 per hour for every hour of extra time. The most expensive plan is $26.95 per month with unlimited connect time.

The Internet programs that come with the MindSpring package are

- ✔ **Eudora Light:** A freeware e-mail program by Qualcomm
- ✔ **Internet Explorer:** The Microsoft Web browser licensed by MindSpring
- ✔ **Netscape Navigator:** A Web browser by Netscape Communications, licensed by MindSpring
- ✔ **Homer:** A shareware FTP client by Toby Smith
- ✔ **Fetch**: A shareware FTP client by Dartmouth College
- ✔ **Anarchie:** A commercial FTP client licensed by MindSpring
- ✔ **StuffIt Expander:** A freeware file-encoding and -decoding utility
- ✔ **JPEGView:** A postcardware graphics viewer by Aaron Giles
- ✔ **SoundMachine:** A shareware sound file player by Rod Kennedy
- ✔ **Newswatcher:** A newsreader by Northwestern University

Some of these programs are also on the CD-ROM as separate programs. In most cases, the separate programs are more recent versions, so you may want to install them rather than the versions from MindSpring.

To install the MindSpring components, follow the steps in the section "Installing the Programs from a Macintosh," near the beginning of this appendix. When you see the main window, open the Connecting folder and then the MindSpring folder. Double-click the MindSpring Install.1 icon and follow the prompts that appear on-screen to complete the installation.

When you install MindSpring on the Mac, the installation program asks you for a key code. Enter **DUMY8579** into the dialog box. Be sure to use all capital letters, just as it's shown here.

The installation program asks whether you want to make a New or Custom installation. A New installation installs all the programs in the preceding list; a Custom installation enables you to pick the ones you want. The installation program prompts you for all the information necessary to open an account with MindSpring, including a credit card number. The program checks your modem, dials an 800 number to register you, and returns with your password and other groovy information.

To run the MindSpring program, double-click the MindSpring Pipeline+ icon in its folder. This action starts the program called the Access Panel, which dials up the ISP and launches the Internet programs you installed.

A full manual of the MindSpring software is on the CD-ROM in the folder Manual under Mindsrng. The file is a Microsoft Word document named manual.doc. You can get help and current information about MindSpring at its Web site at `http://www.mindspring.com`.

NCSA Telnet

NCSA Telnet 2.7b4, from NCSA Software Development, is a telnet shareware program for the Macintosh that lets you connect to other computers over the Internet when more modern routes (such as the World Wide Web) aren't feasible or available.

Telnet lets you log on to another computer as though your PC were a terminal attached to that computer. In the old days (like, way back in 1992), telnet was the way to get lots of information; for example, libraries let you telnet into their card catalogs.

Although telnet is more of a techie tool now, it still has its uses. For example, you may be able to telnet into your PPP and SLIP account (to get access to a UNIX shell) to change your password periodically. If you're on the road and you want to check your mail, you can telnet in via a UNIX shell and run Pine or elm or mail (UNIX mail programs) to read your e-mail without downloading it, which is handy if your disk space is limited or you're on someone else's computer at the time. Also, many people participating in multiuser games (such as MUDs and MOOs) connect via telnet.

To install NCSA Telnet, follow the steps in the section "Installing the Programs from a Macintosh," near the beginning of this appendix. When you see the main window, open the Communicating folder and click and drag the Telnet-2.7b4-fat folder to your hard drive icon.

To run the program, make sure that your modem is turned on and your phone line is hooked in, and double-click the NCSA Telnet 2.6 icon in the Telnet2.6 folder.

For a more detailed explanation of how to use telnet, see our Web page at `http://net.gurus.com/telnet`. For more information about NCSA Telnet, double-click the icon MacTelnet.pdf, which is a PDF document that must be viewed with the Adobe Acrobat Reader program (see the "Acrobat Reader" section); and visit the program's site at `http://www.ncsa.uiuc.edu/SDG/Software/MacTelnet/Docs/index.html`.

Netscape Communicator

Netscape Communicator 4.5, from Netscape Communications, is one of the best-known Web browsers available. Chapters 6 and 7 describe in detail how to use this powerful tool.

To install Netscape Communicator, follow the steps in the section "Installing the Programs from a Macintosh," near the beginning of this appendix. When you see the main window, open the Communicating folder and then the Communicator 4.5 Complete folder. Double-click the * Start Here * icon and then follow the prompts that appear on-screen to complete the installation.

To run Netscape Communicator, double-click the Netscape icon in its folder. You can find information about Netscape Communicator from its Help menu or at its Web site at `http://home.netscape.com`.

StuffIt Expander and DropStuff with Expander Enhancer

StuffIt Expander 4.5, from Aladdin Systems, Inc., is an invaluable file-decompression shareware utility for the Macintosh. Many files you find on the Internet are *compressed,* or shrunken in size via special programming tricks, both to save storage space and to cut down on the amount of time they require to be downloaded. You may also occasionally receive compressed files as e-mail attachments. After you have a compressed file on your hard disk, you should use StuffIt Expander to decompress it and make it useable again.

DropStuff with Expander Enhancer is a complementary product that enables StuffIt Expander to handle a wider variety of compression formats and to decompress files more quickly on Power Macintosh computers.

To install these programs, follow the steps in the section "Installing the Programs from a Macintosh," near the beginning of this appendix. When you see the main window, open the Working Offline folder and double-click the StuffIt Expander 5.0 Installer icon. Follow the prompts that appear on-screen to complete the installation. After you have installed StuffIt Expander, go back to the Working Offline folder and double-click the Install DropStuff w/ EE 4.5 icon, and once again, follow the prompts to complete the installation.

You typically run StuffIt Expander indirectly because it activates automatically when you download a compressed file or double-click a compressed file. When StuffIt has finished its work, you can toss the compressed file in the trash can and use the normal files that have been generated.

For more information about decompressing files, see Chapters 12 and 18. For more information about StuffIt Expander and DropStuff with Expander Enhancer, visit the Web site of these two programs, at `http://www.aladdinsys.com`.

A final note: Although some of the programs on *The Internet For Dummies,* 6th Edition Starter Kit CD-ROM are free, many of them are shareware. As we mentioned near the beginning of this appendix, shareware programs are available to you for an evaluation period, after which you're expected to either stop using them or pay for them. Sending a registration fee to a shareware publisher typically entitles you to technical support and notifications about new versions — and it also makes you feel good. Most shareware operates on an honor system, and it's just plain sensible to support the shareware concept and encourage the continued production of quality, low-cost software by sending in your payment for the programs you use. You can typically get information about where to send your payment for a shareware program by checking its online help system or visiting its Web site.

If You've Got Problems (Of the CD Kind)

We tried our best to compile programs that work on most computers with the minimum system requirements. Alas, your computer may differ, and some programs may not work properly for some reason.

The two likeliest problems are that you don't have enough memory (RAM) for the programs you want to use, or you have other programs running that are affecting installation or running of a program. If you get error messages such as `Not enough memory` or `Setup cannot continue`, try one or more of these methods and then try using the software again:

- ✔ **Turn off any antivirus software that you have on your computer.** Installers sometimes mimic virus activity and may make your computer incorrectly believe that it is being infected by a virus.

- ✔ **Close all running programs.** The more programs you're running, the less memory is available to other programs. Installers also typically update files and programs; if you keep other programs running, installation may not work properly.

- ✔ **In Windows, close the CD interface and run demos or installations directly from Windows Explorer.** The interface itself can tie up system memory, or even conflict with certain kinds of interactive demos. Use Windows Explorer to browse the files on the CD and launch installers or demos.

✔ **Add more RAM to your computer.** This is, admittedly, a somewhat expensive step. However, if you have a Windows 95/98 PC or a Mac OS computer with a PowerPC chip, adding more memory can really help the speed of your computer and enable more programs to run at the same time.

If you still have trouble installing the items from the CD, please call the IDG Books Worldwide Customer Service phone number: 800-762-2974 (outside the U.S.: 317-596-5430).

Glossary

ActiveX   A Microsoft standard for computer program building blocks, known as *objects*.

address   Internet users encounter two important types of addresses: e-mail addresses (for sending e-mail to someone; e-mail addresses almost always contain an @) and Web page addresses (more properly called URLs).

ADSL (Asymmetric Digital Subscriber Line)   A technology that lets you transmit data over phone lines faster — as much as 7 million bps — in one direction than in the other. Not yet widely available, but nice if you can get it.

AltaVista   A search engine used for finding things on the World Wide Web. Its true name is http://www.altavista.com.

America Online (AOL)   A value-added online service that provides many services in addition to Internet access, including access to popular chat groups.

anonymous FTP   A way of using the FTP program to log on to another computer to copy files, even though you don't have an account on the other computer. When you log on, you type **anonymous** as the username and your e-mail address as the password.

applet   A small computer program written in the Java programming language. You can download applets by using a Web browser. Applets must obey special rules that make it difficult for the programs to do damage to your computer.

archive   A single file containing a group of files that have been compressed and glommed together for efficient storage. You have to use a program such as WinZip, PKZIP, tar, or StuffIt to get the original files back out.

ARPANET   The original ancestor of the Internet, funded by the U.S. Department of Defense.

attachment   A computer file electronically stapled to an e-mail message and sent along with it.

backbone   The high-speed communications links that connect Internet providers and other large Internet sites together.

baud   The number of electrical symbols per second that a modem sends down a phone line. Often used as a synonym for bps (bits per second); although this usage is incorrect, only 43 people on the entire planet know why or care. Named after J. M. E. Baudot, inventor of the teletype.

BCC   *B*lind *c*arbon *c*opy. BCC addressees get a copy of your e-mail without other recipients knowing about it. See also *CC.*

binary file   A file that contains information that does not consist of text only. For example, a binary file may contain an archive, a picture, sounds, a spreadsheet, or a word-processing document that includes formatting codes in addition to text characters.

BinHex   A file-encoding system popular among Macintosh users.

bit The smallest unit of measure for computer data. Bits can be *on* or *off* (symbolized by 1 or 0) and are used in various combinations to represent different types of information.

bitmap Little dots put together to make a black-and-white or color picture.

bookmark The address of a Web page to which you may want to return. Netscape lets you maintain a list of bookmarks to make it easy to go back to your favorite Web pages.

bounce To return as undeliverable or redeliver to the appropriate address. If you mail a message to a bad address, it bounces back to your mailbox. If you get e-mail intended for someone else, you can bounce it to her.

bps (bits per second) A measure of how fast data is transmitted. Often used to describe modem speed.

browser A super-duper, all-singing, all-dancing program that lets you read information on the World Wide Web.

byte A group of eight bits, enough to represent a character. Computer memory is usually measured in bytes.

CC *Carbon copy.* CC addressees get a copy of your e-mail, and other recipients are informed of it if they bother to read the message header. *See also* BCC.

CCITT The old name for ITU-T, the committee that sets worldwide communication standards.

channel In IRC, a group of people chatting together. Called "rooms" by value-added providers who use "channel" to mean a major interest area you can get to easily, like a TV channel. In Windows 98, a Web site to which you have subscribed.

chanop In IRC, the *chan*nel *op*erator is in charge of keeping order in a channel. The chanop can throw out unruly visitors.

chat To talk (or type) live to other network users from any and all parts of the world. To chat on the Internet, you use an Internet Relay Chat (IRC) program like mIRC or Microsoft Chat. America Online and CompuServe have similar services.

client A computer that uses the services of another computer or server (such as Usenet, Gopher, FTP, or the Web). If you dial in to another system, your computer becomes a client of the system you dial in to (unless you're using X Windows — don't ask.) See also ***server.***

client/server model A division of labor between computers. Computers that provide a service other computers can use are known as servers. The users are clients. See also ***client, server.***

com When these letters appear as the last part of an address (in `http://net.gurus.com`, for example), it indicates that the host computer is run by a commercial organization, probably in the United States.

communications program A program you run on your personal computer that enables you to call up and communicate with other computers. This type of program makes your computer pretend to be a terminal (that's why it's also known as a terminal program or terminal emulator).

CompuServe (CIS) A value-added online service that provides many services in addition to Internet access, including forums for many popular business topics. Now owned by AOL.

cookie A small text file stored on your computer by a Web site you have visited, used to remind that site about you the next time you visit it.

country code The last part of a geographic address, which indicates in which country the host computer is located, such as `us` for the United States. Country codes are always two letters.

cyber- A prefix meaning the use of the computers and networks that comprise the Internet, as in cyberspace or cybercop.

DES (Data Encryption Standard) A U.S. government standard for encrypting unclassified data. Breakable at some expense, although a newer version, triple-DES, is probably safe.

Dial-Up Networking The built-in Internet communication program in Windows 95 and Windows 98.

digest A compilation of the messages that have been posted to a mailing list during the past few days.

domain Part of the official name of a computer on the Net — for example, `gurus.com`. To register a domain name, go to `http://www.internic.net`.

domain name server (DNS) A computer on the Internet that translates between Internet domain names, such as `xuxa.iecc.com`, and Internet numerical addresses, such as `208.31.42.42`. Sometimes just called a name server.

download To copy a file from a remote computer "down" to your computer.

dummies People who don't know everything but are smart enough to seek help. Used ironically.

edu When these letters appear as the last part of an address (in `http://www.middlebury.edu`, for example), it indicates that the host computer is run by an educational institution, usually a college or university in the United States.

e-mail Electronic messages sent via the Internet.

Eudora A popular mail-handling program that runs on the Macintosh and under Windows.

extranet An Internet technology used to connect a company with its customers and business partners.

FAQ (Frequently Asked Questions) An article that answers questions that come up often. Many mailing lists and Usenet newsgroups have FAQs that are posted regularly. To read the FAQs for all newsgroups, FTP to `http://rtfm.mit.edu`.

Favorites A list of files or Web pages you plan to use frequently. Internet Explorer lets you maintain a list of your favorite items to make it easy to see them again.

FIDONET A worldwide network of bulletin-board systems (BBSs) with Internet e-mail access.

flame   To post angry, inflammatory, or insulting messages. Don't do it!

flame war   Far too much flaming between two or more individuals.

firewall   A specially programmed computer that connects a local network to the Internet and, for security reasons, lets only certain kinds of messages in and out.

freenet   A free (except in Los Angeles) online system offering local communities information and limited access to the Internet.

FTP (File Transfer Protocol)   A method of transferring files from one computer to another over the Net.

FTP server   A computer on the Internet that stores files for transmission by FTP.

gateway   A computer that connects one network with another, where the two networks use different protocols.

GIF (Graphics Interchange Format)   A patented type of graphics file originally defined by CompuServe and now found all over the Net. Files in this format end in .gif and are called GIF files or just GIFs. Pronounced "jif" unless you prefer to say "gif."

giga-   Prefix meaning one billion (1,000,000,000).

Gopher   An Internet system that lets you find information by using menus, made obsolete by the Web.

Gopherspace   The world of Gopher menus. As you move from menu to menu in Gopher, you are said to be sailing through Gopherspace.

gov   When these letters appear as the last part of an address (in `http://cu.nih.gov`, for example), it indicates that the host computer is run by some government body, probably the U.S. federal government.

handle   A user's nickname or screen name.

header   The beginning of an e-mail message containing To and From addresses, subject, date, and other gobbledygook important to the programs that handle your mail.

home page   The entry page, or main page, of a Web site. If you have a home page, it's the main page about you. A home page usually contains links to other Web pages.

host   A computer on the Internet.

hostname   The name of a computer on the Internet (`chico.iecc.com`, for example).

HTML (Hypertext Markup Language)   The language used to write pages for the World Wide Web. This language lets the text include codes that define fonts, layout, embedded graphics, and hypertext links. Don't worry — you don't have to know anything about it to use the World Wide Web. Web pages are stored in files that usually have the extension .htm or .html.

HTTP (Hypertext Transfer Protocol)   The way in which World Wide Web pages are transferred over the Net. URLs for Web pages start with `http://`.

HTTPS   A variant of HTTP that encrypts messages for security.

hypermedia Like hypertext, but including all types of information, such as pictures, sound, and video, not just text. See also *hypertext.*

hypertext A system of writing and displaying text that enables the text to be linked in multiple ways, be available at several levels of detail, and contain links to related documents. The World Wide Web uses both hypertext and hypermedia.

ICQ "I Seek You," a popular paging and instant message system that lets users track which of their friends are online and exchange instant messages with them.

IETF (Internet Engineering Task Force) The group that develops new technical standards for the Internet.

Internet All the computers that are connected together into an amazingly huge global network so that they can talk to each other. When you connect your puny little computer to your Internet service provider, your computer becomes part of that network.

Internet Explorer A Web browser vigorously promoted by Microsoft that comes in Windows, Mac, and (arguably) UNIX flavors.

Internet Relay Chat (IRC) A system that enables Internet folks to talk to each other in real time (rather than after a delay, as with e-mail messages).

Internet Society An organization dedicated to supporting the growth and evolution of the Internet. You can contact it at `http://www.isoc.org`.

InterNIC The Internet Network Information Center, a central repository of information about the Internet. To register a domain name, go to `http.//www.internic.net`.

intranet A private version of the Internet that lets people within an organization exchange data by using popular Internet tools, such as browsers.

ISDN (Integrated Services Digital Network) A faster, digital phone service that operates at speeds as high as 128 kilobits per second.

Java A computer language invented by Sun Microsystems. Because Java programs can run on many different kinds of computers, Java makes it easier to deliver application programs over the Internet.

JPEG A type of still-image file found all over the Net. Files in this format end in .jpg or .jpeg and are called JPEG (pronounced "JAY-peg") files. Stands for Joint Photographic Experts Group.

Kbyte 1,024 bytes. Also written *KB* or just plain *K*. Usually used as a measure of a computer's memory or hard disk storage, or as a measure of file size.

kilo- Prefix meaning one thousand (1,000) or often, with computers, 1,024.

link A hypertext connection that can take you to another document or another part of the same document. On the World Wide Web, links appear as text or pictures that are highlighted. To follow a link, you click the highlighted material. See also *hypertext, WWW.*

ListProc Like LISTSERV, a program that handles mailing lists.

LISTSERV A family of programs that automatically manages mailing lists, distributing messages posted to the list, adding and deleting members, and so on, which spares the list owner the tedium of having to do it manually. The names of mailing lists maintained by LISTSERV often end with -L.

Linux   A freeware version of the UNIX operating system that runs on personal computers and is supported by a dedicated band of enthusiasts on the Internet.

lurk   To read a mailing list or chat group without posting any messages. Someone who lurks is a *lurker.* Lurking is okay and is much better than flaming.

Lynx   A character-based World Wide Web browser. No pictures, but it's fast.

MacBinary   A file-encoding system that's popular among Macintosh users.

MacTCP   TCP/IP for the Macintosh. You can't put your Mac on the Internet without it or a newer product called Open Transport. Comes with System 8.

mail server   A computer on the Internet that provides mail services for mail clients.

mailbot   A program that automatically sends or answers e-mail.

mailing list   A special type of e-mail address that remails all incoming mail to a list of subscribers to the mailing list. Each mailing list has a specific topic, so you subscribe to the ones that interest you. Often managed using ListProc, LISTSERV, or Majordomo.

Majordomo   Like LISTSERV, a program that handles mailing lists.

MBone   The multicast backbone. A special Internet *multicast* subnetwork that transmits live video and other multimedia to many different places on the net simultaneously.

mega-   Prefix meaning one million (1,000,000).

Microsoft Network (MSN)   A commercial online service that provides many Internet services, including e-mail and access to the World Wide Web.

mil   When these letters appear as the last part of an Internet address or domain name (the zone), it indicates that the host computer is run by some part of the U.S. military.

MIME   Multipurpose Internet Mail Extension. Used to send pictures, word-processing files, and other nontext information through e-mail.

mirror   An FTP or Web server that provides copies of the same files as another server. Mirrors spread out the load for more popular FTP and Web sites.

modem   A gizmo that lets your computer talk on the phone or cable TV. Derived from *mo*dulator/*dem*odulator.

moderated mailing list   A mailing list run by a *moderator.*

moderator   The person who looks at the messages posted to a mailing list or newsgroup before releasing them to the public. The moderator can nix messages that are stupid, redundant, off the topic, or offensive.

Mosaic   An older Web browser, now supplanted by Netscape Navigator, Internet Explorer, Opera, and other browsers.

MPEG A type of video file found on the Net. Files in this format end in .mpg. Stands for Moving Picture Experts Group.

MUD (Multi-User Dungeon) Started as a Dungeons and Dragons type of game that many people can play at one time; now, it's an Internet subculture. For information about joining a MUD, consult the Usenet newsgroup `http://rec.games.mud.announce`.

multicast To send the same network information simultaneously to multiple places on a network. Currently only used by the MBone and a few network routing schemes.

net A network, or (when capitalized) the Internet itself. When these letters appear as the last part of an address (in `http://www.abuse.net`, for example), it indicates that the host computer is run by a networking organization, frequently an ISP in the United States.

Netscape Navigator A popular Web browser that comes in Windows, Mac, and UNIX flavors. Part of the Netscape Communicator suite of programs. Pronounced *Mozilla.*

network Computers that are connected together. Those in the same or nearby buildings are called local-area networks, those that are farther away are called wide-area networks, and when you interconnect networks all over the world, you get the Internet!

network computer A computer that lacks a hard disk and gets all its data instead over a computer network, like the Internet.

newbie A newcomer to the Internet (variant: clueless newbie). If you have read this book, of course, you're not a clueless newbie anymore!

news server A computer on the Net that receives Usenet newsgroups and holds them so that you can read them.

newsgroup A topic area in the Usenet news system. (See the Web page `http://net.gurus.com/usenet` for a description of Usenet newsgroups.)

newsreader A program that lets you read and respond to the messages in Usenet newsgroups.

NIC (Network Information Center) Responsible for coordinating a set of networks so that the names, network numbers, and other technical details are consistent from one network to another. The address of the one for names ending in .com, .org, .net, and .edu is `http://rs.internic.net`.

nickname In IRC, the name by which you identify yourself when you're chatting, synonymous with *screen name* or *handle.*

node A computer on the Internet, also called a host.

Opera A small, fast Web browser from Opera Software in Norway, available at `http://www.operasoftware.com`.

org When these letters appear as the last part of an e-mail address or URL (in `http://www.uua.org`, for example), it indicates that the host computer is run by a noncommercial organization, usually in the United States.

packet A chunk of information sent over a network. Each packet contains the address that it's going to and the address from which it came.

page A document, or hunk of information, available by way of the World Wide Web. Each page can contain text, graphics files, sound files, video clips — you name it.

parity   A simple system for checking for errors when data is transmitted from one computer to another. Just say "none" when you're setting up a communications program.

password   A secret code used to keep things private. Be sure to pick one that's not crackable, preferably two randomly chosen words separated by a number or special character. Never use a single word that is in a dictionary or any proper name.

PDF file   A method for distributing formatted documents over the Net. You need a special reader program called Acrobat. Get it at `http://www.adobe.com/acrobat`.

PGP (Phil's Pretty Good Privacy)   A program that lets you encrypt and sign your e-mail, written by Phil Zimmerman. Check out `http://comp.security.pgp.discuss` for more information or point your Web browser to `http://web.mit.edu/network/pgp.html`.

PICS (Platform for Internet Content Selection)   A way of marking pages with ratings about what is inside. Designed to keep kids from getting at the racy stuff, although it has other applications as well.

Pine   A popular UNIX-based mail program. Pine is easy to use (for a UNIX program).

ping   Sending a short message to which another computer automatically responds. If you can't ping the other computer, you probably can't talk to it any other way, either.

PKZIP   A file-compression program that runs on PCs. PKZIP creates a ZIP file that contains compressed versions of one or more files. To restore these files to their former size and shape, you use PKUNZIP or WinZip. See also *ZIP file.*

plug-in   A computer program you add to your browser to help it handle a special type of file.

POP (Post Office Protocol)   A system by which a mail server on the Net lets you pick up your mail and download it to your PC or Mac. A POP server is the computer from which you pick up your mail. Also called *POP3.*

port number   An identifying number assigned to each program that is chatting on the Net. You hardly ever have to know these numbers — the Internet programs work this stuff out among themselves.

posting   An article published on or submitted to a mailing list or Usenet newsgroup.

PPP (Point-to-Point Protocol)   A scheme for connecting your computer to the Internet over a phone line. Like SLIP, only better.

protocol   The agreed-on rules that computers rely on to talk among themselves. A set of signals that mean "go ahead," "got it," "didn't get it, please resend," "all done," and so on.

public key cryptography   A method for sending secret messages whereby you get two keys: a public key you give out freely so that people can send you coded messages and a second, private key that decodes them.

push technology   A way for other computers to send information to you rather than wait for you to ask for it. Push technology enables you to subscribe to channels of information that get updated automatically on your computer. Not that popular (yet?). See also *channel.*

QuickTime   A video and multimedia file format invented by Apple Computer and widely used on the Net.

RealAudio   A popular streaming audio file format that lets you listen to programs over the Net. You can get a player plug-in at http://www.real.com.

RC4   A simple but powerful encryption algorithm developed by Ron Rivest, widely used on the Internet.

RFC (Request for Comment)   A num-bered series of documents that specify how the different parts of the Internet work. For example, RFC-822 describes the Internet e-mail message format.

router   A computer that connects two or more networks.

RTFM (Read The Manual)   A suggestion made by people who feel that you have wasted their time by asking a question you could have found the answer to by looking it up in an obvious place. A well-known and much-used FTP site named http://rtfm.mit.edu contains FAQs for all Usenet newsgroups.

search engine   A program used to search for things on the Web.

secure server   A Web server that uses encryption to prevent others from reading messages to or from your browser. Web-based shopping sites usually use secure servers so that others cannot intercept your ordering information.

serial port   The place on the back of your computer where you plug in your modem. Also called a *communications port* or *comm port.*

server   A computer that provides a service — such as e-mail, Web data, Usenet, or FTP — to other computers (known as clients) on a network. *See also* client.

shareware   Computer programs that are easily available for you to try with the understanding that, if you decide to keep the program, you will send the requested payment to the shareware provider specified in the program. This is an honor system. A great deal of good stuff is available, and people's voluntary compli-ance makes it viable.

Shockwave   A program for viewing interactive multimedia on the Web. For more information about Shockwave and for a copy of the program's plug-in for your browser, go to http://www.macromedia.com/shockwave.

SLIP (Serial Line Internet Protocol)   An obsolete software scheme for connecting your computer to the Internet over a serial line. *See also* PPP.

smiley   A combination of special charac-ters that portray emotions, such as :-) or :-(. Although hundreds have been in-vented, only a few are in active use, and all are silly.

S/MIME   Secure Multipurpose Internet Mail Extension. An extension to MIME that includes encryption (to keep mail confi-dential) and authentication (to prove who sent a message).

SMTP (Simple Mail Transfer Protocol)
The optimistically named method by
which Internet mail is delivered from one
computer to another. An SMTP server is
the computer that receives incoming e-
mail.

socket   On a UNIX or Windows system, a
logical "port" that a program uses to
connect to another program running on
another computer on the Internet. You
may have an FTP program using sockets
for its FTP session, for example, and have
Eudora connect by way of another socket
to get your mail. Winsock is the standard
way that Windows Internet programs use
sockets.

spam   E-mail sent to thousands of
uninterested recipients or usenet messages posted to many uninterested
newsgroups or mailing lists. It's antisocial,
ineffective, and often illegal.

SSL (Secure Socket Layer)   A Web-based
technology that lets one computer verify
another's identity and allow secure
connections.

stop bits   Just say "1" when you're setting
up your communications software.

streaming audio   A system for sending
sound files over the Net that begins
playing the sound before the sound file
finishes downloading, letting you listen
with minimal delay. RealAudio is the most
popular.

StuffIt   A file-compression program that
runs on Macs. StuffIt creates a SIT file that
contains compressed versions of one or
more files. To restore these files to their
former size and shape, you use UnStuffIt.

surfing   Wandering around the World
Wide Web and looking for interesting stuff.

T1   A telecommunications standard that
carries 24 voice calls or data at 1.544
million bps over a pair of telephone lines.

TCP/IP   The way networks communicate
with each other on the Net. It stands for
Transfer Control Protocol/Internet Protocol.

telnet   A program that lets you log in to
some other computers on the Net.

terminal   In the olden days, a computer
terminal consisted of just a screen and a
keyboard. If you have a personal computer
and you want to connect to a big computer somewhere, you can run a program
that makes it *pretend* to be a brainless
terminal — the program is called a
terminal emulator, terminal program, or
communications program.

text file   A file that contains only textual
characters, with no special formatting,
graphical information, sound clips, video,
or what-have-you. Because most computers, other than some IBM mainframes,
store their text by using a system of codes
named ASCII, these files are also known as
ASCII text files. See also *Unicode.*

thread   A message posted to a mailing
list or Usenet newsgroup, together with all
the follow-up messages, the follow-ups to
follow-ups, and so on.

Unicode   An up-and-coming extension of
ASCII that attempts to include the characters of all active written languages.

UNIX   A geeky operating system originally developed at Bell Labs. Used on
many servers on the Net. Linux is now the
most popular version.

upload   To copy your stuff to somebody
else's computer.

URL (Uniform Resource Locator) A standardized way of naming network resources, used for linking pages on the World Wide Web.

URN (Uniform Resource Name) A Web page name that doesn't change when the page is moved to a different computer, proposed as a solution to the broken-link problem.

Usenet A system of thousands of newsgroups. You read the messages by using a *newsreader. See also* newsreader. (See the Web page http://net.gurus.com/usenet for a description of Usenet newsgroups.)

uucp An elderly and creaky mail system still used by a few UNIX systems. Stands for *U*NIX-to-*U*NIX *copy*.

uuencode/uudecode A method of sending binary files as e-mail. Older and cruddier than MIME.

viewer A program to show you files that contain stuff other than text.

virtual reality A 3-D visual computer simulation that responds to your input so realistically that you feel you are inside another world.

VRML A language used for building virtual reality pages on the Web.

VT100 The model number of a very popular terminal made in the early 1980s by Digital Equipment Corporation which became a de facto standard. When you run a terminal emulator you may be asked what type of terminal you have; generally, saying you have a VT-100 works just fine.

WAV file A popular Windows format for sound files (.wav files) found on the Net.

Web page A document available on the World Wide Web.

WebTV An online Internet service that includes hardware (an Internet terminal and remote control) that you connect to your TV.

Winsock A standard way for Windows programs to work with TCP/IP. You use it if you directly connect your Windows PC to the Internet, with either a permanent connection or a modem, by using PPP or SLIP.

WWW (World Wide Web) A hypermedia system that lets you browse through lots of interesting information. The Web will be the central repository of humanity's information in the 21st century.

WinZip A file-compression program that runs under Windows. It reads and creates a ZIP file that contains compressed versions of one or more files.

X.400 A cumbersome, ITU-blessed mail standard that competes, not very successfully, with the Internet SMTP mail standard.

X.500 A standard for white-pages e-mail directory services. It isn't quite as broken as X.400, and Internet people are trying to use it.

XON/XOFF One way for your computer to say "Wait a sec!" when data is coming in too fast; the other way is usually called hardware flow control.

Xmodem A protocol for sending files between computers; second choice after Zmodem.

Yahoo A set of Web pages that provide a subject-oriented guide to the World Wide Web and many other kinds of information. Go to the URL `http://www.yahoo.com`.

ZIP file A file with the extension .zip that has been compressed using PKZIP, WinZip, or a compatible program. To get at the files in a ZIP file, you usually need WinZip, PKUNZIP, or a compatible program.

Zmodem A protocol for sending files between computers; one of the best to use, if it's available.

zone The last part of an Internet host name. If the zone is two letters long, it's the country code in which the organization that owns the computer is located. If the zone is three letters long, it's a code indicating the type of organization that owns the computer.

Index

• K •

IDG Books Worldwide, Inc., End-User License Agreement

READ THIS. You should carefully read these terms and conditions before opening the software packet(s) included with this book ("Book"). This is a license agreement ("Agreement") between you and IDG Books Worldwide, Inc. ("IDGB"). By opening the accompanying software packet(s), you acknowledge that you have read and accept the following terms and conditions. If you do not agree and do not want to be bound by such terms and conditions, promptly return the Book and the unopened software packet(s) to the place you obtained them for a full refund.

1. **License Grant.** IDGB grants to you (either an individual or entity) a nonexclusive license to use one copy of the enclosed software program(s) (collectively, the "Software") solely for your own personal or business purposes on a single computer (whether a standard computer or a workstation component of a multiuser network). The Software is in use on a computer when it is loaded into temporary memory (RAM) or installed into permanent memory (hard disk, CD-ROM, or other storage device). IDGB reserves all rights not expressly granted herein.

2. **Ownership.** IDGB is the owner of all right, title, and interest, including copyright, in and to the compilation of the Software recorded on the disk(s) or CD-ROM ("Software Media"). Copyright to the individual programs recorded on the Software Media is owned by the author or other authorized copyright owner of each program. Ownership of the Software and all proprietary rights relating thereto remain with IDGB and its licensers.

3. **Restrictions on Use and Transfer.**

    (a) You may only (i) make one copy of the Software for backup or archival purposes, or (ii) transfer the Software to a single hard disk, provided that you keep the original for backup or archival purposes. You may not (i) rent or lease the Software, (ii) copy or reproduce the Software through a LAN or other network system or through any computer subscriber system or bulletin-board system, or (iii) modify, adapt, or create derivative works based on the Software.

    (b) You may not reverse engineer, decompile, or disassemble the Software. You may transfer the Software and user documentation on a permanent basis, provided that the transferee agrees to accept the terms and conditions of this Agreement and you retain no copies. If the Software is an update or has been updated, any transfer must include the most recent update and all prior versions.

4. **Restrictions on Use of Individual Programs.** You must follow the individual requirements and restrictions detailed for each individual program in the "About the CD" section of this Book. These limitations are also contained in the individual license agreements recorded on the Software Media. These limitations may include a requirement that after using the program for a specified period of time, the user must pay a registration fee or discontinue use. By opening the Software packet(s), you will be agreeing to abide by the licenses and restrictions for these individual programs that are detailed in the "About the CD" section and on the Software Media. None of the material on this Software Media or listed in this Book may ever be redistributed, in original or modified form, for commercial purposes.

5. **Limited Warranty.**

   (a) IDGB warrants that the Software and Software Media are free from defects in materials and workmanship under normal use for a period of sixty (60) days from the date of purchase of this Book. If IDGB receives notification within the warranty period of defects in materials or workmanship, IDGB will replace the defective Software Media.

   (b) **IDGB AND THE AUTHOR OF THE BOOK DISCLAIM ALL OTHER WARRANTIES, EXPRESS OR IMPLIED, INCLUDING WITHOUT LIMITATION IMPLIED WARRANTIES OF MER-CHANTABILITY AND FITNESS FOR A PARTICULAR PURPOSE, WITH RESPECT TO THE SOFTWARE, THE PROGRAMS, THE SOURCE CODE CONTAINED THEREIN, AND/OR THE TECHNIQUES DESCRIBED IN THIS BOOK. IDGB DOES NOT WARRANT THAT THE FUNCTIONS CONTAINED IN THE SOFTWARE WILL MEET YOUR REQUIREMENTS OR THAT THE OPERATION OF THE SOFTWARE WILL BE ERROR FREE.**

   (c) This limited warranty gives you specific legal rights, and you may have other rights that vary from jurisdiction to jurisdiction.

6. **Remedies.**

   (a) IDGB's entire liability and your exclusive remedy for defects in materials and workmanship shall be limited to replacement of the Software Media, which may be returned to IDGB with a copy of your receipt at the following address: Software Media Fulfillment Department, Attn.: *The Internet For Dummies,* 6th Edition Starter Kit, IDG Books Worldwide, Inc., 7260 Shadeland Station, Ste. 100, Indianapolis, IN 46256, or call 800-762-2974. Please allow three to four weeks for delivery. This Limited Warranty is void if failure of the Software Media has resulted from accident, abuse, or misapplication. Any replacement Software Media will be warranted for the remainder of the original warranty period or thirty (30) days, whichever is longer.

   (b) In no event shall IDGB or the author be liable for any damages whatsoever (including without limitation damages for loss of business profits, business interruption, loss of business information, or any other pecuniary loss) arising from the use of or inability to use the Book or the Software, even if IDGB has been advised of the possibility of such damages.

   (c) Because some jurisdictions do not allow the exclusion or limitation of liability for conse-quential or incidental damages, the above limitation or exclusion may not apply to you.

7. **U.S. Government Restricted Rights.** Use, duplication, or disclosure of the Software by the U.S. Government is subject to restrictions stated in paragraph (c)(1)(ii) of the Rights in Technical Data and Computer Software clause of DFARS 252.227-7013, and in subparagraphs (a) through (d) of the Commercial Computer–Restricted Rights clause at FAR 52.227-19, and in similar clauses in the NASA FAR supplement, when applicable.

8. **General.** This Agreement constitutes the entire understanding of the parties and revokes and supersedes all prior agreements, oral or written, between them and may not be modified or amended except in a writing signed by both parties hereto that specifically refers to this Agreement. This Agreement shall take precedence over any other documents that may be in conflict herewith. If any one or more provisions contained in this Agreement are held by any court or tribunal to be invalid, illegal, or otherwise unenforceable, each and every other provision shall remain in full force and effect.

Installation Instructions

To get started with *The Internet For Dummies,* 6th Edition Starter Kit CD-ROM:

For Windows:

1. **Insert the CD-ROM into your CD-ROM drive. Be careful to touch only the edges of the CD-ROM.**

   If your CD-ROM drive requires a caddy (a protective plastic holder), insert the CD-ROM into an empty caddy and then place the caddy into your drive; otherwise, simply insert the CD-ROM directly into the holder provided by your drive. In either case, be sure to insert the CD-ROM with its printed side up.

2. **If you use Windows 95 or Windows 98, click the Start button (located in the bottom-left corner of your screen) and choose the Run option. If you're using Windows 3.1, choose File from the menu in Program Manager and then choose Run.**

3. **In the Run dialog box that appears, type d:\setup (the letter d, a colon (:), a backslash (\), and the word *setup*). If your CD-ROM drive isn't drive D, type the letter appropriate for your drive rather than d.**

4. **Press Enter or click OK.**

5. **Read the IDG Books Worldwide, Inc. agreement to see if you can stand its terms. When you're ready, click the Accept button. (After you click Accept, you'll never be bothered by the License Agreement again, but if you don't click Accept, you can't use the Installer program; although you can use the individual programs.)**

   After you click Accept, an opening screen appears.

6. **Admire the attractive screen and then click anywhere to continue.**

   A menu displays three software categories: Connecting, for programs that get you connected to the Net; Communicating, for programs that let you interact on the Net; and Working Offline, for programs that help you deal with files you've downloaded from the Net.

7. **Click a category in which you're interested.**

8. **Click a program in which you're interested.**

   A description of the program appears.

9. **To copy the program to your hard disk, click the Install button and then follow the prompts that appear on-screen.**

For details about using the software included with this CD, and for information about using this CD with a Mac, see the "About the CD" Appendix.

IDG BOOKS WORLDWIDE
BOOK REGISTRATION

Register
This Book
and Win!

We want to hear from you!

Visit **http://my2cents.dummies.com** to register this book and tell us how you liked it!

- Get entered in our monthly prize giveaway.

- Give us feedback about this book — tell us what you like best, what you like least, or maybe what you'd like to ask the author and us to change!

- Let us know any other *...For Dummies*® topics that interest you.

Your feedback helps us determine what books to publish, tells us what coverage to add as we revise our books, and lets us know whether we're meeting your needs as a *...For Dummies* reader. You're our most valuable resource, and what you have to say is important to us!

Not on the Web yet? It's easy to get started with *Dummies 101*®: *The Internet For Windows*® *98* or *The Internet For Dummies*, 6th Edition, at local retailers everywhere.

Or let us know what you think by sending us a letter at the following address:

...For Dummies Book Registration
Dummies Press
7260 Shadeland Station, Suite 100
Indianapolis, IN 46256-3945
Fax 317-596-5498

™
·FOR·
DUMMIES

**BESTSELLING
BOOK SERIES
FROM IDG**